Printing and Society in Early America

A Publication of the
American Antiquarian Society Program
in the History of the Book
in American Culture

Printing and Society
in Early America

EDITED BY

William L. Joyce, David D. Hall,

Richard D. Brown, and John B. Hench

WORCESTER

American Antiquarian Society

1983

Library of Congress Cataloging in Publication Data
Main entry under title:
Printing and society in early America.
"A publication of the American Antiquarian Society
Program in the History of the Book in American Culture"
—p.
Proceedings of a conference sponsored by the American
Antiquarian Society.
Includes bibliographical references and index.
1. Printing—United States—History—Congresses.
2. Book industries and trade—United States—History
—Congresses.   3. Books and reading—United States—
History—Congresses.   4. United States—Intellectual
life—Congresses.   I. Joyce, William Leonard.
II. American Antiquarian Society.
Z208.P74   1983   686.2′0973   83–6358
ISBN 0–912296–55–0

Contents

Preface

IN OCTOBER 1980, the American Antiquarian Society convened an international academic conference bearing the same title as this book, 'Printing and Society in Early America.' Seventy-five individuals submitted proposals in response to the Society's call for papers, and nineteen of these were invited to prepare papers. The papers covered a wide range of topics, from analysis of the stock of colonial booksellers to consideration of the changing social function of newspapers to a review of new modes and patterns of communication in the eighteenth and nineteenth centuries. The conference sessions themselves were given over to the delivery of prepared comments on these papers by participants, followed by responses by the paper writers and then by lengthy discussion by all present.

In sponsoring the conference, the Society was attempting to encourage the further development of new approaches to the study of printing in pre-twentieth-century America. Seen in its broadest context, printing history may be viewed as a distinct form of cultural history, a synthesis combining the attention to ideas that is central to intellectual history with the emphasis on patterns of behavior and organization characteristic of social history. One result of the conference was to bring notice to those investigations in American history similar to those carried out by practitioners of what is variously called *livre et société* and *l'histoire du livre*. Finally, the Society desired to provide a forum whereby historians, literary scholars, and bibliographers could begin to recognize the interrelationships among their varied approaches to the same subject and draw upon each other's work more than they have done in the past.

The theme of the conference is closely linked to the stated purposes and historic activities of AAS. As G. Thomas Tanselle commented at the meeting, the study of bibliography is 'climactic' to the Society, and this conference volume is the latest published witness to that truth. From *The History of Printing in America* by Isaiah Thomas, who founded AAS in 1812, through the efforts in this century of Clarence Saunders Brigham, Clifford K. Shipton, and Marcus A. McCorison, scholars associated with the Society have attempted to illuminate aspects of American history and culture through bibliographical inquiry. Moreover, the Society has gathered a comprehensive collection of research materials relating to American printing and publishing history and bibliography through 1876, and by means of its publications, research, and fellowship programs has already supported much basic work in the field. In that tradition, the conference was organized in hopes of linking the interests and scholarly resources of the Society to these recent developments in the scholarship of American social and intellectual history.

Chiefly responsible for organizing the conference was William L. Joyce, then the Society's education officer and curator of manuscripts. A steering committee was established to plan the details. The group consisted of Joyce; David D. Hall, professor of history at Boston University; Richard D. Brown, professor of history at the University of Connecticut; John B. Hench, then research and publication officer at AAS; and Marcus A. McCorison, the Society's director and librarian. Following the conference, the first four named constituted themselves as an editorial committee to see this book through the press.

With the exception of the introduction and afterword added by Professors Hall and Brown respectively, the essays included in this volume are revised versions of papers prepared for the conference. The essays selected for inclusion here are organized into three major sections. The first includes essays on aspects of the Anglo-American book trade. The middle section contains a pair of contributions on 'bibliocultural' topics; that is, they analyze the book as a physical artifact as well as consider the impact of such books on society. The third section includes essays with 'cultural' themes that attempt to measure and describe how and to what extent printing was actually employed in early American society.

Taken together, these essays demonstrate how the world of print changed between the eighteenth and nineteenth centuries, and how that world both shaped and reflected the larger American culture around it. A world of print characterized by scarcity was replaced by a world of abundance. A mode of reading that was centered on the intensive scrutiny of a few key moral or religious texts gave way to a mode characterized by the extensive sampling of a wide range of (increasingly secular) material. And an era in which limited access to print reinforced a cohesive, hierarchical, deferential society was succeeded by a period in which individual taste in print, as in politics, religion, and every other area of choice, made for an increasingly atomized, competitive society.

The editors do not pretend that what is published here constitutes a comprehensive view of this expanding field. Clearly, equal attention was not paid to developments in all parts of the country. There are no treatments of individual printers or publishing houses, no histories of certain kinds of books, no thorough analysis of the different modes of reading. Much more remains to be said on the relationship of bibliographical studies to progress in the field of the history of the book. But, the editors believe, these essays represent a selection of the scholarship undertaken in the early 1980s and will have served their purpose if they point the way to continued research and an eventual synthesis of views on the centrality of the printed word in the development of American culture.

The 1980 conference has begun to bear fruit in another sense as well. Since then, the Society has sought to find ways to continue the intellectual momentum generated by the conference. Further thinking has led to plans for the establishment at AAS of a formal Program in the History of the Book in American Culture. The Program will organize public lectures, conferences, workshops, seminars, and programs of research, fellowships, and publications to stimulate and report on the best possible work in the field. A principal goal of the Program will be to achieve in practice a felicitous union of basic bibliographical research with the French approach to the cultural history of the book.

The American Antiquarian Society is deeply indebted to the individuals and institutions who made the 1980 conference and this book possible. Professors Hall and Brown were instrumental in the formulation of plans and in contributing to the intellectual coherence of the enterprise. All participants—paper-givers, commentators, and invited guests—freely shared their knowledge and insights. All conference expenses and a portion of the costs of publication of this volume were defrayed by generous contributions from the following sources: ABC-Clio, Inc., the George I. Alden Trust, the Elmer L. and Eleanor J. Andersen Foundation, Warren G. Davis, Frank L. Harrington, Sr., the Robert R. McCormick Charitable Trust, Eugene Schwab, University Microfilms International, and the Xerox Foundation. We are pleased to record our gratitude to these donors for their very welcome support of this exciting undertaking.

December 15, 1982

WILLIAM L. JOYCE
New York Public Library

JOHN B. HENCH
American Antiquarian Society

Introduction: The Uses of Literacy in New England, 1600–1850

DAVID D. HALL

JOSEPH BUCKINGHAM AND SAMUEL GOODRICH were entrepreneurs of print in nineteenth-century America, the one as editor of Boston's first daily newspaper, the other as a publisher and author. Goodrich was the man behind the pseudonym 'Peter Parley,' a name attached to children's stories and of such appeal to young readers that unscrupulous publishers stole it for their own ends. Goodrich was not amused by the practice, but his anger was lessened by the sweet smell of success: 'I am the author and editor of about one hundred and seventy volumes, and of these seven millions have been sold!'[1]

In that triumphant sentence from his autobiography lies one characteristic of the new world of print that Goodrich helped to create: a vast expansion in the scale of publishing and reading. Goodrich and Buckingham could remember when things were very different. In their respective autobiographies, both published in the 1850s, the two recalled what life was like in the country towns of late eighteenth-century Connecticut. The contrast between then and now was sharp, for in olden times books were not abundant. Windham farmers owned a mere handful of books: 'The Bible and Dr. Watts's Psalms and Hymns were indispensable in every family, and ours was not without them. There were, also, on the "book shelf," a volume or two of Sermons, Doddridge's "Rise and Progress of Religion," and a very few other books and pamphlets, chiefly of a religious character.'

I want to thank Margaret Spufford for allowing me to read her study of chapbooks while it was still in galleys; and Jennifer Canizares and James McLachlan for their critical readings of an earlier version of this essay.

1 Samuel Goodrich, *Recollections of a Lifetime*, 2 vols. (New York, 1857), 2: 284.

Newspapers were almost as scarce. Buckingham supposed that in the early 1790s, 'there were not more than five or six' being published in the entire state. When a printer came to Windham in 1793 and began to publish a weekly paper, the event marked 'a memorable epoch in our village history.' The sensations Buckingham felt when he bought his first book, a copy of the *New England Primer*, were equally memorable: 'no speculator who makes his thousands by a dash of the pen ever felt richer than I did with my purchase.'[2]

From scarcity to abundance, from one world of print to another, this was the journey Buckingham and Goodrich would make in the course of their lives. It was a journey most Americans and Europeans were making in the decades between the 1770s and the 1850s, for on both sides of the Atlantic a major transformation of print culture was occurring. Several factors coalesced to bring about this transformation: new printing and paper-making technologies that reduced the price of books, improvements in how books were marketed, a rapid increase in the rate of literacy, and a general speeding up of communication. With abundance came the introduction of new literary genres, like the children's stories Goodrich wrote, and a new relationship between writers and their audience. It may be too extreme to say that print was 'democratized.' Yet the mass marketing of 'Peter Parley' indicates that the age of abundance stood in sharp contrast to the age of scarcity.[3]

Goodrich and Buckingham started out in this older system, and because they experienced its transformation, the contrast between old and new became the major theme of their autobiographies. Goodrich and Buckingham carry us back into a veritable 'world we have lost.' In helping us to recover this past, Goodrich and Buckingham provide

[2] Joseph T. Buckingham, *Personal Memoirs and Recollections of Editorial Life*, 2 vols. (Boston, 1852), 1: 15–16, 21, 8.

[3] Richard Altick, *The English Common Reader: A Social History of the Mass Reading Public, 1800–1900* (Chicago, 1963), p. 5; and see the essay by Nathan Hatch that follows in this volume. The history of publishing is plagued by mutually inconsistent assertions as to when the transition to a 'democratic' system occurred. The root of the problem may be that historians have brought different assumptions to bear upon the issue. It is not clear, frankly, that a 'mass' reading public is also a 'democratic' one.

another service that is of even more importance. Because of their life histories, both men were sensitive to the meaning of the book as a cultural artifact. Enriched by their personal experiences of change, the two were instinctively able to discern some of the connections that run between 'the book and society.'

These connections are also the concern of the historians and bibliographers who wrote the essays in this volume. Like Buckingham and Goodrich, these historians regard print as a cultural artifact. Like them, they want to tell a story that moves back and forth between this artifact and its broader context. In some of these essays, the context is intellectual and religious history. In others, it is the economics of the marketplace or the system of authority that infused certain books with extraordinary meaning. And in some essays, the context is one of changing patterns of patronage, taste, and cultural organization. In method these essays are equally diverse. Yet there is common ground among them all in two respects: they share the ambition to achieve a new social history of the book, and they owe this ambition to historians of early modern Europe who have made 'livre et société' so powerful and compelling a field of study.

In saying this I do not mean to scant the American scholarship on which these essays depend, the achievements of bibliographers and historians during the century and three-quarters since Isaiah Thomas wrote his *History of Printing in America*.⁴ Fifty years ago, Samuel Eliot Morison and Perry Miller were making splendid use of probate inventories and book trade records in describing the mental world of the New England colonists.⁵ Most of what we know about the economics of the book trade stems from the scholarship of Rollo Silver, William Miller, and the authors of *The Book in America* (1939). In the work of literary historians such as William Charvat lie clues as to how the traditional relationships among authors, publishers, and readers were radically altered in the middle of the nineteenth century.⁶

4 Isaiah Thomas, *The History of Printing in America* (Worcester, 1810).
5 Samuel Eliot Morison, *The Puritan Pronaos: Studies in the Intellectual Life of New England in the Seventeenth Century* (New York, 1936), chaps. 5 and 6; Perry Miller, *The New England Mind: The Seventeenth Century* (Cambridge, Mass., 1954), pp. 510, 515.
6 Rollo G. Silver, *The American Printer, 1787–1825* (Charlottesville, Va., 1967);

With this work as an intellectual foundation, the 1960s and 1970s were crucial decades in bringing new energies to the history of the book. Those energies originated overseas. They are evident in the two volumes of essays published in 1965 and 1970 under the title *Livre et Société*, in the refounding of the *Revue Française d'histoire du livre* in 1971, and in the rise to fame of the 'bibliothèque bleue.' The rediscovery of the 'bibliothèque bleue' by Robert Mandrou and Geneviève Bollème was especially significant, for it seemed to demonstrate how social history could be integrated with the history of the book.[7] That process of integration was greatly forwarded by Natalie Davis in her essay 'Printing and the People' (1975),[8] and by Robert Darnton in a series of contributions culminating in *The Business of Enlightenment* (1979).[9] As the 1970s ended, 'livre et société' seemed to come of age.[10]

The essays in this volume are hybrids, therefore, owing much to

---

C. William Miller, *Benjamin Franklin's Philadelphia Printing 1728–1766* (Philadelphia, 1974); Hellmut Lehmann-Haupt, Ruth Shepard Granniss, and Lawrence Wroth, *The Book in America: A History of the Making, the Selling, and the Collecting of Books in the United States* (New York, 1939); William Charvat, *The Profession of Authorship in America, 1800–1870*, ed. Matthew J. Bruccoli (Columbus, Ohio, 1968). *The Book in America* was first published in Leipzig in 1937 under the title *Das Amerikanische Buchwesen*; and a second edition appeared in New York in 1951 with the collaboration of Lehmann-Haupt, Lawrence Wroth, and Rollo G. Silver.

7 François Furet et al., *Livre et Société dans la France du xviii siècle*, 2 vols. (Paris, 1965, 1970); Robert Mandrou, *De la culture populaire aux xvii et xviii siècles: La Bibliothèque Bleue* (Paris, 1964); Geneviève Bollème, *La Bibliothèque Bleue; litterature populaire en France du xvi° au xix° siècles* (Paris, 1971).

8 Natalie Davis, 'Printing and the People,' in *Society and Culture in Early Modern France* (Stanford, Calif., 1975).

9 Robert Darnton, 'The High Enlightenment and the Low-Life of Literature in Pre-Revolutionary France,' *Past and Present* 51 (May 1971): 81–115; 'Trade in the Taboo: The Life of a Clandestine Book Dealer in Prerevolutionary France,' in *The Widening Circle: Essays on the Circulation of Literature in Eighteenth-Century Europe*, ed. Paul J. Korshin (Philadelphia, 1976), pp. 11–83; *The Business of Enlightenment: A Publishing History of the Encyclopédie, 1775–1800* (Cambridge, Mass., 1979); 'What Is the History of Books?' *Daedalus* 111 (1982): 65–83.

10 Raymond Birn, 'Livre et Société after Ten Years: Formation of a Discipline,' *Studies on Voltaire and the Eighteenth Century* 154 (1976): 287–312; G. Thomas Tanselle, 'From Bibliography to Histoire Totale: The History of Books as a Field of Study,' *Times Literary Supplement*, June 5, 1981, pp. 647–49; John Feather, 'Cross Channel Currents: Historical Bibliography and l'Histoire du Livre,' *The Library*, 6th ser. 2 (1980): 1–15. Mention should also be made of Lucien Febvre and Henri-Jean Martin, *The Coming of the Book: The Impact of Printing 1450–1800* (London, 1976).

native traditions, but owing even more to the vigor and excitement of a field of study that arose among historians of early modern Europe. Like all hybrids, these essays are selective in how they represent their parents. Some of the methods and assumptions of the European literature fail to reappear. Why is it that no essay deals with the cheapest, most 'popular' forms of print in America, or that none employs the quantitative, *histoire sérielle* approach so favored by the authors of *Livre et Société*? Generally speaking, these essays are silent on the topic of literacy, as though it were not the problem in America that it is in early modern Europe.[11] But the resemblances are also strong. Historians on both sides of the Atlantic are contending with the same problems: whether 'oral' culture was different from and in conflict with the world of print; the relationship between 'culture savante' and 'culture populaire'; the role of intermediaries; and how diffusion happened.[12] In several of these papers, as in much of the European literature, the relationship of the book to traditional structures of authority —an established church, a social hierarchy, a political elite—is an important issue. Were books subversive or conserving of these systems? Other papers address what may be the most intractable of such questions, the process of reading and what it was that people actually took from the books that came their way.

As these issues were debated at the conference on 'Printing and Society in Early America,' answers to one or two began to emerge. The most explicit of these answers concerned the changing nature of print culture in the century between 1750 and 1850. Several of the papers throw more light on the world that Buckingham and Goodrich recall so richly in their autobiographies. In others, the transformation from old to new was sharply visible from another vantage point, be it the reordering of cultural authority via the lecture system of the 1840s

---

11 François Furet and Jacques Ozouf, eds., *Lire et écrire: l'alphabétisation des Français de Calvin à Jules Ferry*, 2 vols. (Paris, 1978); David Cressy, *Literacy and the Social Order: Reading and Writing in Tudor and Stuart England* (Cambridge, 1980).

12 Georges Duby, 'The Diffusion of Cultural Patterns in Feudal Society,' *Past and Present* 39 (April 1968): 3–10; Henri-Jean Martin, 'Culture écrite et culture orale, culture savante et culture populaire dans la France d'Ancien Régime,' *Journal des Savants* (July–Sept. 1975; Oct.–Dec. 1975): 225–82.

or the emergence of 'genteel' songbooks in the 1790s.[13] On the issue of oral culture and the world of print, these papers reflect a rough consensus that these modes were less in conflict than some historians have argued. In this regard, there was a restlessness at the conference with analytical categories that seemed too rigid or that did not bear upon American circumstances. A decade ago, Robert Darnton brought home to historians of 'livre et société' the limitations of forcing all books of a given period into categories like 'religious' or 'historical,' as though any world view were actually composed of such airtight little units.[14] Do concepts such as oral culture have similar limitations that outweigh their usefulness?

One way of reflecting on such questions is to return to Buckingham, Goodrich, and the uses of literacy in early New England. I want to develop more fully the framework they present, borrowing as I do so from the other essays in this volume to fill out their description. I also want to review the literature on 'livre et société,' looking again at the major problems in the European historiography and how they bear on the history of the book in America. My purpose is finally to suggest some ways of connecting books and readers. It is the 'uses of literacy' that concern me, the modes of using print that seem predominant in the first two centuries of New England life. To inquire into the uses of literacy is not to ask about the distribution of literacy as a skill, but to explore how reading functioned as a cultural style.[15] In reconstructing that style, we may come closer to a history of the book that is also social history.

I

Of all the kinds of information that bear upon the history of the book, none is more important than descriptive bibliography. As Robert Winans points out in his essay in this volume on book trade catalogues

[13] See the essays by Donald Scott on the lecture system and that on music publishing by Richard Crawford and Donald Krummel that follow in this volume.
[14] Robert Darnton, 'Reading, Writing, and Publishing in Eighteenth-Century France: A Case Study in the Sociology of Literature,' *Daedalus* 100 (1971): 214–56.
[15] I have borrowed the phrase and this meaning for it from Richard Hoggart, *The Uses of Literacy* (London, 1957).

and the importation of fiction, bibliography is essential to an understanding of the book trade. His is a precise example of the general thesis, that assertions about reading patterns and their cultural implications must rest on an adequate foundation of bibliography.[16] Given this imperative, historians of the book in early America can regard themselves as extremely fortunate. In Charles Evans's *American Bibliography* and its supplements, they possess a listing of books and other printed matter that grows steadily more complete and accurate. Within the shelter of this great edifice, there have grown up dozens of more specialized bibliographies—listings for colonies, states, and towns, of Bibles, primers, songsters, and children's books, of individual printers and their shops, to cite but a few.[17] The North American Imprints Program, now underway at the American Antiquarian Society, will produce a thorough revision, in computerized form, of the canon of early American bibliography begun by Evans and continued by Roger Bristol.

All of these listings invite the curiosity of the historian who wants to explore themes and problems in the development of American culture. Merely to glance through Hills's *The English Bible in America* is to realize that the American book trade in the early nineteenth century was extraordinarily decentralized; for example, one or more editions of the Bible or New Testament were printed at twenty-four separate locations in Massachusetts. In the same source we can trace the rapid contraction of this network after 1850, until the business of printing Bibles shrank to only Boston and Cambridge. The mere fact that Bibles in English were not printed in America until the Revolution underscores another

---

[16] Robert B. Winans, 'The Growth of a Novel-Reading Public in Late Eighteenth-Century America,' *Early American Literature* 9 (1975): 267–75; and see the essay by Winans that follows in this volume.

[17] For example: Hazel A. Johnson, *A Checklist of New London, Connecticut, Imprints, 1709–1800* (Charlottesville, Va., 1978); Marcus A. McCorison, *Vermont Imprints 1778–1820* (Worcester, Mass., 1963); Charles F. Heartman, *The New-England Primer Issued Prior to 1830* (New York, 1934); Irving Lowens, *A Bibliography of Songsters Printed in America Before 1821* (Worcester, 1976); d'Alté A. Welch, *A Bibliography of American Children's Books Printed Prior to 1821* (Worcester and Barre, Mass., 1972); Charles L. Nichols, *Isaiah Thomas, Printer, Writer & Collector* (Boston, 1912). In general, see G. Thomas Tanselle, *Guide to the Study of United States Imprints*, 2 vols. (Cambridge, Mass., 1971).

aspect of the book trade, its provincial relationship to England. Most of the books that Americans bought and read throughout the early period were imported from London.[18]

Given this provincial dependence, the history of the book in early America must be understood as part of a larger story. Whether the setting is eighteenth-century France, seventeenth-century England, or colonial New England, that story unfolds as a dialectic between certain fixed, intractable circumstances on the one hand, and flexible, ingenious strategies on the other. The essential constraint was a chronic lack of capital in the industry. This shortage of capital was in part a function of printing practices, and in part of limited sales for most types of publications. The pace of book production fluctuated from week to week, a factor that master printers had to reckon with in pricing their services. Robert Darnton's reconstruction of printing office practices confirms the picture of a fluctuating rhythm of production.[19] Entrepreneurs in the book trade, like Darnton's Parisians who were out to market the *Encyclopédie*, were always on the hustle seeking to finance press runs larger than the normal size. Printing houses could not afford to tie up capital in paper, the most expensive of the ingredients in bookmaking. In any case, the market could not ordinarily absorb large quantities of most forms of print. Books cost too much to be items of frequent purchase by any but professionals and the affluent.[20]

[18] Margaret T. Hills, ed., *The English Bible in America* (New York, 1961). The privilege of publishing the Bible in English was a legal monopoly of the king's printers in the British empire.

[19] Donald McKenzie, 'Printers of the Mind: Some Notes on Bibliographical Theories and Printing-House Practices,' *Studies in Bibliography* 22 (1969): 1–75; Darnton, *The Business of Enlightenment*, chap. 5.

[20] On price, see McKenzie, 'Printers of the Mind'; F. R. Johnson, 'Notes on English Retail Book-Prices, 1550–1640,' *The Library*, 5th ser. 5 (1950): 83–112; Edwin H. Miller, *The Professional Writer in Elizabethan England* (Cambridge, Mass., 1959), p. 41; Altick, *The English Common Reader*, pp. 21–23, 51–53; and the references and information in the essays by Stephen Botein and Gregory and Cynthia Stiverson that follow in this volume. On the size of editions, see H. S. Bennett, *English Books and Readers, 1475 to 1557* (London, 1952), p. 228, and the relevant sections of succeeding volumes in this series: *English Books and Readers, 1558 to 1603* (Cambridge, 1965) and *English Books and Readers, 1603 to 1650* (Cambridge, 1970).

Hence the search for ways around these limitations. For some book sellers, the answer lay in patronage, though this had ceased to be significant by 1640.[21] For others, and especially in the eighteenth century, the ways to finance a book and to build an audience for it included publishing in parts and advertising for subscriptions. Publishing by subscription was how Daniel Henchman and Benjamin Eliot dared to print Samuel Willard's *The Compleat Body of Divinity* in 1726, the first book in folio to be published in New England.[22] Another way of saving money was to not pay the author. The usual practice was for authors to receive their 'pay' in copies, the rule of thumb being 10 percent of an edition. Among themselves, moreover, booksellers made exchanges on the basis not of cash but of copies. If someone wished to carry the books of a competitor in his store, the way of doing so was to swap one set of books for another. The undercapitalization of the *American* book trade is also evident in Robert Winans's discovery that American printers chose to republish only that British fiction which was short. The two or three volumes of a *Pamela*, or even the complete text of a *Robinson Crusoe*, were usually beyond their resources.[23]

In the nineteenth century the book trade became transformed in its capital structure. For Americans and the French, the change came after 1830.[24] Change was already well underway in Britain, where the structure of the book trade was shifting after 1780 'from a series of independent but cooperative bookselling firms into a group of large corporate enterprises. . . . The extent of this transformation is indicated by the number of booksellers that went out of business during

---

21 Bennett, *English Books and Readers, 1558 to 1603*, chap. 2; Miller, *The Professional Writer*, p. 129.

22 No comprehensive study of publishing by subscription in early America has been undertaken, to the best of my knowledge. Individual lists of subscribers invite analysis as evidence of readership and diffusion patterns. Cf. the references in fn. 29, below, and Samuel G. Drake, *Some Memoirs of the Life and Writings of the Rev. Thomas Prince* (Boston, 1851), for the interesting subscribers' list to Prince's *Chronological History of New England* (1728).

23 Winans, 'Growth of a Novel-Reading Public.'

24 Roger Chartier, 'L'ancien régime typographique: reflexions sur quelques travaux recents,' *Annales E.S.C.* 36 (1981): 191–209, esp. 201ff.

these years [1780 to 1820].'[25] The golden age of local publishing in America came between 1800 and 1840, when almost anyone could set up shop. Alexis de Tocqueville's astonishment at the quantity of newspapers Americans could absorb—the highest per capita in the world—was related to the ease with which an Anthony Haswell and a William Lloyd Garrison could publish.[26] Carey, Lea in Philadelphia and the Harpers in New York were of a different order of magnitude, and their emergence by the 1830s signaled a process of consolidation. This process, with all of the advantages accruing to publishers who seized a metropolitan location, was essentially complete by the Civil War, when the village printer-bookseller was rapidly becoming a figure of the past.[27] Gone were the days when the many each produced a few for a limited audience; now a few produced great quantities for an audience that numbered in the millions.

This analysis of the book trade depends on the work of bibliographers. They have less to say, however, about the interaction between books and readers. Here, alas, the evidence for saying *anything* is much more elusive and fragmentary. Every source has its limitations. Probate inventories are incomplete—characteristically they lump most books together in a single category, or do not mention them at all—and offer no means of distinguishing between books that were merely owned and books that mattered.[28] Bibliographers can tell us that certain books went through many editions, but not the reasons for this popularity. Two of the essays in this volume are based on booksellers'

[25] Leslie Chard, 'Bookseller to Publisher: Joseph Johnson and the English Book Trade, 1760 to 1810,' *The Library*, 5th ser. 32 (1977): 138, 150.

[26] Alexis de Tocqueville, *Democracy in America*, ed. Phillips Bradley, 2 vols. (New York, 1954), 1: 193.

[27] The story may be followed in Milton W. Hamilton, *The Country Printer: New York State, 1785–1830* (New York, 1936).

[28] The absence of books in so many inventories is open to conflicting interpretation. Margaret Spufford argues that certain books had so little value that no one bothered listing them; Peter Clark argues against ownership at all. Margaret Spufford, *Small Books and Pleasant Histories: Popular Fiction and Its Readership in Seventeenth-Century England* (Athens, Ga., 1982), p. 48; Peter Clark, 'The Ownership of Books in England,' in *Schooling and Society*, ed. Lawrence Stone (Baltimore, 1976), pp. 95–111. Spufford and Clark agree that chapbooks and their ilk were easily destroyed and thus perhaps not likely to turn up in inventories.

account books, which for once permit us to associate specific books with individuals. Subscription lists can also serve to link books and readers,[29] as do the records of circulating libraries.[30] Among French historians of the book, a common method is to assign the books in inventories or a national bibliography to certain categories—'religious,' 'historical,' and the like—and to argue that changes over time in the relative size of these categories informs us of shifting preferences among their readers. But as Darnton has pointed out, this method has its limitations.[31]

How then do we proceed with a history of the book that extends to culture and society? Any such history must confront certain fundamental problems. Two of these are illiteracy and the role of oral culture. In early modern Europe, the relationship between books and readers was powerfully affected by illiteracy. The half or two-thirds of the population that could not read were presumably excluded from the book trade. In this context, it is easy to overstate the impact of the book. But it is just as easy to swing to the other extreme of denying that print ever penetrated the oral culture of the peasantry. If the impact of printing must not be overstated, so too the role of oral culture must yield to a common-sense recognition of its limits.[32] One of the weaknesses of the concept is its holistic implications, as though the mental world of the peasantry were thoroughly self-contained. It is also weakened by the evident fact that Europe had been a literate culture for a millennium. David Buchan has proposed a useful distinc-

[29] Sarah L. C. Clapp, 'The Beginnings of Subscription Publication in the Seventeenth Century,' *Modern Philology* 29 (1931–32): 199–224. See also Peter J. Wallis and Francis J. G. Robinson, 'The Potential Uses of Book Subscription Lists,' in *The Art of the Librarian*, ed. A. Jeffreys (Newcastle, England, 1973); F. J. G. Robinson and P. J. Wallis, *Book Subscription Lists. A Revised Guide* (Newcastle, England, 1975).

[30] Paul Kaufman, 'The Eighteenth-Century Forerunner of the London Library,' *Papers of the Bibliographical Society of America* 53–54 (1955–56): 89–100, reprinted with many other studies in Kaufman, *Libraries and Their Users* (London, 1969).

[31] See the essays in Furet et al., *Livre et Société*, vol. 1; and Darnton, 'Reading, Writing, and Publishing.'

[32] Elizabeth Eisenstein, *The Printing Press as an Agent of Change*, 2 vols. (Cambridge, 1979), p. 130; Cressy, *Literacy and the Social Order*, p. 14; Ian Watt, *The Rise of the Novel* (Berkeley and Los Angeles, 1957), p. 196; François Furet and Jacques Ozouf, 'Trois siècles de métissage culturel,' *Annales E.S.C.* 32 (1977): 488–502.

tion between 'oral,' referring to 'the tradition of non-literate societies,' and 'verbal,' referring to 'the word of mouth tradition of a literate culture.'[33] Early modern Europe would seem to fall into the second of these categories, where oral knowledge is always touched by print. The situation in early modern Europe was one in which apparent barriers were constantly breached by intermediaries—the peddlers with their *littérature du colportage*, the village curés who knew a little Latin, the fathers who read aloud in households.[34]

Certain forms of print most certainly were intermediaries. Geneviève Bollème has suggested that French almanacs of the sixteenth and seventeenth centuries were available to the illiterate because they were composed in a system of 'signs' meaningful to everyone.[35] The 'bibliothèque bleue,' the classic *littérature du colportage*, was another intermediary. This literature was the dust bin of Western culture, its myths and commonplaces reduced to almost incoherent rubbish. But when the French peasant came in touch with this debris, something stuck. Like it or not, he was in contact with the culture of the learned. Altogether, there seems reason to believe that the distance between print and oral culture has been overemphasized.

Leaving these categories aside for the moment, we can turn in their absence to intellectual history as a means of connecting books and readers. Each of the great movements of thought that swept across Europe and America in the sixteenth and seventeenth centuries became embodied in print. Historians of the book have done notable work in describing the diffusion of these movements. To cite an American example, we know that Princeton undergraduates in the 1770s drew on the classics for the pseudonyms which were used in the rituals of debate. As reconstructed by James McLachlan, this little world of books and readers becomes a microcosm of the impact and penetration of the Whig mentality that was so crucial for Americans in the Revo-

---

[33] David Buchan, *The Ballad and the Folk* (London, 1972), pp. 1–2.

[34] Peter Burke, *Popular Culture in Early Modern Europe* (New York, 1978), chap. 4 and p. 257.

[35] Geneviève Bollème, *Les Almanachs populaires aux xvii⁰ et xviii⁰ siècles* (Paris, 1969), pp. 7–15.

lutionary period.[36] In another American example, Elizabeth Reilly suggests, in an essay included in this volume, that the business of the Boston bookseller Jeremiah Condy may have flourished because of intellectual affinities between him and his customers. Condy and his customers were more advanced in their thinking than the majority of colonists.[37] It may well be that in such circumstances we can more readily connect books and their readers.

Most historians prefer to work with books that are popular. The scholarship on popular literature has often remained at a very general level.[38] More recently, historians have been focusing on particular genres or types of literature: the almanac or chapbook, or products like the 'bibliothèque bleue de Troyes,' the little paperbound books that were churned out on a veritable assembly line and peddled across the countryside. Seventeenth- and eighteenth-century printers could produce astonishing quantities of single-sheet books. In a good year, the London publishers of almanacs in the latter decades of the seventeenth century turned out 400,000 copies, and perhaps as many ballads. Meanwhile the partnerships devoted to the publishing of chapbooks were printing these inexpensive items at a rapid pace.[39]

In a recent study of English chapbooks, Margaret Spufford demonstrates that they were printed in remarkable quantities—at his death, one publisher had enough copies in his warehouse to supply one out of every fifteen families in England—and that the methods of distribu-

---

[36] James McLachlan, 'Classical Names, American Identities: Some Notes on College Students and the Classical Tradition in the 1770s,' in *Classical Traditions in Early America*, ed. John W. Eadie (Ann Arbor, Mich., 1976), pp. 81–98. Cf. David Lundberg and Henry F. May, 'The Enlightened Reader in America,' *American Quarterly* 28 (1976): 262–93.

[37] See the essay that follows in this volume.

[38] James D. Hart, *The Popular Book in America* (New York, 1950); Frank Luther Mott, *Golden Multitudes* (New York, 1947); Russel B. Nye, *The Unembarrassed Muse: The Popular Arts in America* (New York, 1970).

[39] Cyprian Blagdon, 'The Distribution of Almanacks in the Second Half of the Seventeenth Century,' *Studies in Bibliography* 11 (1958): 107–16; Blagdon, 'Notes on the Ballad Market in the Second Half of the Seventeenth Century,' *Studies in Bibliography* 6 (1954): 161–80; Spufford, *Small Books and Pleasant Histories*, chap. 4. An informal general history is Leslie Shepard, *The History of Street Literature* (Newton Abbot, England, 1973).

tion were surprisingly efficient. She moves to a thematic analysis of the chapbooks, and especially those on religious subjects, on the assumption that books which were so widely bought and read inform us of beliefs among the general population. In support of this argument, she has collected stories of people's reading and book ownership—as of the two books that Bunyan's wife included in her dowry—that bespeak the significance of easily available books. Here as with Bollème and Mandrou, we sense that we are on the verge of uncovering the mental categories of a world view that would otherwise lie largely hidden from our sight.[40]

The question can still be asked of chapbooks, almanacs, and their kin: is this a literature 'of' or 'for' the people? By the end of the seventeenth century, a recognizable group of writers and booksellers in Britain were earning their livelihoods producing books and ballads for the people. John Shirley cranked out bastardized versions of traditional stories at the rate of two or three a year.[41] Richard Sault invented the story of *The Second Spira*, which tells of an atheist who suffered the most extraordinary pangs of conscience as he was dying.[42] Professional writers were delighted to feed a public taste for sensationalism by providing 'one-signature tracts on earthquakes, macabre events, or some new freak with two heads recently born in a remote shire of England.'[43] Reports of apparitions and wonders, as of the Devil appearing in the guise of a bear or wheat pouring from the sky, were nearly always fictional.[44]

This is certainly a literature *for* the people, but in what sense is it *of* them? The answer to this question may be as simple as observing that the 'people' had nowhere else to go for reading matter than to

[40] Spufford, *Small Books and Pleasant Histories*; John Bunyan, *Grace Abounding to the Chief of Sinners*, ed. Roger Sharrock (Oxford, 1962), p. 8. The two books were *The Plain Mans Pathway to Heaven* and *The Practice of Piety*.

[41] Barbara L. Magaw, 'The Work of John Shirley, an Early Hack Writer,' *Papers of the Bibliographical Society of America* 56 (1962): 332–45.

[42] [Richard Sault], *The Second Spira*, 6th ed. (Boston, 1715, from the 1692 London ed.). See fn. 95, below.

[43] Miller, *The Professional Writer*, pp. 54–55.

[44] Hyder E. Rollins, ed., *The Pack of Autolycus, or Strange and Terrible News of Ghosts, Apparitions, Monstrous Births, Showers of Wheat* (Cambridge, Mass., 1969), pp. 36, 40, 219.

the London market. Willy-nilly, the mentality of artisans and hus-
bandmen was shaped by the booksellers who assembled the ballads,
broadsides, almanacs, and chapbooks that sold so widely. The booksellers' social identity was ambiguous, and the cultural message of
their products fluctuated within a wide range. A good many chapbooks were mildly pornographic.[45] This circumstance, together with
the persistence of sensationalism as a motif of street literature, suggests
that the producers of these items were attuned to the reading tastes
of the barely literate.[46] On the other hand, the chapbook editions of
Richard Baxter's *Call to the Unconverted* would indicate that some printers were intermediaries between evangelicalism and the culture we
want to call popular.[47]

Those who served as go-betweens in the making of popular books
must have been conscious of not one, but several reading publics for
their wares. Historians of the book could profit from thinking along
these lines themselves. As it is, the category 'popular' is stretched this
way and that to fit quite different groups. Many of the books that John
Sommerville describes as 'popular' religious reading in Restoration
England were written by ordained ministers, most of whom were Anglicans.[48] In seventeenth-century Britain the readers of this devotional literature—undoubtedly quite numerous —were probably different from
the readers of ballads and the more traditional chapbooks. The distance between these groups could be large, as the following account
of 'peasant' reading in early eighteenth-century England may suggest:
'The peasant father of the poet John Clare, though barely able to
read, doted on such penny treasures as Nixon's Prophesies, Mother

---

[45] Roger Thompson, ed., *Pepys' Penny Merriments* (London, 1976); Thompson,
'Popular Reading and Humour in Restoration England,' *Journal of Popular Culture*
9 (1975): 653–71.

[46] Margaret Spufford argues, and I feel convincingly, that all social groups or
classes in seventeenth-century England relished 'bawdy' humor. The same point
has been made in studies of Shakespeare's 'bawdy.' Spufford, *Small Books and Pleasant Histories*, chap. 7. On sensationalism, see Martha Vicinus, *The Industrial Muse:
A Study of Nineteenth Century British Working-Class Literature* (New York, 1974), chap. 1.

[47] Spufford, *Small Books and Pleasant Histories*, chap. 8.

[48] C. John Sommerville, *Popular Religion in Restoration England*, University of Florida Social Science Monographs, No. 59 (Gainesville, Fla., 1977).

Bunches Fairy Tales, and Mother Shipton's Legacy, and late in the century Clare himself learned to read from chapbooks like Cinderella, Little Red Riding Hood, and Jack and the Beanstalk.'[49]

A literary historian has divided seventeenth-century fiction and its readers into two categories. In one of these, the books were 'sturdily old-fashioned, presenting both in appearance and content antiquated, indeed anachronistically retarded, tastes . . . [they] continue [their] popularity right through the century with no regard for fashion in literary style or material; [their] appeal is exotic, dealing as [they do] in wondrous feats of arms, strange locales and descriptions of lushly opulent displays, and enchantments, prophecies and spells.' The other type consisted of the 'fashionable' literature of the day: the 'secret histories' translated from the French, the duodecimos of 'exotic amorous adventures.'[50] Presumably the first of these categories was relegated to readers lower down in the social scale; while the other was consumed by a metropolitan audience that had more advanced tastes and consciousness.

In late seventeenth- and early eighteenth-century Wales, an evangelical literature of devotion was widely read and much republished. Many of the classics of the Puritan tradition—*Pilgrim's Progress*, Baxter's *Call*, Joseph Alleine's *Alarm*—were translated into Welsh and went through innumerable editions. But, as in the case of other genres, literacy, education, and wealth were factors that intervened to shape the distribution of these books: 'Of those below the level of the gentry, only professional men, substantial farmers, merchants and tradesmen, skilled artisans and craftsmen were consistently able to afford elementary education for their children. Subscription lists and probate material confirm that these were the groups that bought books, created a demand for more books, and set a high premium on literacy.' In Wales as elsewhere, the popular literature of devotion circulated in specific milieus.[51]

[49] Altick, *The English Common Reader*, p. 38.
[50] Charles C. Mish, 'Best Sellers in Seventeenth-Century Fiction,' *Papers of the Bibliographical Society of America* 47 (1953): 356–73, esp. 370–72.
[51] Geraint H. Jenkins, *Literature, Religion and Society in Wales, 1660–1730* (Cardiff, Wales, 1978), p. 300 and chap. 10.

These bits and pieces of description point toward two or three broad groupings within the general rubric of the popular book: readers of devotional literature, whether Anglican or evangelical; readers of 'fashionable' books, especially fiction; and readers of traditional prophecies, fairy tales, and romances. I do not mean to insist on these groups. In real life they must have overlapped, and certain books must have circulated among them all. But distinctions of this kind are in order lest we stretch the term 'popular' to cover every kind of circumstance.[52]

Certainly the seventeenth-century reader was aware of distinctions. The learned and the fashionable mocked the tastes of the 'vulgar.' Moralists decried 'bad' books, enjoining readers young and old to restrict themselves to books that qualified as 'good.' 'When thou canst read,' Thomas White cautioned in 1702, 'read no Ballads and foolish Books, but the Bible.' In a chapbook of the same period, the author warned, 'Let not your Children read these vain Books, profane Ballads, and filthy songs. Throw away all fond and amorous Romances, and fabulous Histories of Giants, the bombast Achievements of Knight Errantry, and the like; for these fill the Heads of Children with vain, silly and idle imaginations.'[53] Here the anger seems to focus especially on the motifs and forms of print—ballads, chapbooks, and broadsides —favored by or most accessible to readers in the lowest social groups, like John Clare and his father.

Anger means conflict. If the history of the book and the history of society are ever to converge, the most fruitful bond between them may be their common interest in the conflicts that reverberate through early modern history. Print may have worked in several different ways in regard to conflict. It could have served as an agent of control, extending and enhancing the legitimacy of an established, hierarchical system. But in a fluid, multilayered marketplace, the book could

---

[52] Robert Mandrou, 'Cultures Populaires et Savante: Rapports et Contacts,' in *The Wolf and the Lamb: Popular Culture in France, from the Old Regime to the Twentieth Century*, ed. Jacques Beauroy, Marc Bertrand, and Edward T. Gargan (Saratoga, Calif., 1977), pp. 17–38, urges that we speak in terms of several 'cultures populaires.'

[53] Thomas White, *A Little Book for Little Children* (Boston, 1702), p. 19; Victor Neuberg, *The Penny Histories: A Study of Chapbooks for Young Readers over Two Centuries* (New York, 1969), p. 20.

also have been a means of asserting cultural independence. In certain situations the book became the vehicle of far-reaching dissent.

Protestantism provides the perfect example of this latter process in sixteenth- and seventeenth-century Europe. Protestantism owed its rapid growth to the book. Martin Luther turned at once to the vernacular as a means of spreading his new faith. By 1523 he had mated the Protestant critique of Rome to the chapbook genre of remarkable prodigies and portents.[54] In England, Margaret Spufford has documented the importance of vernacular Bibles that drifted into the hands of Cambridgeshire farmers.[55] A church trial of the 1530s turned up striking evidence of how such books—illegal though they were—were welcomed and transmitted. A fifteen-year-old boy caught owning a primer and New Testament described how 'divers poor men in the town of Chelmsford . . . bought the new testament of Jesus Christ and on sundays did sit reading [aloud] in lower end of church, and many would flock about them to hear their reading then I came among the said readers to hear them . . . then thought I will learn to read english, and then I will have the new testament and read thereon myself.' Such scenes must have been multiplied a thousand times over in early modern Europe, even down to the detail of hiding the illegal book in the 'bedstraw.'[56] The rise of Protestantism was closely tied to the diffusion of such books, all written in the vernacular, and all aimed at lay readers.

So too in seventeenth-century England, evangelical Protestants who had been defeated in their ecclesiastical ambitions turned to the press, creating a devotional literature that was rapidly absorbed by pious householders. As this process unfolded in late seventeenth-century Wales, it involved not only translating into Welsh the classic texts of

---

[54] Eisenstein, *The Printing Press*, chap. 4; L. H. Buell, 'Elizabethan Portents: Superstition or Doctrine,' in *Essays Critical and Historical Dedicated to Lily B. Campbell* (Berkeley and Los Angeles, 1950), pp. 27–41. See also R. W. Scribner, *For the Sake of Simple Folk: Popular Propaganda for the German Reformation* (Cambridge, 1981).

[55] Margaret Spufford, *Contrasting Communities: English Villagers in the Sixteenth and Seventeenth Centuries* (Cambridge, 1974), chap. 8 and p. 247.

[56] Charles C. Butterfield, *The English Primer, 1529–1545* (Philadelphia, 1953), p. 202.

the evangelical tradition, but also exploiting the popularity of certain vernacular literary genres: 'Many Welsh religious reformers . . . realized that the easiest and most natural way of instilling Reformation truths was by casting scripture, private devotion and moral codes into popular verse-form. Among semi-literate folk in particular, verse had the mnemonic advantages of rhythm and rhyme. That is why so many authors chose to turn the catechism, the decalogue, the Lord's Prayer, and even parts of devotional books into verse.'[57]

The same process of mating devotional themes with verse and other popular genres was at work in England and New England. Benjamin Harris, a zealous Protestant and a London bookseller who lived briefly in Boston, published and probably wrote a *History of the Bible* in verse. It was also Harris who assembled the *New England Primer*, which blended piety with anti-Catholic propaganda.[58]

Like evangelical Protestantism with its primers, chapbooks, and versified devotion, every social movement had a literary arsenal. The conflict between Royalists and Parliamentarians was mirrored in competing versions of astrological and portent literature of the Civil War period.[59] At Douai on the continent, and at secret presses scattered about England, recusants created a vernacular literature of martyrology and devotion to sustain a beleaguered community of English Catholics.[60] In an essay included in this volume, Rhys Isaac considers how certain books in eighteenth-century Virginia functioned as symbolic tokens of social and ecclesiastical authority.[61] Few, if any, books were neutral in the early modern period. Instead they were caught up in tangled webs of controversy, be it Catholic versus Protestant, evangelical versus standpatter, Royalist versus Parliamentarian; or,

---

[57] Jenkins, *Literature, Religion and Society*, esp. p. 52.

[58] Charles L. Nichols, 'The Holy Bible in Verse,' *Proceedings of the American Antiquarian Society* 36 (1926): 71–82; Worthington C. Ford, 'Benjamin Harris, Printer and Bookseller,' *Proceedings of the Massachusetts Historical Society* 57 (1924): 34–68.

[59] The rival astrological predictions of William Lilly and John Gadbury are a case in point; and see Bernard Capp, *English Almanacs 1500–1800* (Ithaca, 1979), pp. 47–50, 79, 86.

[60] John Bossy, *The English Catholic Community, 1570–1850* (London, 1975), pp. 170–71 and chap. 15.

[61] See the essay by Isaac that follows in this volume.

at a deeper level yet, the world of 'magic' that Keith Thomas has
so magisterially described versus the rationalist mentality of the bour-
geoisie.[62]

The history of the book thus leads readily to issues that engage the
historian of culture and society: the ways in which a social order can
maintain itself or be subverted; the distribution of popular belief; the
rise of Protestantism or rationality. These issues are common to Europe
and America, though the differences are also interesting to consider.
The New England colonists, for example, were very largely literate,
and because they were two or three generations removed from the
coming of a vernacular religious literature, they were comfortably
accustomed to a fusion of identity, print, and religion that the Welsh
would not experience until the very end of the seventeenth century.
It is difficult to believe, moreover, that a full-blown 'peasant' culture
made its way across the Atlantic, though enough 'bad' books did to
worry the authorities.[63] As in eighteenth-century Virginia, the book
in colonial New England was closely tied to certain structures of authority. We would not expect otherwise in a society that proclaimed itself
to be a single, covenanted whole. But in time there was opposition,
and with opposition came a pluralistic culture of the book.

II

In *Recollections of a Lifetime*, Goodrich remembered the Ridgefield of
1790 as a self-contained, self-sufficient community. People lived sim-

---

[62] Keith Thomas, *Religion and the Decline of Magic* (London, 1971).
[63] No fully adequate study of literacy exists for New England. Kenneth Lockridge has used the method of signature counts in *Literacy in Colonial New England*
(New York, 1974), which measures the distribution of the skill of writing. But as
Margaret Spufford and others have argued (*Contrasting Communities*, chaps. 7 and
8), many persons, and especially women, could read but not write. This point is
crucial to my description of traditional literacy, below. For an argument that Lockridge's figures for the eighteenth century should be adjusted upwards, see Ross W.
Beales, Jr., 'Studying Literacy at the Community Level: A Research Note,' *Journal
of Interdisciplinary History* 9 (1978): 93–102. When I say that peasant culture did not
become transplanted to New England, I have in mind the ideal type that Robert
Muchembled describes in *Culture Populaire et Culture des Elites dans la France Moderne*
(Paris, 1978). Many attitudes among the colonists—e.g., toward property, gender
roles, sexuality, and health—were of course rooted in tradition.

ply, making their own clothes and raising most of what they ate. Access to books and printing was limited, for in this as in other modes of material life the town kept to itself. As if in compensation for the limits on supply, people read with care the texts that came to hand. The reading style of olden times was deliberate and reverential.

The amusements were then much the same as at present—though some striking differences may be noted. Books and newspapers—which are now diffused even among the country towns, so as to be in the hands of all, young and old—were then scarce, and were read respectfully, and as if they were grave matters, demanding thought and attention. They were not toys and pastimes, taken up every day, and by everybody, in the short intervals of labor, and then hastily dismissed, like waste paper. The aged sat down when they read, and drew forth their spectacles, and put them deliberately and reverently upon the nose. These instruments were not as now, little tortoise-shell hooks, attached to a ribbon, and put off and on with a jerk; but they were of silver or steel, substantially made, and calculated to hold on with a firm and steady grasp, showing the gravity of the uses to which they were devoted. Even the young approached a book with reverence, and a newspaper with awe. How the world has changed!

The very gestures that Goodrich describes for us—sitting down to read, or putting glasses on 'deliberately'—bespeak a distinctive relationship to print.[64]

Another characteristic of the relationship between books and readers was that people read aloud. Often this happened in the context of religious devotion. 'In her devotional exercises,' Buckingham recalled, 'my mother often introduced passages from Watts and Doddridge. One of them now recurs to me, as having been so often repeated as to become almost a part of her daily devotion.' Where he lived as a servant, Buckingham spent every Saturday evening reciting the Westminster Catechism and 'such Psalms or Hymns as I might have committed to memory in the course of the week. There was a time when I could recite Watts's version of the Psalms from beginning to end, together with many of his Hymns and Lyric Poems.' In that same household it was his duty to read aloud from the Bible.

64 Goodrich, *Recollections of a Lifetime*, 1: 71–72, 75, 86.

For a number of years . . . I read every day, [in the presence of his master
and mistress] at least one chapter, and often two or three chapters in the
Bible. . . . I have no doubt that I read the Bible through *in course* at least
a dozen times before I was sixteen years old, with no other omissions than
the jaw-breaking chapters of the Chronicles. The historical parts I had
read much oftener, and the incidents and the language became almost as
familiar as the grace . . . said before and after meals,—neither of which
ever varied a word during . . . nine years.

As for the Goodrich household, every morning after breakfast Samuel,
senior, read a chapter. 'In our family Bible it is recorded that he thus
read that holy book through, in course, thirteen times, in the space
of about five and twenty years.'[65]

In recalling this practice of reading aloud, Goodrich and Buckingham also alert us to its consequences. People came to know certain
texts by heart, sometimes because the religious customs of the day
demanded it—Goodrich and Buckingham both had to memorize the
Westminster Catechism—but more often through the force of repetition. This was especially true of Scripture, parts of which became the
basis of everyday conversation. Looking back upon his own immersion
in this text, Goodrich realized that he could not write without invok-
ing in some manner the key motifs and narrative style of the Bible.
His imagination was founded on a language he had learned almost
unconsciously.[66] Because Buckingham had absorbed this same language from the earliest moments of his life, he was able as a very
young child to *read* the Bible, and this without the benefit of any
formal instruction. Literacy flowed directly from his household experiences. 'I have no recollection of any time when I could not read. . . .
In December, 1784, the month in which I was five years old, I went
to a master's school, and, on being asked if I could read, I said I could
read in the Bible. The master placed me on his chair and presented
a Bible opened at the fifth chapter of Acts. I read the story of Ananias
and Sapphira falling down dead for telling a lie. He patted me on the

    [65] Buckingham, *Personal Memoirs*, 1: 11, 16, 19; Goodrich, *Recollections of a Life-
time*, 1: 157.
    [66] Goodrich, *Recollections of a Lifetime*, 1: 157–58.

head and commended my reading.'[67] Goodrich learned to read at
school, though for him as for Buckingham organized schooling was
intermittent. But in telling us that he learned a little Latin by over-
hearing the lessons of an older brother and piecing out the words in a
battered Corderius, he provides a parallel example of how reading
aloud became the route to literacy.[68]

To trace out all the consequences of reading aloud is eventually
to arrive back at Goodrich's description of the relationship between
books and readers. People approached print with 'reverence,' he reports, because books were scarce. But the stories that he and Buckingham tell of their experiences with print make it clear that 'reverence'
was also a response to the religious context in which reading seems to
have begun. The books that figured in devotional practice and that
were also the stuff of elementary reading—descriptions of the spiritual
life, like Doddridge's *Rise and Progress of Religion in the Soul*, catechisms,
psalmbooks, and religious verse—had an aura of the sacred. People
returned to such texts many times over, whether in public ceremonies
or in reading silently. This repetition of a few books made it easy for
children to memorize and eventually to become readers of these texts
themselves. All of these factors—the religious context, the scarcity of
print, the habit of repetition—were cumulatively involved in the pace
and quality of reading as a style. Reading in early New England was
an act that took place slowly and with unusual intensity, in contrast
to the faster pace and casualness of mid-nineteenth-century reading.

Let me refer to the older style as 'traditional literacy.'[69] Traditional
literacy prevailed on both sides of the Atlantic in the seventeenth and
eighteenth centuries; it is another of the fundamental continuities
between European and American history in the early modern period.

[67] Buckingham, *Personal Memoirs*, 1: 8–9.
[68] Goodrich, *Recollections of a Lifetime*, 1: 152–53.
[69] What I mean by this term is not quite the same as what François Furet and
Jacques Ozouf mean by 'restricted literacy,' a term they borrow from Jack Goody.
Cf. Furet and Ozouf, 'Trois siècles de métissage culturel,' pp. 491–92. Some historians speak of certain social groups in early modern Europe as 'semiliterate.' Carlo
Ginzburg's portrait of Menocchio is a brilliant reconstruction of a curiously naive
style of literacy: *The Cheese and the Worms: The Cosmos of a Sixteenth-Century Miller*,
trans. John and Anne Tedeschi (New York, 1982).

Generalizing from what I have already noted of its nature, we can identify traditional literacy in terms of four characteristics:

1. People valued learning to read over learning to write; and the first was taught prior to the other as a skill, often in the household or else at 'dame schools.'

2. Children learned to read by memorizing certain texts, most of which also had a role in church services and devotional practice. Memorizing occurred in situations where reading aloud was practiced, and where children were expected to recite from memory.

3. People came in contact with a limited number of books. Most persons had the use of, or owned, a Bible, psalmbook, primer, and catechism. Almanacs were widely available. Otherwise, the factors of cost and distribution were barriers to extensive reading.

4. Certain books nonetheless circulated widely, and had an extremely long life among the reading public. Such 'steady sellers' were staple reading in the culture of traditional literacy.

What Buckingham and Goodrich have to say about this system, and especially about the coherence of its parts, can scarcely be improved upon. Each came to literacy by the road of recitation and reading aloud; each began to read in a context of devotional practice. The books that circulated in their households were true examples of the steady seller—Watts and Doddridge, the *New England Primer*, and most important, the Bible. Other than these books and the almanac, they had little access to print.

All of their description is borne out in other sources. For example, Goodrich and Buckingham imply that children learned to read before they learned to write. There is frequent evidence that the two skills were kept separate, with reading ranked first in order of priority. Town records distinguish between 'woman schools' that taught reading, and 'Masters Schools' where children learned to write. Many children went off to school already knowing how to read. When the Reverend Peter Thacher took on a new student in 1680, he noted in his journal that 'I was to perfect him in reading, and to teach him to write.'[70] In his autobiography, Samuel Johnson of Connecticut

[70] 'Extracts from Salem School Committee Records,' *Essex Institute Historical Col-*

tells of a typical experience—typical in that he learned to read at home by a process of listening and memorizing: 'This Samuel was early taught to read by the care of his grandfather, who was very fond of him and, being apt to learn, he taught him many things by heart, beginning with the Lord's Prayer and Creed, and as he delighted to read the Scriptures, he got many passages of them by heart, which his grandfather, carrying him about with him to visit the ancient people, his contemporaries, made him recite *memoriter*, in which he much delighted.' As for learning to write, Johnson indicates that it happened 'after' the death of his grandfather.[71]

In this statement Johnson touches on two other aspects of learning to read, the household context and the role of recitation. Most New England autobiographies report that it was the mother who taught reading to her children; and though there are exceptions, it was the father who taught his children to write. 'I lived in my Fathers Family 12 years,' Increase Mather remembered, 'I learned to read of my mother. I learned to write of Father.' In 1704, Deacon John Paine wrote of his mother's cares to have him educated: 'carefull mother eke She Was / unto her children all / in teaching them gods word to read / when as they were but Small.'[72] In such households, the act of learning to read was inextricably linked with the practice of reading aloud. Fathers often played a major role as readers. The husband of Sarah Goodhue 'read aloud' each Sunday from his transcriptions of the minister's sermons. Samuel Sewall read the Bible aloud 'in course' to his children, and as they grew older each had to join in the exercise.[73]

---

lections 91 (1955): 53; Peter Thacher, Journal, MS, p. 644, Massachusetts Historical Society, Boston. I am grateful to Ross W. Beales, Jr., for these references and also for those in fn. 72.

71 Herbert and Carol Schneider, eds., *Samuel Johnson, President of King's College, His Career and Writings*, 4 vols. (New York, 1929), 1: 3–4.

72 'The Autobiography of Increase Mather,' ed. Michael G. Hall, *Proceedings of the American Antiquarian Society*, 71 (1961): 278; 'Deacon John Paine's Journal,' *Mayflower Descendants* 8 (1906): 230.

73 Thomas Waters, *Ipswich in the Massachusetts Bay Colony*, 2 vols. (Ipswich, Mass., 1905), 1: 523; *The Diary of Samuel Sewall*, ed. M. Halsey Thomas, 2 vols. (New York, 1973), 1: 115, 384, 404.

For children who were just beginning to encounter print, reading aloud, reciting, and memorizing were acts that fused together. Samuel Johnson's is a key statement: he began by learning 'things by heart'—the Lord's Prayer, the Apostles' Creed—and by an almost intangible progression found himself able to read, meanwhile continuing to memorize from Scripture. All this he accomplished when he was but four or five years old. Johnson was probably using a *New England Primer* or something like it, for such books ordinarily added the Lord's Prayer, the Apostles' Creed, a catechism, and selections from the Bible to an alphabet and lists of words. From cover to cover, the material in the *Primer* was designed to be memorized. At home as in school, the children chanted aloud, sounding out words and memorizing texts before they could actually read.

In early New England, school books like the primer were among the most widely owned and distributed kinds of books, rivaled only by catechisms, psalmbooks, and the Bible. All of these books owed their wide distribution partly to official regulations, which themselves grew out of the Puritan supposition that reading was a 'great help' to 'salvation.'[74] From time to time the Massachusetts government would order house-to-house inspections to see if every family owned a Bible; and there were similar inspections of children's knowledge of the catechism.

Other than the Bible and its kin, books were scarce, as Buckingham and Goodrich both suggest. The situation in England and New England was one of small press runs and limited circulation for most items. Press runs for quartos and octavos could dip as low as 300 or 400 copies, and rarely went above a maximum of 1,500. The economics of publishing—the shortage of capital, the inefficiencies of distribution—made larger editions unusual. Taking these figures into account, David Cressy has calculated that the entire production of London printers in 1640 could have been absorbed by the households of the gentry, the clergy, and professionals. On the eve of the English Revolution, the London book trade may have scarcely touched the

[74] Waters, *Ipswich*, 1: 277; Israel Loring, *The Duty and Interest of Young Persons* (Boston, 1718), pp. 21–22.

artisans and yeomanry of the countryside save for occasional chap-books and broadsides.[75] No one has made similar calculations for New England, where in any case the substantial business in importations makes local figures of less use. But here as in England, press runs were small, prices high, and distribution a matter of catch-as-catch-can.[76] As Edward Taylor headed west to become the first minister of a new Connecticut River Valley town, he carried with him a precious hoard of manuscript copies he had personally made of books in Cambridge and Boston. Ministers were exceptional in building up substantial libraries, though we may know more about the large collections than the small. In most probate inventories, however, books fail to appear.[77]

If the situation in New England was not quite as bright as it is often painted, the situation in mid-eighteenth-century Virginia was one of real limits on the circulation of print. The publisher of the *Virginia*

[75] Cressy, *Literacy and the Social Order*, p. 47. 'Though it is pleasant to envision the Elizabethan cottage with its faded and tattered ballads on the wall, and the cottager crouching over the feeble fire spelling out the words of a chapbook . . . , it would be a mistake to imagine that reading had any but the most incidental place in the life of the masses.' Altick, *The English Common Reader*, p. 29. The paradox is nonetheless that (as Margaret Spufford and others argue) certain inexpensive forms of print were remarkably abundant.

[76] Rollo G. Silver, 'Financing the Publication of Early New England Sermons,' *Studies in Bibliography* 11 (1958): 163–78; Silver, 'Publishing in Boston, 1726–1757: The Accounts of Daniel Henchman,' *Proceedings of the American Antiquarian Society* 66 (1956): 17–36; Silver, 'Government Printing in Massachusetts, 1751–1801,' *Studies in Bibliography* 16 (1963): 161–200; Marcus A. McCorison, ed., 'A Daybook from the Office of the *Rutland Herald* Kept by Samuel Williams, 1798–1802,' *Proceedings of the American Antiquarian Society* 76 (1966): 293–395.

[77] Norman Grabo, *Edward Taylor* (New Haven, Conn., 1961), p. 25. Thomas Goddard Wright, *Literary Culture in Early New England, 1620–1730* (New Haven, Conn., 1920), reprints a number of ministers' library inventories; for others, see the references in Miller, *The New England Mind*, pp. 509–11. Comprehensive studies of book holdings in a particular community tend to indicate that between half and two-thirds of surviving inventories do not include books. See, for example, Harriet S. Tapley, *Salem Imprints* (Salem, Mass., 1927), p. 164; Minor Myers, Jr., 'Letters, Learning, and Politics in Lyme: 1760–1800,' in *A Lyme Miscellany 1776–1976*, ed. George Willauer, Jr. (Middletown, Conn., 1977), pp. 48–80; Christopher M. Jedrey, *The World of John Cleaveland: Family and Community in Eighteenth-Century New England* (New York, 1979), p. 103 (the figure here is 13 percent). Hart, *The Popular Book in America*, p. 8, has a figure of 60 percent for Middlesex County in the seventeenth century. This seems improbable.

Almanac managed an annual press run of 5,000 copies, at a time when New Englanders were buying up to 60,000 copies a year of a single almanac, and sustaining several others. Gregory and Cynthia Stiverson, in an essay included in this volume, have calculated that the most active bookseller in mid-eighteenth-century Virginia sold books to perhaps no more than 250 customers a year. And not very many books at that: a total of 2,028, excluding almanacs, for a white population that exceeded 130,000 persons.

The celebrated autobiography of Devereux Jarratt adds to the gloom of these figures, for Jarratt remembered provincial Virginia as a veritable desert in regard to books. Wanting to know something of 'philosophy, rhetoric and logic,' he discovered that 'there were no books on such subjects among us.' In order to learn arithmetic he 'borrowed a plain book, in manuscript.' The very 'first sermon book I ever had seen, or, perhaps, heard of,' had been 'left, by some one,' at a neighbor's. When he had been spiritually awakened and became curious to understand the meaning of the Bible, he found that 'I had not a single book in the world, nor was I able to buy any books, had I known of any for sale. But, by some means, I got hold of a little old book, in a smoky condition, which I found to be Russel's seven sermons. I borrowed the book, and read the sermons again and again.' Later on, by word of mouth, 'I was told of a very large book, belonging to a gentleman, about five or six miles distant across the river, which explained all the New Testament. I resolved to get the reading of that book, if possible.' Only when he came into contact with a Presbyterian minister—from whom he heard his first sermon—did Jarratt finally have access to 'a number of very excellent books, written by men of the greatest eminence for learning and piety, such as Baxter, Watts, Doddridge, Young, etc.'[78]

Through the story of this search for books runs another motif of traditional literacy, the importance of certain 'steady sellers' in the reading done by ordinary people. Steady sellers were books that remained in

[78] Devereux Jarratt, *The Life of the Reverend Devereux Jarratt . . . Written by Himself* (Baltimore, 1806), pp. 24–26. Compare Rhys Isaac's interpretation of this same material in his essay that follows.

print for several decades. Some of these books showed an astonishing longevity, circulating among a popular audience for at least 200 years. Nowhere is there evidence of total sales for any of these titles. Once or twice we hear of press runs—Joseph Alleine's *Alarm for the Unconverted* was published, we are told, in 'one Impression' of 30,000 copies, and altogether 70,000 were sold in the space of a few years.[79] But for the most part the evidence that these books were popular, and *that they were also readily available*, lies half-obscured in bibliographies, booksellers' catalogues, probate inventories, and memoirs such as those by Goodrich, Buckingham, and Jarratt. Steady sellers were never available in the same quantities as psalmbooks, primers, catechisms, and the Bible. But they turn up so many times and in so many places that they must be seen as cultural artifacts of a special kind. No less than the Bible and the catechism, steady sellers stand at the very center of traditional literacy.[80]

The identity of some of these books is revealed in occasional recommendations of 'good' reading. In one of these statements, an English clergyman in 1702 advised young people to 'read the Bible, and get the *Plain Mans Pathway to Heaven*, a very plain holy book for you, get the *Practice of Piety*, Mr. Baxters *Call to the Unconverted*, Mead's *Almost Christian*, Vincents *Advice to Young Men*, and read the Histories of the Martyrs that died for Christ, and in the *Book of Martyrs*.'[81] In another,

[79] These figures are cited on the inside back cover of the 1767 Boston ed. of *Alarm to the Unconverted*.

[80] Steady sellers are books that went through five or more editions in New England in a period of at least fifty years. In the late seventeenth century, Boston booksellers repeatedly ordered certain titles from London; most of these were or became steady sellers. A guide to these books is Worthington C. Ford, *The Boston Book Market, 1679–1700* (Boston, 1917). Steady sellers were a phenomenon of the book trade in seventeenth- and eighteenth-century Germany, Netherlands, and France; in these countries, as in Britain and America, books of devotion and their kin were frequently reprinted and widely owned. Albert Ward, *Book Production, Fiction and the German Reading Public 1740–1800* (Oxford, 1974), p. 4; Julien Brancolini and Marie-Thérèse Bouyssy, 'La vie provinciale du livre à la fin de l'Ancien Régime,' in Furet et al., *Livre et Société*, 2: 3–37. Ministers in late seventeenth-century Wales were translating familiar titles into the vernacular; cf. Jenkins, *Literature, Religion and Society*, p. 133.

[81] White, *A Little Book for Little Children*, p. 19. Two of these titles were in Bunyan's dowry.

a young widower of Bennington, Vermont, in the early nineteenth
century urged women to spend their days 'diligently reading the Scriptures through in course every year, in selecting and committing to
memory several hundred of the most striking passages of scripture,
which may appear of the highest doctrinal and practical importance,
in reading the writings of Baxter, Flavel, Bunyan, Berkitt, Henry,
Saurin, Mason, Watts, Guyse, Doddridge, J. Edwards, Davies, Hopkins, John Newton ... Young's Night Thoughts, and a few of the best
histories.'[82] Even though this nineteenth-century list has all of the eighteenth to draw upon, the similarities of title and of type are striking.

Steady sellers also figured significantly in the production of country
printers in New England. These books originated in the metropolitan
book trade of London and Boston, but in the course of their existence
became increasingly the business of the country or provincial printer.
As printing offices sprang up outside Boston in ever increasing numbers during the eighteenth and early nineteenth centuries, each new
entrepreneur looked around him for items he was sure of selling. The
local writer and the local patron provided some work in the form of
funeral, ordination, and election sermons, and perhaps an almanac.
But to get more work, every country printer turned eventually to the
titles that were known to everyone, and that always seemed to sell.

Consider E. Merriam, & Co., founded in the Worcester County
town of Brookfield, Massachusetts, in 1798. The Merriams were more
ambitious than most country printers. Their list included a few novels, two songbooks, a dictionary, and some spellers, all sandwiched in
among the usual funeral sermons and orations. But much of their
business for the first twenty years lay in printing steady sellers: four
editions of Isaac Watts and two of Doddridge's *Rise and Progress of
Religion*, together with single editions of Baxter's *Call to the Unconverted*
and *The Saints Everlasting Rest*, Thomas Shearman's *Divine Breathings*,
captivity narratives by Mary Rowlandson and John Williams, and
Young's *Night Thoughts*. The steadiest of the 'steady sellers' on the
Merriam list was Robert Russel's *Seven Sermons*, published by them in

---

82 *The Religious Experience of Mrs. Emerson* (Bennington, Vt., 1809), p. 53n.

1818, but originally appearing before 1700. This was the 'little old book, in a smoky condition' that Jarratt came across in Virginia, a stray from one of the *forty-three* printings this book had in America between 1701 and 1820, when it finally ceased being published.[83]

Early and late, printers in New England relied on steady sellers for their business. The pattern holds for nearly everyone who entered the book trade, be it James Franklin in his Newport days, the Greens in Hartford and New London, Isaiah Thomas in Boston and Worcester (though Thomas had wider interests), or Anthony Haswell in Bennington. In search of printers and their consciousness of steady sellers, we can return to the seventeenth century and the two men who ran the Cambridge press in the 1660s and 1670s. Marmaduke Johnson and Samuel Green kept a sharp eye on the London book market for titles that would sell in New England. One or two of their reprints were sensations of the moment, like a nobleman's account of Mount Aetna in eruption. But most were books that already qualified as steady sellers, or would soon become so: *Old Mr. Dod's Sayings*; William Dyer's *Christs Famous Titles*; Thomas Vincent's *Gods Terrible Voice*, a powerful sermon on the great plague and London fire (still of interest to a printer in Windham, Connecticut, in 1795); Thomas Wilcox's *A Choice Drop of Honey* (at least fifty English editions, and reprinted in Boston as late as 1807); and books by two of the colonists, in one case printed originally abroad, Shepard's *The Sincere Convert* and Wigglesworth's *The Day of Doom*.

The world of steady sellers is revealed to us, finally, in the stories people tell of their reading. From these stories we learn something else of equal importance: these books were read in a special manner that befit their religious or devotional contents. Samuel Goodrich has already told us of the 'awe' and 'reverence' with which people came to books. His words are borne out in advice on how to read, and in the simple and naive statements people left behind of their experience as readers.

A motif of all such statements is intensity. Here is Thomas White

---

[83] The original date of imprint in England is impossible to determine. An edition *was* published after 1820 in Mountain Valley, Va. (1853).

telling readers how to use a book: 'As you read (if the Books be your own) Mark in the margin, or by underlining the places you find most relish in, and take most special notice of, that that doth most concern thee, that you may easily, and more quickly find them again.'[84] And here is the anonymous author of *The Life and Writings of Miss Eliza Waite* (1813) on why it is worthwhile to read the journals of pious young ladies: 'The end of reading is not attained by getting through the book, but by receiving those serious and deep impressions, which will have a practical influence upon the future life.'[85]

In line with this advice, people read with care, returning again and again to the same text to ensure they got its meaning. Robert Keayne of Boston, the man who left so long and famous a will, bequeathed to his son, 'As my special gift to him my little written book in my closet upon 1 Cor. 11, 27, 28, which is a treatise of the sacrament of the Lord's Supper. . . . [It is] a little thin pocket book bound in leather, all written with my own hand, which I esteem more precious than gold, and which I have read over I think 100 and 100 times. . . . I desire him and hope that he will never part with it as long as he lives.'[86]

As in Keayne's '100 and 100 times,' people read slowly—so slowly, and so repeatedly, that parts of these texts became embodied in their memories. Let me offer some examples. Sarah Osborn went to nurse her eldest son:

He was given over by the doctors and all friends, who lamented him, and did the best for him in their power, as to the body. But alas! my great concern was for that precious jewel, his immortal soul. I endeavored to improve

---

[84] White, *A Little Book for Little Children*, p. 19. He continues: 'I would have you learn some Sentences out of the Scripture by heart; of which you may have constant use.'

[85] *Life and Writings of Miss Eliza Waite* (Hallowell, Me., 1819), p. 246. There is no shortage of instructions on how to read. 'Be diligent in reading the scriptures: First, you must every morning and evening, read a chapter in your bible, or else some part of a godly sermon; and when you read, you must not run it over, and then leave it, you had as good do nothing as do so; but when you read, you take especial heed, what you be reading of; and when you have done, look back a little upon what you have read.' Robert Russel, *Seven Interesting Sermons* (Boston, 1767), p. 127.

[86] *The Apologia of Robert Keayne*, ed. Bernard Bailyn (New York, 1965), pp. 28–29.

every opportunity to discourse with him, and read to him such portions of scripture as I thought suitable, with passages out of Mr. Allein's Alarm.[87]

Like Goodrich, Buckingham, and so many others, a young man was especially responsive to Isaac Watts:

For about twenty four hours before he died [he] seemed to be in an extasy of joy, and so remained till he could speak no longer; and when he was speechless he by signs desir'd the Company to sing praises to God; and when they seem'd backward, he was the more earnest, and took Dr. Watts' hymns and turned them to the third hymn of the second book of Spiritual Songs, and by signs urged them to sing, which they did; and he endeavoured to join them as well as he could; and then with Eyes and Hands lift up, fell asleep.[88]

A minister recalled the time when, temporarily out of school, he

read over all the vollums of Foxes Acts and Monuments, which I much delighted in, and know much of espetially the two last vollums, which I read over diverse times, where, in my young years, I showd a tendr heart, yet could not forbare melting into tears, when I read of the cruelty showd against the Masters and blessed servants of Jesus Christ.[89]

The mother of Carteret Rede remembered that when

I came up into her Chamber, I found her reading Mr. *John Janeway's* Life and Death; she was all in Tears, she said to me, Oh! that I were such a Worm as this was! that God would give me Repentance unto Life! Oh! that I were in the Bosom of Jesus! Oh! that my Sorrow might be true Sorrow![90]

Or consider the fusion of world view, reading, and emotion in the life of Joseph Croswell. Born in 1712 in Charlestown, Croswell was converted during the Great Awakening and became a lay itinerant preacher. His 'favorite' authors, an anonymous biographer informs us, 'were those of the Calvinistic description, such as Flavel, Erskine, Bolton, Edwards, &c.' The statement is borne out by the journal in

---

87 Samuel Hopkins, *Memoirs of the Life of Mrs. Sarah Osborn* (Worcester, 1799), p. 66.
88 *The Christian History, Containing Accounts of the Revival and Propagation of Religion in Great-Britain & America. For the Year 1744* (Boston, 1745), p. 112.
89 Lilley B. Eaton, *Genealogical History of the Town of Reading, Mass.* (Boston, 1874), p. 53.
90 [Mrs. Sarah Rede], *A Token for Youth* (Boston, 1729), p. 12.

which he recorded his reading and the impact that it had upon him. Often as he read he experienced 'quickenings.' Thus,

In the evening realized some quickenings in reading the believer's journey to the heavenly Canaan, by Mr. Erskine.

Experienced quickening influences of the Divine Spirit whilst reading an account of the joyful deaths of young people at Haverhill about 22 years past, which was occasioned by the throat-distemper.

But Croswell's most passionate responses as a reader were to Scripture, the steadiest of all the steady sellers: 'I know not when I have experienced greater consolation in reading the word of God. Blessed be its glorious and gracious Author. Sweetly regaled in the afternoon by the heavenly south breezes of the divine Spirit, whilst repeating scripture passages.' And having memorized one part of the Bible—'I have this day repeated the whole book of Canticles by heart'—he returned to the exercise again and again: 'Some enlivening about noon while passing through woods and repeating the last three chapters in the Canticles. . . . Refreshed in repeating passages from the Canticles.'[91]

Traditional literacy culminates in the intense relationship between book and reader recounted in these episodes. To understand the reasons why, we need to look beyond the cultural process of becoming literate to consider the contents of the steady sellers. All of them were concerned with religion as a mode of living and a mode of dying.[92] As they define it, the religious life encompassed four great crises or rites of passage. The conversion process in all of its amplitude was the dominating event in the steady sellers; many of them were specifically about the process, and each assumed that it was fundamental. Other steady sellers focused on the imperative for self-scrutiny when coming to the Lord's Table to receive communion.[93] Still others dramatized the experience of 'remarkable' afflictions. A final group taught the

91 *Sketches of the Life, and Extracts from the Journals, and other Writings, of the Late Joseph Croswell* (Boston, 1809), pp. 8, 14–40.

92 I am indebted to Charles Hambrick-Stowe's splendid study of Puritan devotional practice, *The Practice of Piety* (Chapel Hill, N.C., 1982), for this argument concerning the relationship between reading and the structure of the religious life.

93 Two examples that were widely read in New England were Thomas Doolittle, *A Treatise Concerning the Lords Supper* (London, 1665, and many subsequent eds.),

art of dying well, of turning the terror of death into the joy of eternal life with Christ.[94] The steady sellers told stories of specific people and their ways of dealing with these crises. Children underwent conversion and died in bliss in James Janeway's *A Token for Children*. Martyrs suffered the most terrible punishments, but withstood them because of God's assistance. In one of Robert Russel's *Seven Sermons*, Devereux Jarratt came across the history of Francis Spira, and was 'deeply impresst' by this vivid narrative of the agonies of conscience suffered by an apostate from Protestantism. 'Spira' was a commonplace of diaries and the sermon literature, so widely known that people used this single word to convey a wealth of meaning.[95] The people who read or listened to such stories came to feel that their structure coincided with the very 'plot' of human life: the pilgrimage from sin to grace, from bondage to salvation. The distance between books and life was very short, if any real distance existed in the first place. The hymns of Watts that Buckingham learned from his mother, and could still quote after half a century, were reality to people who lived within the boundaries of traditional literacy.

Let us suppose, therefore, that traditional literacy evokes a world view. This world view was embodied not only in the steady sellers but also in much of the street literature of Anglo-American print culture, the broadsides, chapbooks, and almanacs that were dispersed quite widely. Some of this street literature was devoted to 'amazing' por-

---

and Jabez Earle, *Sacramental Exercises* (London, 1707), which Samuel Sewall was reading in 1715. *The Diary of Samuel Sewall*, 2: 790.

94 The longest-lived of these was doubtless Charles Drelincourt, *The Christian's Defence against the Fears of Death* (Boston, 1744), which was originally published in France in the middle of the seventeenth century. Flora Thompson, in *Lark Rise to Candleford* (London, 1954), p. 110, remembers *Drelincourt on Death* as a staple of cottager reading in north Oxfordshire in the 1880s.

95 Leonard Hoar, *The Sting of Death and Death Unstung* (Boston, 1680), p. 9; Andrew Jones, *The Black Book of Conscience* (Hartford, 1767), p. 14; *Thomas Shepard's Confessions*, ed. George Selement and Bruce C. Woolley, *Publications of the Colonial Society of Massachusetts* 58 (Boston, 1981): 168. I am grateful to Patricia Caldwell for this last reference. John Bunyan 'did hit upon that dreadful story of that miserable mortal, Francis Spira; A book that was to my troubled spirit as salt, when rubbed into a fresh wound.' *Grace Abounding*, p. 49.

tents and prodigies that were God's warning voice to man. Some
of it recounted the behavior of criminals awaiting execution, who in
their final words always warned the young to avoid their sad fate.[96]
The almanacs catered to a Protestant self-awareness with their talk
of 'popery.' 'Penny godlies' taught the difference between right and
wrong ways of dying.[97] Broadside elegies described the saint in flight
to heaven.[98] Altogether the most 'popular' forms of print in England
and New England shared much in common with the steady sellers.

By one route or another, the world view of these texts became the
world view of most New Englanders. The social boundaries of this
world view were broad, encompassing both the highly educated and
the barely literate.[99] In seventeenth-century England, the reformation of manners was visibly incomplete, and the process of replacing
traditional rural culture with evangelical Christianity involved open
conflict between the social orders. Perhaps because the colonists had
undergone this process before migrating, conflict in New England is
less evident than consensus. Here, the ministry spoke the same language as the farmers and artisans who paid their salaries. Here too,
the Baptists and Quakers who opposed the 'New England Way' of
organizing churches continued at more basic levels to share the mentality of those in the majority.[100] Even the curse that ordinary people
exchanged so often in the street—'the devil take you'—owed its being
to a common set of ideas.[101]

The alternatives to this traditional mental world were unsystematic
and intermittent in seventeenth- and early eighteenth-century New

---

[96] Increase Mather, *A Sermon Occasioned by the Execution* (Boston, 1686), pp. 27ff.

[97] Spufford, *Small Books and Pleasant Histories*, chap. 8; and see Hyder E. Rollins,
Old English Ballads, 1553–1625, Chiefly from Manuscripts (Cambridge, 1920), pp. ix–xvi.

[98] Ola E. Winslow, ed., *American Broadside Verse* (New Haven, Conn., 1930).

[99] The intellectual world of the 'learned' in New England embraced a wider
range of reading than the steady sellers. Some of this reading, or its possibilities,
are indicated in Norman S. Fiering, 'The Transatlantic Republic of Letters: A Note
on the Circulation of Learned Periodicals to Early Eighteenth-Century America,'
William and Mary Quarterly, 3d ser. 33 (1976): 642–60.

[100] [Thomas Maule], *New-Englands Persecutors Mauld with Their Own Weapons*
([New York, 1697]), sig. A2 recto, pp. 9, 19, 32.

[101] [Cotton Mather], *The Young Mans Preservative* (Boston, 1701), p. 64; *Records
and Files of the Quarterly Courts of Essex County*, 9 vols. (Salem, Mass., 1911–75), 1:134.

England. Two such divergences can be distinguished. To give one a more elaborate name than it deserves, we can speak of the culture of the alehouse. Like ordinary people everywhere, the colonists gathered at the local tavern to down their rum or beer. Winter evenings, they told stories of thieving lawyers and cuckolded husbands. They sang 'wicked' ballads and swapped copies of dirty books, including most likely that illicit steady seller, *Aristotle's Master Piece*. Certainly, they laughed. Guilt and fear were the province of the meetinghouse; release and humor the province of the tavern.[102]

Occasionally the almanacs play up to this world. In Tully's almanac for 1688 the sober plainness of the almanac tradition in New England was challenged by a closing 'prognostication' in verse:

> January's Observations.
> The best defence against the Cold,
> Which our Fore-Fathers good did hold,
> Was early a full Pot of Ale,
> Neither too mild nor yet too stale.

Under February, young men

> Do present their Loves
> With Scarfs . . .
> And to show manners not forgot all,
> Give them a lick under the 'Snot-gall.'

The 'prognostication' for February concludes in kind: 'The Nights are still cold and long, which may cause great Conjunction betwixt the Male and Female Planets of our sublunary Orb, the effects wherof

---

102 Peter Clark, 'The Ale-house and the Alternative Society,' in *Puritans and Revolutionaries: Essays Presented to Christopher Hill*, ed. D. Pennington and K. Thomas (Oxford, 1978), pp. 47–72; Benjamin Wadsworth, *An Essay to Do Good. Being a Disswasive from Tavern-haunting, and Excessive Drinking* (Boston, 1710); John Barnard, *The Nature and Danger of Sinful Mirth. Exhibited in a Plain Discourse* (Boston, 1728); Otho T. Beale, 'Aristotle's Master-Piece in America: A Landmark in the Folklore of Medicine,' *William and Mary Quarterly*, 3d ser. 20 (1963): 207–22. I am grateful to Roger Thompson for this reference. He informs me that this and other dirty books are frequently mentioned in cases involving sexual offenses in the Middlesex County (Mass.) court records for the seventeenth century. Cf. Thompson, 'The Puritans and Prurience: Aspects of the Restoration Book Trade,' in *Contrast and Connection*, ed. H. C. Allen and Roger Thompson (London, 1976), pp. 36–64.

may be seen about nine months after, and portend great charges of Midwife, Nurse, and Naming the Bantling.'[103]

But before these verses become tokens of an anti-Puritan mentality —an overdue revolt of the long-repressed masses—the peculiar history of Tully's almanacs must be taken into account. In 1688 Tully inserted Anglican saints' days and secular holidays into his calendar, while referring in his chronology to 'blessed Charles martyr' and 'Oliver the tyrant.' This vigorous trampling on New England sensibilities grows out of a single circumstance: Tully had chosen to write for the tiny community of Anglicans and Royalists then in command of civil government in New England, a community that constituted the other alternative. When the Revolution of 1689 swept this group from office, Tully changed directions, stripping his almanacs of all saints' days and licentious verse, and reverting to the New England norm. His almanac for 1688 is nonetheless a straw in the wind. Puritan culture in New England had been breached by cosmopolitanism. As the decades passed, the influence of this alternative would gradually increase. Thanks to this tendency, a century later Boston had a professional theater, dancing schools, and subscription libraries concentrating on fiction. But to look this far ahead brings us back to Goodrich and Buckingham and the transformation of print culture they had taken part in.

III

To Goodrich and Buckingham the first half of the nineteenth century was a time of rapid progress out of 'barbarism.' The upward 'march of civilization' was as evident in print as in the temperance movement. Goodrich could remember when 'a half-pint of [rum] was given as a matter of course to every day-laborer' who worked on a Connecticut farm. But no longer: the standards of morality had changed, leaving demon rum behind. The improvements in communications and material comforts were equally marked. At the turn of the century Ridgefield was breaking out of its isolation. As local farmers abandoned native wares in favor of the latest styles in furniture, the 'homely'

103 John Tully, *An Almanack* (Boston, 1687), pp. 15–16.

picture of 'half a century ago' shifted to one of 'Kidderminster car-
pets—made at Enfield or Lowell—mahogany bureaus, gilt looking-
glasses, and a small well-filled mahogany bookcase.'[104]

The same improvements in technology that opened up Ridgefield
to the world were carrying books and newspapers into such towns at
a faster rate. Goodrich knew that his mid-nineteenth-century readers
would be struck by the scarcity of books in the Ridgefield of memory. He
made this point repeatedly in terms of children's literature, juxtaposing
his own excitement as a child at owning two or three precious books
to the abundance of opportunities children of the new age enjoyed.

It is difficult now, in this era of literary affluence, almost amounting to
surfeit, to conceive of the poverty of books suited to children in the days
of which I write. Except the New England Primer . . . I remember none
that were in general use among my companions. When I was about ten
years old, my father brought from Hartford, Gaffer Ginger, Goody Two
Shoes, and some of the rhymes and jingles, now collected under the name
of Mother Goose,—with perhaps a few other toy books of that day. These
were a revelation.

In casting my mind backward over the last thirty years—and comparing
the past with the present, duly noting the amazing advances made in every
thing which belongs to the comfort, the intelligence, the luxury of society—
there is no point in which these are more striking than in the books for
children and youth. Let any one who wishes to comprehend this matter,
go to such a juvenile bookstore as that of C. S. Francis, in Broadway, New
York, and behold the teeming shelves—comprising almost every topic . . .
—and let him remember that nineteen twentieths of these works have come
into existence within the last thirty years.[105]

Somewhere in his consciousness, Goodrich must have realized that
books in such abundance were no longer 'revelations' to their readers,
and that he as Peter Parley was expendable. But any ambivalence he
might have felt about the age of abundance was minimized in his rush
to extol the progress of children's literature.

---

[104] Goodrich, *Recollections of a Lifetime*, 1: 69, 82.

[105] Ibid., pp. 165–66, 174. Books of this sort were being advertised as 'Little
Books for the Instruction and Amusement of Children, adorn'd with a Variety of
Cuts and bound in Gilt Paper,' in *A Catalogue of A Very Large Assortment of the Most
Esteemed Books* (Boston, [1772]). Isaiah Thomas would make a specialty of such
items, most of them copied from the publications of John Newbery.

That motif applied as much to the moral contents of children's literature as to its availability. The Mother Goose rhymes his father gave him had in retrospect been 'painful' reading:

I recollect, while the impression was fresh in my mind, that on going to bed, I felt a creeping horror come over me, as the story [Little Red Riding Hood] recurred to my imagination. As I dwelt upon it, I soon seemed to see the hideous jaws of a wolf coming out of the bedclothes, and approaching as if to devour me. . . . at last I became so excited, that my mother was obliged to tell me that the story was a mere fiction.
'It is not true, then,?' said I.
'No,' said my mother, 'it is not true.'
'Why do they tell such falsehoods, then,?' I replied.

'False' is but the mildest of the epithets he uses for the stories of his childhood. Jack the Giant Killer teaches readers 'to forgive, nay, to love and approve, wickedness,—lying, deception, and murder.' Puss in Boots teaches its readers to 'cheat, lie, and steal,'—in effect, 'to hate virtue itself.' Such tales inculcate 'the love of the horrible, the monstrous, the grotesque.' Their moral standard is 'debased' and 'coarse.' They have, concludes Goodrich, no place in the Christian home.[106]

This reaction has little to do with how Mother Goose stories were perceived in the eighteenth century, but much to do with Goodrich in his adult identity as Peter Parley. As a writer he proposed to enter the marketplace and drive out all wicked stories, replacing them with 'nursery books . . . [that] consist of beauty instead of deformity, goodness instead of wickedness, decency instead of vulgarity.' The models for the stories he would write were the moral tales of Hannah More, an English Evangelical who preached the virtues of poverty and strict temperance to English workers.[107] Hannah More and Samuel Goodrich shared in common a ferocious antipathy to the uses of literacy they had known as children. In *The Fortune Teller*, Hannah More derides the mentality of a farm girl who delights 'in dream books,' buys 'very wicked ballads' from an old woman peddler, and takes all

---

[106] Goodrich, *Recollections of a Lifetime*, 1: 166–70.
[107] Ibid., p. 172. Cf. Harry B. Weiss, *Hannah More's Cheap Repository Tracts in America* (New York, 1946).

kinds of portents seriously. Sally Evans, the antiheroine of the tale, is betrayed by her world view into abandoning an honest lover for a man who has no morals. Sally dies, and the old woman fortune teller who has led her astray is declared a criminal and transported.[108]

Goodrich is less specific but no less hostile in the Peter Parley stories. The children who move through these stories are gentle, loving, and full of heart. The natural world which they encounter is personified as smiling and benevolent. Implicit in these settings is a theology at odds with the theology of the *New England Primer*; the God of Samuel Goodrich was as smiling and benevolent as the sunshine, flowers, animals, and children of his stories. Contrary to the *Primer*, and contrary to the practices of his own youth, Goodrich believed that children must be educated with special care:

> Children are simple, living, true—
> 'Tis God that made them so;
> And would you teach them?—be so, too,
> And stoop to what they know. . . .
> Begin with simple lessons, things
> On which they love to look;
> Flowers, pebbles, insects, birds on wings—
> These are God's spelling-book!

That Goodrich was aiming to reverse a traditional consciousness is directly suggested in a story that ends with an analysis of thunder and lightning. He is at pains to demonstrate the purely natural origins of the phenomena, for in the rational world of Peter Parley an older mentality, with its fearful awareness of the supernatural, was to be discarded.[109] Something seems at work in these stories that can only be described as a fundamental shift of sensibility. Goodrich and Buckingham indicate another aspect of the changes taking place in their mature reflections upon Scripture. In hindsight, Buckingham regretted his absorption in the Bible. Using language akin to Goodrich's, he remembered

---

108 Hannah More, *The Fortune Teller* (Philadelphia, [1807]), pp. 8, 11–12, 25.
109 [Samuel Goodrich], *Peter Parley's Juvenile Tales* (Boston, 1830); [Samuel Goodrich], *One of Peter Parley's Winter Evening Stories* (Boston, 1830), pp. 7, 16.

being terrified by what he read, and especially by the apocalyptic
chapters:

What agonies have I not felt, after reading the description of the opening
of the seals, the pouring out of the seven vials, with the sounding of the
trumpets!—when, if alone, in the evening I dared not turn my eyes to look
behind me, lest I should see the pale horse with death, and hell following,
or the dragon vomiting a flood to drown the woman clothed with the sun.
. . . The passages referred to, and indeed almost every chapter of the book,
is adapted to fill the mind of a child with terror, and it is, in my humble
judgement, a piece of gratuitous and unprofitable cruelty . . . to place
before him any thing to inspire terror or produce affright. Why should
children be made to read what they cannot comprehend?[110]

Goodrich had a parallel reaction to the *New England Primer*. His contempt for this book seeps through the description he provides for readers who had never seen it: 'The New England Primer—the main contents of which were the Westminster Catechism—and some rhymes,
embellished with hideous cuts of Adam's Fall, in which "we sinned
all;" the apostle and a cock crowing at his side, to show that "Peter
denies his Lord and cries;" Nebuchadnezzar crawling about like a
hog, the bristles sticking out of his back, and the like.' By association,
the *New England Primer* lay on the wrong side of the line that separated
vulgarity from moral truth, barbarism from civilization.[111]

In the context of this reaction, we can begin to understand why so
many of the steady sellers limped into the nineteenth century and
expired. A few were kept alive by tract societies, but we can regard
these printings as artificial in comparison to the dozens of locally
produced editions that had once made such titles plentiful. With one
or two exceptions the steady sellers of the seventeenth and eighteenth
centuries reached their end by 1830. Several of the genres of print
that had been companions of the steady sellers also vanished, like
broadside elegies and the literature on portents and prodigies. The
almanac lost much of its importance. The *New England Primer*, after

---

[110] Buckingham, *Personal Memoirs*, 1: 17. Nor could he abide Wigglesworth's *The
Day of Doom*.
[111] Goodrich, *Recollections of a Lifetime*, 1: 165.

passing through 450 editions by 1830, was rapidly displaced by more secularized and cosmopolitan school books. The old style of 'lining out' in church music also vanished, though not without much conflict.[112]

A broader unsettling of authority seems to have occurred in the years on either side of 1800, as the old moral and social order came under attack. Radical democrats wanted to tear down all hierarchies of wealth and privilege. As Nathan Hatch describes their campaign in an essay in this volume, these democrats made effective use of journalism, turning its expansion to political advantage. In ironic counterpoint to democratization, the new publishers of secular sheet music were catering to the urban rich, who may have stood apart from the great evangelical revival. These diverging tendencies could have pulled American society asunder had other forces not been at work to create some kind of center. As Donald Scott argues in an essay in this volume, the public lecture system that came into being after 1840 functioned to consolidate a diverse and disorganized society. Amid the discordant sounds of conflict, the voices that spoke for an emerging civil religion—the American version of Victorianism—grew stronger all the time, as did the vehicles of print that echoed this synthesis.

The vehicles of print that created and embody this synthesis were fiction, journalism, and children's literature. Fiction had existed in the seventeenth and eighteenth centuries, but was barred from wide distribution by factors of cost and of cultural hostility. The second of these barriers had begun to weaken by the middle of the eighteenth century. Thereafter, in Europe and America, fiction steadily gained on religious and devotional literature as a percentage of total book production. The transition to an age of fiction was complete by the 1850s.[113] The progress of journalism was equally rapid, culminating in the emergence of the 'penny press' in the 1830s and 1840s. Child-

---

112 Winslow, ed., *American Broadside Verse*, p. xxv; Neuberg, *The Penny Histories*, p. 47. On conflict and change in music, see the essay by Richard Crawford and Donald Krummel that follows in this volume, and David P. McKay and Richard Crawford, *William Billings of Boston* (Princeton, N.J., 1975).

113 Ward, *Book Production*, chap. 2; Ilsedore Rarisch, *Industrialisierung und Literatur: Buchproduktion, Verlagswesen und Buchhandel in Deutschland im 19. Jahrhundert* (Berlin, 1976); Altick, *The English Common Reader*, chap. 13.

ren's literature was slower to emerge. The annus mirabilis was 1745, when the Englishman John Newbery began to publish attractive, inexpensive editions of children's stories, some old, some new. But many children continued to read 'adult' books like the Bible well into the next century.

These new genres were both cause and consequence of changes in the book trade. Fiction was costly. Unlike the steady sellers, it was also expendable, in that patrons craved fresh reading. Circulating and subscription libraries, which came into being in the middle of the eighteenth century, were a means of spreading the cost while offering variety. In America, subscription libraries first appeared in the 1760s. Their number slowly rose until the 1790s, when it abruptly doubled.[114] As book prices began to fall in the nineteenth century, publishers were also introducing serialized fiction into magazines. The combination of these several techniques made the genre increasingly accessible. The very scale of the reading public for fiction, together with the possibilities for distribution that the railroad opened up, pushed the book trade toward consolidation. As the country printer vanished, his place was taken by massive firms like Harper's, armed with steam presses and a railroad to distribute cheap products—mainly fiction— all across America.

According to Goodrich and Buckingham, the very style of literacy changed to one more in keeping with the new genres. A shift in rhythm was already evident in 1713, when Richard Steele complained of the 'unsettled way of reading' and its 'transient satisfactions.'[115] Describing the older style, Goodrich had emphasized the stateliness and 'reverence' of the act of reading. In the new age of fiction and daily journalism, people moved 'hastily' from one day's paper to the next, and from one novel to another. No book, not even the Bible, retained the aura that certain texts had once possessed. Bit by bit, the structure

---

[114] Winans, 'The Growth of a Novel-Reading Public'; Winans, *A Descriptive Checklist of Book Catalogues Separately Printed in America 1693–1800* (Worcester, Mass., 1981), p. xvii.
[115] Watt, *The Rise of the Novel*, p. 48. It is tempting to speculate that, with novels, the practice of reading aloud slackened.

of traditional literacy unraveled, as print became abundant, school books were secularized, and the steady sellers vanished. These changes betoken the decay of one mentality and the emergence of another. This is not to say that traditional literacy and its world view disappeared overnight. Aspects of it lingered on in nineteenth-century Evangelicalism. Tract societies and denominational publishers continued to reprint Baxter, Wilcox, and Alleine. In Lyman Beecher's household, little Harriet still had to memorize some chapters from the Bible.[116] Certain works of fiction were transitional. *Clarissa* has a section on death which Richardson regarded as in keeping with conduct manuals on how to die. But the 'rise of the novel' can also be linked with fundamental shifts in the value system of the middle class. The old awareness of time as an eternal present gave way to an understanding of time as merely chronological. Fiction catered in its social ethos to individualism, or, as in Peter Parley's stories, to sentimentalism. Goodrich himself had become a Unitarian. Like so many other religious liberals, he transmuted his new faith into children's stories, school books, and fiction, the themes of which were utterly opposed to evangelical Calvinism.[117]

The social correlations of literacy were also changing in the eighteenth and early nineteenth centuries. In the culture of traditional literacy, the distinction between elite and popular belief had not been consequential, at least in New England. With relatively few exceptions, the colonists in 1650 or 1700 were all engaged with the same forms of reading, the same popular culture. But by the 1740s certain groups were beginning to withdraw from this common world into a new gentility. The coming of gentlemen's libraries, together with dancing assemblies, the tea ceremony, and the theater, were steps in the making of a cosmopolitan alternative to the culture of traditional literacy.[118] Not surprisingly, the taste of those who used the Redwood

116 Charles Edward Stowe, *Life of Harriet Beecher Stowe* (Boston, 1889), p. 8.

117 Watt, *The Rise of the Novel*, pp. 22–24 and chap. 3; Ann Douglas, *The Feminization of American Culture* (New York, 1977); David S. Reynolds, *Faith in Fiction: The Emergence of Religious Literature in America* (Cambridge, Mass., 1981).

118 Rodris Roth, 'Tea Drinking in 18th-Century America: Its Etiquette and Equipage,' *Contributions from the Museum of History and Technology* (Washington, D.C.,

Library, founded at Newport in 1741, was for other reading matter
than the steady sellers, not one of which was purchased for the collection.[119] The withdrawal of urban merchants and their allies from the
older culture is also evident in their discomfort with 'enthusiasm,'
their scorn for 'superstitions,' like taking comets as portentous,[120] and
in the vogue of *Mrs. Chapone's Letters to Her Niece*, an English conduct
book. Like Goodrich and Buckingham, Mrs. Chapone urged her readers not to begin upon the Bible until they were mature enough to cope
with its language. According to her calculations, young ladies should
wait until they were fifteen. Even then, she urged them to skip the
prophetic books. Mrs. Chapone regarded skill in dancing and French
as essential 'accomplishments.' She would not exclude fiction (of a
moral nature) from her pupils' reading.[121]

Yet by the 1850s the old hostility between the genteel and the evangelical was waning. Fiction brought these groups together in the culture we call Victorianism. Writing in the 1850s of the transformation
they had witnessed, Goodrich and Buckingham remind us often of its
benefits. What they could not see so clearly were the drawbacks. The
story papers and the dime novels that were also making their appearance in the 1850s catered to a reading public that lay beyond the
reach of liberal moralists.[122] Once or twice Buckingham and Goodrich
acknowledged that all was not well—that the daily press had grown
'licentious,' and that publishers no longer treated authors with due
respect.[123] But the faults and failures of the new age were less apparent

---

1969), pp. 61–91. Cf. Laurel T. Ulrich, *Good Wives: Image and Reality in the Lives of
Women in Northern New England 1650–1750* (New York, 1982), pp. 115–16; 'Extracts
from a Journal of a Gentleman Visiting Boston in 1792,' *Proceedings of the Massachusetts Historical Society* 12 (1871–73): 60–66.

[119] Marcus A. McCorison, ed., *The 1764 Catalogue of the Redwood Library Company
at Newport, Rhode Island* (New Haven, Conn., 1965).

[120] Andrew Oliver, Jr., *An Essay on Comets* (Salem, Mass., 1772), p. 3.

[121] [Hester Chapone], *Letters on the Improvement of the Mind* (Boston, 1783), pp.
19, 26–28, 49, 190, 205.

[122] Q.D. Leavis, *Fiction and the Reading Public* (New York, 1979), chap. 7; David
D. Hall, 'The Victorian Connection,' *American Quarterly* 27 (1975): 561–74.

[123] Buckingham, *Personal Memoirs*, 2: 37; Goodrich, *Recollections of a Lifetime*, 2:
253–60.

than its differences from the eighteenth-century world in which Goodrich and Buckingham had begun. Their autobiographies are crucial testimony of the journey they and many others made from scarcity to abundance.

The Anglo-American Book Trade before 1776: Personnel and Strategies

STEPHEN BOTEIN

I

EIGHTEENTH-CENTURY English books carried both old and new ideas across the ocean to colonial readers. The purpose of the essay that follows is to outline a framework for understanding the transatlantic book business as a mechanism of cultural transmission in early American history. Since many aspects of the subject are obscure or elusive, this is an undertaking that will raise as many questions as it answers.

A few general observations are relevant here, the most important of which is simply that the Anglo-American book trade originated in London and therefore must be examined from an English as well as a colonial angle of vision. Little of the literature on 'the book in America' adopts the 'imperial' perspective of metropolitan London; on the other hand, few of the many scholars who have investigated the book trade in eighteenth-century England have shown much interest in exportation to the colonies. One elaborate exercise in macro-statistical analysis is available,[1] and several articles have described the only transatlantic business correspondence of long duration that is well documented, between William Strahan in London and David Hall in Philadelphia,[2] but an overview of basic entrepreneurial trends is still lacking. So far, too, no study of this Anglo-American topic has

[1] Giles Barber, 'Books from the Old World and for the New: The British International Trade in Books in the Eighteenth Century,' *Studies on Voltaire and the Eighteenth Century* 151 (1976): 185–224, and see discussion in Sec. IV below.
[2] This correspondence is discussed repeatedly in what follows, where the appropriate references may be found; Robert D. Harlan has made the major contribution here.

drawn effectively on the abundant information contained in trade records of large mid-century auctions, where major London dealers sold or acquired quantities of books and fractions of copyright.[3] The literary historian investigating the book trade is inclined to keep an eye out for a Smollett here or a Fielding there; the political historian is intrigued to learn that the first Thomas Longman supplied an American bookseller, Boston's Thomas Hancock, with a personal set of *Cato's Letters*.[4] But surely it is misleading to focus on a few titles now certified as 'classics' of English literature, even if they were popular in their day, or to emphasize politics when this was a subject 'rather unnecessary for the generality of readers'—according to a book buyer's guide that traveled across the ocean during the Revolutionary era.[5] Students of the 'Enlightenment in America' might want to revise their definitions of that phenomenon after inspecting a miscellany of invoices sent to colonial importers.[6] Most titles in such lists represent the detritus of eighteenth-century English culture. This in itself may say something about the nature of the transatlantic book business.

It has to be recognized also that the long-term cultural effects of

---

[3] Three overlapping sets of printed auction catalogues have survived; many have handwritten notes about prices, purchasers, etc. See Cyprian Blagden, 'Booksellers' Trade Sales 1718–1768,' *The Library*, 5th ser. 5 (1950–51): 243–57; Terry Belanger, 'Booksellers' Trade Sales, 1718–1768,' *The Library*, 5th ser. 30 (1975–76): 281–302. It will take some time before scholars learn how to process the data contained in these documents and what may thereby be ascertained of trade conditions in the mother country.

[4] Thomas Hancock to Thomas Longman, June 4, 1737, Hancock Papers, Baker Library, Harvard Business School, Cambridge, Mass. (hereafter cited as BLHBS). Longman was a partner in this particular publication.

[5] *Directions for a Proper Choice of Authors to Form a Library* (London, 1766), p. 33; the author was one 'N.N.' For an example of a colonial dealer ordering (twelve) copies of this book, see David Hall to William Strahan, Jan. 31, 1767, Hall Papers, American Philosophical Society, Philadelphia, Pa. (hereafter cited as APS). Recognizable political categories seldom appeared in listings of books; see generally Robert B. Winans, *A Descriptive Checklist of Book Catalogues Separately Printed in America, 1692–1800* (Worcester, Mass., 1981).

[6] Colonial American tastes are called 'standard and unexciting' in David Lundberg and Henry F. May, 'The Enlightened Reader in America,' *American Quarterly* 28 (1976): 262–71, but even in this article the methodology is to search through printed catalogues for preselected titles.

wholesaling printed matter to the colonies are indistinct. For reasons that will be suggested below, the trade between London and American dealers tended to be sluggish until the middle of the eighteenth century. Personal correspondences may have been more instrumental than commercial exportation in moving books across the ocean.[7] Seen from the English publishing world, the colonial market was underdeveloped. Newspaper advertising indicates that exploitation of a 'reading public' was far more intensive in the mother country than in America. According to one calculation, books accounted for less than 10 percent of advertisements in the colonial press at mid-century; in the English press, for more than 35 percent.[8] No one could fail to appreciate the general disadvantages of trying to sell any English product from afar to an overwhelmingly agricultural population, much of it scattered beyond the range of the most aggressive mercantile operator. In addition, despite the relatively high literacy rates of some colonial groups,[9] the book trade to America had its own peculiar liabilities. In London, where overall his business flourished, William Strahan complained of the 'exceeding trifling Profit' to be derived from colonial trade.[10] Entrepreneurial incentives were weak on both sides. David Hall might place orders with Strahan for books worth more than £1,000 per annum, which doubtless yielded a respectable tradesman's income to supplement the printing that he did in partnership with Benjamin Franklin, but this was not the way to great wealth.[11] In Boston, Thomas Hancock amassed a fortune equivalent

---

[7] See discussion in Sec. III; there is simply no dependable way to estimate the difference in volume between these two channels of transmission.

[8] These are unpublished data drawn from the sample analyzed in Stephen Botein et al., 'The Periodical Press in Eighteenth-Century English and French Society: A Cross-Cultural Approach,' *Comparative Studies in Society and History* 23 (1980–81): 464–90. The figure for provincial newspapers in England is upward of 40 percent.

[9] See, for example, Kenneth A. Lockridge, *Literacy in Colonial New England: An Enquiry into the Social Context of Literacy in the Early Modern West* (New York, 1974).

[10] William Strahan to David Hall, Feb. 6, 1750, Miscellaneous Collections, Historical Society of Pennsylvania, Philadelphia, Pa. (hereafter cited as HSP).

[11] Robert D. Harlan, 'William Strahan's American Book Trade, 1744–1776,' *Library Quarterly* 31 (1961): 243. Details of Hall's dealings with Strahan may be found in British Library Add. mss., 48800 (Strahan folio ledger). On income from the book trade in relation to printing, see Stephen Botein, ' "Meer Mechanics" and

to that of a leader in the London book trade only by branching out into more lucrative sectors of transatlantic commerce.[12] The sluggishness of colonial business for book wholesalers in the mother country, before mid-century, seems to confirm impressions of the cultural as well as geographical distance that separated England and America.

New trade strategies did emerge in the 1750s and 1760s, pointing toward greater integration of a larger colonial readership with the London publishing world. But the commercial structures underlying such change remained in a state of incomplete development before 1776. The Revolutionary crisis interrupted a process of transformation that had yet to make an enduring mark on American consumption of English printed matter. Thus, study of the book trade promises no surprising insights into what eighteenth-century Americans were in the habit of reading, much less thinking. Considered within a 'counterfactual' context, however, it does promise at least a preliminary mapping of new access routes that in a longer-lived transatlantic empire might have altered the relationship between colonial modes of thought and English models.[13] As with the geography of linguistic innovation,[14] so with the circulation of print in society—the raw fact of distance, depending on circumstances, might or might not be a barrier that enforced cultural isolation.

II

The Anglo-American book trade took form within networks of religious affiliation. This pattern was most conspicuous in late seven-

an Open Press: The Business and Political Strategies of Colonial American Printers,' *Perspectives in American History* 9 (1975): 140–50.

12 Graham Pollard, 'The English Market for Printed Books,' *Publishing History* 4 (1978): 30; and see generally William T. Baxter, *The House of Hancock: Business in Boston, 1724–1775* (Cambridge, Mass., 1945).

13 Other access routes also need to be charted. For a discussion along these lines, in which the book trade appears secondary to personal correspondence, see Norman S. Fiering, 'The Transatlantic Republic of Letters: A Note on the Circulation of Learned Periodicals to Early Eighteenth-Century America,' *William and Mary Quarterly*, 3d ser. 33 (1976): 642–60.

14 There are suggestive comments in this regard in Peter Trudgill, *Sociolinguistics: An Introduction* (Harmondsworth, Middlesex, 1974), chap. 7.

teenth-century New England, and reflected the distinctive ideals that had prompted migration there. In 1682, at his own risk ('without ordre'), a prominent London dealer named Robert Boulter selected and shipped a consignment of books to Boston's John Usher. In the next few years, after Boulter had died and been succeeded by one Richard Chiswell, Usher himself drew up four orders for English titles. The difference between the shipments of Boulter and Chiswell—the first based on the judgment of a London supplier, the other representative of local demand—was pronounced. Secular items that may be loosely categorized as 'romance' accounted for about 20 percent of Boulter's exports but no more than 5 percent of Chiswell's. Usher knew best what would suit his customers. Mainly, it seemed, they wanted what has been called 'intensive' reading matter—pious school books, Bibles, and devotional literature.[15] As John Dunton reported shortly afterward, having landed in Boston with a large stock of English publications, ministers were 'generally the greatest Benefactors to Booksellers' in New England. Not only did they make purchases for their personal libraries, but they influenced the taste of the laity. 'So that my paying them a Visit,' Dunton explained, 'is but in other words to go among my Customers.'[16]

Intricate personal and ideological alliances connected New Englanders with publishing circles in the mother country. Dunton shrewdly predicted that he would not be the last of the 'honest Men' in the English book trade to depart from his homeland and glimpse a less 'uneasie' life in New England. Moreover, although he boasted of having 'broke the Ice,' neither was he the first to have done so.[17] Late

[15] Worthington Chauncey Ford, *The Boston Book Market, 1679–1700* (Boston, 1917), p. 44 and apps.; the discussion here takes account of Roger Thompson, 'Worthington Chauncey Ford's *Boston Book Market, 1679–1700*: Some Corrections and Additions,' *Proceedings of the Massachusetts Historical Society* 86 (1974): 67. On 'intensive' (and 'extensive') literature, see David D. Hall, 'The World of Print and Collective Mentality in Seventeenth-Century New England,' in *New Directions in American Intellectual History*, ed. John Higham and Paul K. Conkin (Baltimore, 1979), pp. 166–80, and his essay in this volume.

[16] W. H. Whitmore, ed., *John Dunton's Letters from New-England* (Boston, 1867), p. 254.

[17] Ibid., pp. 144–46.

Stuart policies and depressed trade conditions had combined to drive a small band of Nonconformist printers and booksellers across the ocean to the religiously congenial town of Boston.

Dunton himself had originally been expected to follow three generations of his family into the ministry. When he chose bookselling instead, care was taken to apprentice him to Thomas Parkhurst, a Presbyterian who would subsequently earn a reputation for publishing the literary output of New England's clergy (including Cotton Mather's *Magnalia*). Dunton also strengthened his credentials for a New England venture by marrying the daughter of the Reverend Samuel Annesley, a leading dissenter with useful Boston contacts. In the early 1680s, it appears, Dunton acted as London agent for Samuel Phillips, an important Boston bookseller, and probably dealt with others in the New England trade. To some of these men, his arrival in February 1686 was 'as welcome . . . as sowr Ale in Summer.' John Usher tried hard to buy up the newcomer's stock and send him home. Dunton persisted, however, fortified by the kindnesses of Richard Wilkins, a bookseller and religious refugee from Limerick, and encouraged by promises of patronage from various gentlemen as well as ministers. It had never been his intention to settle permanently in the region; before returning to London he appointed a resident factor, and afterward continued to conduct business with Bostonians.[18]

Others in the book trade—like Wilkins—came to stay, or at any rate remained in Boston for more than an exploratory visit. One was John Allen, a London printer who sailed on the same ship that had carried Dunton to the Bay Colony. Allen had already recommended himself to New Englanders by producing Increase Mather's first English publication, and he had an uncle who was a minister at Boston's First Church. Another émigré was the bookseller John Griffin. In 1685, six years after crossing the ocean, he arranged an American printing of the *Protestant Tutor*, a fiery piece of anti-Papist propaganda that had been brought out in London by the printer-bookseller Ben-

[18] Charles Knight, *Shadows of the Old Booksellers* (London, 1865), chap. 2; Whitmore, ed., *Dunton's Letters*, pp. 94n, ix–xi, 77–78, 63, 248–49, 257–59, 306–7; Ford, *Boston Book Market*, pp. 21–25.

jamin Harris, for whom Griffin may have been acting as a colonial agent. Harris, for his part, was what Dunton called 'a brisk asserter of English liberties,' a trait that had caused him chronic trouble with the English government. From the mid-1680s, for a period of about ten years, he moved back and forth between London and Boston, where he and his son Vavasour soon established an active business.[19]

Outside New England, in the formative era of the Anglo-American book trade, both family ties and religious commitments could also be the makings of success. William Bradford I, for example, was advantageously positioned to start printing and selling books in Pennsylvania, as a son-in-law and former apprentice of Andrew Sowle—probably the outstanding Quaker publisher of seventeenth-century England. Bradford had adopted his wife's religion. Appearing in Philadelphia in 1685, he made his way with the help of a letter from George Fox recommending such a 'sober young man' to Quakers in all of North America. '& w^t Books you want,' urged Fox, 'he may supply you or answers against apostates or wicked Professors Books, he may furnish you wth our answers for he intends to keep a correspondence wth ffriends that are stattioners or Printers here in England, and so whatever Books come out and are printed by ffriends here they may send some of each sort over every year.' For the next seven years or so, Bradford distributed Quaker books, many published by his father-in-law, up and down the Atlantic seaboard. This convenient arrangement ended when he chose to follow George Keith out of the Quaker fold. As a result, Bradford would later complain, 'all my relations in England (being Quakers) are offended with me to the highest degree; and as my concerns have lain among that People their prejudice has been to my very great disadvantage.'[20]

---

[19] Whitmore, ed., *Dunton's Letters*, pp. 28, 57, 76; George Emery Littlefield, *Early Boston Booksellers, 1642–1711* (Boston, 1900), pp. 129–37, 159, 109–10; Isaiah Thomas, *The History of Printing in America*, 2 vols. (Worcester, Mass., 1810), 1: 282–83, 287–89; Worthington C. Ford, 'Benjamin Harris, Printer and Bookseller,' *Proceedings of the Massachusetts Historical Society* 57 (1923–24): 34–68.

[20] Anna L. Littleboy, *A History of the Friends' Reference Library with Notes on Early Printers and Printing in the Society of Friends* (London, 1921), esp. pp. 6–10; *The Historical Magazine* 4 (1860): 52; Gerald D. McDonald, 'William Bradford's Book Trade and John Browne, Long Island Quaker, as his Book Agent, 1686–1691,' in

The subsequent history of the Bradford family illustrates how earlier religious affiliations were likely to become blurred as the Anglo-
American book trade expanded in the course of the eighteenth century. Having moved to New York, William Bradford I sought com-
pensatory patronage from the Church of England. His son Andrew
was an Anglican too, but managed to assert family claims to a share
of Quaker business when he reestablished his father's office in Philadelphia. Andrew Bradford imported books from Tace Sowle Raylton,
Andrew Sowle's daughter, who was a skilled printer in her own right
as well as the dominant figure among Quaker publishers in London
through the middle of the eighteenth century. Raylton's support
could occasionally be burdensome, as when Bradford turned out to
be 'a Looser' for having taken from her and been unable to market
some 700 second edition copies of Sewel's *History of the People Called
Quakers*.[21] In the early 1740s, however, she was capable of lending assistance to William Bradford III, Andrew's nephew, who—disowned
by his uncle on account of a family feud—had journeyed to England
to make the connections that he needed to conduct business on his
own. 'She did some thing for me while with her,' the youngest Bradford wrote an English acquaintance after he had returned to Philadelphia. The record does not say what. A good guess would be that
Raylton introduced Bradford to someone in the trade who was better
situated than she to serve him.[22]

As the Anglo-American book trade grew more elaborate, colonial
importers came to rely increasingly on diversified dealers at the center

---

Essays Honoring Lawrence C. Wroth, ed. Wilmarth S. Lewis (Portland, Me., 1951),
pp. 220–22; Beverly McAnear, 'William Bradford and The Book of Common
Prayer,' *Papers of the Bibliographical Society of America* 43 (1949): 105–6. Bradford
may have exaggerated the harm done, by way of currying Anglican favor.

21 McAnear, 'William Bradford,' pp. 105–6; Anna Janney De Armond, *Andrew
Bradford, Colonial Journalist* (Newark, Del., 1949), pp. 25–26, 31; R. S. Mortimer,
'Biographical Notices of Printers and Publishers of Friends' Books up to 1750,'
Journal of Documentation 3 (1947–48):121–22; Nathan Kite, 'Antiquarian Researches
among the Early Printers and Publishers of Friends' Books,' *The Friend: A Religious
and Literary Journal* 17 (1843): 45.

22 De Armond, *Andrew Bradford*, p. 30; Thomas, *History of Printing*, 2: 48–49;
William Bradford to John White, May 11, 1742, Bradford Papers, HSP.

of the business in London. Simply termed 'booksellers,' they combined many of the roles associated in modern times with both publishing and wholesaling.[23] Because evidence is sparse, it is impossible to identify every English bookseller who exported to the colonies. Because the chief colonial importers in such port towns as Boston, Philadelphia, and New York acted themselves as wholesalers to smaller tradesmen in the same vicinity and in the countryside,[24] it may well be that the number of Londoners involved in the colonial trade was never considerable. As of mid-century, the total number of substantial wholesalers in the London book world probably did not exceed thirty,[25] of whom it is doubtful that many more than half had a serious interest in American business. Enough names of those dealing with the colonies are known to show that a specialized printer like Raylton, who did not belong to the select circle that regularly attended book trade auctions, was not likely to meet the needs of American importers.

Although religious and personal associations still counted in the networks of correspondence that underlay the transatlantic book business, a more formalized system of trade was emerging. Impersonal and ideologically neutral modes of transaction were superimposed on earlier relationships. With the passage of time, fewer colonial dealers were immigrants from the mother country who could appoint close relatives or former trade associates as their London agents. Moreover, outside Boston, most of the major colonial importers were also printers

[23] That is, they owned fractions of copyright and also kept extensive stock. For the purposes of this essay, the word 'publisher'—which in the eighteenth century was apt to be a synonym for 'author,' 'editor,' or 'compiler'—is used to mean the person who risked capital to print and sell a piece of writing. See, for example, R. W. Chapman, 'Authors and Booksellers,' in *Johnson's England*, ed. A. S. Turberville, 2 vols. (Oxford, 1952), 2: 310; Terry Belanger, 'From Bookseller to Publisher: Changes in the London Book Trade, 1750–1850,' in *Book Selling and Book Buying: Aspects of the Nineteenth Century British and North American Book Trade*, ed. Richard G. Landon (Chicago, 1978), pp. 7–16.

[24] For an indication of the routes by which English printed matter might be transmitted beyond the major importers, see Benjamin Franklin to William Strahan, Nov. 27, 1755, *The Papers of Benjamin Franklin*, ed. Leonard W. Labaree et al., 22 vols. (New Haven, Conn., 1959–82), 6: 277–79.

[25] See, for example, Pollard, 'English Market for Printed Books,' p. 31.

whose natural trade allies in London—their 'brother Types'—had nearly all come to be excluded from investment and marketing opportunities in the book world. Usually, then, transatlantic correspondence crossed occupational boundaries,[26] with the result that traditional networks became further attenuated. To whatever limited extent those networks facilitated transmission of a dissenting political outlook to America, as was the case most specifically and radically when the first Thomas Longman sent *Cato* to Boston's Thomas Hancock, the strength of such influence had to diminish.

Of those trade 'insiders' who exported books to the colonies at mid-century, several of the most prominent could be said to have made the transition themselves from old to new ways of doing business overseas. At first, William Bradford III seems to have bought from John Oswald, a frequent purchaser at trade auctions from the 1730s, whose original interest in the colonial market may have been cultivated through Nonconformist circles. In 1743, Oswald published a pastoral statement by the New England clergy on the Great Awakening, and four years later he issued the second edition of Daniel Neal's *History of New-England*.[27] After his death, Oswald's firm was taken over by Edward Dilly, later to be joined by his brother Charles. Together, retaining a portion of Bradford's correspondence, they continued to sponsor popular dissenting authors, although by the 1760s their list was less religious in emphasis.[28]

The first Thomas Longman was another important figure in London who appears to have entered the colonial trade with a Noncon-

---

[26] See generally Botein, ' "Meer Mechanics," ' pp. 130–60. Thomas, *History of Printing*, 1: 209–10, 301, 2: 423, 441, comments on the relative influence of printers and booksellers in Boston.

[27] Oswald is mentioned in Benjamin Franklin to William Strahan, Feb. 12, 1745, *Franklin Papers*, 3: 13–14; and see H. R. Plomer et al., *A Dictionary of the Printers and Booksellers Who Were at Work in England, Scotland and Ireland from 1726 to 1775* (Oxford, 1932), pp. 186–87. Attendance at trade auctions is conveniently indexed in Terry Belanger, 'Booksellers' Sales of Copyright: Aspects of the London Book Trade, 1718–1768' (Ph.D. diss., Columbia University, 1970), app. C.

[28] Sylvester H. Bingham, 'Publishing in the Eighteenth Century with Special Reference to the Firm of Edward and Charles Dilly' (Ph.D. diss., Yale University, 1937), esp. chap. 1. For a record of later Dilly dealings with the Bradford firm, see Invoice Book (1767–69), Bradford Papers, HSP.

formist orientation but then enlarged the range of his enterprise. His father-in-law, a London bookseller named John Osborn, had produced an edition of the Bay Psalm Book in 1712—'For the use edification and comfort of the Saints in publick and private, especially in New England.' This publication probably resulted from the death just the previous year of Richard Chiswell, who had been exporting to New England since John Dunton's day and had been responsible for earlier editions of the Bay Psalm Book. Although Osborn did not acquire the bulk of Chiswell's trade, this one item may have been transferred separately. Along with other devotional items, Osborn and then later Longman brought out a number of Bay Psalm Books over the years, possibly picking up much of Chiswell's New England trade.[29]

Tradition credits the second Thomas Longman—who inherited his uncle's business in 1755—with initiating a major expansion of the firm's colonial business, but in fact the senior Longman had been selling a wide variety of books to Boston for several decades before his death. Among his customers were not only Thomas Hancock but Hancock's father-in-law, Daniel Henchman, whom Isaiah Thomas remembered as 'the most eminent and enterprising bookseller that appeared in Boston, or, indeed, in all British America, before the year 1775.' In 1761, when his father-in-law died, Hancock requested that the younger Longman carry on a correspondence with Henchman's successors, two former apprentices named John Wharton and Nicholas Bowes. By the 1770s, Longman was also wholesaling to Henry Knox, previously an employee of Wharton and Bowes, and to other 'good friends' in the area. By this time, after many years of steady purchasing at London's trade auctions, the Longman firm had put its imprint on a large unspecialized list of publications.[30]

[29] Cyprian Blagden, *Fire More than Water: Notes for the Story of a Ship* (London, 1949), p. 40; Ford, *Boston Book Market*, pp. 12–21; Wilberforce Eames, ed., *A List of Editions of the 'Bay Psalm Book' or New England Version of the Psalms* (New York, 1885), pp. 10–11, 13–14.

[30] Harold Cox and John E. Chandler, *The House of Longman* (London, 1925), p. 12; Thomas, *History of Printing*, 2: 423; William T. Baxter, 'Daniel Henchman, A Colonial Bookseller,' *Essex Institute Historical Collections* 70 (1934): 1–30; Rollo G.

Still another major London firm with an interest in the colonial market could trace the history of that connection to the religious networks of an earlier era. Charles Rivington entered the book trade in 1711 as Richard Chiswell's principal successor. Both he and his son John were Anglicans, however, and the Rivington business soon lacked the special orientation that had recommended Chiswell to Puritans in seventeenth-century New England. John Rivington, indeed, became a friend of Archbishop Secker, and in 1760 obtained a valuable appointment as an official publisher for the Church of England. William Bradford III was perhaps his most substantial American customer.[31] James Rivington, John's younger brother, began to develop a colonial clientele of his own in the early 1750s, while still associated with the family firm; this operation soon turned into a flamboyant if ultimately unsuccessful attempt to engross the entire American trade.[32]

Whatever the particular reasons for their original involvement in the colonies, these were not secondary figures in the English book trade looking for the main chance, but large-scale businessmen engaged in exploitation of a peripheral market. Trade auction records make clear that the main entrepreneurial arena for all these dealers was the London publishing world. By mid-century, the colonial trade had come to intrigue other booksellers of similar stature.

Some merely seem to have experimented with a few trial shipments to this or that colonial dealer; such was the nature of Charles Hitch's business with David Hall in Philadelphia.[33] Samuel Birt, who in 1753

Silver, 'Publishing in Boston, 1726–1757: The Accounts of Daniel Henchman,' *Proceedings of the American Antiquarian Society* 66 (1956): 17–36; Thomas Hancock to Thomas Longman & Co., May 1, 1761, Hancock Papers, BLHBS; Worthington Chauncey Ford, ed., 'Henry Knox, Bookseller, 1771–1774,' *Proceedings of the Massachusetts Historical Society* 61 (1927–28): 227–35; and see Thomas Longman to Henry Knox, July 21, 1772 and May 14, 1774, in ibid., pp. 241–42, 288.

31 Henry Curwen, *A History of Booksellers, the Old and the New* (London, 1873), pp. 296–312; and see generally Septimus Rivington, ed., *The Publishing House of Rivington* (London, 1894); John Rivington to William Bradford, Sept. 15, 1759, Bradford Papers, HSP.

32 See discussion in Sec. IV below.

33 William Strahan to David Hall, Feb. 6, 1750, Miscellaneous Collections, HSP; and see the Hitch account for 1748–50 in Account Book (1748–67), Hall Papers, APS.

issued a London edition of William Stith's *History of the First Discovery and Settlement of Virginia*, developed a more sustained consignment trade first with William Parks and then with William Hunter, Parks's successor in Williamsburg.[34] Joseph Royle, Hunter's successor, was supplied by William Johnston, who had entered the London trade in 1748 at a cost of some £3,000 and could boast of owning shares in three-quarters of the books published in the mother country.[35] Thomas Cadell, a younger wholesaler, had started as an apprentice of Andrew Millar, a Scotsman who loomed large in the mid-century London book world. Cadell became Millar's partner in the 1760s and began sending heavy shipments of books to the Bradford firm in Philadelphia.[36] Another important wholesaler, Joseph Richardson, is known to have dealt in volume with Boston's Jeremy Condy, and no doubt would have extended his colonial business had he not died in 1763.[37] Perhaps the most adventurous London dealer to show an interest in exploiting the possibilities of the colonial trade, before James Rivington, was the younger Thomas Osborne. In 1747 he sponsored an edition of Cadwallader Colden's *History of the Five Indian Nations*, and was thereafter reported by Benjamin Franklin to be 'endeavouring to open a Correspondence in the Plantations for the Sale of his Books.' Parcels from Osborne reached Virginia, New York, and Philadelphia. For an Osborne to deal with the colonies was something of

---

[34] Plomer et al., *Dictionary*, p. 26; *The Virginia Gazette Daybooks, 1750–1752 & 1764–1766*, Microfilm Publication 5, University of Virginia Library (Charlottesville, Va., 1967), segment I. A detailed discussion of this and the next correspondence is presented in Cynthia Z. Stiverson and Gregory A. Stiverson, 'The Colonial Retail Book Trade: Availability and Affordability of Reading Material in Mid-Eighteenth-Century Virginia,' in this volume.

[35] *Virginia Gazette Daybooks*, segment II; Plomer et al., *Dictionary*, p. 142.

[36] Theodore Besterman, ed., *The Publishing Firm of Cadell & Davies: Select Correspondence and Accounts, 1793–1836* (London, 1938), pp. viii–x; Invoice Book (1767–69), Bradford Papers, HSP. In this collection, too, may be found a price list from Thomas Carnan and one of William Nicoll's business cards, but it is unclear whether Bradford dealt regularly with these two London booksellers.

[37] On this connection in particular, and the Boston business in general, see Elizabeth Carroll Reilly, 'The Wages of Piety: The Boston Book Trade of Jeremiah Condy,' in this volume.

a family tradition; the elder Osborne, who died in 1743, had been an exporter of books to the British West Indies.[38] Finally, there was William Strahan, David Hall's boyhood friend from Scotland and one of the very few printers who had managed to force his way into the exclusive fraternity of London's booksellers, originally with the support of his compatriot Andrew Millar. After 1750, as the annual cash income of his printing firm climbed toward and then beyond £10,000, Strahan began to invest in copyright. 'The Booksellers always consider me as one of them,' he could boast to Hall as early as 1758. By 1771, he owned shares in some 200 different English publications, having thus taught his fellow craftsmen 'to emancipate themselves from the Slavery in which the Booksellers held them.' Moreover, he had built up an impressive wholesale stock through the practice of accepting books as payment for printing work. By so doing, he explained to Hall, he induced booksellers to give him more jobs, since otherwise they would have 'to part with . . . *ready Money itself*.'[39] Although he was a printer, Strahan was much like the other 'insiders' of the trade who exported to the colonies, except that possibly he was attracted to an overseas market because it spared him the awkwardness of having to compete vigorously with the clientele for whom he printed. Hall was a personally loyal correspondent who not

[38] Plomer et al., *Dictionary*, pp. 185–86; Benjamin Franklin to William Strahan, Oct. 19, 1748, *Franklin Papers*, 3: 321–23, and see also 170n; *Virginia Gazette Daybooks*, segment 1, Sept. 6, 1751; Benjamin Franklin to David Hall, Apr. 8, 1759, *Franklin Papers*, 8: 317–22, and see also 57n, 169–70n; John Nichols, *Literary Anecdotes of the Eighteenth Century*, 9 vols. (London, 1812–15), 5: 471n. Osborne's books were 'very high charg'd,' according to Franklin; his ventures in America appear to have been mostly unsuccessful, but see discussion in sec. III below.

[39] William Strahan to David Hall, July 11, 1758, Hall Papers, APS; William Strahan to David Hall, July 15, 1771, Feb. 6, 1750, Jan. 30, 1764, Miscellaneous Collections, HSP. In addition to the references in fn. 11 above, Strahan's business may be better understood by consulting J. A. Cochrane, *Dr. Johnson's Printer: The Life of William Strahan* (Cambridge, Mass., 1964), esp. chaps. 6, 8; R. A. Austen Leigh, 'William Strahan and His Ledgers,' *The Library*, 4th ser. 3 (1922–23): 261–87; Robert D. Harlan, 'David Hall's Bookshop and Its British Sources of Supply,' in *Books in America's Past: Essays Honoring Rudolph H. Gjelness*, ed. David Kaser (Charlottesville, Va., 1966), pp. 2–23; Robert D. Harlan, 'A Colonial Printer as Bookseller in Eighteenth-Century Philadelphia: The Case of David Hall,' *Studies in Eighteenth-Century Culture* 5 (1976): 355–69.

only bought in quantity but, through his partnership with Franklin, provided access to a far-flung group of colonial dealers. On Franklin's word, Strahan occasionally sold books to New York's James Parker, Thomas Smith in Antigua, and others.[40]

Such were the circumstances of English personnel involved in the Anglo-American book trade around mid-century. All these book-sellers operated from a common base in the heavily capitalized publishing business of metropolitan London. Some, like the Dillys and Cadell, were sympathetic to the more strident varieties of opposition politics in the mother country; others, like Strahan, were not.[41] Certainly it was the entrepreneurial structure of London publishing that shaped their strategies of exportation to the colonies. Even as that structure imposed constraints on the transatlantic business in books, it defined opportunities. The history of the trade in the decades before 1776 suggests where entrepreneurial logic was leading, and what the consequences might have been had the British Empire held together longer.

III

Although colonial importers from John Usher onward were apt to be stubborn in their insistence that books sent from London suit the interests of local readers rather than the convenience of their correspondents, there were compelling reasons for a London wholesaler to try to make his own selection of titles for exportation to the colonies. Anxious to avoid overstock, like their counterparts in the English provinces, colonial booksellers tended to resist this strategy. For the transatlantic trade in books to accelerate, dealers on both sides of the ocean had to find an alternative to the conventional pricing system established by the London trade.

A London wholesaler had to supply books at prices that would per-

---

[40] Nichols, *Literary Anecdotes,* 1: 151n; on Franklin's role in the Strahan-Hall correspondence, see Benjamin Franklin to William Strahan, Sept. 25, 1746, Oct. 19, 1748, July 3, 1749, May 9, 1753, Dec. 19, 1763, *Franklin Papers,* 3: 82–84, 321–23, 381–83, 4: 487–88, 10: 406–8.
[41] See Cochrane, *Dr. Johnson's Printer,* chap. 13, and fn. 98 below.

mit colonial retailers to survive competition from those booksellers in the mother country who sold directly to individual colonists or their agents. This was far from a simple assignment. It was generally agreed that no London dealer should charge a retail customer in the colonies at anything below the going 'gentleman's price' in London— 'which is reasonable,' commented Strahan, 'for how could a Book-seller in America live, if every Gentleman could buy as cheap in England as he?' A colonist ordering directly from overseas would also be expected to pay shipping costs. If he employed a personal agent, there might be an additional fee of perhaps 2.5 percent. The 'gentleman's price' in London was sometimes open to interpretation, however, and there were no controls to prevent a bookseller from quietly offering bargains to a particular colonist.[42]

This, it seems, explained David Hall's surprising discovery in 1752 that a potential client of his was able to order books from one John Shuckburgh in London at prices lower than the discounted rate that Hall himself paid Strahan. 'As to what you write about Mr Chew's Prices of Books from Mr Shuckburgh,' Strahan replied, 'I really don't know what to say, nor can I devine from what Motives, or by what means he is induced to sell him so much under the known Retale Price here.' One clue was that Shuckburgh himself had bought at least one of the books in question from the younger Thomas Osborne —who, said Strahan, 'sells them sometimes cheaper sometimes dearer, just as he happens to want Money, and often just as the Whim takes him.'[43] Such a transaction indicates why Hall had found few comers even when he volunteered to serve local clients on a modest commis-sion basis. 'I believe I must let them for the future, send for their own Books,' he had concluded in 1750, 'for I cannot convince them that

42 William Strahan to David Hall, Feb. 6, 1750, Miscellaneous Collections, HSP. The analysis that follows is of course highly generalized; since lack of unifor-mity is a major premise, there are no formulas that will comprehend all recorded transactions.
43 David Hall to William Strahan, Mar. 21, 1752, Hall Papers, APS; William Strahan to David Hall, Aug. 26, 1752, in 'Some Further Letters of William Strahan, Printer,' ed. J. E. Pomfret, *Pennsylvania Magazine of History and Biography* 60 (1936): 465–66.

they come so cheap charged, as they can have them from their own Correspondents.' Later, Hall would revive his commission business with somewhat more success,[44] but it was a frequent complaint of colonial dealers that they could not offer low enough prices to suppress direct retail competition from London.

The main advantage enjoyed by a colonial retailer was that he might be able to satisfy a customer immediately, by means of stock kept on hand. This would appear to have been more likely to occur with some titles than with others. For a fashion-minded clientele that valued the most recent fiction from London and was prepared to buy it on 'impulse' at comparatively high prices,[45] it made sense to import novels. Such 'extensive' literature was a growing component of the American retail trade after mid-century.[46] Literature for 'intensive' reading still preponderated, however, particularly if this category is understood to include the many authoritative manuals offering secular advice and expertise that people of the time seem to have required, and which they consumed much like devotional works. Except perhaps for cheap school books and the like, this market looked problematic. To judge by the perceptions of retailers, it is evident that the average colonial reader did not regard one practical guide or volume of religious prose as interchangeable with another; titles acquired reputations, whether by word of mouth or by reviews in the English monthlies that circulated in America.[47] If the available item was unsatisfactory on grounds of content or price, or both, the customer could wait. It might well be preferable, therefore, to order generally through a personal correspondent in London.

Understandably, booksellers in the colonies were eager to reduce the prices they had to pay their London suppliers. The problem was

---

[44] David Hall to William Strahan, June 2, 1750, Sept. 25, 1764, Hall Papers, APS.

[45] See, for example, Stiverson and Stiverson, 'Colonial Retail Book Trade.'

[46] Harlan, 'A Colonial Printer as Bookseller,' p. 365; Robert B. Winans, 'The Growth of a Novel-Reading Public in Late-Eighteenth-Century America,' *Early American Literature* 9 (1975): esp. p. 271. See also fn. 15 above.

[47] See discussion below. David Hall to William Strahan, Sept. 21, 1767, Hall Papers, APS, includes a specific request for books that had been favorably reviewed.

that the traditional pricing system in the mother country normally gave wholesalers very little leeway in their dealings with the colonies. According to a well-known analysis of the book trade made in 1776 by Dr. Johnson, a 'regular profit' of 10 percent was what wholesalers to provincial England expected. That much of Dr. Johnson's thesis was approximately correct. Constructing his model of the wholesale trade from the publishing history of one hypothetical book, however, Johnson specified price arrangements that are somewhat misleading as a representation of trade circumstances in the previous few decades. Probably because his purpose was to persuade the Clarendon Press to deal generously with the trade, in the interest of stimulating consumption, he gave the impression that a London wholesaler would automatically be granted a ready-money discount of at least 25 percent from the 'gentleman's price,' and that a country retailer would then receive a discount upward of 15 percent.[48] This ignored the variability of operations in the eighteenth-century book trade. Prices were sometimes calculated in terms of markup, sometimes in terms of discount, and often by very rough estimates in order to avoid inconvenient monetary formulas. Not until 1760 was there any regular effort in London to publish a general listing of 'gentlemen's prices'; subsequent catalogues provided this information for books in quite different conditions—some in sheets, others simply sewn, most in the usual bindings.[49] Johnson's figures are of uncertain significance because they omit the fact that a country retailer customarily preferred to acquire books in sheets, partly to economize on the carriage costs for which he was also responsible. If the 'gentleman's price' stipulated by

[48] Samuel Johnson to Dr. Wetherell, Mar. 12, 1776, *Boswell's Life of Johnson*, ed. Sydney Roberts (London, 1960), 1: 602–5. Most accounts of the eighteenth-century English book trade try to explain prices by interpreting this particular document. Johnson himself did not calculate discounts but simply identified a sequence of prices as the book moved from publisher to reader.

[49] For a description of most of these catalogues, see A. Growoll, *Three Centuries of English Booktrade Bibliography* (New York, 1903), pp. 85–89. *A General Catalogue of Books in All Languages, Arts, and Sciences* (London, 1779) provides abundant evidence of variability, close to the date of Johnson's letter. For glimpses of the complexity of trade pricing at the start of the century, see Norma Hodgson and Cyprian Blagden, eds., *The Notebook of Thomas Bennet and Henry Clements* (Oxford, 1956), pp. 16–17, 72–73.

Johnson is regarded as that of a bound book sold in London, which is the only reasonable basis for calculating percentages in a general discounting system, then the country dealer who took sheets at the price cited in Johnson's model was really getting nowhere near 15 percent off.[50] Furthermore, there was no guarantee of a wholesaler getting 25 percent or more as a discount. Much depended on the quantity desired and on the marketing tactics of those who at the moment owned the copyright of any particular book, for which a managing partner was supposed to supervise a mutual pricing policy. Presumably, a smaller wholesaler's discount meant a smaller discount to retailers. The wholesaler's discount would be still smaller if the books were already bound. The retailer's would also be smaller in that case, as it would be if the wholesaler himself arranged for and assumed the costs of binding.[51]

In all, even though Johnson remarked on the narrowness of profit margins for both the country retailer ('if he trusts a year') and the London wholesaler ('at the hazard of loss, and the certainty of long credit'), his price model implied more favorable circumstances for trading to the provinces than those commonly understood around and after mid-century. Standardized discounts of the magnitude he described or greater were a trend for the future, it seems,[52] but the earlier situation was rather fluid. As the elder Thomas Osborne had once indicated in negotiations with the Society for the Encouragement of Learning,[53] a wholesaler who could not get much better than

---

[50] Pollard, 'English Market for Printed Books,' pp. 15–16, draws this conclusion. Less understandably, he appears to assume that the country retailer was obliged to sell the book (once bound) at the 'gentleman's price' in London. Still other readings of Johnson's letter are possible; none that has been advanced makes complete sense of it. For further discussion of prices, see Marjorie Plant, *The English Book Trade: An Economic History of the Making and Sale of Books*, 2d ed. (London, 1965), esp. pp. 243–45, 257–58.

[51] See Pollard, 'English Market for Printed Books,' p. 33; coordination of pricing could be intricate, it should be kept in mind, because copyright was often divided into many small shares that might be sold and resold year by year. The root of the difficulty here, in a sense, was a failure to recognize fully the function of 'jobbers.'

[52] Ibid., p. 42; profit margins continued to be narrow for wholesalers.

[53] Thomas Osborne to Alexander Gordon, Dec. 26, 1739, British Library Add. mss., 6190, and see miscellaneous other material in the same collection.

a 15 percent discount on a book in sheets was not in a position to attract the business of country retailers. In that worst of cases, their discount on the book would be only 6 or 7 percent, which would require charging customers enough above the 'gentleman's price' in London to persuade at least some that direct purchases from the metropolis were more feasible. A wholesaler who could get 20 percent taken off a book in sheets was perhaps on the borderline of marketability. Circumstances were obviously unstable. Opportunities existed for profitable wholesaling to the provinces, but overall this could not be an expansive business environment as long as cautious pricing habits prevailed.

The surviving evidence suggests that substantial colonial dealers who ordered from London were fortunate if they could obtain discounts that were the equivalent of the best accorded to provincial English booksellers. For importers like David Hall, who took advantage of cheaper labor costs in the mother country by ordering bound books wherever possible,[54] this appears to have meant about 10 percent off the 'gentleman's price.' Ten percent was tolerable, if not greatly attractive to colonial dealers. From Thomas Hancock's response, for example, it is clear that he considered the first Thomas Longman's offer of such a discount, in 1736, to be entirely fair, although he would have preferred to operate on commission. In 1759, John Rivington was at pains to please William Bradford III when he sent him books 'at the price I put them to the Country Booksellers with whom I trade in this Island,' by which he also seems to have meant roughly a 10 percent discount on bound merchandise. Strahan's prices to Hall were similar.[55] At this rate, after a markup that

[54] Harlan, 'David Hall's Bookshop,' p. 6. For reasons noted above, there was no way effectively to insist on uniformity in this respect.

[55] Thomas Hancock to Thomas Longman, Apr. 10, 1736, Hancock Papers, BLHBS; John Rivington to William Bradford, Sept. 15, 1759, Bradford Papers, HSP. Rivington's and Strahan's discounts have been estimated by selective matching of their prices with information in *A Catalogue of All the English Books That Have Been Published* (London, 1764). The prices of the former are taken from an invoice of Sept. 11, 1759, Bradford Papers, HSP; of the latter, from invoices of June 10, 1758, and Nov. 17, 1760, Hall Papers, APS. There are many uncertainties involved, since the 'gentleman's price' in London was subject to change and precise biblio-

had to take into account carriage costs as well as profit, the colonial dealer was plainly inviting retail competition from London, but his position was not appreciably weaker than that of the country bookseller in the mother country. If he chose to buy in sheets,[56] the operational differences appeared minimal.

Ten percent was unattractive, indeed barely tolerable, from the perspective of a London wholesaler operating within the framework of prices outlined above. This was so because of the special disadvantages involved in dealing with the colonies. The key issue was credit. When trading with provincial retailers, as John Rivington informed William Bradford III, credit was ordinarily given for periods of three to six months.[57] For colonial dealers this was unsatisfactory, although doubtless the vigor of their continual protest was often intensified by a desire to stretch capital resources. According to Thomas Hancock, every colonial merchant, whatever his line of merchandise, was used to giving his country customers two years' credit or more. Between one colonial printer or bookseller and another, it appears, twelve months was the normal term, and this was what English wholesalers were requested to extend as well. Six months 'is so short,' Hall advised Strahan of another wholesaler's proposals, 'I cannot make it worth my while.' Payment would be due before much of a cargo could be sold.[58] An extra half year or more of credit, however, put additional

---

graphical descriptions are lacking for titles listed in the invoices. Ten percent is not an average, but rather the discount that appears to have been approximated most frequently.

[56] Jeremy Condy did this, for example; see Reilly, 'Wages of Piety.' In addition to savings on carriage and a better discount, the retailer might benefit from running a bindery on the side. Because of higher binding costs, however, the long-range consequence of this practice in the colonies might be to inhibit market growth.

[57] John Rivington to William Bradford, Sept. 15, 1759, Bradford Papers, HSP; and see generally B. L. Anderson, 'Money and the Structure of Credit in the Eighteenth Century,' *Business History* 12 (1970): 85–101. It was normal English commercial practice to charge interest on overdue payments and to give discounts for cash in advance; these arrangements could be applied to the colonies, but the length of the original term was crucial.

[58] Thomas Hancock to John Rowe, June 20, 1739, Hancock Papers, BLHBS; Daniel Fowle to Henry Knox, May 21, 1773, in Ford, ed., 'Henry Knox, Bookseller,' p. 258; David Hall to William Strahan, Sept. 27, 1750, Oct. 7, 1755, Hall Papers, APS.

pressure on the profit margins of London dealers in the transatlantic trade. The difference might well be equivalent to three more percentage points on the discount offered retailers, which in Strahan's case could make things look very tight.[59]

Long credit, costly as this might be to a London wholesaler, was distinctly better than no payment at all, yet the latter also had to be anticipated as a particularly significant risk of selling to the colonies. 'The Truth is,' Strahan admitted to Hall, 'I am not fond of dealing with many People at such a Distance.' It was all very well to supply a man like Hall—'on whose Ability, Honesty, and Punctuality I can absolutely depend.' At times, out of friendship, Strahan even expressed concern that Hall was being overpunctual. Most of his other American correspondents proved disappointingly unreliable, however, and legal or extralegal remedies were problematic with an ocean in between.[60] A London bookseller exporting to the colonies had to live with the large risk that he would never be paid for his cargoes, but neither this possibility nor the cost of lengthier credit could be readily countered by reducing the colonial retailer's discount, since that course eventually would turn away local customers.

Thus, the conventional pricing arrangements of the London book trade presented only minimal incentive for expansion of transatlantic business. Like wholesalers in other fields, the major figures of the publishing world knew perfectly well that credit could be an effective

59 If the value of money is considered at 5 or 6 percent per annum, which is not excessive, the situation of an exporter like Strahan appears precarious—within the context of the foregoing analysis. According to William Strahan to David Hall, Mar. 3, 1755, Hall Papers, APS, it seems that a well-connected wholesaler shipping bound books might have to pay out in cash about 85 percent of their value at the 'gentleman's' rate, whether he acquired them bound or had the binding done himself. With a healthy discount and a year's credit to the colonial retailer, there would be no profit margin left at all.

60 William Strahan to David Hall, June 29, 1763, Hall Papers, APS; William Strahan to David Hall, Feb. 21, 1763, in 'Correspondence between William Strahan and David Hall, 1763–1777,' *Pennsylvania Magazine of History and Biography* 10 (1886): 87–90; William Strahan to David Hall, May 4, 1750, Miscellaneous Collections, HSP; William Strahan to David Hall, Feb. 13 and July 27, 1751, in Pomfret, ed., 'Some Further Letters of William Strahan,' pp. 458–59, 460–61; Benjamin Franklin to William Strahan, Dec. 19, 1763, *Franklin Papers*, 10: 406–8.

instrument for creating or capturing markets,[61] but there had to be misgivings whether this was a market worth the effort. As it happened, there was an important opportunity for maneuvering outside the confines of the system. As Strahan told Hall, a decent profit could always be made by exporting a simply definable category of books— 'those in which one has a Share of the Copy Right.' The reason for this critical exception was straightforward enough. Although a London exporter had to pay a wholesaler's price or more when he bought merchandise from another bookseller, in effect he laid out only the expenses of publication when he sent titles of which he was a partial owner. Depending on the terms of partnership for a particular book, this could double or triple his profit margin. Thus, where possible, a wholesaler would prefer to export items from his own copyright list. Or, as Strahan also noted, it was sometimes convenient to exchange one's own copyright books for those of another bookseller, and thereby fill additional parts of an order at publication cost.[62]

Hence, in large measure, the requirement that booksellers exporting to the colonies be 'insiders' of substance—without extensive copyright, it was difficult to glean a reasonable profit from the transatlantic business. Hence, too, arose a further impediment to standardization of a 25 percent wholesaler's discount. If the partners in a particular title could dispose of an entire printing themselves, by wholesaling or by exchange, they would be less likely to have or make copies available at a price below what they charged retailers. These considerations applied to the provincial wholesale business as well, although there the need to widen profit margins was not quite as urgent.

[61] See Anderson, 'Money and the Structure of Credit,' p. 93; and Jacob M. Price, 'Capital and Credit in the British-Chesapeake Trade, 1750–1775,' in *Of Mother Country and Plantations: Proceedings of the Twenty-Seventh Conference in Early American History*, ed. Virginia Bever Platt and David Curtis Skaggs (Bowling Green, Ohio, 1971), p. 9.

[62] William Strahan to David Hall, Feb. 26, 1761, Hall Papers, APS; William Strahan to David Hall, Jan. 30, 1764, Miscellaneous Collections, HSP. By buying a share of copy in a given title, it seems, a bookseller acquired a right to receive as stock a proportional number of the books produced in all future impressions, as well as an obligation to pay the appropriate fraction for printing and other charges (including paper, advertising, storage, and management). *Any* bookseller, wherever his customers were located, would be interested in disposing of copyright stock.

To understand what copyright meant for the Anglo-American book trade, it is instructive to compare sales records of Samuel Birt's exports on consignment to William Hunter in Virginia, from 1750 to 1752, with trade auction catalogues itemizing his possessions after his death in 1756. Four years had intervened, and it is by no means certain that all of Birt's property was put up for auction. Still, of all titles in which he was recorded as owning one-quarter of the copyright or more, about one-third appear at least once in the very incomplete accounts preserved from Williamsburg. Of all titles listed in those accounts, almost half appear in the later auction records of Birt's property. If a complete list of Birt's exports to Virginia were known and could be matched against a complete list of his property in precisely the same years, the overlap would surely be much greater. By shipping his own copyright books, Birt could turn a dubious enterprise into a sound business proposition.[63]

It was the incentive provided by the possibility of such overlap that drew large London dealers into the colonial trade, despite the special risks that narrowed the real value of the margin between their wholesaler's discount and the colonial retailer's. Unpromising as the pricing system of the London book trade might seem at mid-century, copy holdings—and exchanges based on those holdings—allowed exporters to perceive prospects of gain in the American market.

In the 1750s some colonial importers began to rely less on all-purpose correspondences with London suppliers. Instead, a dealer in the colonies might purchase from several exporters at once. Such arrangements made mutual sense, most of all if conducted on a consignment basis, because they maximized the number of transactions in which London wholesalers exported titles from their copyright. So, for example, a leading London bookseller named Thomas Waller shipped parcels from his line of law books to the colonies; so John Newbery,

---

[63] *Virginia Gazette Daybooks*, segment 1; Longmans catalogues #70 (Feb. 5, 1756), #71 (Oct. 7, 1756), British Library. The latter figure of almost 50 percent refers to Birt's stock as well as copyright. Because of the usual bibliographical uncertainties, these data must be considered merely approximations; a more precise rendering would be illusory.

known for his children's books, opened transatlantic correspondences.[64] Foreshadowed here was the emergence in early nineteenth-century England of publishers who would function as the exclusive wholesalers of their own imprints and handle no one else's.[65]

Trade strategies had to change, sooner or later, lest the constrictions of discounting in London continue to impede the growth of a colonial market. Nevertheless, like their counterparts in the English provinces, American importers complained repeatedly of being sent unsolicited merchandise that would not 'answer.' Hall urged Strahan to be careful, when assembling books for an order, not to 'leave the Booksellers pick them out; for I Know, in that Case, they will send what suits themselves, and not the Person they send to.' Just the right selection of 'Intirely new' and modish publications might be welcome, but Hall fretted continually that Strahan and other suppliers seldom seemed to get the magical combination, whatever their intentions.[66] From time to time, colonial dealers had to take a stand. In 1761, Boston's Jeremy Condy returned 43 copies of *An Easy Introduction to Practical Gunnery*, by Francis Holliday, which apparently Joseph Richardson had 'sent without Order.' Unsurprisingly, when Richardson's widow finally auctioned off the business five years later, 395 copies and the entire copyright of this book were listed.[67] Here was a strategy of exportation that Hall and others like him in the colonial trade were determined to rebuff.

The pressures for a more adventurous policy were intensifying, however, to the point of irresistibility. Although from force of habit colonial dealers might hope to keep doing business as usual, overseas wholesalers had begun to move aggressively in the direction of trans-

[64] *Virginia Gazette Daybooks*, segment 1; Plomer et al., *Dictionary*, p. 254; *Pennsylvania Gazette*, Nov. 15 and Dec. 11, 1750; and see generally Charles A. Welsh, *A Bookseller of the Last Century* (London, 1885). See also Harlan, 'David Hall's Bookshop,' pp. 10–16.

[65] Pollard, 'English Market for Printed Books,' pp. 35–36.

[66] David Hall to William Strahan, Mar. 21, 1752, Hall Papers, APS; David Hall to Rivington and Fletcher, June 18 and Aug. 9, 1759, Hall Papers, APS.

[67] Condy Account Book, 1759–70, p. 57, Manuscript Collections, American Antiquarian Society; Longmans catalogue #144 (Jan. 14, 1766), British Library.

forming the Anglo-American book trade even further, into a mechanism for disposal of surplus English goods.

IV

Some thirty years after mid-century, a bookseller named James Lackington introduced what he advertised as a dramatically new technique in the English publishing world. Rather than destroy some of his overstock and then sell the rest at full retail value, as he claimed other booksellers were wont to do, Lackington undertook to acquire and sell large quantities of slow-moving books at sharply reduced prices, thus increasing his volume of business and cutting storage costs.[68] By energetically publicizing himself as the father of remainder bookselling, Lackington managed not only to win a small share of fame but also to obscure the historical record.

It was true that many London booksellers before him had been inclined to let their stock pile up, instead of selling it off quickly at prices responsive to low demand. One notorious ploy favored by less scrupulous members of the trade—including the younger Thomas Osborne—was to change the title page of an overprinted book and then promote it at full price as something new.[69] In the 1750s, however, miscellaneous merchandise started to circulate within the London trade in a series of massive auctions. By 1771, as Strahan told Hall, the bookselling business was in disarray, 'after so many large Stocks . . . lately brought to market.' Dealers in town were naturally concerned to find outlets for their excess wares. 'I have had pretty good success, thank God,' one reported in 1765, 'in lightening my shelves of some of their loads.'[70] An effective way to do this was to

---

[68] James Lackington, *Memoirs of the First Forty-Five Years* (London, 1791), pp. 220–21, 224, 230–32; and see Richard G. Landon, 'Small Profits Do Great Things: James Lackington and Eighteenth-Century Bookselling,' *Studies in Eighteenth-Century Culture* 5 (1976): 390–92.

[69] Hodgson and Blagden, eds., *Notebook of Bennet and Clements*, p. 79; Nichols, *Literary Anecdotes*, 6: 198n, 1: 151n.

[70] Blagden, 'Booksellers' Trade Sales 1718–1768,' p. 253; Stephen Parks, 'Booksellers' Trade Sales,' *The Library*, 5th ser. 24 (1969–70): 241–43; William Strahan to David Hall, July 15, 1771, Miscellaneous Collections, HSP; James Robson to Rev. John Robson, Dec. 21, 1765, in George Smith and Frank Benger, *The Oldest London Bookshop, A History of Two Hundred Years* (London, 1928), pp. 88–89.

remainder, but there was still a reluctance to destabilize the trade by flooding London with bargain items.

What better place to try to dump unwanted books than in the colonies? As Philadelphia's Robert Bell was well aware, remaindering was 'the mode practised in all other countries' to 'realizeth dead stock into live CASH.'[71] The colonial market was attractive for this purpose precisely because it was peripheral. 'Rum books,' meaning unsalable titles, was an expression said by some to have originated in the elder Thomas Osborne's procedure of sending such stock to Jamaica in exchange for a more popular commodity.[72] As early as the mid-1750s, James Rivington began to undersell his competitors in the London wholesale trade by offering an extraordinary bound book discount of 16 percent (allowing one year's credit and the return of unsold items) to colonial dealers. He did this in part by shipping what William Hunter told Strahan were 'a great many extreme dull Books.' At the same time, 'as a Bait,' Rivington shrewdly included a few lively titles ('loss leaders' in modern parlance), and so enticed some in America to sign up for his entire line. It was a 'pretty extensive' scheme, according to Strahan, and would have thoroughly disrupted the transatlantic trade if Rivington—and James Fletcher, with whom he formed a partnership after separating from his brother John—had not gone bankrupt in early 1760. As it was, briefly, the younger Rivington had nearly 'got the whole into his Hands.' Strahan's comments on the quality of Rivington's merchandise registered curiosity as well as indignation. 'And yet very often,' he wrote to Hall, 'I am told, Books of that kind may be sold in America—Did you think it adviseable to order a Cargo consisting partly of such as these, I could afford you . . . a larger Discount, and venture also to take back what you could not sell in a reasonable time.'[73]

---

[71] Robert Bell, *Observations Relative to the Manufactures of Paper and Printed Books* (Philadelphia, 1773).

[72] Nichols, *Literary Anecdotes*, 5: 471n. Evidently, this explanation was incorrect.

[73] William Strahan to David Hall, Mar. 3, 1755, July 11, 1758, Mar. 24, 1759, Hall Papers, APS. See also Leroy Hewlett, 'James Rivington, Tory Printer,' in Kaser, ed., *Books in America's Past*, pp. 166–68.

What were the characteristics of a 'rum book'? During 1764 and 1765, at trade auctions in London, at least 100 different titles that were listed in quantities of 100 copies or more seem to have gone un- bought at any price; it may be assumed that they were virtually un- marketable.[74] Only a very few of these titles were contemporary fic- tion. Some items were unappealing on odd but obvious grounds—for example, volume 4 of *Gil Blas* translated by Smollett ('old Ed.') and Raleigh's *History of England* ('no Cuts'). Three categories that ac- counted for about three-quarters of the titles were school books, reli- gious works, and practical manuals. The last was the largest, com- prising about 30 percent of all unbought items; the first may be least significant, because the inexpensiveness of such books meant that the quantities involved were not exactly comparable to those of the others. That religion might be hard to sell was predictable. A couple of decades earlier, Fielding's bookseller in *Joseph Andrews* had dis- missed sermons as 'mere drugs.' The trade was already so 'vastly stocked' with such materials that he would not handle any unless they had 'the name of Whitefield or Wesley, or some other such great man, as a bishop, or those sort of people.' In Philadelphia, somewhat later, David Hall's judgment was the same. Divinity, he reported in 1758, 'moves very slowly here, except it be some Things of an extraordinary Character indeed.'[75]

Whether they were religious or secular, the great majority of 'rum books' may be classified as 'intensive' literature, if that term is used broadly. Unlike novels, the most up-to-date of such items were not necessarily the most desirable. It has been noted of one New York bookseller's catalogue, issued in 1755, that as many titles had been in print a half-century or more as had originally appeared within the

---

[74] Longmans catalogues ⚹128–46 (Jan. 26, 1764–Nov. 12, 1765), British Library. Since the handwritten notes in this set are incomplete, or sometimes difficult to interpret, it cannot be established with certainty that each of the titles in the list analyzed here was passed over, and it may be assumed that many more put up for auction were 'rums.' Nevertheless, there is no reason to doubt that the sample is approximately representative.

[75] David Hall to Hamilton and Balfour, Apr. 24, 1758, Hall Papers, APS. The Fielding novel (in which see bk. 1, chap. XVII) first appeared in 1742.

preceding decade.[76] Novelty could well be a risk—in an age, after all, when the oldest legal precedent was often regarded as most authoritative. Francis Holliday's guide to gunnery, which Jeremy Condy sent back to Joseph Richardson, is a good illustration. The book, published in 1756, had been received unenthusiastically by the *Critical Review*,[77] and seems not to have been much in demand anywhere. At first, no one was willing to buy the 395 copies that Mary Richardson still had on hand ten years later; at her second closing auction, John Rivington took them at the very low price of one and a half pence each.[78] Part of the problem may have been that the author, a clergyman, had chosen to address himself pragmatically to an audience of 'young Gentlemen' in grammar school, and had omitted the lengthy historical discourse that conventionally prefaced such a work. A subsequent edition of 1774, produced in a more expensive format, aimed self-consciously at a well-established adult clientele.[79] Probably, however, readers among the gentry shared the preferences expressed in a contemporary survey of English-language books, which left out Holliday in favor of treatises with longer pedigrees.[80] Not every book buyer in England was an Uncle Toby, who swore by military expertise that was a century old,[81] but Sterne's comic imagination only

[76] Robert B. Winans, 'The Beginnings of Systematic Bibliography in America up to 1800: Further Explorations,' *Papers of the Bibliographical Society of America* 72 (1978): 24–25.

[77] *Critical Review* 2 (1756): 327–31; the main point was that the author left out some basics while intending to instruct beginning students.

[78] See fn. 67 above, and Longmans catalogue #147 (Sept. 18, 1766), British Library.

[79] Compare *An Easy Introduction to Practical Gunnery* (London, 1756), pp. iii, vii–viii, with *An Easy Introduction to Fortification and Practical Gunnery* (London, 1774), pp. ix–x. The first edition was a duodecimo at three shillings, the second an octavo at six shillings. Holliday is identified in both as the master of a grammar school in Nottinghamshire.

[80] *Directions for a Proper Choice of Authors*, p. 28 (see fn. 5 above), mentions the names Gray and Robins, apparently meaning the former's *A Treatise of Gunnery* (London, 1731) and the latter's *New Principles of Gunnery* (London, 1742), both octavos. A weighty five-volume work is also recommended.

[81] As of 1760, when the first volumes of *Tristram Shandy* appeared, perhaps not every reader was aware that Stevinus—Uncle Toby's 'favorite author' (bk. II, chap. 12)—may have been most accessible to early eighteenth-century England through his *Nouvelle manière de Fortification par Escluses* (Leyden, 1618), in folio.

exaggerated the habitually regressive taste of the many English gentlemen who were consumers of 'intensive' literature.

Little wonder, then, that William Strahan was unsure if 'rum
books' would 'answer' overseas. There was no telling whether or how
the colonists could be induced to speculate on unfamiliar authors
whose wisdom or knowledge had yet to be verified. With the price
right, however, here was an experimental strategy of marketing that
might conceivably pay off.

Besides James Rivington's challenge, there was another reason for
a London bookseller like Strahan to be tempted by the prospect of
shipping 'rum books' to the colonies. Competition from the Scots, and
occasionally the Irish,[82] increased the pressure on London's wholesalers to offer more alluring terms to their colonial correspondents.
Despite a defensive price war organized by the English trade in the
late 1750s, printers and booksellers in Edinburgh and Glasgow moved
determinedly against what they called the 'monopolising schemes'
that had made them 'no more than Retailers to the great London
Booksellers.' Because they refused to recognize English copyright law,
the Scots had one important advantage in lowering costs. (This was a
kind of economy that had inspired Rivington to dabble in piracy.) In
1764, Alexander Donaldson, whom Strahan termed 'the Rivington of
Scotland,' was so bold as to open 'a shop for cheap books' in London,
offering them at 30 to 50 percent below his neighbors' prices. 'Good
allowance,' he announced, 'is made to merchants who buy for exportation, and to country-booksellers.'[83] Hall was one of those in the

---

[82] Notorious as literary pirates, the Irish do not seem to have gained a permanent
foothold in the colonial market. For evidence of their interest in America, see Benjamin Franklin to William Strahan, July 29, 1747, *Franklin Papers*, 3: 165–66; David
Hall to William Strahan, Mar. 21, 1752, June 28, 1761, David Hall to James Mag-
gee, Feb. 4, 1766, Hall Papers, APS. At least from the 1760s, it appears, customs
officers managed to discourage the importation of Irish books. See David Hall to
John Balfour, Nov. 20, 1764, Hall Papers, APS; David Hall to John Balfour, Apr.
15, 1769, Hall Letter Book, Salem County Historical Society, Salem, N.J.

[83] A. S. Collins, *Authorship in the Days of Johnson* (London, 1927), chap. 2; *Considerations on the Nature and Origin of Literary Property* (Edinburgh, 1767), p. 14; *Some
Thoughts on the State of Literary Property, Humbly Submitted to the Consideration of the
Public* (London, 1764), pp. 11–17, 2, 24; William Strahan to David Hall, July 11,
1758, Mar. 24 and July 17, 1759, Nov. 30, 1764, Hall Papers, APS.

colonies who received a letter of solicitation from Donaldson. His terms, Hall advised Strahan, 'will induce many People to make Trials of him at least.' Joseph Royle, in Williamsburg, did just that. Although Strahan scorned the quality of Donaldson's books, he realized very well that many Scottish publishers, including some old personal acquaintances, could easily undersell him in America. The firm of Hamilton and Balfour, he conceded to Hall in 1759, could deal on 'much better Terms' than members of the London trade. Perhaps because of lower binding costs, the Scots even seem to have managed to reexport London imprints to America at prices that competed with those asked by Strahan and his associates.[84]

Amid such a flurry of marketing, it was James Rivington who made the most innovative effort to develop a colonial outlet for English books. In 1760, after undergoing bankruptcy proceedings, he decided to relocate in New York, at the heart of the market area that he intended to exploit. Bringing along a load of what impressed Strahan as 'very heavy' stock, Rivington proclaimed to the public his 'early Intimacy with the Characters and Prices of Books,' and proposed—so Hall reported back to Strahan—'to undersell us all.' Colonial booksellers, Rivington let it be known, had been kept 'quite in the Dark' by their English correspondents as to the 'real Prices' of what they imported.[85] By taking up residence in the colonies, Rivington was well situated to publicize and distribute his goods, instead of having to rely on the good will and acumen of distant agents. Some twenty-five years before, there had been a precedent of sorts for such an approach, when Thomas Cox of London opened a Boston bookshop under his own name. He stayed in the mother country, however, leaving management of the operation in local hands; without the

[84] David Hall to William Strahan, Sept. 25, 1764, Hall Papers, APS; *Virginia Gazette Daybooks*, segment II, June 1764, May 1765; William Strahan to David Hall, July 17, 1759, David Hall to John Balfour & Co., Apr. 26, 1763, Hall Papers, APS; Robert Urie to James Rivington, Dec. 14, 1757, British Library Add. mss., 28275.

[85] *Weyman's New-York Gazette*, Nov. 17, 1760; William Strahan to David Hall, Oct. 6, 1761, David Hall to William Strahan, Dec. 22, 1760, Hall Papers, APS; and see Winans, *A Descriptive Checklist*, pp. 29–30. The Rivington bankruptcy papers, British Library Add. mss., 38730, indicate that he had proved solvent at the end of the proceedings.

presence in America of a dynamic sponsor, little came of this undertaking.[86] Rivington, perhaps by force of circumstances, was embarked upon a more ambitious project. If English wholesalers were unable from afar to persuade dealers in America that 'rum books' might be salable by energetic promotion, possibly a Londoner himself could directly propagandize a colonial clientele.

In more stable political times, American book buyers might have been susceptible enough to such an appeal that Rivington's career would have become a famous success story. Their estimate of things English was so high that a false London imprint could seem an effective way to sell a local publication.[87] And although they showed the characteristic provincial trait of insisting on metropolitan standards of 'correctness,'[88] unwittingly here and there they had deviated from the orthodoxies of London. Their peculiar political culture, so strongly influenced by minor libertarian authors of an earlier era, was indeed one result.[89]

If not for the Revolutionary crisis, which interrupted transatlantic commerce in books as well as other merchandise (and incidentally claimed a political casualty in Rivington),[90] wholesalers in the mother country might soon have been exporting far more briskly to the colonies. It appeared to be a sign of what lay ahead that such an eminently respectable London bookseller as Charles Dilly made a busi-

---

[86] Thomas Cox, *A Catalogue of Books* (Boston, 1734); and see Thomas Hancock to Thomas Longman, Apr. 10, 1736, Dec. 15, 1737, May 14, 1738, and Jan. 11, May 10, Oct. 29, Dec. 10, 1739, Hancock Papers, BLHBS.

[87] This does not appear to have been a frequent stratagem, but there is evidence that genuine London imprints could compete effectively against American editions of the same title; see Reilly, 'Wages of Piety.'

[88] See, for example, Daniel J. Boorstin, *The Americans: The Colonial Experience* (New York, 1958), chap. 42.

[89] Politics may not be a helpful entry point for understanding the book trade, as suggested at the outset of this essay, but an understanding of the book trade might well illuminate the history of early American political thought. A detailed entrepreneurial study of *Cato's Letters*, for example, could produce information of more than passing significance.

[90] For an intriguing effort to unravel his bizarre later career, see Catherine Snell Crary, 'The Tory and the Spy: The Double Life of James Rivington,' *William and Mary Quarterly*, 3d ser. 16 (1959): 61–72.

ness trip to the colonies in 1764.[91] Eventually, the London trade might have played a decisive role in expanding the range of English printed matter available to colonial readers, driving down prices and stimulating the growth of a larger and more 'impulsive' consuming public—wherever urban market skills could reach. Robert Bell's public book auctions in Philadelphia[92] pointed toward a future that had not quite materialized before Independence, but the makings of a new transatlantic trade structure were visible. Although cautious dealers like David Hall remained as unimaginative at disposing of speculative parcels from overseas as Thomas Hancock had been a generation earlier,[93] the situation argued cogently for the development of new commercial strategies.

The statistical record of books exported from London to the colonies is revealing in this respect.[94] Before 1750, volume increased at approximately the same rate as the American population. In the 1750s, however, book exports to the colonies were about two and a half times what they had been over the previous decade. The 1760s was a stagnant period, reflecting temporary conditions of overstock and later the vicissitudes of transatlantic politics, which to David Hall's mind made the book trade 'not worth following.'[95] Most sug-

[91] Lyman H. Butterfield, ed., 'The American Interests of the Firm of E. and C. Dilly, with Their Letters to Benjamin Rush,' *Papers of the Bibliographical Society of America* 45 (1951): esp. 293–94. It was also a sign of changing times that Dilly wanted to make contact with American authors.

[92] See Carl Bridenbaugh, 'The Press and the Book in Eighteenth Century Philadelphia,' *Pennsylvania Magazine of History and Biography* 65 (1941): 16; on public remaindering in the colonies, see also William Hart to William and Thomas Bradford, Nov. 3, 1770, Bradford Papers, HSP, and David Hall to John Knox, Aug. 9, 1771, Hall Letter Book, Salem County Historical Society, Salem, N.J.

[93] Thomas Hancock to Thomas Longman, Oct. 14, 1746, Hancock Letter Book, Massachusetts Historical Society, Boston.

[94] Barber, 'Books from the Old World,' pp. 219–24. Only data for the continental colonies have been analyzed here. As Barber explains, the customs data available are rather crude and therefore will not sustain much in the way of more specific conclusions.

[95] David Hall to John Balfour, Apr. 15, 1769, Hall Letter Book, Salem County Historical Society, Salem, N.J.; see also James Parker to Hamilton and Balfour, June 13, 1767, Franklin Papers, APS.

gestive of all are the figures for 1771 and 1772, a relatively peaceful interlude prior to the acute stage of the imperial controversy. In each of those two years, the volume of books exported to the colonies was more than double the annual average for the boom decade of the 1750s.

What was happening in the Anglo-American book trade may be considered part of a more general transformation of transatlantic marketing that threatened to flood the colonies with English products after mid-century. James Rivington's innovations were undoubtedly 'derivative' from new practices in other fields of commerce.[96] Whether or not the term *anglicization* is applicable, there is reason to think that colonial America was in the process of being incorporated into the provincial orbit surrounding the cultural metropolis of the mother country.[97] Since this process did not imply exact replication of metropolitan norms, there is no troubling paradox in the fact that it took place in an age of intensifying colonial assertiveness. One indirect effect of acceleration in the book trade may have been to quicken the pulse of Anglo-American debate during the 1760s and 1770s. Transmission was perhaps facilitated in both directions; some of the English firms that published American pamphlet literature relating to the crisis, such as the Dillys, were major exporters to the colonies.[98]

Nevertheless, it is difficult to specify the consequences of uneven and unsystematized change in the transatlantic book business. From a broader point of view, it could be said that the most important

[96] This and related modes of 'innovation' are discussed generally in Fritz Redlich, *Steeped in Two Cultures* (New York, 1971), pp. 163–71. For an overview of the new marketing, see Marc Egnal and Joseph A. Ernst, 'An Economic Interpretation of the American Revolution,' *William and Mary Quarterly*, 3d ser. 29 (1972): 11–16.

[97] The strongest statement concerning anglicization remains John M. Murrin, 'The Legal Transformation: The Bench and Bar of Eighteenth-Century Massachusetts,' in *Colonial America: Essays in Politics and Social Development*, ed. Stanley N. Katz (Boston, 1971), pp. 415–49.

[98] See Thomas R. Adams, 'The British Pamphlet Press and the American Controversy, 1764–1783,' *Proceedings of the American Antiquarian Society* 89 (1979): 53–54. Thomas Cadell is another example. On the other hand, someone like John Almon was obviously trying to exploit the crisis from a peripheral position in the trade.

questions in need of answering are when and to what extent Independence reversed the anglicizing tendencies of late colonial American culture. The indications are that it did not have a decisive impact for as much as half a century.[99]

[99] See, for example, James D. Hart, *The Popular Book: A History of America's Literary Taste* (New York, 1950), chap. 5.

The Wages of Piety:
The Boston Book Trade of Jeremy Condy

ELIZABETH CARROLL REILLY

WHEN JEREMY CONDY opened his bookstore in Boston 'across from the Concert Hall,' he was a controversial minister whose troubled First Baptist Church could no longer offer enough financial support to sustain him and his family. A decade later Condy died, having in the meantime left the ministry and moved his shop to Union Street 'opposite the sign of the Cornfield' in the heart of Boston's market district.[1] His death was noted in the *New Hampshire Gazette* as well as the major Boston newspapers, and Richard Draper devoted the first page of the *Boston Weekly News-Letter* to eulogizing him as 'a Gentleman well known among us, and much respected for his superior abilities, both natural and acquired.'[2]

There is no evidence in Jeremy Condy's estate inventory of the financial hardship that drove him into the Boston book trade. At the time of his death, his 'mansion house' was assessed at £400, and its contents included mahogany, pewter, silver, and gold. He owned a horse and carriage as well as many other items that speak of financial

I am indebted to David D. Hall and to William J. Gilmore for a number of references in this paper and for their thoughtful advice.

[1] For a biographical sketch of Condy see Clifford K. Shipton, ed., *Sibley's Harvard Graduates*, vol. 8, 1726–30 (Boston, 1951), pp. 20–30. See also Nathan Wood, *The History of the First Baptist Church of Boston 1665–1899* (Philadelphia, 1899), pp. 233–44. It is possible that Condy began to sell books as early as 1750, when he advised his church that he was in debt and could not support his family on his salary. If this was the case, no records survive.

[2] The notice in the *New Hampshire Gazette*, Sept. 9, 1768, was copied from the *Boston Weekly News-Letter*, Aug. 28, 1768. His death was also noted in the *Boston Gazette*, Aug. 28, 1768. Richard Draper devoted the front page of the *Boston Weekly News-Letter*, Sept. 1, 1768, to eulogizing Condy.

well-being, and kept two servants.[3] Although his estate did not place him among the wealthiest merchants of Boston, it bore the marks of a successful storekeeper.[4] Jeremy Condy had achieved success in a decade of financial upheaval, a decade that encompassed the great fire of 1760, the end of the Seven Years' War, and the commencement of difficulties with England. Boston's population was changing both economically and politically, and to build a viable business required skill and planning as well as good fortune. Condy would have had to have worked well with both his suppliers and his customers and to have understood the marketplace to make himself such a successful contender in a highly competitive book trade.

The character of Jeremy Condy's book trade and the strategies that Condy employed in developing it are the subjects of this essay; a larger investigation is still in progress. My evidence is drawn from the records and few surviving letters of Condy's years as a Hollis fellow at Harvard and as a liberal Baptist minister in the stormy years of the Great Awakening and the provocative climate of dissenting Whigs in England. Condy's business and career are illuminated by an account book that he, and later his son, kept in the years from 1758 to 1770—most of the period of his book trade—and by the probate inventory of his estate taken shortly after his death in 1768.[5] These records are enriched by the extant papers of other Boston booksellers: the letters of Henry Knox, who ran the London Bookstore and corresponded with many of the same people Condy had as customers; and the daybook of Benjamin Guild's Boston Bookstore, which represents the kind of daily record of transactions that Condy would have kept.[6] Together with the information gathered by Robert Har-

[3] Suffolk County Probate Records, vol. 67, (1768), pp. 188–98, microprint copy, Boston Public Library.

[4] For a sense of where Condy fit on the scale of material possessions, see Jackson Turner Main, *The Social Structure of Revolutionary America* (Princeton, N.J., 1965), esp. pp. 134–37.

[5] Jeremy Condy's account book is held in the Manuscript Collections of the American Antiquarian Society. For a description of the account book see Appendix I. The inventory of Condy's bookshop and house are in the Suffolk County Probate Records, 67: 188–98.

[6] Worthington Chauncey Ford examined the Massachusetts Historical Society's

lan on David Hall's Philadelphia business and by Hannah French on Andrew Barclay's bookbinding practice, they complement the material that relates directly to Condy's trade.[7]

What we are striving to understand in looking at Jeremy Condy's business is not a static structure but a process. The book trade involves a commodity that moved, over space and time, through a centralized urban structure and out to rural villages. As this process comes into focus, it reveals the community of readers in colonial America. We learn how books and the ideas within them came into the hands of consumers of print. Jeremy Condy is, in this regard, the agent of a process and a network. His experience as a bookseller threads through the structure of the Boston book trade and its processes of distribution. Ultimately his particular story serves as a key to a network of readers, the books they read, and the ideas they espoused.

The decade of the 1760s witnessed the growth of the Boston book trade in a difficult economic environment. On March 23, 1760, a great fire began in Cornhill and burned south and east, destroying important portions of the trade.[8] With the end of the Seven Years' War a period of relatively vigorous trade and prosperity came to an end. In Boston as elsewhere the war was followed by a recession.[9]

---

collection of letters relating to Henry Knox's book trade in 'Henry Knox and the London Book Store in Boston, 1771–1774,' *Proceedings of the Massachusetts Historical Society* 61 (1927–28): 227–303. The Henry Knox Papers belong to the New England Historical and Genealogical Society and are on deposit at the Massachusetts Historical Society, Boston. The daybook for Benjamin Guild's Boston Bookstore covers the years 1785–90; it is in the collection of the Baker Library Archives at the Graduate School of Business Administration, Harvard University, Cambridge, Mass.

7 Robert Harlan has made an extensive examination of David Hall's book trade. Two of the most helpful articles for purposes of this study have been 'David Hall's Book Shop and Its British Sources of Supply,' in *Books in America's Past: Essays Honoring Rudolph H. Gjelsness*, ed. David Kaser (Charlottesville, Va., 1966); and 'A Colonial Printer as Bookseller in Eighteenth-Century Philadelphia,' *Studies in Eighteenth-Century Culture* 5 (1976): 355–69. Hannah French examined the various aspects of Andrew Barclay's business in 'The Amazing Career of Andrew Barclay, Scottish Bookbinder of Boston,' *Studies in Bibliography* 14 (1961): 145–62.

8 See *The Boston Post-Boy and Advertiser*, Mar. 24, 1768; also Gerard B. Warden, *Boston 1689–1776* (Boston, 1970).

9 See James A. Henretta, 'Economic Development and Social Structure in Colo-

During the years of political and economic crisis that ensued, currency was in short supply. The Philadelphia bookseller David Hall found that, 'except for school texts and a few perennial best sellers,' his 'book stock was moribund.'[10] The lack of cash posed a difficult problem for tradesmen, who relied on a steady supply of currency to enable them to stock their shelves. One answer to their problem came in long terms of credit granted by wholesale suppliers to the tradesmen and offered in turn to substantial customers. Other arrangements were also developed to address the difficult task of maintaining a balance of monies moving in and out of the business.[11]

Throughout this difficult period, Jeremy Condy managed to thrive in his business. Like other Boston booksellers, he relied on English books to stock his shelves, but he enjoyed far more direct contact with English culture than most of his competitors.[12] As a young Baptist clergyman, Condy had traveled to England in 1735 and for the next three years 'moved in the best religious and literary groups in dissenting London.'[13] Though he returned to Boston in 1738 to take over the pulpit of Elisha Callender, he remained deeply attached to the ideas and attitudes of English dissenting clergy whose work he had known at Harvard and whose ideals had been central to his English literary circle.[14] His familiarity with books and with the English literary world, especially with its moral and religious literature, prob-

---

nial Boston,' *William and Mary Quarterly*, 3d ser. 22 (1965): 75–92; and James Lemon and Gary Nash, 'The Distribution of Wealth in Eighteenth-Century America,' *Journal of Social History* 2 (1968): 1–24.

[10] Robert Harlan, 'David Hall and The Townshend Acts,' *Papers of the Bibliographical Society of America* 168 (1974): 24. Harlan cites Hall to Strahan, May 26, 1767, Hall Collection, American Philosophical Society, Philadelphia.

[11] For a helpful examination of this complex issue, see John McCusker, *Money and Exchange in Europe and America, 1660–1775* (Chapel Hill, N.C., 1978).

[12] Other booksellers came from London and Scotland where they had worked in the English book trade. John Main and William MacAlpine were contemporaries of Condy. However, Condy's contact with the books had been the close contact of a reader and scholar.

[13] See Shipton, ed., *Sibley's Harvard Graduates*, vol. 7, 1722–25, p. 22. Also Jeremiah Condy to John Sparhawk, in *New England Historical and Genealogical Register* 24 (1870): 114–15.

[14] Shipton, ed., *Sibley's Harvard Graduates*, 8: 22ff. Condy named his sons after his benefactor, Thomas Hollis, and his friend and colleague, John Foster.

ably figured in his decision to enter the book trade when the income provided by his church was no longer sufficient to meet his needs. The contacts he had made during his years in England remained extremely important to Condy throughout his life. They strengthened his own intellectual leanings while enmeshing him in a literary network that remained important to him as a bookseller. Although his decision to specialize in English books was not unique, he was especially well equipped to do so.

Late in the summer of 1760 Jeremy Condy, by then a bookseller, returned to England to renew his stock and to enlarge his connections with members of the London book trade.[15] That he took such a trip suggests that he had a well-established business by 1760. Condy stayed in England for a year, returning to Boston in July 1761.[16] His account book, which he apparently brought up to date after his return, notes his whereabouts by bills of exchange that were drawn in his behalf on several London firms and by notes alluding to his involvement in various transactions. During his year abroad Sarah Condy, his wife, managed the bookshop.[17]

The importance of strong ties with the English book trade is evident in the correspondence between David Hall of Philadelphia and his British agent, William Strahan, as well as in the letters from the London bookseller Thomas Longman to Henry Knox of Boston.[18] By the mid-eighteenth century, the English trade was highly structured and extremely competitive; American booksellers, facing disadvantages of time and distance between orders placed and filled, had to rely for accuracy and speed on their relationships with agents in London. By the 1760s, except for a small drop in the number of books sent to New England between 1762 and 1765, British books

---

[15] Condy set sail on Aug. 11, 1760, and returned on the first week in July 1761. See Shipton, ed., *Sibley's Harvard Graduates*, 8: 27; and Condy to Curwen, July 19, 1760, Curwen Family Manuscripts, Box 3, American Antiquarian Society.

[16] Shipton, ed., *Sibley's Harvard Graduates*, 8: 27.

[17] Apparently Sarah Condy used only a daybook during Condy's absence; when Condy returned he transferred all the credit accounts to the extant account book, noting as he did so that his wife had transacted the business. See Condy, Account Book, p. 157.

[18] Harlan, 'David Hall's Book Shop,' p. 9.

sent directly to the colonies and via the West Indies comprised about half of all British book exports.[19] Trade was expanding rapidly. Parallel to the rise in British exports ran a growing American relish for English and European news, customs, and ideas.

Joseph Richardson, a London bookseller and publisher, was Jeremy Condy's major, but not his only, source of English books. On July 14, 1759, Condy owed Richardson more than £1,500 sterling for books sent from England. In the next six years Condy purchased books valued at wholesale at more than £3,500 sterling from Richardson's firm.[20] Unlike David Hall, Jeremy Condy purchased his books unbound and had them bound to order in Boston. By doing so, he profited from the higher sale price of bound books and also paid much lower prices and probably lower shipping charges than Hall, who imported books already bound in England.[21]

Richardson extended Condy lengthy terms of credit on his purchases. While the usual term of credit was six months, Condy's payments to Richardson lagged far behind that term, and the bills of exchange he sent to England seldom erased the balance due Richardson. Two years after the last purchase recorded in the extant account book, the account was still open and being paid.[22]

[19] For an examination of the number of books leaving England see Giles Barber, 'Books from the Old World and for the New: The British International Trade in the Eighteenth Century,' *Studies on Voltaire and the Eighteenth Century* 151 (1976): 185–224.

[20] The Richardson account begins with the notation 'No. 4, page 34,' referring to the previous account book used to record Condy's purchases from Richardson. Condy probably had been doing business with Richardson for a number of years and already stocked many of Richardson's books. Condy, Account Book, p. 57. After Richardson's death in 1763 Condy dealt with his estate and then with the widow, Mary Richardson.

[21] Harlan, 'David Hall's Book Shop,' p. 6. Apparently no bookbinders worked in Philadelphia at that time. Also see Harriet Tapley, *Salem Imprints 1768–1825* (Salem, Mass., 1927), p. 233. On Dec. 19, 1760, Condy's supplier of bond books for the Salem Library enclosed the following note with a large shipment of books: 'J. Richardson has this observation to make, that the price of Binding of Books is advanced more than 10 per cent within this six months owing to the dearness of Leather.' Condy could decrease the cost of binding by importing unbound books and having them bound where the supply of leather was more abundant.

[22] Elsewhere in the trade, although there were general limits to the terms on which credit was extended, the limits appear to have been crossed frequently, and

Condy also purchased books from Thomas Longman and from the Edinburgh firm of Kincaid and Bell.[23] Notes in the account book record the complex nature of those purchases. Books were sometimes sent without having been ordered, orders were often incomplete, and other things could go wrong.[24] It is difficult to tell how much control Condy actually had over the books that were sent to him, but his notation that he was returning books sent without an order suggests that he probably had generally firm control over the books he stocked. The fact that the inventory of his estate contains multiple copies of his most popular titles suggests that Condy was able to stock books according to public demand for them.[25]

If the English character of his stock was the outstanding feature of

monies were owed for long periods of time. The problems of long terms of credit are discussed in Main, *The Social Structure of Revolutionary America*, pp. 136–37. Certainly the letters from the London bookseller Thomas Longman to his Boston customer Henry Knox reveal a world of business transactions in which very long terms of credit were a fact of life. See Ford, 'Henry Knox,' pp. 274, 277–78. The letters reprinted by Ford were sent by Thomas Longman and by the stationery firm of Wright and Gill and refer to long periods of credit.

23 Condy, Account Book, pp. 157–58. This was probably the same firm referred to by Harlan, 'David Hall's Book Shop,' pp. 12–13. That firm held the Bible patent in Scotland.

24 A letter to William Williams of Deerfield gives one a sense of the nature of transactions between America and England and the frustrations of those transactions. See Jeremiah Condy to William Williams, Jan. 24, 1758, Williams Family Papers, Massachusetts Historical Society.

Boston January 24th 1758

Sir,

Not having the History of England 3V4o I have accordg to your desire sent for it to London; but perhaps my Correspondt, as he is the Proprietor of that Work, will, with his next Parcell, send some of the Books without Order; as he has sometimes done; if so you shall have a sett, without waiting for them till my last list for London is sent [*illegible*]

No magazines yet, the Vessells waiting a prodigious while for Convoy. I think they were [*illegible*] to sail the beginning of October

I am,Sir (in the greatest
Hurry) yr respectful serv't
Condy

Condy practiced the same kind of speculation in books, sending unordered books to merchants in New England and giving the customer the option of returning them. See Condy, Account Book, Nathaniel Parsons account, p. 192.

25 Condy, Account Book, p. 57; Harlan, 'David Hall's Book Shop,' p. 11; and Suffolk County Probate Records, 67: 188–98.

Condy's bookstore, the diversity of that stock was also striking. Although Condy was first and foremost a bookseller, he was also a stationer, mercer, and shopkeeper who stocked a wide variety of items, from mathematical instruments, eyeglasses, and prints to shoes, china, and glassware. The importance of this diversity needs to be underscored. In 1766 Samuel Johnson declared that 'the country bookseller cannot live; for his receipts are small and his debts sometimes bad.'[26] Stationery and other sidelines were taken up by small booksellers in provincial England to supplement the profit from books. The sale of patent medicines was a particularly common sideline for England's provincial booksellers and for some American booksellers like Benedict Arnold and Henry Knox.[27] In the colonies, stationery supplies, cloth, tinware, medicines, and jewelry were usually found in some combination in the shops of large and small Boston printers and booksellers. This diversity ran counter to the comparatively specialized stock of large firms of London booksellers. Although booksellers in Boston were not as straitened as the rural booksellers mourned by Johnson, colonial booksellers faced some of the problems of their provincial English counterparts. While American booksellers could buy on lengthy terms of credit and could—even had to—extend lengthy terms of credit to large customers, the daily rhythm of their businesses had to generate a flow of cash on the profits from smaller sales.[28]

Since no paper was made in the colonies during this period, imported stationery supplies such as paper, quills, ink, and wafers for sealing letters were first in importance among the other items sold by booksellers. Jeremy Condy's account book and estate inventory

[26] Quoted in Marjorie Plant, *The English Book Trade: An Economic History of the Making and Sale of Books* (London, 1965), p. 255.

[27] Ibid., p. 97. See also the broadside catalogue advertising Benedict Arnold's supply of patent medicines and books, New Haven, 1765, Evans 41515 (Charles Evans, *Evans' American Bibliography*, 14 vols. [Chicago, 1903–59]); and the correspondence of James Rivington and Henry Knox, The Henry Knox Papers, Massachusetts Historical Society.

[28] The same problem was attacked differently by other booksellers. See Richard G. Landon, 'Small Profits Do Great Things: James Lackington and Eighteenth-Century Bookselling,' *Studies in Eighteenth-Century Culture* 5 (1975): 387–99.

bear witness to the importance of paper and writing supplies to the bookseller. The records of Condy's daily cash sales, were they available, would probably show the importance of stationery supplies even more vividly. Benjamin Guild's daybook recounts frequent daily sales of playing cards, writing paper, quills, and wafers. Almost all booksellers' advertisements and catalogues mention the availability of stationery and other supplies; but since the notation generally follows an itemized list of books, we tend to overlook the importance of this other stock.[29] The very title of 'bookseller' fails to take into account how much the colonists saw booksellers and stationers in combination. An example of this perception is found in a 1771 letter written in response to a letter by Henry Knox to the London firm of Wright and Gill. Knox was just starting out in business, and wrote to Wright and Gill, the stationers who supplied most of Condy's paper, placing an order for books and stationery. In reply the stationers explained that they specialized in stationery and did not carry books.[30] To anyone in the Boston book trade, such specialization was unheard of.[31]

Jeremy Condy stocked a large supply of stationery. His main supplier was the firm of Wright and Gill on Church Lane in London. Unlike David Hall, who depended on William Strahan to act as his agent in acquiring stationery as well as books, Jeremy Condy appar-

[29] See Robert B. Winans, *A Descriptive Checklist of Book Catalogues: Separately Printed in America, 1693–1800* (Worcester, Mass., 1981).

[30] Ford, 'Henry Knox,' p. 240.

[31] In its attachment to stationery, the eighteenth-century Boston book trade greatly resembled the provincial book trade in England. In a paper delivered before members of the London Bibliographical Society, John Feather emphasized the crucial importance of stationery to the provincial book trade in eighteenth-century England. Feather pointed out that country traders and shopkeepers in rural England and in provincial population centers relied on the sale of paper even more than books. Thomas S. Willan's study of the eighteenth-century shopkeeper Abraham Dent of Kirkby Stephen reveals the substantial amounts of stationery and the relatively small number of books sold by Dent. Dent was a stationer, grocer, and hosier; and books were subsumed under the heading of stationery. John Feather, 'Cross-Channel Currents: historical bibliography and l'histoire du livre,' *The Library, Papers of the London Bibliographical Society*, 6th ser. 2 (Mar. 1980): 1–15, esp. 6–8; and Thomas S. Willan, *An Eighteenth-Century Shopkeeper: Abraham Dent of Kirkby Stephen* (Manchester, England, 1970), pp. 15–17, 32–33.

ently acted in his own behalf.[32] The first purchase from Wright and Gill was made while Condy was in London from 1760 to 1761. It was a sizable, though not itemized, purchase, valued at £112.6.2 and shipped to Boston on April 6, 1761. In the next six years Condy purchased stationery supplies valued at more than £800 from Wright and Gill. When the inventory of Condy's shop was taken shortly after his death in 1768, the approximately forty reams of paper, eighteen dozen double packages of ink powder, numerous Dutch quills, and other writing supplies were valued at nearly £35, which, even allowing for differences in evaluating these items, points out the large supplies of stationery being bought and sold by Condy.[33]

One of the most interesting aspects of the account book is that relatively little stationery is charged in it despite Condy's large orders from Wright and Gill. Most credit accounts that included stationery belonged to school teachers or butlers at Harvard College who were responsible for supplying students with paper, pens, and other supplies. For example, in one year that stretched from March 1764 to March 1765, Andrew Eliot, Jr., butler at Harvard College, bought 1,100 quills, 9 reams of paper, and 200 stone pencils from Jeremy Condy; and between August 1765 and August 1766, Joseph Willard, butler at Harvard College, bought more than 14 reams of paper, 1,200 quills, 650 pens, and more than 2,000 wafers from Condy. In June 1759 William Eastman of South Hadley, a deacon, bought 100 quills and one-half ream of Superfine Fools Cap from Condy. Nathaniel Oliver, a schoolmaster in Boston, bought a number of blank books in 1765 and 1766. But individual credit customers from outside Boston and Cambridge seldom bought their stationery supplies from Condy, perhaps because they could purchase stationery from local shopkeepers. The few local stationery customers to whom Condy did give credit were substantial members of the community. The Reverend Charles Chauncy bought considerable amounts of paper, sealing wax, and other supplies from Condy between 1759 and 1768. And Ezekiel

[32] Harlan, 'David Hall's Book Shop,' pp. 16, 19; Condy, Account Book, pp. 109, 232, 234.
[33] Suffolk County Probate Records, 67: 192–93.

Goldthwait, one of John Singleton Copley's most elegant subjects, bought many rolls of paper hangings (wallpaper) from Condy's shop.[34]

We are left with evidence of large amounts of stationery being imported by Condy from Wright and Gill in London and a relatively small amount of paper being bought by his credit customers. Knowing from Knox's correspondence that Wright and Gill were not involved in supplies other than stationery, we are faced with accounting for the market for this paper. Perhaps most of Condy's market for paper was a local street market. Like Benjamin Guild's daybook, Condy's daybook may have recorded a constant market for paper, playing cards, blank books, pens, quills, and ink. The location of Condy's shop, in the center of the busiest part of Boston, makes this all the more possible. In turn, the daily cash sales of paper could have provided Condy with a steady flow of currency.

Condy's customers could also buy a variety of cloth and sewing supplies as well as china, shoes, and glassware. Condy's source for these goods is not clear. They are probably the contents of his purchases from the London firm of Kilby and Barnard and Co. Beginning with purchases made while Condy was in England, the British firm shipped 'Sundry parcells Goods' to Boston from August 1761 through January 1764. The purchases totaled more than £925. Similarly, the London firm of Barnard, Harrison and Barnard accumulated £902.14.0 of credit in the usual form of bills of exchange in Condy's favor for unspecified purchases by Condy between August 1763 and the end of October 1765.[35]

As in the case of paper, Condy's credit customers do not account for large quantities of cloth and other goods, though their purchases certainly included a variety of items. Besides three yards of striped cotton, one-half ounce of green silk, and four yards of Cambrick, Pres. Edward Holyoke of Harvard purchased three pairs of shoes, two pairs of earrings, six China petty pans, one Chip Hat, one book, and some sealing wax from Condy. Rev. Samuel Checkley, Jr., bought

34 Condy, Account Book, Eliot and Willard, pp. 169, 198, 213; Eastman, p. 4; Oliver, p. 104; Chauncy, p. 20; Goldthwait, p. 18.

35 Ibid., Kilby and Barnard and Co., p. 111; Barnard, Harrison and Barnard, p. 112.

seven yards of 'best shalloon,' six yards of 'Tamy,' and a pattern for breeches; and Dr. William Lee Perkins included one yard of lawn and two handkerchiefs among his book purchases. Mary Warren of Roxbury bought ten yards of Irish linen, five yards of 'stuff,' three yards of 'Check,' a little silk, a pair of shoes, and one testament. Catharine Upham of Brookfield purchased a decanter and wine glasses along with paper hangings and borders. These are random examples from a fairly small field. The probate inventory of Condy's shop lists a wide variety of cloth, shoes, glassware, and other goods that Condy offered for sale.[36] As in the case of stationery, only small amounts of cloth and other goods appear in the records of large shipments of books to provincial merchants. The same is true of the local merchants Condy named in his account book. The main market for items like cloth, shoes, china dishes, and glassware must have come from purchases paid for in cash by customers who wandered in off the street.

As an importer of British goods, Jeremy Condy dealt with two other London suppliers besides Wright and Gill. From Benjamin Martin he bought optical supplies. Martin was probably also the source for the mathematical and scientific instruments sold in Condy's shop. Scioptic balls, Gunter's scales, microscopes, and cases of mathematical instruments appeared frequently among the purchases of Condy's customers. Beginning in May 1761, while Condy was in England, and continuing into November 1767, Benjamin Martin sent goods valued at £471.11.11½ to Condy's bookstore. Over a similar period of time Robert Sayer of Fleet Street, London, a printseller, sent prints to Condy's shop in Boston where they were sold both to private individuals and to other shopkeepers.[37]

Like provincial British booksellers, Jeremy Condy seems to have relied on diversity to provide him with a profitable business. Since paper, cloth, and other goods he sold were not produced in the colonies, Condy could, through contacts made in England, make himself

---

[36] Ibid., Holyoke, p. 83; Checkley, p. 77; Perkins, p. 84; Warren, p. 11; Upham, p. 133. Suffolk County Probate Records, 67: 193–95.

[37] Condy, Account Book, Martin, p. 108; Sayer, p. 110.

a central source for a variety of imported goods. Able to purchase large quantities from British wholesalers, Condy could then balance the credit trade in books against the cash flow generated by the local sale of stationery, mercery, and miscellaneous items like glassware, shoes, and china.

It is curious that Condy does not seem to have supplied American merchants with goods other than books. Whether or not it was more profitable for merchants outside Boston to order paper and cloth but not books directly from England needs more exploration, as does the rural market for those goods. The rural English shopkeeper Abraham Dent ordered his goods directly from London wholesalers, and his counterpart in New England might have done the same. If so, we should examine the degree to which rural American shopkeepers traded directly with England for books as well. Perhaps other, more specialized colonial suppliers were more attractive to provincial customers in need of cloth and paper than Condy was; or perhaps it was most profitable for Condy to sell cloth and paper on a retail basis only. Like provincial English booksellers, Condy turned to London wholesalers to supply his more diverse stock. But his relatively large business then became, like the London wholesale houses, a centralized source for books for rural and urban shops. Paper, cloth, and other goods seem to have been marketed almost wholly in a retail trade that appealed to local customers.

Alongside the imported books, stationery, cloth, and other goods in his shop lay the fruits of Condy's ventures into publishing. It is not certain how many books and pamphlets he published, since his name did not appear in any colophons. But the account book records his part in bringing out a number of works while the presence of hundreds of copies of certain titles in the inventory of his shop strongly suggests his financial involvement in others.

Compared to the dealings of his English counterparts, the extent of Jeremy Condy's publishing business, like that of other American printers and booksellers, was relatively small. Publishing was not a particularly profitable business in the colonies; Americans could not equal the ability of London firms to muster large amounts of both capital and credit to finance their ventures. Wealthy English publishers like Strahan, Longman, and Richardson invested thousands of pounds in the rights to titles and the cost of printing the volumes they would sell to Condy and his contemporaries.[38] This fundamental difference was accentuated by the system of copyright and monopoly within the British empire. Before the Revolution no American could publish an edition of the Bible in English, since the right to do so was a legal monopoly of the king's printers.[39] Nor could Americans print editions of books that remained in copyright. Booksellers in London depended on 'Property in Copies'—that is, a given share of a particular copyright—for much of their profits.[40] These rights to publication were jealously guarded by the booksellers who struggled successfully to sustain monopolies over classic and popular works in spite of laws that limited their rights.[41] American booksellers did not have the capital to compete for the rights to large and popular books. Nor did they have the political and financial strength to defy the London booksellers.[42] Thus, colonial publishers had to live within the restric-

[38] R. A. Austen Leigh, 'William Strahan and His Ledgers,' *The Library*, 4th ser. 3 (1923): 261–87; R. W. Chapman, 'Authors and Booksellers,' in *Johnson's England*, ed. Arthur S. Turberville, 2 vols. (Oxford, 1933), 2: 310–20.

[39] Daniel Henchman secretly published an edition of the Bible in English about 1752 and also an edition of 2,000 copies of the New Testament about the same time. Both bore imprints that are likenesses of the royal imprint. See Isaiah Thomas, *History of Printing in America*, ed. Marcus McCorison (Barre, Mass., 1970), pp. 103, 120.

[40] Harlan, 'A Colonial Printer as Bookseller,' p. 358. The quotation appeared in a letter from Strahan to Hall, Jan. 30, 1764, Strahan MSS, American Philosophical Society.

[41] According to the Statute of Anne a publisher's rights extended from fourteen to twenty-one years. See A. S. Collins, 'Some Aspects of Copyright from 1700 to 1780,' *The Library*, 4th ser. 7 (1926): 67–81; also Lyman Ray Patterson, *Copyright in Historical Perspective* (Nashville, Tenn., 1968), pp. 151–79. By 1759, British publishers, incensed over attempts to undercut their monopolies, had circulated agreements that ostracized any bookseller, urban or provincial, who pirated or published the works that originally belonged to another publisher—even though the copyright might have expired. See A. S. Collins, *Authorship in the Days of Johnson* (London, 1927), p. 91.

[42] Mid-eighteenth-century England was the scene of a lively battle between Alexander Donaldson, a Scottish bookseller, and the London booksellers. Donaldson succeeded at publishing popular titles claimed by other booksellers and selling

tions imposed by their lack of capital and by the rules of the British trade.

Jeremy Condy appears to have been an astute observer of the business of publishing and, given his resources, a wise entrepreneur. In response to the restrictions of the American trade, he concentrated his finances in two areas of print. The first was reprints of English works. For instance, Condy's estate inventory contained 457 copies of 'Doddridge on Family Religion.'[43] The forty-three page pamphlet was written by Philip Doddridge, one of the most popular religious writers of the day. The inventory also contained 491 copies of Michaiah Towgood's pamphlet *Recovery from Sickness* and 275 of Towgood's *The Dissenting Gentleman's Answer*, in sheets; both pamphlets were works of multiple editions.[44] Hundreds of copies of 'Christoph Weiland's *The Trial of Abraham*,' the eighth edition of Henry Grove's *A Discourse Concerning the Lord's Supper*, and John Smith's *An Essay on Universal Redemption*, all of which were published in Boston in the mid-1760s, appear in the inventory.[45]

What all of these works have in common is their brevity and their proven popularity. Throughout the eighteenth century American booksellers had to import most of the large books they sold, because books of any size were expensive to print. By and large, unless they had the financial backing of subscribers to bring out a large work,

---

them more cheaply than his competition. See James Boswell, *The Life of Samuel Johnson* (Garden City, N.Y., 1946), pp. 160–61; and W. Forbes Gray, 'Alexander Donaldson and the Fight for Cheap Books,' *Juridical Review* 180 (1926): 38; also James Boswell, *Boswell for the Defense: 1769–1774*, ed. William K. Wimsatt, Jr., and Frederick A. Pottle (London, 1960), pp. 240–41.

43 This citation in Condy's estate inventory probably refers to the 4th or 5th ed., or both, of Philip Doddridge's *A Plain and Serious Address to the Master of a Family on the Important Subject of Family Religion* published in Boston in 1766 and 1767 respectively.

44 The references are to [Michaiah Towgood], *Recovery from Sickness*, 4th ed. (Boston, 1768), published by the Fleets; and [Michaiah Towgood], *The Dissenting Gentleman's Answer*—the only extant Boston edition was the 5th ed. printed by Rogers and Fowle in 1748; the appearance of the title in the estate inventory in 1768 suggests a later edition.

45 The citations probably refer to [Christopher Martin Wielson], *The Trial of Abraham* ([Boston], 1764); Henry Grove, *A Discourse Concerning the Lord's Supper*, 8th ed. (Boston, 1766); and John Smith, *An Essay on Universal Redemption* (Boston, 1767).

Americans published imprints that were fairly short.[46] This need to be brief for financial reasons meshed with the necessity of publishing works that were less tightly held in copyright and thus more available to American booksellers. Condy, like other successful publishers, chose to publish works that he knew would sell. He concentrated on the briefer works of well-known English writers and published titles that had withstood the test of multiple editions. They were also the works of authors whose religious views coincided with his own and who belonged, in some cases, to the English religious circle with which Condy had contact. Condy's one venture into handling a larger and widely popular English book was a 1761 edition of Solomon Gessner's *Death of Abel*.[47]

The second thrust of Condy's publishing was toward timely works written by friends and acquaintances in New England. Balancing the British monopoly over large, steady sellers, American printers and publishers found a reliable market for imprints that provided information and entertainment. People read newspapers, almanacs, pamphlets, and broadsides to keep abreast of the changing times and

---

[46] Robert Winans finds that 'American printers, at least until near the end of the century, could not compete profitably with imported English editions of longer novels.' See his essay in this volume. American printers did print some editions of popular English books. It is not yet known how publishers obtained the rights to those books; they were probably financed by subscribers and represented a small percentage of American books. See James D. Hart, *The Popular Book. A History of America's Literary Taste* (New York, 1950); and Frank Luther Mott, *Golden Multitudes. The Story of Best Sellers in the United States* (New York, 1947). I take issue with Samuel Rogal's assertion that the publication of British books by American printers is a reliable measure of the popularity of a given title. See his study 'A Checklist of Eighteenth-Century British Literature Published in Eighteenth-Century America,' *Colby College Quarterly* 10 (1973): 232.

[47] In the account of John Perkins, a bookbinder who worked on Union Street and had a number of varied dealings with Condy, there is the following note on the debit side of the account: 'April 15, 1765 One half of the Death of Abel borrowed & used at the press for a new Edition in which we were jointly and equally concerned; bound and lettered cost .2/10—1.5.' Condy, Account Book, p. 200. This is the only reference to that transaction, and there is no record of any Boston edition of the book in that year. Gessner's extraordinarily popular book was published in Boston, and printed by Fowle and Draper in 1762 (Evans 9126) and in the same year in Philadelphia by William Bradford (Evans 9125). It was published in New York by Hugh Gaine in 1765 and 1766 (Evans 9981 and 10313).

of situations that affected their daily lives. Thus, American printers and booksellers rushed to bring out pamphlets chronicling religious disputes and vied for control of the most popular almanacs and newspapers.[48] Such imprints were less costly to produce, while the local character of the contents gave Americans an edge over English competitors. Thus, it becomes clear that Jeremy Condy chose to publish timely works that he knew would have special appeal to the customers whose names appear in his credit account book.

In 1755 Condy published some of the sermons of Jonathan Mayhew, whose Arminian tendencies had already made him a controversial writer.[49] As a fellow member of the ministry, Mayhew was a colleague of Jeremy Condy; but Mayhew's point of view would have been untenable to many members of Condy's Baptist congregation. The fact that Condy became one of Mayhew's publishers only underlines the turmoil that was taking place within Condy's First Baptist Church of Boston.

Condy's major publishing venture was *The History of Massachusetts Bay*, written by his Harvard friend Thomas Hutchinson.[50] Condy published the two volumes that Hutchinson wrote in the colonies, and Hutchinson's *Collection of Papers* was about to be published at the time of Condy's death in 1768.[51] The credit account book is full of references to the printing, binding, and distribution of these books, and even bears references to the English edition of volume 2 that Condy had printed and distributed in London as well as in the colonies.[52]

---

[48] For an example of this competition see Stephen Botein, ' "Meer Mechanics" and an Open Press: The Business and Political Strategy of Colonial American Printers,' *Perspectives in American History* 9 (1975): 125–225; and Lawrence Wroth, *The Colonial Printer*, 2d ed. (Portland, Me., 1938), pp. 217ff.

[49] *Newport Historical Magazine* 4 (1883–84): 125.

[50] Shipton, ed., *Sibley's Harvard Graduates*, 8: 27–28. See Massachusetts Archives, XXVI, 121, 125, 272. Condy had Hutchinson's work printed in Boston by the Fleets, but he also published a London edition to which there are many references in his account book; e.g., opposite p. 109.

[51] Shipton, ed., *Sibley's Harvard Graduates*, 8: 28. See also *Boston Weekly News-Letter*, Sept. 1, 1768.

[52] Condy, Account Book; e.g., Wright and Gill account, opposite p. 109; John Mein account, p. 230.

The most revealing records of Jeremy Condy's publishing ventures are the account book references to his part in publishing the writings of the controversial Newbury minister, John Tucker. What makes those writings and Condy's part in publishing them particularly interesting are the issues debated in the Tucker controversy and their relationship to Condy's own religious position. Jeremy Condy resigned his ministry of the First Baptist Church in August 1764 after twenty-five years of controversy and decline.[53] His relatively liberal religious attitudes clashed with the stricter beliefs of many members of his own congregation and with members of other Baptist churches outside of Boston. Like the English dissenters John Foster and Thomas Hollis, after whom he named his sons, and like other Harvard-educated Congregationalists in both Massachusetts and Connecticut, Condy emphasized the importance of toleration and of the Christian way of life as opposed to emphasizing dogma. Those convictions led him to actions and words that cost him not only the support, financial and otherwise, of his congregation, but also the presidency of Rhode Island College.[54] At Condy's death in 1768 Richard Draper wrote: 'The religious sentiments which distinguished his denomination were, all along in life, a great disadvantage to him in worldly respects. He was more than once tampered with to renounce them and go over to another communion of Christians; but as his principles were the result of due enquiry into the mind of Christ, he conscientiously and steadfastly adhered to them under pressing difficulties; hereby discovering the integrity of his heart.'[55]

Like Jeremy Condy, John Tucker found himself at the center of heated debate within his church. Tucker, ten years Condy's junior,

---

[53] Shipton, ed., *Sibley's Harvard Graduates*, 8: 28–29. For more extensive accounts of the situation in the First Baptist Church in Boston see Isaac Backus, *A History of New England with Particular Reference to . . . Baptists* (Boston, 1777), vol. 1, esp. pp. 419–20; and Wood, *The History of the First Baptist Church of Boston*, pp. 233–44.

[54] Shipton, ed., *Sibley's Harvard Graduates*, 8: 291; *The Massachusetts Gazette and Boston News-Letter*, Sept. 20, 1764; and Andrew Eliot to Thomas Hollis, *Collections of the Massachusetts Historical Society* 4: 431. The name of Rhode Island College was changed to Brown University in 1804.

[55] *Boston Weekly News-Letter*, Sept. 1, 1768.

graduated from Harvard in 1741. Upon accepting the ministry of the First Congregational Church of Newbury, Tucker found himself in the midst of a bitter clash between Old Lights and New Lights. Though Tucker appears to have been more conservative than Condy, his battle with the New Lights in his parish must have stirred memories of Condy's similar controversy with his own parishioners.[56] On March 31, 1767, the New Lights in Tucker's church filed a complaint that Tucker had denied 'the doctrine of original sin, as explained agreable to the holy scriptures, in the protestant confessions of faith,' that he had neglected 'to preach, explain and enforce the peculiar doctrines of grace,' and that he had 'openly preached and printed against all creeds and human confessions of faith as standards or summaries of Christian doctrine, by which any, either ministers or private Christians, should have their principles examined.'[57] Those were almost exactly the same complaints that had been filed against Condy on September 29, 1742, by the New Light faction of his church, a move which led to the suspension and secession of that faction and the formation of the Second Baptist Church of Boston. Like Condy, Tucker received widespread support from the Harvard-educated clergy throughout New England.

Jeremy Condy published several of the pamphlets written by Tucker during the years of most heated debate. The first of these, *A Brief Account of an Ecclesiastical Council*, was published in 1767. It was followed by *A Letter to the Rev. Mr. James Chandler*, also published in 1767. That Tucker was the popular victor in his fight and spoke for his Harvard colleagues was shown by the fact that in 1768, while the controversy still raged, he was given the great honor of delivering the annual address to the convention of the Congregational clergy of Massachusetts.[58] Condy's knowledge of Tucker's popularity must certainly have played as much of a part in the elder man's decision to publish Tucker's writings as did Condy's personal sympathy with

---

[56] Shipton, ed., *Sibley's Harvard Graduates*, 8: 25 and vol. 11, 1741–45, p. 81.
[57] Ibid., 11: 82; see Tucker's pamphlet *A Brief Account of an Ecclesiastical Council. So Called, Convened in the First Parish of Newbury*, 2d ed. (Boston, 1767), p. 2.
[58] Shipton, ed., *Sibley's Harvard Graduates*, 8: 24; 11: 87, 90.

Tucker's parish troubles and with Tucker's intellectual position in the debate.

Condy's records of his work in publishing Tucker's writings are the clearest examples we have of how Condy went about the process of publishing. Those records also lead us into the crucial matter of how and with what strategies Condy distributed his stock, both the books and other goods that he imported and the books and pamphlets that he published.

In assuming the responsibilities of a publisher, Jeremy Condy became a financier and coordinator of the printing and distribution of a given work. In the case of Tucker's pamphlets, this meant that Condy supplied the paper; arranged and paid for printing and advertising; had copies sewn and, in the case of a large work, bound; and took part in distributing the work, whether to merchants, to other members of the book trade, or to individual customers. Tucker accepted part of the financial responsibility by repaying Condy for some of his costs. Condy and Tucker both reaped profits from sales of the pamphlet, though pamphlets were not high-profit items. But Condy's rewards may have been other than monetary, for in publishing Tucker's work Condy extended himself further into a network of faithful customers, i.e., the New England ministry.

The first transaction mentioned in the extant account book refers to the publication of Tucker's 'Ordination Sermon,' doubtless Tucker's pamphlet *A Sermon Preached at the Ordination of . . . Amos Moody . . . in Pelham, in New Hampshire, November 20, 1765.* On February 20, 1766, Condy charged Tucker a total of £8.4.2 for the work of 'Tho. and John Fleet printing . . . , Demy Paper for printing the sermon' (£3.9.8), and 'Thomas Rand bookbinder for folding and sewing 600 sermons at 3 shillings per 100' (£0.18.0). Three months later Condy received cash for the work. What had happened was that Condy had supplied paper to the Fleets, while paying them in March with cash and copies of Hutchinson's *History of Massachusetts* to their ongoing account. On February 25, 1766, Thomas Rand charged £0.18.0 for 'gathering, folding and sewing 600 Tucker's Ordination Sermon,' and Condy, who already had a little more than a shilling's credit because of ink powder sent to Rand the previous May, paid in cash on March 7, 1766.

On April 14, 1767, Tucker was charged for the publication of 'A Brief Account of an Ecclesiastical Council . . . March 31, 1767.' Condy charged Tucker £0.2.5 for 'Cash pd Richard Draper advertising in the *Boston Weekly News-Letter*,' £1.10.0 to the Fleets for printing 214 copies, and £0.2.5 to Thomas Rand for folding and sewing the same. He charged £0.8.5 for the paper used in the printing. On April 29, Condy forgave the account £0.10.0 for 'Cash rec'd for 21 of the Acct. of the Council,' and on May 28 he received the remaining £1.13.3 in cash. Neither Rand's account nor that of the Fleets contains a specific note on what they were being paid for doing, but both accounts had been brought up to date with paper, cloth, and stationery supplies. Both Rand and the Fleets were accumulating large accounts with Condy, accounts that were frequently brought up to date, largely with supplies of paper and some cash. This brisk business is reflected by the fact that between February 1765 and February 1767 Condy had paid the Fleets £85.4.6.[59]

The account book follows the publication of others of Tucker's writings, in which there were similar dealings with the printers John Mein and John Fleeming, the Fleets, Thomas Rand, and Richard Draper. In each case the sequence of charges and payments is similar. Apparently Condy was able to pay the printers, advertisers, and binders with both paper and cash.[60]

The size of the Fleets' account was probably due to the fact that they were the printers of Hutchinson's sizable *History of Massachusetts*.

---

[59] Condy, Account Book, Tucker, pp. 31, 152, 226; Fleets, p. 206; Rand, pp. 200, 209.

[60] The account book refers to another edition of Tucker's *A Brief Account*, but refers to it as 'Narrative of Ecclesiastical Council and Sermon' (Boston, [1767]). Whether that is Evans 10789 or 10788 is not clear. It was printed by Mein and Fleeming, folded and stitched by Thomas Rand, and advertised by Richard Draper and by the Fleets in their respective newspapers. See Condy, Account Book, p. 152. The account book refers to three other publications by Tucker; they appear to be *A Letter to the Rev. Mr. James Chandler* (Boston, 1767), *A Reply to Mr. Chandler's Answer* (Boston, 1768), and *Remarks on a Sermon of the Rev. Aaron Hutchinson* (Boston, [1767]). See Condy, Account Book, pp. 152 and 226.

Condy's sales of the books that he published were, as with the Tucker pamphlet of April 1767, sometimes used to repay the expenses he had incurred. Doubtless the sale of these publications was, after the expenses were paid, largely a matter of profit for Tucker and for Condy. If 21 of the pamphlets sold for £0.10.0 and the total cost of publishing 214 was £2.3.3, it would take less than half the edition to repay the costs of the publication. There was a profit to be made, even though it was relatively small. Exactly what arrangement Condy had with Tucker is unclear, since Condy did not list his own fees on the debit side of Tucker's account and there is also no notation on the credit page opposite. Possibly, after the cost of publication was met, Condy had a portion of the publication to sell and could profit from its entire retail or wholesale cost to the customer.

The network of suppliers and craftsmen who traded by exchanging goods and services rather than cash was a key element in the American book trade. Printers, binders, and booksellers lived and worked in close proximity to each other. Jeremy Condy's bookshop 'across from the sign of the Cornfield' on Union Street was near Dock Square in the heart of Boston's market district. He moved there in 1763 from adjacent Hanover Street, 'across from the Concert Hall,' where he seems to have begun keeping shop about 1756.[61] Both locations were near the north end of town where Condy lived, at least until 1754, and where he preached at the First Baptist Church until he resigned his ministry in 1765.[62] The area north of Dock Square was tightly

[61] Shipton, ed., *Sibley's Harvard Graduates*, 8: 26. The implication in *Sibley's* is that Condy started his business about 1754. Isaiah Thomas notes 1758 as the first year that Condy worked as a bookseller. See his *History of Printing in America*, p. 207. The account book Condy began using in 1758 is no. 5 so he must have been in business for a while as of 1758. On the other hand, Condy first advertised his shop as 'near Concert Hall,' and Walter Whitehill placed the Concert Hall on Hanover Street and wrote that it was built in 1756. See his book *Boston, A Topographical History* (Cambridge, Mass., 1959), p. 66. Condy probably began selling books at the earlier date and used the colophon only after 1756.

[62] Condy sold his house in North Square in 1754. Shipton, ed., *Sibley's Harvard Graduates*, 8: 26. It is not clear where he moved at that point. Hanover Street, the location of his first shop, led out of the North End. The Baptist church where Condy continued to preach until 1765 was located on Back Street near North Square. The North End was heavily populated, especially by merchants and ship-

populated with shops, though most of the shops of members of the book trade were south of Dock Square on King Street, in Cornhill, and on Marlborough and Newbury streets. By working north of Cornhill, Condy managed to avoid the great fire of 1760, which began in Cornhill and spread south and east, destroying 174 houses and 175 shops.[63] Whether the losses of that fire had an impact on his business is unknown, but six months after the fire Condy went to England to further develop his trade by making added contacts with wholesalers in London. Condy's shop on Union Street was advantageously located as the first bookshop approached from the town's North End, where a large part of Boston's population lived and where students from Harvard coming to Boston to shop left the ferry which brought them from Charlestown.[64]

Although most of Boston's printers and booksellers worked south of Dock Square, Condy's shop was close to some of the craftsmen of the book trade and certainly not far from the shops of King Street and Cornhill. John Perkins's bookbinding shop was near Condy's on Union Street. Perkins bound books for Condy who, unlike David Hall, ordered his books from London unbound.[65] Perkins also sold books on consignment for Condy. In fact, although Sarah Condy was in charge of the shop while Condy was in England between the summers of 1760 and 1761, it appears that Condy placed a large portion of his stock in Perkins's hand with an agreement that Perkins would receive 5 percent on all sales.[66] In February 1762 Perkins col-

---

builders. The elegant houses of William Clark and Thomas Hutchinson were there. Nearby were the merchants' wharves and warehouses. The area was noisy and bustling with activity.

63 See Warden, *Boston 1689–1776*, p. 149.

64 Whitehill, *Boston*, pp. 28–29; see also the 1769 version of the Bonner Map.

65 Condy could buy unbound books from England at a much lower price than Hall had to pay for bound editions. By having Perkins bind them, Condy could then sell them for a greater profit. I have not looked into comparative prices for English and American bound and unbound editions, nor have I, at this point, examined the leather trade in America. In Frank A. Mumby, *Publishing and Bookselling* (London, 1930), esp. p. 9, the author stressed that it was comparatively easy to get into the bookselling trade by buying unbound works.

66 Isaiah Thomas indicated that Perkins served an apprenticeship with Joshua Winter, a Union Street binder and bookseller, and that Condy's first dealings with

lected £10.8.0 from Condy for selling £207.14.0 worth of books. He returned books valued at £297.0.0 because they had not sold, and continued working with Condy for the next six years.[67]

Other members of the book trade lived and worked near Union Street. Thomas Rand, another binder with whom Condy did business, lived on adjacent Anne Street.[68] Nearby, on the south side of Dock Square, King Street stretched down to Long Wharf. John Mein's London Bookstore stood at the head of King Street; Mein distributed copies of Hutchinson's *History of Massachusetts* for Condy and also printed one of Tucker's pamphlets in 1767.[69] A short distance away, at the shop of Benjamin Edes and John Gill, Condy sold paper in return for printing and advertising.[70] And in Cornhill, off King Street, the Fleets printed Hutchinson's *History of Massachusetts*, Tucker's writings, and other pamphlets. Andrew Barclay bound them 'At the Bible in Cornhill.'[71] In return for Barclay's work, Condy helped the binder stock his shop with a small number of books from England. Stretching out from Cornhill were Marlborough and Newbury streets, where Richard Draper printed the *Boston Weekly News-Letter* and where John Hodgson bound numerous books for Condy in return for books and cash.[72]

Condy appears to have had four types of financial arrangements with local members of the book trade. One was consignment, as in the case of John Perkins. Another was simply cash payment, though cash was scarce and would probably have been used reluctantly. A

Perkins took place before Winter's death, i.e., between the summer of 1760 and the autumn of 1761; but there is no indication of what the relationship between Winter and Perkins was at that time. Possibly Perkins was just beginning the business on his own and Condy's books formed a new stock for him. See the Condy account book, pp. 96–101, and Isaiah Thomas, *History of Printing in America*, pp. 206–9.

[67] Condy, Account Book, p. 101.

[68] Condy, Account Book, pp. 200, 209.

[69] The London Bookstore had previously been operated by James Rivington, the sometimes scurrilous printer and bookseller from New York. For Mein's transactions with Condy see the Condy account book, p. 230.

[70] Condy, Account Book, pp. 225–26.

[71] Ibid., pp. 206, 203. Also on Barclay, see French, 'The Amazing Career of Andrew Barclay,' pp. 145–62.

[72] Condy, Account Book, p. 178.

third was the use of goods to pay for services such as printing, binding, and advertising. This third method of payment would have been appealing as a means of distributing stock and paying debts because Condy could buy goods wholesale and trade them at a higher value. Through this method of local distribution, Boston printers and binders could diversify their stock, draw more people into their shops, and generate an important flow of currency.[73] Finally, Condy sold books on credit to other Boston booksellers and merchants. He was paid in cash by terms of credit that often stretched over years and only sometimes included interest.

Jeremy Condy bought goods from London, had them shipped to Boston, and then sold them to customers throughout the northern colonies. His trade was both urban and rural, local and distant. It was also both wholesale and retail; that is, his customers included merchants and other booksellers as well as individuals. Examining the web of relationships that stretched over the northern colonies, linking people and places by transportation systems but also by letters, newspapers, and word of mouth, is crucial to our understanding of Condy's business.

In Boston, the books that Condy published and imported were distributed by Boston merchants, artisans, and small shopkeepers. From those shops the books fanned out to customers from nearby houses as well as students from Cambridge and people from distant towns and villages who had traveled to Boston. Only one-sixth of the customers in Condy's account book of credit sales were from Boston, a figure that must understate the extent of local business, probably because Condy extended credit to individuals mainly for reasons of distance from his shop. Most of the Bostonians listed in the account book were either merchants, men who bore the title of esquire, or artisans to whom Condy owed payment. Selling books, stationery, and other goods from his shop for cash was probably a major means of distributing goods, especially stationery, but as in the daybooks of the *Virginia Gazette*, we are left with almost no records of individual

---

[73] Botein, ' "Meer Mechanics," ' pp. 144–45.

cash sales.[74] Benjamin Guild's daybook of the Boston Bookstore records a bustling local trade that probably paralleled Condy's. The best view we have into sales to local customers coming into the shop from the street are the accounts of those Harvard students who bought books on credit listing their home towns so that parents could be held responsible for payments. Many of the Harvard listings bear notes that payments were made by family members. There are 151 accounts belonging to Harvard students among the 600 accounts in Condy's extant account book. Those accounts record hundreds of visits to Condy's shop by students who probably arrived in the North End by ferry and made the easy walk to the shop. For these students and other local customers Condy kept one shelf of books 'to be lett,' thus affording readers a small circulating library.[75]

More than half the accounts in Condy's credit book belonged to customers who lived outside Boston and Cambridge.[76] Many were tradesmen, but most were not. All of them testify to an elaborate distribution network through which Condy's books were marketed. Those hundreds of customers who lived outside Boston were scattered throughout Connecticut, Rhode Island, Massachusetts, and New Hampshire in 134 towns. At a time when most goods were consumed where they were produced, books and paper were traveling long distances as commercial commodities.[77] Relatively few of the towns listed in the account book contained more than a tiny number of customers. Many had only one. Newbury, Providence, and Springfield were exceptional, containing between ten and fifteen customers. What all of the outlying towns listed by Condy have in common is that, when plotted on a map, they fall universally along trade routes; i.e., they lie along the coast, along rivers, or on stage routes. These

[74] See Cynthia Z. Stiverson and Gregory A. Stiverson, 'The Colonial Retail Book Trade: Availability and Affordability of Reading Material in Mid-Eighteenth-Century Virginia' in this volume.

[75] Suffolk County Probate Records, 67: 192.

[76] The more than 150 Harvard students in the account book are counted as Cambridge residents, and thus as local customers, even though their home towns are listed in the account book.

[77] See the same point discussed by Feather, 'Cross-Channel Currents,' p. 8.

routes were important not only in getting the books to their purchasers, but also in carrying word of new books to potential purchasers.

Newspapers and booksellers' catalogues traveled along the water and land routes used by ships, stages, and horses. As in England, newspapers and book catalogues were the major means for booksellers to advertise their stocks.[78] In 1759 the printers of Boston's newspapers refused to advertise an Ames almanac published by booksellers; the booksellers complained, in broadside form, of the printers' ability to deprive them of 'the Benefit of their usual Channel of Conveyance to the Publick.'[79] Similarly, Robert Harlan cites the importance of David Hall's *Pennsylvania Gazette* to Hall's book sales.[80] Worthington Ford has emphasized the importance of newspaper advertising to the Boston book trade of Henry Knox and his contemporaries.[81] The advertisements themselves often contained appeals to rural as well as urban readers, thereby testifying to their wide circulation in rural areas.

Jeremy Condy advertised his stock in the *Boston Weekly News-Letter* of Richard Draper, in Thomas and John Fleet's *Boston Evening Post*, and in Benjamin Edes and John Gill's *Boston Gazette*.[82] He also published at least one catalogue of books.[83] Booksellers used catalogues, often in the form of broadsides, to advertise recently received shipments of books or selections from their general stock of books and stationery. Condy may well have issued a number of such catalogues and sent them via ships, stages, and postriders to the merchants and individuals with whom he did business.

[78] Ibid., pp. 8ff. Roy McKeen Wile's examination of this subject was published shortly after his death; it was to have been preliminary to a larger study. See his article 'The Relish for Reading in Provincial England Two Centuries Ago,' in *The Widening Circle: Essays on the Circulation of Literature in Eighteenth-Century Europe,* ed. Paul Korshin (Philadelphia, 1976), pp. 87–116.

[79] Botein, ' "Meer Mechanics," ' p. 148; 'To the Publick,' broadside, Dec. 21, 1759, Boston.

[80] Harlan, 'A Colonial Printer as Bookseller,' p. 357.

[81] Ford, 'Henry Knox,' pp. 227–30. Ford cited John Foster Condy's use of the *Boston Evening Post* for advertising his books, p. 230.

[82] Condy, Account Book, pp. 152, 206, 225–26.

[83] Winans lists a Condy catalogue published on Sept. 30, 1766. See Winans, *A Descriptive Checklist of Book Catalogues,* p. 39.

Condy's carefully kept records of his business transactions track the books he sent out along the distribution networks. Thus, he noted that Col. Jonathan Moulton of Hampton received books via 'the Stage Coach W[est],' and that Benjamin West, the famous almanac maker of Providence, received his books through Dexter Brown, as did Sarah Goddard, partner and mother of William Goddard of Providence. Brown was probably a carrier or postrider.[84] A parcel for John Waite of Brookfield was ordered and paid for by the Deerfield merchant Elijah Williams, Esq., and sent by Condy to Brookfield probably via the stage.[85] Trunks, parcels, and postage frequently appear as charges in the account book. Ships carried trunks and smaller parcels of books down the coast of Rhode Island and Connecticut so that customers in Newport, Kingston, and Westerly, Rhode Island, received books by water as did customers in Groton, New London, Lyme, New Haven, Stratford, and Stamford, Connecticut. For example, Roger Sherman, the wealthy merchant and future signer of the Declaration of Independence, received large orders from Condy by ship.[86]

This network was also reciprocal in that Condy often received payments via the same means of distribution. John White, Elisha White, Robert Rice, and Captain Burroughs were only four of many ship's captains who paid Condy cash on various accounts.[87] Condy received cash sent by Rev. David Rowland of Plainfield, Connecticut, from 'Brown the Waggoner,' and accounts were often brought up to date by monies given the postrider Peter Mumford or 'Silens Wilde, Post Rider.'[88] In some cases, Condy appears to have gone to Cambridge, Providence, or Newport and received payments there.[89] Whether he made the trips specifically to collect debts is not clear.

[84] Condy, Account Book, pp. 103, 69, 201, 210–11, 105, 231, 204.

[85] Ibid., p. 7; James Putnam of Worcester, one of Condy's customers, wrote to Knox about an order for books, 'Let them be carefully done up in brown paper to prevent rubbing as they are to come up in saddle bags.' See Ford, 'Henry Knox,' p. 224.

[86] Condy, Account Book, pp. 174–75.

[87] Ibid., pp. 174, 199.

[88] Ibid., pp. 122, 19, 36, 74, 62.

[89] Ibid., e.g., pp. 32, 126.

A common intermediary for transporting payments and orders was another person from the customer's village or town, often a family member, who had traveled to Boston on business. Condy's book frequently notes payments on account by people other than the customer. In this connection, one of Knox's customers, Joseph Clarke of Northampton, wrote to the bookseller in 1773 ordering a manuscript book to be bound and adding, 'Mr. Lyman, the bearer hereof will stay in Boston some time I suppose. I would therefore be glad if you would get it ready to send by him when he comes out. . . . If you desire it Mr. Lyman will pay you.'[90] The letter probably referred to Gad Lyman, who also settled accounts with Condy for Joseph Hawley.[91] Condy's account book and letters from Hawley to Knox record many other instances of this practice.[92]

Perhaps the most striking fact about this distribution system is not that Condy's customers lived along trade routes, but that no one who did not live along the trade routes bought books from Condy. Of the more than 600 separate customers in the account book, only 26 have not been accounted for in terms of location. These people probably lived in Boston since the credit customers for whom Condy neglected to list occupation or location tended to be close at hand and well known to their creditor. The rest of Condy's customers, though they lived at considerable distance from Boston, in small as well as in larger towns, testify to the lines of influence that moved along trade routes borne by newspapers and by the books they advertised. These trade routes were also lines of cultural demarcation; the sparsely populated areas beyond them appear from Condy's book to have been cut off from the books that moved along main access routes by boats, stages, and postriders. Whether this was indeed the case is a difficult question to answer; certainly we need to look for evidence, not present in Condy's account book, that will follow tradesmen off the major roads and along the paths used by peddlers.

90 Ford, 'Henry Knox,' pp. 249, 259–60.
91 Condy, Account Book, p. 37.
92 Ibid., p. 37; and Ford, 'Henry Knox,' pp. 249, 259–60.

The geographical web of Jeremy Condy's customers was spread broadly across New England; yet in other ways that same web of customers was surprisingly close knit. The large proportion of Harvard students in Condy's credit account book bears repeating; of the 600 separate accounts in the book, 151 were students at Harvard College. Even more striking is that of the remaining three-quarters of Condy's credit customers, 200 had graduated from Harvard College. Ninety of these had not only graduated from Harvard but were also ministers.[93] One hundred and six customers were neither graduates of Harvard College nor listed with their occupations, but a large proportion of those bear the titles of colonel, doctor, or esquire; they were apparently gentlemen of property and standing and can be traced with relative ease. Of the remaining names on Condy's list, 44 were merchants, a few were listed as widows, others were artisans, and still others were members of the book trade in Massachusetts, i.e., artisans and shopkeepers. The Harvard graduates who were not ministers were generally listed as merchants, attorneys, or physicians, or simply bore the title of esquire.

Condy's business as a bookseller appears to have been built largely on the support of colleagues in the ministry and other Harvard graduates and undergraduates. Those men sometimes bought stationery and cloth or china goods, but first and foremost they bought books.[94]

The web of Harvard-trained ministers was large and influential. Although Jeremy Condy was a Baptist minister, he was extremely popular among Massachusetts Congregationalists. From the moment of his ordination—when he offended many Baptists by his insistence on the presence of Congregational clergymen, including his future customer Rev. Nathaniel Appleton—and throughout his life as he preached the relatively liberal views of Harvard-trained ministers, Condy was respected and befriended by a large proportion of his fellow clergy. The widespread respect for Condy is evidenced by his

[93] The figures on Harvard graduates in the Condy account book have been obtained using Shipton, ed., *Sibley's Harvard Graduates*.

[94] T. S. William found that ministers did not buy their books from the rural shop of Abraham Dent. Perhaps English ministers, like those in America, were ordering from well-stocked urban bookstores. *An Eighteenth-Century Shopkeeper*, p. 22.

OCCUPATIONS OF CONDY CUSTOMERS
AS LISTED IN ACCOUNT BOOK

Harvard students	151
Ministers	89
Esquire (no occupation listed)	55
Merchant	44
Book trade (English and American—includes printers, booksellers, stationers, bookbinders, etc.)	28
Artisans	19
Doctors	19
Col., Capt., Maj.	13
Physicians*	6
Deacons	3
Miscellaneous†	20
No occupation or title listed:	
Boston resident	28
Non-Boston resident	94
No occupation or location	8

*Customers whom Condy listed as physicians never bore the title of doctor; however, most of the men who were listed as doctor were probably physicians in the current sense.

†Includes listings for widows, teachers, milkmen, barbers, brewer collectors, postriders, and wharfingers—few of these customers were book-buying customers.

being elected four times to the committee to visit the schools. He also served as chaplain of the Province Council and the General Court and was invited to preach the election sermon in 1759.[95]

Jeremy Condy understood the support he enjoyed among members of the clergy and was careful to nourish that support. His decisions regarding the books and pamphlets he chose to publish reflect his sensitivity to the interests of his audience. As part of the network of liberals, Condy understood the interest that would greet Mayhew's pamphlets, Hutchinson's *History*, and Tucker's arguments. Being in the midst of his community of readers and an active intellectual as well, Condy also understood which English titles were of special interest and could feel confident of his ability to shape a desirable stock of books.

Condy's well-educated readers, whether they lived in Boston or in outlying towns and villages, formed their own complex communications networks that drew together patterns of friendship, family, and proximity. Letters and conversations, as well as newspapers, perpetuated the bookseller's provincial business; and loyalty to a Harvard colleague probably played a part. Time and again, connections turn up among Condy's customers. One example of these little networks is the case of Rev. Robert Breck.[96] Breck was a controversial figure even in his student days at Harvard, from which he graduated in 1730. Condy was teaching at Harvard at that time, and must have witnessed the good and bad moments of Breck's student years. Like Tucker, Condy, and many other New England ministers, Breck's liberal ideas met with heated resistance in the years leading up to and during the Great Awakening. In Western Massachusetts and Connecticut feelings were especially intense. Breck moved from Harvard to Windham, Connecticut, and in the mid-1730s he became the controversial minister of the First Church of Springfield. Like Condy he continued to concentrate his preaching on the problem of toleration and orthodoxy; like Condy, he met with problems.[97]

95 Shipton, ed., *Sibley's Harvard Graduates*, 8: 24.
96 Ibid., pp. 661–80.
97 Ibid., p. 675.

Robert Breck became one of Condy's customers after Condy took up bookselling.[98] Breck's son, Robert, went to Yale to study—a curious choice given the nature of his father's difficulties—and Condy sent books to him there. When the younger Breck graduated he apparently became a merchant in Springfield, for he appeared in Condy's book in that capacity and began to make larger purchases from Condy.[99] Robert's sister Lois married Rev. Joseph Whitney, another Yale graduate, and settled in Pomfret, Connecticut. Whitney and other members of the Pomfret community also became Condy's customers.[100] Although the line of communication between Lois's family and her husband was not necessarily responsible for Whitney and the other Pomfret customers, it probably was. Similarly, Rev. Chauncy Whittlesey of New Haven, with whom the elder Breck had dealings, turned out to be another of Condy's customers.[101] Whittlesey's orders for eighteen copies of Hutchinson's *History of Massachusetts* and twenty-four copies of *The Death of Abel*, which he could distribute to his parish, further trace the dissemination of Condy's books.[102] The important point is not exactly what conversation or letter might have included a discussion of Condy's business. Rather it is that all of these men inhabited an environment in which there were considerable opportunities for contact as well as many common points of interest.

Others of Condy's customers had political rather than religious affiliations with one another. Names that appeared on various sides of the developing struggles with England also appear in the account book. Andrew and Peter Oliver, Thomas Hutchinson, James Otis, Samuel Adams, Robert Treat Paine, Joseph Hawley, Josiah Quincy, Joseph Warren, and Roger Sherman are some of the most prominent.[103] Whether Condy was actively involved in politics in Boston

[98] Condy, Account Book, p. 22.

[99] Ibid., pp. 42, 92.

[100] Ibid., p. 144. Ebenezer Chaplin, Ebenezer Craft, Josiah Dana, and Rev. Aaron Putnam were a few of Condy's other customers from Pomfret.

[101] Condy, Account Book, p. 66.

[102] Ibid., p. 66.

[103] Ibid., Adams, p. 84; Hawley, p. 37; Hutchinson, p. 75; the Olivers, pp. 40, 166, 35, 41, 180; James Otis, pp. 18, 73; Robert Treat Paine, p. 16; Josiah Quincy, p. 22; Roger Sherman, pp. 53, 174–75; Joseph Warren, pp. 45, 61, 124.

in the mid-1760s is not a matter of record, but his sympathies are clear in Richard Draper's remark: 'His country was a more special object of his good wishes. He rejoiced in those liberties both religious and civil and ardently desired the continuance of them and that all attempts to deprive it of them, in whole or in part, might be frowned upon in providence and brought to nothing.'[104]

The artisans who appeared in Condy's credit account book were not book buyers; however, they attest to the activity and apparent success of Condy's book-oriented business life as it was reflected in his personal life. The eighteen artisans in Condy's account book provided services or supplied goods to Condy and he repaid them in cash, cloth, paper, and other goods, but they did not take books as payment nor did they appear as outright purchasers of books.

William Bell, a mason, took six china cups and saucers, one 'Barcelona Hankerchief,' and a considerable amount of cloth in November 1767 and January 1768 for unspecified work performed for Condy in October 1767.[105] Similarly, Job Walker of Roxbury, a shoemaker, received cloth and writing paper in return for '1 pair Shoes for Foster [Condy's son], 1 pair Do [ditto] for Cloe and Do for Cato'; Cloe and Cato were probably the servants listed in Condy's estate inventory and mentioned elsewhere in the account book.[106] 'Mr. Gideon Frost, Milkman,' received shoes and cloth as payment for 138½ quarts of milk and for keeping a horse for 125 nights.[107] Condy also received cordwood, chocolate, beer, wine, rum, tea, rainwater, shoes, and wigs as well as the services of a housewright, a glazier, a truckman, a tailor, and a barber.[108] He seldom paid cash; instead he used his own stock as payment. By trading goods for goods and services Condy

[104] *Boston Weekly News-Letter*, Sept. 1, 1768.
[105] Condy, Account Book, p. 209.
[106] Ibid., p. 227, and see May 13, 1766 entry, Hodgson, p. 178.
[107] Ibid., p. 199.
[108] The following pages in the Condy account book contain the accounts of artisans and shopkeepers who supplied Condy with goods and services for himself and his family: Billings, p. 140; Brown, p. 184; Champney, p. 212; Davis, p. 80; Jackson, p. 103; Joy, p. 132; Lloyd, p. 217; Marret, p. 17; Moody, pp. 121, 161; Newell, pp. 137, 233, 234; Russell, p. 24; Saller, pp. 89, 94; Spear, p. 80; Swan, p. 227.

avoided using the scarce commodity of cash and paid with goods that he had purchased wholesale.

As the structure and practices of Jeremy Condy's book trade unfold, the character of that trade becomes increasingly clear and provocative. We are driven to explore the connections between books and society. How were the lenses with which Condy's readers saw their world and the troubles of the 1760s colored by the titles they purchased from the Boston bookseller? What sociology of knowledge do we find in New England? How far did the ideas in such books filter into colonial society? What forms did they take?

If we ever reach the answers to such questions, we will do so only after many more questions about how the book trade functioned in eighteenth-century America have been persistently explored and answered. And answers cannot be arrived at without looking at the books themselves.

While the statistics on the titles in Condy's account book are not yet fully computed or analyzed, and thus only bear mention here, the titles themselves do not present us with surprises. Those that leap to attention from sheer repetition are the same as those recorded in Condy's estate inventory. They are works known to have been extremely popular among colonial readers.[109] Many were books that enjoyed simultaneous popularity in rural and urban England.[110]

Although American scholars have emphasized the popularity and importance of the writings of John Locke, John Trenchard, and Thomas Gordon to American readers of the mid-eighteenth century, Jeremy Condy's account book records that these authors were less popular with his customers than several others. And, in fact, the libraries of colonial Americans, like the account book, testify to the

---

[109] Mott, *Golden Multitudes*; Hart, *The Popular Book*; and David Lundbert and Henry F. May, 'The Enlightened Reader in America,' *American Quarterly* 28 (1976): 262–93. That the same books were popular over a broad geographical area is evidenced in Richard Beale Davis, *A Southern Colonial Bookshelf* (Athens, Ga., 1979), pp. 65–90.

[110] See William, *An Eighteenth-Century Shopkeeper*, pp. 15–17; and Caroline Robbins, *The Eighteenth-Century Commonwealthman* (Cambridge, Mass., 1961).

immense popularity of books that were religious in nature and devotional in mode. Compared to the writings of Philip Doddridge, the sermons of John Tillotson, the works of Isaac Watts, Robert Dodsley, the Swiss Solomon Gessner, and Edward Young, Locke's *An Essay Concerning Human Understanding* appeared relatively infrequently in Condy's account book. Doddridge and company deserve more careful attention than historians have given them.[111] Generally speaking, these writers urged that religion be rooted in practice, not in systematic doctrine. Their religious ideas and instructions as to how to practice them in daily life reached a broad spectrum of New England readers. Jeremy Condy's bookstore was one channel through which these books passed.

Condy himself had been steeped in the teachings of Tillotson, Doddridge, and that network of writers while he was a student at Harvard and especially in the 1730s when he spent three years in England. During those years Condy's friendship with the English writer John Foster put him in the company of writers and thinkers whose works were so popular in America in the eighteenth century.[112] Condy shared their beliefs in the importance of benevolence and toleration. Ironically, his practice of those virtues caused him a great deal of trouble and controversy with laymen and clergy whose readings of the same books did not inspire them to Condy's actions or attitudes.[113] Few of Condy's congregation at the First Baptist Church

[111] As G. R. Cragg has described them, the ideas presented in their works derived from the Cambridge Platonists and moved through religious thought in lines that were gradually paralleled in the secular philosophies of the Enlightenment. G. R. Cragg, *From Puritanism to the Age of Reason* (Cambridge, 1966), p. 17, passim.

[112] Shipton, ed., *Sibley's Harvard Graduates*, 8: 22. Also Jeremiah Condy to John Sparhawk, *New England Historical and Genealogical Register* 24 (1870): 114-15.

[113] References to Condy's troubles and his devotion to the idea of toleration are made in his obituary, *Boston Weekly News-Letter*, Sept. 1, 1768. The books by dissenting clergy are found in many libraries and inventories of people who held ideas opposed to Condy's; for example, see William McLoughlin, *Isaac Backus and the American Pietistic Tradition* (Boston, 1967), p. 191. George Whitefield apparently found that remarks he made against Tillotson met with such resentment among potential followers that he published an explanation. See his pamphlet 'A Letter . . . wherein He Vindicates His Asserting that Archbishop Tillotson Knew No More of Christianity than Mahomet,' in *Three Letters from the Reverend Mr. G. Whitefield* (Philadelphia, 1740). Brief mention is made of this controversy in another

shared his views. Nevertheless, the writers with whom Condy sympathized and from whom he drew inspiration continued to grow in popularity among New Englanders, and attitudes that drove Condy from the ministry were swept into the slow process of accommodation and change.

Jeremy Condy's account book also bears witness to the popularity of more secular works, the most popular of which was Alexander Pope's *Essay on Man*. Pope's work, like the writings of James Thomson and William Wollaston, is an excellent example of a literature that was both religious and secular in tone and message. The following passage illustrates that tone:

> All nature is but art unknown to thee;
> All Chance, direction which thou canst not see;
> All discord, harmony not understood;
> All partial evil, universal good;
> And, spite of pride, in erring reason's spite,
> One truth is clear, Whatever is, is right.[114]

This passage evokes the natural religion that developed out of Newtonian physics. The order of the universe, the workings of nature are examples and proof of God's attention to the world. These themes were echoed in the writings of Watts, Young, Wollaston, and Thomson, some of the frequently cited authors in the account book.[115]

Greek and Roman classics enjoyed contemporary popularity throughout the colonies. Most popular with Condy's customers were the works of Cicero, Xenophon, Seneca, and the Roman historian Tacitus. Most of the classics that Condy imported were translations rather than Latin and Greek texts. A considerable part of the allure of the translations was the fact that they were accompanied by lively

---

context in Alan Heimert, *Religion and the American Mind* (Cambridge, Mass., 1966), pp. 36–37.

[114] From *Essay on Man*, quoted in Mott, *Golden Multitudes*, p. 45.

[115] In Condy's account book, popular titles by these religious and secular writers were as follows: Isaac Watts, *Horae Lyricae*; Doddridge, *The Rise and Progress of Religion* and *The Family Expositor*; Tillotson, *Sermons*; Gessner, *The Death of Abel*; James Thomson, *The Seasons*; Edward Young, *Night Thoughts*; William Wollaston, *Religion of Nature*; James Hervey, *Meditations and Contemplations*; and Robert Dodsley, *The Oeconomy of Human Life*.

introductions that applied the classical text to current events or ideas. For example, Condy specified 'Gordon's Tacitus' as the translation purchased by his customers. In Condy's account book the popularity of this classic ranked with the most popular religious titles. Scholars have attributed the widespread popularity of Gordon's translations to the fact that the text treated historical crises as moral issues and that Gordon, a famous pamphleteer and publisher, set the classical text into a political environment in which the text argued for political and social virtues that had contemporary application.[116]

Condy sold many histories, the most popular of which was Paul Rapin's history of England. David Hume's *History of Great Britain* was less popular though it was bought occasionally. Condy sold a large number of Thomas Hutchinson's *History of Massachusetts*, of which he was the publisher. Rousseau's *Émile* and Defoe's *Robinson Crusoe* were most frequently cited of the relatively small number of narratives and romances bought from Condy's shop. Among the numerous self-help books in Condy's inventory, John Love's *Surveying*, Thomas Salmon's *Grammer* and *Gazeteer*, and John Ward's *Mathematics* and *Everyman His Own Lawyer* appeared frequently.

What stands out in looking at the broad picture presented by the titles in Jeremy Condy's account book and by the probate inventory of his estate is an internal balance. There is a visible order to Condy's stock, achieved by a balance of intensive and extensive reading matter. The devotional works of English writers form a kind of intensive literature that could be counted on to have a large and regular market. As such they provided Condy with steady sellers that could be imported with confidence.[117] Against that stock Condy set a stock of more timely books.

---

116 D. L. Jackson, 'Thomas Gordon's *Works of Tacitus* in Pre-Revolutionary America,' *Bulletin of the New York Public Library* 69 (1965): 58–64, esp. 59 n. 11; Meyer Reinhold, comp., *The Classick Pages* (University Park, Pa., 1975), p. 99; Bernard Bailyn, *The Ideological Origins of the American Revolution* (Cambridge, Mass., 1967), p. 25; Robbins, *The Eighteenth-Century Commonwealthman*, p. 117.

117 The distinction between ways of reading and the use of the terms 'intensive' and 'extensive' first came to my attention in David D. Hall, 'The World of Print and Collective Mentality in Seventeenth-Century New England,' in *New Directions in American Intellectual History*, ed. John Higham and Paul K. Conkin (Baltimore,

When Jeremy Condy died, late in August 1768, his bookstore passed into the hands of his son, James Foster Condy, who continued in business until the Revolution. The probate inventory is thus the inventory of an active business. The inventory recorded a stock of more than 1,500 magazines, many of them published in 1767.[118] Their early dates were probably not evidence of any lack of popularity, since Condy's account book records the sale of magazines, bound in sets and also unbound, that were bought well after their dates of publication. *The Gentleman's Magazine*, the *Museum*, the *London Magazine*, and many others were among Condy's most popular stock. Thousands of copies left his shop during the decade recounted by his credit account book. Condy profited from the serial nature of such popular literature.

Unlike Zechariah Fowle, whose nearby shop specialized in chapbooks, broadsides, and inexpensive popular books, and unlike the extremely successful London bookseller James Lackington, who made a fortune on remaindered stock, Jeremy Condy does not appear to have carried a large inventory of cheap, expendable books. He stocked a supply of almanacs that he received from John Perkins and other members of the Boston book trade.[119] But his chief venture into this market was the subscription sale of pamphlets imported for 'Governor Bernard and others' and for 'Samuel Phillips Savage and others.'[120] Beginning in January 1761 while Condy was still in England, and for the next three years, the account book records lengthy and frequent lists of pamphlets imported for those reliable groups of customers. The pamphlets and books were fully paid for in advance by the subscribers, and Condy simply acted as agent and thus received an undisclosed

---

1979). Hall notes that his use of the distinction is made with the influence of Norman Fiering and Rolf Engelsing, *Analphabetantum und Lekture: Zur Sozialgeschichte des Lesens in Deutschland zwischen feudaler und industrieller Gesellschaft* (Stuttgart, 1973). See also Hall's article in this volume.

118 Suffolk County Probate Records, 67: 192.

119 Condy, Account Book, account of John Perkins, in which Perkins sold Condy almanacs (thirty Wests and twelve Ames in Dec. 1766), opposite p. 228.

120 Condy, Account Book, pp. 114–19.

profit.[121] Thus, Condy was able to profit without risk from those popular books and pamphlets.

Jeremy Condy was a wise and careful businessman. He was a bookseller who was closely acquainted with both the books he stocked and the customers to whom he sold those books. He understood the issues toward which his readers gravitated and carefully steered his ventures in publishing along those lines. A well-respected figure in Boston, he enjoyed the business that came from Harvard-educated readers who lived both locally and in rural parts of the northern colonies. Lacking complete evidence of his sales of books, stationery, cloth, and other goods, we cannot make any unqualified pronouncement on the degree of success that Jeremy Condy met with in his pursuits. But the personal expenditures recorded in the account book and the material comfort evidenced in the probate inventory give us a picture of a man who enjoyed financial success, a man whose circumstances had improved considerably from the time he entered the Boston book trade.

The available biographical sketches of Jeremy Condy and the records that document his life and work are lenses through which we can view the world of print as it was experienced by eighteenth-century New Englanders. In broad ways that world resembled its English counterpart. Many of the same books were popular in both places. There are similarities in the way books moved from London out to provincial centers in England and New England; after all, Boston was still another provincial center to the London wholesale market. But the account book is also our key to more specific environments—the world of Harvard College and rural New England in the decade before the American Revolution. The picture we receive from Condy's account book reveals a tightly knit, well-educated, and financially stable, even comfortable, network of readers that extended from Boston out into the New England countryside along well-traveled routes. Those readers, dispersed as they were, were part of an intel-

---

121 Ibid.; note that the orders were paid for in advance.

lectual community that maintained strong links among its members. Jeremy Condy, by belonging to the community which gave him his livelihood, enjoyed special advantages—advantages that he understood and pursued with care.

APPENDIX I

The Condy Account Book

The surviving account book of Jeremy Condy's Boston bookstore is held in the Manuscript Collections of the American Antiquarian Society. The book records the purchases, paid for on credit, by 600 separate customers or suppliers between 1758 and 1770, two years after Condy's death when his son John Foster Condy had taken over the business. There seem to be no criteria for inclusion in the book other than the credit nature of the transactions. The surviving account book incorporates a broad range of people from Boston as well as scores of rural towns. In the same book Condy recorded the accounts of merchants, booksellers, and library and subscription groups; i.e., large purchases, as well as the accounts of individual customers. He also recorded the accounts of people in the book trade to whom he owed money; i.e., London booksellers and stationers, Boston binders and booksellers, and printers who advertised his stock and printed the books he published. With those customers and business dealings Condy included personal accounts in which he owed money to shoemakers, smiths, tailors, and other artisans mentioned in the body of this paper.

The accounts are not set in any particular order though in general the earliest entries appear toward the front of the book. As space filled up in a previously begun account book, Condy transferred the account to this extant book; and as the pages in this book became crowded, accounts were transferred to another book. The extant book must have been designated no. 5 because the notes that preface many accounts in this book record that the account is being transferred from no. 2, no. 3, and most often no. 4 (for a few examples see pp. 94, 16, 38, and 7, 13, 30). Although accounts in the surviving account book run all the way to 1770, Condy had put another credit book into use by the early 1760s. The book was referred to as the Quarto Book, the 4° Book, and the Quarto Marble Book (e.g., opposite pp. 64 and 51, and p. 108). After Condy's death on August 28, 1768, entries were usually transferred to the Administration Account Book, 4° Marble Covers (e.g., pp. 162, 191, 203, 211, and 229).

Given these boundaries, what information can we gather from Condy's extant account book? For a business that spanned a period from the mid- to late 1750s to the spring of 1768 when Condy was gravely ill, we know that we are missing all of Condy's daybooks (like the book of Benjamin Guild at the Baker Library at Harvard Business School) and all of Condy's business correspondence (analogous to the papers of Henry Knox held at the Massachusetts Historical Society or those of David Hall at the American Philosophical Society). What we do have is a large credit book, kept over the decade from 1758 through 1768 when Condy did most of his business in Boston. We cannot be certain of the size of Condy's business from the remaining book though accounts of major suppliers like Joseph Richardson, the London bookseller, appear complete for the period of their inclusion in the book. We can get a *sense* of the success of his business from the account book combined with his biography and his estate inventory. The personal accounts recorded in the account book and the notes which accompany them give us a further sense of Condy's lifestyle and thus of his social and financial standing.

There are special features to Condy's account book of credit purchases that make it particularly valuable as a research tool. Probably because of his desire to collect any money owed him, Condy recorded the location and occupation of almost every customer in the account book. Armed with that information he could keep track of customers over the long terms of payment taken by many colonial purchasers. In some cases we find that Condy collected money owed him in these various locations either in person or through a postrider. Most of the traceable customers for whom no occupation or location were listed turn out to have been men of property and standing in Boston, i.e., customers whom Condy could easily recognize and contact.

The nature of this account book means that the information it contains is necessarily skewed toward a kind of customer who would need or request credit from Condy. The account book is skewed toward students, merchants who were making sizable purchases, and customers who lived outside Boston. The book misses Condy's traffic from the street and thus probably misses small purchases and buyers who paid in cash.

Within this book each separate account seems to be complete for the period of its inclusion. Thus, what we do have is an invaluable list of the names, occupations, and locations of about 600 individuals in the important decade before the Revolution, and a list of the books and other items they purchased from Condy. Moreover, we have important information about a Boston bookseller as importer, publisher, and salesman. The fact that other data from other bookstores survives helps to fill out our picture of Condy's shop. The inventory of his estate and records of his education and life provide us with important materials to expand the depth and scope of that picture.

APPENDIX II

Books Listed in the Inventory of
Jeremy Condy's Estate Taken October 6, 1768

The following list of books has been transcribed from Suffolk County Probate Records, volume 67, pp. 188–98. The books formed the book stock of Condy's shop at the time of his death. The assessments of the values of books have not been included since values were given to several books at a time rather than to individual books. Brackets enclose questionable and illegible listings and words that were taken for granted as understood by the reader.

1	Sett 4 Vols Doddridges Expositor	3	Watts on the Mind
1	Dictionary Arts	3	History England
8	Preceptors	6	Gazeteer
7	Salmons [Grammar]	14	Lexicons
7	Gordons Grammar	12	Caesar
5	Lockes Essays	10	Xenophon
3	[Pl]iny's Letters	5	Horace Delph
1	Newton on Prophecys	12	Terrence
6	Brooks Practice	5	Sallust
2	[Orr]erys Pliny	8	Longinus
2	Sharps Surgery	5	Gentlemans Library
2	Medica Physica	1	[*illeg.*] Works
2	Butlers Analogy	1	Attorney Pocket Book
11	Reid on the Mind	1	dº [Attorney] Practice
4	Swans Siderham	6	Brittish Grammar
8	James Dispensatory	4	Hudibrass
4	Quarto [Bibles]	2	Leeds Works
4	Octo Bibles	7	Gilbert on Tennuus Ejectments
13	Watts Logic	2	Barnes Notes

1	Officium Clarici Pa[*illeg.*]	1	do Trigono
3	Watts Essay	1	History Calefornia
4	Patoun Navigation	3	Harvies Life
3	Euclid	3	Sharps Enquiry
3	Martins Grammer	1	do Surgery
1	Turkish spy	3	Loves Surveying
1	Elaboratory	3	Davidsons Horace
4	Spectators	2	Boehaves Lectures
6	odd Vols. of Nature displayed	6	Huxham on Fevers
1	Shaftburys Character	1	Johnson Sophocles
1	Tales [Fairies]	1	Cheyne on Regemen
2	Bennets Oratory	1	do Natural Method
1	Gentleman instructed	2	Nelsons Festivals
2	Thompsons Seasons	1	[Levinsons] Oratory
2	Durhams Ash?	2	Quincy [Sanitorius]
1	Scougal Works	1	Lock Miscellanies
5	Every Man his own Lawyer	20	Bayleys [Dictionary]
4	History Religion	10	Johnsons Dictionary
5	[R]ennits Antiquities	17	Youngs Dictionary
2	Lock on Understanding	2	Quincys Dispensatory
2	Hebrew Psalter	1	Masons Sermons
2	Quincy Lexicon	1	Collins Scheme
3	Willsons Surveying	1	Fosters Answer
2	Cheselden Anatomy	1	Cold Bath
2	Whyst on Newes	1	Life of Holt
3	Daltons Sermons	1	Cheyne on Fevers
1	Boehave	2	do Malasy
1	Italian Library	2	do Hand
20	Willsons Navigation	2	Watts Horace
1	Clarks Sermons	1	Virgil
1	Berry [street] do	6	Bayleys Ovid
2	Martins Philo	2	Clarks Ovid
		2	Nepos
		3	Justin
		3	Cicero

30	Second hand Books sundry sorts	1	Cadet
1	Walls Astronomy	1	Calvinist Cabinet
2	Short on Tea	14	Holmes Rhetoric
1	Fredrican Code	1	Antient History
1	[Votters] Antiquities	1	Indep. Wigg
2	Hills Sermons	2	Annual Register 1763
1	Williams do	1	Rowes Letters
1	[*illeg.*] Magazine	1	Smellie Midwife
1	Mead on Poisons	2	Diseases of Women
1	do Medical [*illeg.*] on Pulse	1	Fordyce on Education
1	History Engld	1	Handmaid to Arts
1	Mathers Apology	1	Blands Military
1	[Howells] Letters	22	Wollaston Religion Nature
1	West on Resurrection	5	Life of David
1	Colmans Parable	14	Wards Mathematicks
1	Duty Man	109	History Massachusetts Vol. 1
1	Ladies Dispensatory	40	ditto——2
1	[*illeg.*] Animal Oec. ?	27	ditto——2 sticht
1	Arbuthnot Aliments	450	ditto——in sheets—
1	Lawsons Oratory	105	Dillworth
1	Mariners Kallender	11	Gignoux spelling Books
11	Compass	44	Testaments
4	Assistant	188	Small Books for use of Latin School
1	Boyers Dictionary	21	[R]ichers Companion
2	do Grammer	2	Guthries Tryal
8	French Books	12	[*illeg.*] Godliness
1	Livis Admirals	17	Book Knowledge
1	[*illeg.*] Travels	3	Fishers
3	Livys History	15	Cockers
11	Duncans Cicero	3	[J]ennings Arithmetick
1	Meditations do	15	Russells Sermons
2	Virgill	12	pilgrims progress
3	Burnes Justice		

5	History England	2	Bacon ABridgem!
4	Kings Heathen Gods	6	Woods Institutes
4	Doddridge Rise	1	Jacobs Law Dictionary
5	Sermons	4	Hawkins [*illeg.*]
5	power & grace	1	[*illeg.*] Conveyance
5	History Rome	1	Woods Civil Law
2	History Greece	3	Stackhouse Body
2	[Rule] Life		Divinity
2	[pleasing] Instructor	1	Burket New Testament
6	Holy Wars	1	Flavels Works
3	Bunyans Temple	1	Bates Works
2	[*illeg.*] Anatomy	1	Henrys exposition
2	Culpeppers Physician		6 Vol.s
2	Monro on Dropsy	2	pools Annotations
1	Cheyne on Long life		2nd Hand
1	Vicar Wakefield	1	Rapius History
27	Bibles different Sorts	1	Locks Works
6	Prayer Books do	7	Doddridges Lectures
3	Tate and Bradys Psalms	18	Fergusons Astronomy
5	Church primmers	6	Crudens Concordance
24	Mayhews 14 Sermons	1	[Fl]eisters Surgery
12	Tansur [Melody]	1	Ainsworths Dictionary
18	Williams Melody	5	Gravesand Philosophy
15	Latin Gramar	1	Hedrici Lexicon
1	Duncans Cicero	1	Shaws Boerhave
9	Davidsons Virgil	1	Fosters Discourses
2	Norfolk Militia	1	Newmans Chemistry
1	Plutarch's Lives	1	Whitbys Commentarys
1	Popes Odeysey	1	Franklins Sophocles
1	Iliad	1	Halsys Tables
6	[*illeg.*] Polity	1	Estranger Touph[a]s
1	Household Furniture	1	[*illeg.*] Test^a
1	White on Isaiah	1	on Creed
1	Burnet [Mortuum]	1	Life Pope Alex.
1	Gales Serm.	1	Lives Eminent Men

1   Ambrose looking to
        Jesus
1   Emersons Mechanicks
1   [*illeg.*] Maps
491   Recovery from Sickness
        Pamphlets
192   Smiths Essay d°
457   Doddridge Family
        Religion d°
134   Grove on Sacrament
        ½ bound
22   Death of Able Tryal
        of Abraham d°
156   death Abel
158   Tryal Abraham in sheets
10   [Gratus]
1   Childrens Grammar
1   [Dacius] Plato
10   Mem° Books
3   Baxter
5   Baxters rest old
1   Orphans Legacy
1   [*illeg.*] on Psalms old
1   Biblia [*illeg.*] 6 Vol
        folio old
1   Greek and Lattin book
15   Rhetor[u]s Elementa
        ½ bound
11   Parchment Books with
        Clasps
3   Watts Lyric[ae]
2   Psalms
    Boyles Voyage
    Hamsons [*illeg.*] Prucia
        Memoirs

2   Voltairs Annals
3   Origin Evill
2   Mason on Knowledge
1   Burnet Reform.ᵃ
1   History N & S America
1   Rogers on Revolution
1   Blackerbys Justice
1   Telemaque French
1   [*illeg.*] Britain
3   Gardiners Life
5   Religious Courtship
2   [*illeg.*]
1   Polnits Memoirs
1   Life Marlbrough
2   Fox on Time
1   Castalio Bible 4 Vol.ˢ
1   Sidney Biddelph
1   Swignes Letters
1   Life Charles 12:
1   Family Instructor
1   Humorist
1   [S]andeman on Theron
1   Discription Animals
1   Allins Alarm
2   on Prayer
3   Young Mans Calling
1   Plaything
1   Dilworth
1   University
1   Shaws Immᵃ
1   Student
1   Crusoe
1   Dyre
1   Generosity
1   [*illeg.*]

20	Fishers Tutor	1	Anatomy
7	[F]ennings spelling book	3	Copper plate Books
18	Doddridge on Education	20	old plays
16	Setts Doddridge Tract	134	Country Town Officer
2	de Concientia		sewd
1	Vincent	236	ditto in sheets
	Sundry books on a Shelf	40	Dissenting Gentlemans
	which are kept to		answer sewd
	be lett	275	dº in sheets
	a parcel old Books	1513	Magazines chiefly for
	4½ doz primmers		1767
	1 Magazine Museum	56	Small Acct Books differt
	for 1766		sizes in parchment
	1 Mercury [pt] of 1753	20	ditto in marble paper
6	Martin use of Globes	15	Alphabets
	sticht	2	setts Slips 8ᵈ
19	Oeconomy Life dº	6	doz 9 Writing Books
2	Architect		

The Colonial Retail Book Trade: Availability and Affordability of Reading Material in Mid-Eighteenth-Century Virginia

CYNTHIA Z. STIVERSON *and* GREGORY A. STIVERSON

V IEWING THE DEVASTATION at Yorktown shortly after Cornwallis's defeat, the Abbé Robin, a chaplain with the French army, noticed a number of books piled in heaps among the ruins of the town. Hoping to get an 'idea of the taste and morals of the inhabitants,' Robin stopped to examine the books in the rubble. What he found were:

treatises of religion or controversial divinity; the *history* of the English nation, and their foreign settlements; *collections* of *charters* and *acts* of parliaments; the works of the celebrated *Alexander Pope*; a translation of *Montaigne's Essays; Gil Blas de Santillane*, and the excellent *Essay upon Women*, by *Mr. Thomas*.[1]

Robin's brief listing of the books discovered in the streets of Yorktown is more tantalizing than informative. He did not know who owned the books, he failed to note how frequently he came upon the same titles, and he was most interested in books authored by Frenchmen. But historians would generally agree with Robin's assumption that some measure of understanding about men can be gained by discovering what books they read, and would only wish that he had been more explicit about the books owned by the residents of Yorktown. As much as he might envy Robin's opportunity, however, the historian can never project himself back in time to personally examine all of the

---

[1] Claude C. Robin, *New Travels Through North-America: In a Series of Letters* (Boston, 1784), p. 58.

books owned by the people of the society in which he is interested. Some books have survived with bookplates or signatures that identify the original owner, but in most cases the historian must rely on other evidence—the 'rubble' of past generations fortuitously preserved in public and private papers—to discover what was owned and read.

In recent decades, a number of scholars have attempted to assess the character of literary culture in colonial America by employing a variety of methodologies. Perry Miller's analysis of the Puritan mind and Bernard Bailyn's essays on the intellectual origins of the American Revolution are but two examples of studies that rely in part on determining what was read by colonial elites.[2] Others, such as Louis B. Wright and George K. Smart, have examined estate inventories to establish what books were owned, and presumably read, by the colonists.[3] Still another approach has been to examine booksellers' advertisements and library catalogues to define the extent and content of printed material available in the colonies, as in the work of H. Trevor Colbourn and Howard Mumford Jones.[4] Because of problems presented by the evidence upon which each of these types of studies is based, scholars such as Richard Beale Davis have more

[2] See esp. Perry Miller, *The New England Mind: The Seventeenth Century* (New York, 1939), and *The New England Mind: From Colony to Province* (Cambridge, Mass., 1953), and Bernard Bailyn's essays on the intellectual origins of the American Revolution, particularly his introduction to *Pamphlets of the American Revolution, 1750–1776*, vol. 1 (Cambridge, Mass., 1965). See also the following works by Bailyn: *The Ideological Origins of the American Revolution* (Cambridge, Mass., 1967); *The Origins of American Politics* (New York, 1969); and 'The Central Themes of the American Revolution: An Interpretation,' in *Essays on the American Revolution*, ed. Stephen G. Kurtz and James H. Hutson (Chapel Hill, N.C., 1973).

[3] Louis B. Wright, *The First Gentlemen of Virginia: Intellectual Qualities of the Early Colonial Ruling Class* (San Marino, Calif., 1940), is based primarily on inventories of prominent seventeenth-century Virginia aristocrats. George K. Smart, 'Private Libraries in Colonial Virginia,' *American Literature* 10 (Mar. 1938): 24–52, examines the books in about 100 Virginia inventories. To obtain his sample of 100 libraries, Smart had to encompass the years 1650 to 1787, yet the books were not listed by title in over a quarter of the inventories he included ('Private Libraries,' pp. 29–30).

[4] H. Trevor Colbourn, *The Lamp of Experience: Whig History and the Intellectual Origins of the American Revolution* (Chapel Hill, N. C., 1965); Howard Mumford Jones, 'The Importation of French Literature in New York City, 1750–1800,' *Studies in Philology* 28 (Oct. 1931): 235–51, and 'The Importation of French Books in Philadelphia, 1750–1800,' *Modern Philology* 22 (Nov. 1934): 157–77.

recently adopted a multidimensional approach, considering a variety of evidence in their investigations of colonial culture.[5]

While each of these methods has contributed substantially to our understanding of literary taste in the colonial period, none offers a truly satisfactory means of assessing the role of books and reading in the pre-Revolutionary period. Studies of the elite invariably fail adequately to relate the presence of a few great libraries, in the possession of men with distinguished minds, to the thoughts and actions of the masses. Estate inventories too often mentioned only a 'parcel of books,' the recording of inventories was skewed in favor of the well-to-do, and studies based on inventories generally ignore the preponderance of estates that included no books at all. Titles listed in library catalogues and advertisements may never have circulated or been sold, and extremely popular books that had wide currency required no more space to list in an advertisement or catalogue than a book that was never purchased or read.[6] The multidimensional approach, by widening the quantity of sources consulted but not necessarily with a corresponding qualitative refinement of the data, too often results in little more than overlong recitations of ever expanded lists of titles discovered. The sheer energy required to identify and compile the masses of information that appear in multidimensional studies can give the illusion that the conclusions presented have greater validity than those obtained from other approaches. In fact, the profusion of detail may add little

[5] While the bibliography of Richard Beale Davis's writings is extensive, the culmination of his years of research on the Southern mind is presented in his award-winning *Intellectual Life in the Colonial South, 1585–1763*, 3 vols. (Knoxville, Tenn., 1978). For the purposes of this study, the most pertinent sections are found in chap. IV.

[6] Booksellers' advertisements can also be deceptive because all titles in stock were not always listed. John Edgar Molnar, for example, in his 'Publication and Retail Book Advertisements in the *Virginia Gazette*, 1736–1780' (Ph.D. diss., University of Michigan, 1978), found only 1,632 titles advertised for sale in the period covered by his study, 122 of which were printed locally. But in the forty-seven months encompassed by the periods July 1750 to June 1752 and January 1764 to January 1766, William Hunter and Joseph Royle, proprietors of the Williamsburg printing office and two of the printers of the *Virginia Gazette* included in Molnar's study, stocked at least 997 different titles and they sold 10,066 copies of 671 of those titles. For a discussion of book sales by Hunter and Royle, see below.

to the precision of argument or extent of knowledge about who actually read what.

The student of literary culture in Virginia has available a unique source for investigating colonial reading habits. Though not entirely free from methodological problems itself, it at least offers a different means of determining what was available to be read and what was actually purchased by the reading public. Two daybooks have survived from the Williamsburg printing office that, in conjunction with published advertisements, make possible a partial reconstruction of the inventory of colonial Virginia's largest retail bookstore and the identification of hundreds of people who bought books there.[7] The data from the daybooks can be used to complement, and in some cases correct, the conclusions reached in studies based on other types of evidence. Our purpose here, however, is limited to utilizing the daybooks as a means for exploring the operation of a large retail bookstore in the colonial South.

I

'Virginia,' wrote Hugh Jones in 1724, 'is esteemed one of the most valuable gems in the crown of Great Britain.' Established in 1607, Virginia was the oldest and largest British colony, claiming by its charter land as far west as the Mississippi River. Virginia's financial success was due to tobacco, a crop first shipped from the colony in

---

[7] The Hunter and Royle daybooks were deposited in the University of Virginia Library by their owner, James Southall Wilson, in 1946. In 1950 they were purchased from Mr. Wilson and became part of the Tracy W. McGregor Library at the University of Virginia. Nothing is known about the history of the daybooks from the time they were written until they came into the possession of Mr. Wilson, nor have any companion volumes been found. Paul P. Hoffman, ed., *Guide to the Microfilm Edition of the Virginia Gazette Daybooks, 1750–1752 & 1764–1766* (Charlottesville, Va., 1967), was prepared by the Department of Research, Colonial Williamsburg Foundation, Williamsburg. The daybooks are not paginated, but page numbers were added for the purpose of indexing the volumes. Further references in this study will cite the page numbers assigned by the indexers. Wilson recognized the value of the daybooks for studying reading habits and published his own conclusions in 'Best-Sellers in Jefferson's Day,' *Virginia Quarterly Review* 36 (Spring 1970): 222–37.

1614 and by 1619 its most valuable export. The transportation and marketing of tobacco was a major source of income for British merchants and the English treasury, and the trade provided Virginians with a constant supply of goods and services from England.[8]

Throughout most of the eighteenth century, Williamsburg was the capital of the rich and extensive province of Virginia. Although it has been called the 'seat of empire,' Williamsburg's physical proportions inadequately reflected its importance as the administrative center of the colony. Established by act of assembly in 1633, Williamsburg— or Middle Plantation as it was then called—had grown little by 1699 when the colonial capital was moved there from Jamestown. The College of William and Mary, chartered in 1693, was located in Williamsburg, as was a powder magazine, a few stores, and some private dwellings, but little else distinguished the site from the surrounding countryside.[9]

Because of its inland situation, Williamsburg would never attain the size of port cities like Philadelphia, New York, or Boston, but being the seat of government provided some impetus for growth. The construction of public buildings, foremost of which were the capitol and the governor's residence, and additions to the college—including Brafferton Hall, the president's house, and wings to the Wren Building—formed a nucleus for the mile-long town. These buildings were augmented by stores, taverns, and private homes built to serve the city's residents and transient visitors.[10] Despite the expansion, an Eng-

---

[8] Hugh Jones, *The Present State of Virginia: From Whence Is Inferred A Short View of Maryland and North Carolina*, ed. Richard L. Morton (Chapel Hill, N.C., 1956), p. 83. For a comprehensive history of colonial Virginia to the year 1763, see Richard L. Morton, *Colonial Virginia*, 2 vols. (Chapel Hill, N.C., 1960).

[9] The most detailed discussion of Williamsburg is Rutherfoord Goodwin, *A Brief & True Report Concerning Williamsburg in Virginia* (Williamsburg, Va., 1941). See also Carl Bridenbaugh, *Seat of Empire: The Political Role of Eighteenth-Century Williamsburg* (Williamsburg, Va., 1950); Jane Carson, *We Were There: Descriptions of Williamsburg, 1699–1859* (Williamsburg, Va., 1954); and John W. Reps, *Tidewater Towns: City Planning in Colonial Virginia and Maryland* (Williamsburg, Va., 1972), pp. 141–93.

[10] In 1760 the population of Philadelphia was approximately 23,750, that of New York 18,000, and that of Boston 15,631. Carl Bridenbaugh, *Cities in Revolt: Urban Life in America, 1743–1776* (New York, 1955), p. 5. Comparable population

lish visitor in 1732 estimated that 'the Metropolis' contained only about 100 houses,[11] and a decade later another Englishman called the town a 'most wretched contriv'd Affair for the Capital of a Country.'[12] As late as 1760, when Williamsburg had nearly reached the apogee of its growth, Andrew Burnaby noted that the town was 'far from being a place of any consequence.'[13]

Eighteenth-century visitors frequently made disparaging remarks about Virginia's capital because they were inadequately attuned to the nature of provincial society. Virginia was overwhelmingly agricultural, and to the members of its rural population, who often lived miles from their nearest neighbor, the small town with dusty streets was indeed the metropolis. Innumerable landings on the extensive river network that laced the province and the prevalence of neighborhood stores operated by planters and Scottish factors reduced the need for a central marketplace. A few urban centers, such as Norfolk, Fredericksburg, and Richmond, arose to serve the backcountry, but the Virginia landscape remained predominantly rural. Throughout the colonial period the vast majority of the colony's citizens never saw a city of more than two or three thousand population.[14]

It was Virginia's rural character that caused Williamsburg to assume

---

data for Williamsburg are not available, but the town probably had little more than 1,000 residents in 1760, half of whom were blacks. Thad W. Tate, *The Negro in Eighteenth-Century Williamsburg* (Williamsburg, Va., 1965), pp. 27–28. For a description of major structures in the town, see Marcus Whiffen, *The Public Buildings of Williamsburg, Colonial Capital of Virginia* (Williamsburg, Va., 1958), esp. pp. 1–17.

[11] William Hugh Grove, 'Virginia in 1732: The Travel Journal of William Hugh Grove,' ed. Gregory A. Stiverson and Patrick H. Butler III, *Virginia Magazine of History and Biography* 85 (Jan. 1977): 24.

[12] [Edward Kimber], 'Observations in Several Voyages and Travels in America in the Year 1736,' *William and Mary Quarterly*, 1st ser. 15 (Apr. 1907): 223.

[13] Andrew Burnaby, *Travels Through the Middle Settlements in North-America. In the Years 1759 and 1760. With Observations upon the State of the Colonies*, 2d ed. (London, 1775), p. 6.

[14] Arthur Pierce Middleton, *Tobacco Coast: A Maritime History of Chesapeake Bay in the Colonial Era* (Newport News, Va., 1953), esp. chaps. 2–4; Thomas Jefferson, *Notes on the State of Virginia*, ed. William Peden (Chapel Hill, N.C., 1955), p. 108; Joseph A. Ernst and H. Roy Merrens, ' "Camden's turrets pierce the skies!": The Urban Process in the Southern Colonies during the Eighteenth Century,' *William and Mary Quarterly*, 3d ser. 30 (Oct. 1973): 549–57.

an importance to the colony's inhabitants that was rarely appreciated by English visitors. In addition to being the administrative capital of the colony, Williamsburg was the social and cultural center of the 'country' of Virginia. Williamsburg was the place of residence of the royal governor, whose style of living the country gentry assiduously emulated; it was the site of the College of William and Mary, the only institution of higher learning in the colony; and it was the home of some of Virginia's most powerful, intelligent, and genteel residents. Because it was the focal point of the colony's politics and the center of its culture, to many Virginians Williamsburg must have seemed the nucleus of the universe.[15]

Williamsburg served as the locus of colonial Virginia culture in a variety of ways, and the printing office, located on the north side of Duke of Gloucester Street, was a preeminent source of information for Virginians during the last four decades of the colonial period. Its successive proprietors published the *Virginia Gazette* for distribution throughout the province, the shop housed the Williamsburg post office, and at least from the early 1740s it was the site of the colony's largest bookstore. Since the printing office bookstore was located in the colonial capital, it served a much larger audience than stores elsewhere in the province.[16] Persons visiting the city for business or pleasure could select books personally, and because the bookstore's owner was also the colony's postmaster, books could be ordered by letter and delivered by return mail. Consequently, books sold at the printing office reflect more than the reading preferences of the inhabitants of one small town. The Williamsburg bookstore served a province-wide audience, and what was purchased there is indicative of the reading needs and interests of people from all sections of the colony.

---

[15] Jane Carson, *Colonial Virginians at Play* (Williamsburg, Va., 1965), chap. 4; James H. Soltow, *The Economic Role of Williamsburg* (Williamsburg, Va., 1965), pp. 6–19; Bridenbaugh, *Seat of Empire*, pp. 29–31.

[16] According to the Scottish tobacco factor William Cunninghame, a store in Virginia drew most of its customers from a 'Circle of twelve or fourteen miles.' William Cunninghame to John Turner, Oct. 6, 1771, William Cunninghame & Co. Letter Books, 1767–74, National Library of Scotland, Edinburgh (microfilm copy, Research Department, Colonial Williamsburg Foundation).

The Williamsburg printing office was founded nearly a century after printing had begun in New England. It could be argued that the reason for the late introduction of printing in Virginia was that residents of the southern colonies were less interested in reading than were people who settled in the North.[17] But Virginians were different from New Englanders and had less need for local printing facilities. Immigrants to New England were religious dissenters who felt compelled to publicize their particular beliefs concerning religion and society; most Virginians were Anglicans, and were in substantial agreement with the mainstream of English thought. Furthermore, New Englanders settled in towns, but Virginians quickly dispersed to isolated farms and plantations, relying on London merchants to supply most of the goods and many of the services that they required from an urban center. Finally, the early establishment of public schools to thwart 'that old deluder, Satan,' the founding of Harvard College in 1636, and the high percentage of well-educated clergymen in the region stimulated the growth of a native literary culture in New England, whereas Virginians long remained content to import their culture, like their furniture and clothing, from England. In short, the absence of printing in Virginia does not necessarily imply that Virginians were uninterested in reading, but rather that their requirements for reading materials could be better served by alternative sources.[18]

---

[17] See Carl Bridenbaugh, *Myths and Realities: Societies of the Colonial South* (Baton Rouge, La., 1952), p. 40. The following discussion of printing in Virginia and the proprietors of the Williamsburg printing office is based on Lawrence C. Wroth, *William Parks: Printer and Journalist of England and Colonial America* (Richmond, Va., 1926), pp. 9–29; Lawrence C. Wroth, *The Colonial Printer*, 2d ed. (Portland, Me., 1939), pp. 38–39, 42–43; Mary Goodwin, 'The Printing Office' (research report, Research Department, Colonial Williamsburg, 1952), pp. 8–38, i–liii; and Douglas C. McMurtrie, *A History of Printing in the United States*, vol. 2, *Middle & South Atlantic States* (1932; reprint ed., New York, 1969), pp. 276–88.

[18] For positive assessments of literary life in colonial Virginia, see Wright, *First Gentlemen*, p. 2; Richard Beale Davis, *Literature and Society in Early Virginia, 1608–1840* (Baton Rouge, La., 1973), pp. 151–52; and Jay B. Hubbell, ed. *The South in American Literature, 1607–1900* (Durham, N.C., 1954), p. 10. See also Richard Beale Davis, C. Hugh Holman, and Louis D. Rubin, Jr., eds., *Southern Writing, 1585–1920* (New York, 1970), pp. 3–12; and Smart, 'Private Libraries,' p. 26n. For a statement regarding differences between Virginia and New England libraries, see William Harwood Peden, 'Thomas Jefferson: Book-Collector' (Ph.D. diss., University

Actually, printing occurred in Virginia as early as 1682, three years before the first printer began work in Pennsylvania. A press was erected by William Nuthead at Jamestown under the patronage of John Buckner, a local merchant and landowner, but it was banned by royal order shortly after it began operations.[19] The suppression of Nuthead's press was in accord with sentiments expressed by Governor William Berkeley a decade earlier when he wrote to the Commissioners of Trade and Plantations concerning Virginia: 'I thank God, *there are no free schools* nor *printing*, and I hope we shall not have these [for a] hundred years; for *learning* has brought disobedience, and heresy, and sects into the world, and *printing* has divulged them, and libels against the best government. God keep us from both!'[20] As long as this attitude prevailed on the part of the colony's officials, no printer could hope to practice his craft in the province.

The next attempt to establish a press in Virginia—this time with the approbation of the royal governor, William Gooch—succeeded, but it was half a century in coming. In 1730 William Parks was invited to set up a press in Williamsburg. Parks, an immigrant from England, had been a printer in Maryland since 1726, and his Williamsburg office was operated initially as a branch of his Annapolis firm. Parks immediately began printing laws and pamphlets with the Williamsburg imprint, however, and by 1731 he had moved his residence to the town.[21]

Like other colonial printers, Parks retailed books from his printing shop.[22] In addition to his own publications, Parks sold Bibles, prayer

---

of Virginia, 1942), p. 6; and Louis B. Wright, 'Literature in the Colonial South,' *Huntington Library Quarterly* 10 (May 1947): 297. For an extravagant appraisal of intellectual life in the eighteenth-century Chesapeake, see Richard Beale Davis, 'The Intellectual Golden Age in the Colonial Chesapeake Bay Country,' *Virginia Magazine of History and Biography* 78 (Apr. 1970): 131–43.

[19] Wroth, *Colonial Printer*, p. 38; McMurtrie, *History of Printing*, 2: 276–78; John T. Winterich, *Early American Books & Printing* (Boston, 1935), pp. 61–62.

[20] William Waller Hening, ed., *The Statutes at Large; Being a Collection of All the Laws of Virginia, from the First Session of the Legislature, in the Year 1619*, 13 vols. (New York, 1810–23), 2: 517.

[21] Wroth, *William Parks*, pp. 14–15.

[22] As with printing, a large retail bookstore was late in coming to Virginia. The colonial book trade was centered in New York, Philadelphia, and Boston, with the

books, and school books, nearly all of which he imported from England.[23] Parks's inventory of books was small, however, and bookselling remained a minor segment of the printing office business until the early 1740s. In 1742 the faculty of the College of William and Mary noted in their journal that Parks intended to 'Open a Booksellers Shop' in Williamsburg.[24] An advertisement from the October 17, 1745, issue of the *Virginia Gazette* indicates that the bookstore was well supplied by that date: 'Just imported, and to be Sold by *William Parks*, in *Williamsburg*, a considerable Quantity and great Variety of Books, on Divinity, History, Physick, Philosophy, Mathematicks, School-Books, in Latin and Greek, among which are some very neat Classicks. A large Quantity of large Church and Family Bibles and Common Prayer Books, Sermons, Plays, etc. too tedious to mention.' Although we do not know what titles were included in his store's stock, Parks certainly had a fully operational bookstore by 1745, and his business continued to expand.[25] When Parks died in 1750, the bookstore's inventory encompassed a large selection of books, the bulk of which he had imported from London booksellers.[26]

Parks's establishment of a bookstore in Virginia greatly increased the availability of printed material in the colony. Other Virginia merchants sold books in their stores, but the number of copies and variety of titles they had on hand were always small. Many dealers in general merchandise imported a dozen or more Bibles, New Testaments, prayer books, and psalters each year, as well as a smaller number of devotional tracts, primers, and English spelling books. The larger mer-

---

latter having at least twenty booksellers between 1669 and 1690. Louis B. Wright, *The Cultural Life of the American Colonies, 1607–1763* (New York, 1957), p. 152.

[23] C. Clement Samford and John M. Hemphill II, *Bookbinding in Colonial Virginia* (Williamsburg, Va., 1966), pp. 9–10; *Virginia Gazette*, Sept. 29, 1738.

[24] Mary Goodwin, 'Printing Office,' p. v; *William and Mary Quarterly*, 1st ser. 2 (July 1893): 51.

[25] Parks probably had a well-stocked bookstore at the printing office earlier than Oct. 1745. No issues of Parks's *Virginia Gazette* for the years 1741 through 1744 have survived, however, so earlier advertisements that might have described the stock of books at the printing office are missing.

[26] Payment to Thomas Waller, bookseller of London, William Parks Estate Settlement, York County Wills and Inventories, 1745–59, vol. 20, p. 324; Wroth, *William Parks*, p. 25; *Virginia Gazette* Daybook, 1750–52.

chants also stocked two or three copies of perennial favorites such as the *Spectator*, an assortment of children's chapbooks, and a single copy of a dozen or so other titles that they thought might appeal to their customers. But no Virginia merchant whose activities are documented came close to Parks and the succeeding owners of the Williamsburg printing office in the number and variety of books offered for sale to the public.[27]

Most of the books sold at the printing office were imported from England, but Parks augmented his stock with books and pamphlets printed on his Williamsburg press. One of his first publications was John Markland's *Typographia*, printed during the first year of operation of the Williamsburg press. The work was a poetic tribute to the art of printing dedicated to Governor William Gooch in recognition of his role in securing a printer for the colony. Two years later, Parks issued Governor William Gooch's *A Dialogue between Thomas Sweet-Scented, William Oronoco, Planters, and Justice Love Country*, a propaganda tract addressed to opponents of the recently passed tobacco inspection act. In 1734 Parks printed *Every Man His Own Doctor*, a home medical manual ascribed to a Virginian, John Tennent, that was later reprinted in both Williamsburg and Philadelphia. Two years later, Parks issued the first locally printed legal guide for local officeholders, George Webb's *Office and Authority of a Justice of Peace*. In 1742 Parks published the first cookbook printed in the American colonies, E. Smith's *Compleat Housewife*, followed in 1747 by William Stith's *History of the First Discovery and Settlement of Virginia*, an early history of the colony written by a native Virginian. These are only a few of the more important works published by Parks during his twenty years in the

[27] Roger Atkinson Account Book, 1762–89, p. 20, Alderman Library, University of Virginia, Charlottesville, Va.; 'Inventory of Goods on Hand at Mr. James Ritchie and Company's Upper Store, Brooksbank in Essex County,' May 28, 1776, James and Henry Ritchie Account Books, 1771–77, Manuscript Division, Library of Congress; William Allason Invoice and Inventory Book, 1761–64, pp. 5, 27, Virginia State Library, Richmond; William Allason to James Knox, Nov. 3, 1769, William Allason Letter Book, Mar. 18, 1757–May 30, 1770, Virginia State Library. For a discussion of the books sold at a general store in backcountry North Carolina, see Elizabeth Cometti, 'Some Early Best Sellers in Piedmont, North Carolina,' *Journal of Southern History* 17 (Aug. 1950): 324–37.

Williamsburg printing office, the quality and quantity of whose total output was outstanding in colonial America.[28]

Parks's publication of books and pamphlets did much to foster the growth and dispersal of knowledge in Virginia, but it was not his only contribution to the colony. In 1736 Parks established the colony's first newspaper, the *Virginia Gazette*. With the assistance of the Philadelphian Benjamin Franklin, Parks erected a paper mill on the outskirts of Williamsburg in 1743, the first of its kind south of Pennsylvania. When the intercolonial postal service reached Williamsburg in 1738, the printing office became the local post office, and Parks extended postal service south to Edenton, North Carolina. Finally, in his role as public printer Parks published the first collection of the colony's laws published in Virginia and issued numerous assembly journals, acts, and official proclamations.[29]

In short, when William Parks died at sea on his way to England in 1750, he left behind in his adopted home a legacy matched by few colonial printers. Not the least of his accomplishments was that by establishing a bookstore in the printing office he made available to Virginians a wide variety of locally printed and imported books. Although Parks's impact on the intellectual development of Virginia is difficult to assess, he certainly did as much as any other individual to facilitate the communication of ideas within the province.

When Parks embarked for England in the spring of 1750, he left the printing office in the care of William Hunter, his longtime employee and shop foreman. Following Parks's death, Hunter managed the printing office until 1751, when he acquired ownership of the property at a sheriff's sale. Hunter operated the printing office much the same as Parks had, publishing the *Virginia Gazette* and *Virginia Almanack*, running the post office, printing books and pamphlets, and selling books imported from England. Fortuitously, a daybook that provides

28 Wroth, *William Parks*, pp. 37–70; William Clayton-Torrence, *A Trial Bibliography of Colonial Virginia*, 2 vols. (Richmond, Va., 1908, 1910), 1: 104–41.

29 Rutherfoord Goodwin, *The William Parks Paper Mill At Williamsburg* (Lexington, Va., 1939), pp. 7–14; Fairfax Harrison, 'The Colonial Post Office,' *William and Mary Quarterly*, 2d ser. 4 (Apr. 1924): 82.

detailed information concerning the operation of the printing office has survived for the first two years of Hunter's management.[30]

The first entry in Hunter's daybook is dated July 28, 1750, and the ledger continues without interruption until June 29, 1752, for a total of almost exactly twenty-three months. During this period the printing office was open Monday through Saturday each week. Every credit sale was entered in the daybook in the order that it occurred. A typical entry includes the date, the customer's name, and a list of items purchased and their prices. Cash sales were not recorded, but at the end of each month the value of all cash transactions was listed. A comparison of the monthly summaries of charge and cash sales reveals that most persons charged their purchases. Just 26.8 percent of the nonbook sales and 31.4 percent of the book sales were paid for in cash (see Tables 1 and 2). If almanacs are excluded, cash book sales accounted for just 27.4 percent. The practice of deferring payment by purchasing on credit was common throughout colonial Virginia, necessitated by a chronic shortage of currency and by the fact that

TABLE 1

VALUE OF NONBOOK SALES,
OCTOBER 1750–JUNE 1752

Nonbook accounts	Charge sales*	Cash sales	Total sales	% cash sales
Binding	£232.04.07	£87.03.06½	£319.08.01½	27.3
Advertisements	174.12.09	31.03.08	205.16.05	15.2
Blanks	45.03.09½	59.11.10	104.15.07½	56.9
Printing	84.09.02	08.07.04½	92.16.06½	9.0
Postage	45.10.00	15.07.07	60.17.07	25.3
Paper	43.12.00	13.13.00½	57.05.00½	23.8
Stationery	30.06.06	18.11.09	48.18.03	38.0
Virginia Gazette	00.07.06	05.15.02	06.02.08	93.9
Total	£656.06.03½	£239.13.11½	£896.00.03	26.8

SOURCE: Daybook, 1750–52.

*Monetary values are in Virginia currency.

[30] Mary Goodwin, 'Printing Office,' pp. 16–27; McMurtrie, *History of Printing*, 2: 282–88. For a discussion of the Hunter daybook, see below.

planters usually received payment for their crops only once each year.[31] Therefore, although some goods were purchased for cash, the predominance of credit sales strongly suggests that the entries in Hunter's daybook accurately represent the kinds of purchases made at the printing office in the early 1750s.

The monthly accounts in Hunter's daybook indicate the relative importance of the different branches of the printing office business. Hunter failed to record his cash sales until October 1750, but his accounts are complete from that month through June 1752. As Table 1 shows, binding accounted for the largest percentage of sales of nonbook items. Hunter continued Parks's practice of binding old and new books, employing John Stretch as bookbinder. Stretch's work encompassed everything from binding local publications in plain leather covers to stamping elegant gilt lettering and ornaments on volumes owned by persons who wanted to improve the appearance of their libraries. Most of the work charged to the binding account, however, was for making the blank books and ledgers used by planters and merchants for registering accounts and recording copies of their correspondence.[32]

The second largest of the nonbook accounts was for advertisements inserted in the *Virginia Gazette*. Most advertisements cost seven shillings per week, although an unusually long one could cost as much as thirteen shillings and a brief notice as little as three shillings. The next most important category was blanks, which consisted of all preprinted forms such as ship manifests, bonds, bills of exchange, and deeds. The fourth largest account, printing, encompassed the special printing jobs done at the printing office, such as handbills and admission tickets for balls given in Williamsburg during court and assembly sessions. Postage ranked fifth among the nonbook accounts, and consisted of the income derived from the operation of the post office. The sixth

31 Soltow, *Economic Role*, pp. 124–55.

32 Samford and Hemphill, *Bookbinding*, pp. 15–17. Sometime after 1759, Stretch severed his connections with the printing office, and at the time of his death in Aug. 1764 he appears to have been a bookseller in Williamsburg. Ibid., pp. 16–17. See also 'Statement of Wm. Johnston,' n.d., Loyalists Claims, T. 79/114, pp. 196–99, Public Record Office, London, England.

account was labeled 'paper,' which included everything from writing paper of various sizes and grades to cartridge paper for gunpowder. The stationery account was seventh largest and included sales of fancy paper with gilt edging and black-edged paper for death notices, as well as writing supplies such as quill pens, ink powder, pencils, and sealing wax. The final category, that for the *Virginia Gazette*, included only two charge sales, one for a two months' and the other for a four months' subscription to the newspaper. Because the *Virginia Gazette* had a wide circulation, Hunter must have recorded most subscriptions in another book. With the exception of the *Gazette* account, however, Hunter's daybook appears to contain a complete record of all nonbook sales made during the twenty-three months it covers. Cash and credit sales for the period totaled just over £896.[33]

TABLE 2

VALUE OF BOOK SALES,
OCTOBER 1750–JUNE 1752

Book accounts	Charge sales*	Cash sales	Total sales	% cash sales
Bought Books	£276.00.00½	£98.06.02½	£374.06.03½	26.3
Almanacs	59.07.04	69.02.07½	128.09.11½	53.8
Bibles	74.10.07½	33.06.10	107.17.05½	30.9
S. Birt	69.03.01	16.11.11½	85.15.00½	19.4
T. Waller	46.01.02	13.11.03	59.12.05	22.7
Laws (1752)	21.10.00	27.02.01½	48.12.01½	55.8
Davies's *Poems*	16.18.06	01.16.00	18.14.06	9.6
Stith's *Sermon*	10.18.00	02.17.00	13.15.00	20.7
Webb's *Justice*	05.10.00	04.00.00	09.10.00	42.1
Sherlock's *Letter*	02.10.07½	00.04.04½	02.15.00	8.0
Total	£582.09.04½	£266.18.04½	£849.07.09	31.4

SOURCE: Daybook, 1750–52.

*Monetary values are in Virginia currency.

[33] Unless otherwise noted, all monetary sums are expressed in Virginia currency. When exchange stood at par, £100 sterling was equal to £125 Virginia currency. See John J. McCusker, *Money and Exchange in Europe and America, 1600–1775* (Chapel Hill, N.C., 1978), p. 206.

As with nonbook items, Hunter's daybook contains a daily record of books sold on credit at the bookstore as well as a monthly summary of cash book sales. As shown in Table 2, Hunter divided his stock of books into several categories. The largest volume of sales was from the bought books account, those books that Hunter had purchased outright for resale on his own account. A few of the titles in the account were secondhand books purchased in Virginia; some were publications that had been sent to Williamsburg by the Philadelphia printer and bookseller Benjamin Franklin; but the majority were volumes that Hunter had imported from English booksellers. The second largest category was for sales of the locally printed *Virginia Almanack*. The *Almanack* was the least expensive publication sold at the printing office, costing as little as seven and one-half pence per copy. Because of its low cost, over half of the *Almanacks* sold were purchased for cash. The third largest category of books was the Bible account, which also included prayer books and Testaments. Although the source of the books in the Bible account is not given, all were probably imported from England.[34] The next largest account, labeled 'S. Birt,' was a selection of titles on a wide variety of subjects that had been sent to Williamsburg by the London bookseller Samuel Birt.[35] The 'T. Waller' account was for law books acquired from another London bookseller, Thomas Waller.[36] Both the Birt and Waller books were sold on commission. The remaining book categories were for individual titles printed in Williamsburg by William Hunter or by his predecessor, William Parks. Book sales amounted to £849.7.9 in the period covered by Hunter's daybook, nearly as much as the proceeds from the

[34] Robert Aitken, a Philadelphia printer, published the first American edition of the Bible in English in 1782. Winterich, *Early American Books*, pp. 36, 58–59, 120–21.

[35] Samuel Birt's bookshop was located at the sign of the Bible in Ave Mary Lane, off Ludgate Street, in London. *Complete Guide to All Persons Who Have Any Trade or Concern with the City of London, and Parts Adjacent*, 6th ed. (London, 1755), p. 120; R. M. Wiles, *Serial Publication in England Before 1750* (Cambridge, 1957), p. 357; Henry R. Plomer, George H. Bushnell, and E. R. McC. Dix, *A Dictionary of the Printers and Booksellers Who Were At Work in England, Scotland and Ireland from 1726 to 1775* (London, 1932), p. 26.

[36] Thomas Waller's bookstore was under the sign of the Crown and Mitre, opposite Fetter Lane, in Fleet Street, London. Wiles, *Serial Publication*, p. 365; Plomer, Bushnell, and Dix, *Dictionary*, p. 254.

sale of all nonbook items. Even allowing for the underrecording of income from subscriptions to the *Virginia Gazette*, the bookstore accounted for a larger volume of sales than any other branch of Hunter's business.

Although his daybook ends in June 1752, Hunter continued to operate the printing office until his death in 1761. The goods and services he offered to the public appear to have remained substantially the same as those that are documented in the daybook. Hunter's interest in the intercolonial post office was enhanced in 1753 when he and Benjamin Franklin were jointly appointed deputy postmaster for North America. Hunter continued to issue publications from the Williamsburg press, but most were official acts, proclamations, and assembly journals, rather than the type of original work that had distinguished his predecessor. Hunter did publish a few items of special interest, however, particularly George Washington's *Journal* in 1754, which recounted the events of the young major's trip to the Ohio country to observe French military positions, and the pamphlets by Landon Carter and Richard Bland that opened the 'great paper controversy' known as the 'Parsons' Cause.'[37]

William Hunter died in August 1761. He was succeeded by Joseph Royle, who, like Hunter at the time of Parks's death, was the printing office foreman. A political conservative, Royle came under increasing attack during his last years as manager of the printing office for his refusal to print antigovernment articles submitted to the *Virginia Gazette*. Thomas Jefferson later wrote, 'We had but one press, and that having the whole business of the government, and no competitor for public favor, nothing disagreeable to the governor could be got into it.'[38] Because of Royle's restrictive policies, leaders of the opposing political faction invited William Rind to establish a rival press. Rind moved to Williamsburg from Annapolis in 1766, and from that date to

---

[37] Mary Goodwin, 'Printing Office,' pp. 20–27; Clayton-Torrence, *Trial Bibliography*, 1: 141–49, 2: 3–29.

[38] Jefferson's comment, written in a letter to Isaiah Thomas in July 1809, is printed in Isaiah Thomas, *The History of Printing in America, with a Biography of Printers, and an Account of Newspapers*, 2d ed., 2 vols. (Albany, N.Y., 1874), 2: 336n.

the end of the colonial period Williamsburg had at least two printers.[39]

Royle died before Rind arrived in Williamsburg, however, and the daybook that survives for his last two years as manager of the printing office covers a period when Virginia still had only one printer and one major bookstore. The first entry in Royle's daybook is for January 7, 1764, and the last is dated January 19, 1766, so that the period covered is slightly more than twenty-four months. Like the Hunter accounts, Royle's daybook lists the name of each person who bought goods on credit, followed by a description of the items purchased and their prices.[40] Unlike Hunter's daybook, Royle's accounts do not include the value of cash sales; but there is no reason to suspect a marked reduction in credit transactions between the early 1750s and the mid-1760s, and the majority of Royle's customers must also have charged what they purchased at the bookstore.

Royle offered the public essentially the same goods and services as had his predecessor. He continued to print the *Virginia Gazette* and the *Virginia Almanack*, although because of the Stamp Act Royle suspended publication of the newspaper in November 1765 and he did not issue an almanac for 1766.[41] Most important for this study, Royle continued to operate the bookstore, selling both locally printed titles and an ever increasing number of imported books.

Royle arranged his daybook accounts differently than Hunter. As Table 3 shows, the largest nonbook category was the stationery account, which encompassed Hunter's stationery, paper, and blanks accounts. Thus, in addition to writing paraphernalia, the account included preprinted forms as well as the different types of paper stocked at the printing office. The second largest nonbook account was for the *Virginia Gazette*, which included both subscription fees and charges for advertising in the newspaper. Royle's *Gazette* account provides a much better idea of the income derived from the newspaper than the obvi-

---

[39] McMurtrie, *History of Printing*, 2: 290–91.

[40] For a discussion of the Royle daybook, see below.

[41] The Stamp Act was passed Mar. 22, 1765, but did not go into effect until Nov. 1 of that year. For the text of the act, see Edmund S. Morgan, ed., *Prologue to Revolution: Sources and Documents on the Stamp Act Crisis, 1764–1766* (Chapel Hill, N.C., 1959), pp. 35–43. See also Mary Goodwin, 'Printing Office,' pp. 29–33.

TABLE 3

VALUE OF CREDIT NONBOOK SALES,
JANUARY 1764–JANUARY 1766

Nonbook accounts	*Charge sales**
Stationery	£855.18.01 ½
Virginia Gazette	485.09.00
G.A.O. (General Account of Office)	222.07.04 ½
N.P.L. (Northern Postal Line)	158.10.10 ¼
V.P.O. (Virginia Post Office)	20.13.08
Total	£1,742.19.00

SOURCE: Daybook, 1764–66.
*Monetary values are in Virginia currency.

ously incomplete figures in Hunter's daybook. The third largest account was labeled 'G.A.O.,' for 'General Account of Office.'[42] This account encompassed the operation of the bindery, fees charged for printing handbills, and charges for composing advertisements for the *Virginia Gazette* that were withdrawn prior to publication. The final two accounts covered the operation of the post office. The larger of the two, the 'N.P.L.,' was for the intercolonial northern postal line; the smaller, the 'V.P.O.,' was for the intracolonial Virginia post office. Credit sales of nonbook goods and services totaled nearly £1,743 for the twenty-four month period covered by Royle's daybook, nearly double the combined amount of cash and credit sales for the twenty-three months covered in Hunter's ledger a decade and a half earlier.

Most of Royle's book sales were subsumed under one heading simply labeled 'books' (see Table 4). Prints and books of plates imported from the London printer and mapmaker Robert Sayer were kept in a separate account, as were local publications.[43] Sales of the *Virginia*

[42] The meaning of the initials 'G.A.O.' is made clear in Royle's will, which is recorded in York County Wills and Inventories, vol. 21, pp. 264–71. See also Mary Goodwin, 'Printing Office," p. xxxiv.
[43] Robert Sayer was a map- and printseller at the Golden Buck in Fleet Street, London. John Chaloner Smith, *British Mezzotinto Portraits*, vol. 4, div. 2 (London, 1878–83), p. lii. See also Plomer, Bushnell, and Dix, *Dictionary*, p. 223; and *Sayer and Bennetts Enlarged Catalogue of New and Valuable Prints* (1775; reprint ed., London, 1970).

TABLE 4

VALUE OF CREDIT BOOK SALES,
JANUARY 1764–JANUARY 1766

Book accounts	Charge sales*
Books	£1,189.03.09
Sayer's Prints	115.10.03
Virginia Almanack	90.12.04
John Camm's pamphlets	09.15.00
Richard Bland's pamphlets	05.11.03
Landon Carter's pamphlets	04.12.03
Buckner Stith's *Treatise on Tobacco*	02.15.00
John Wily's *Treatise on Sheep*	01.00.00
Richard Henry Lee's pamphlet	00.11.03
James Horrocks's *Upon the Peace*	00.10.00
Total	£1,420.01.01

SOURCE: Daybook, 1764–66.
*Monetary values are in Virginia currency.

Almanack dominated the accounts devoted to locally printed works, with credit purchases amounting to over £90. All of the other local publications were inexpensive pamphlets, none of which accounted for more than a small percentage of the total income from book sales. Royle's credit sales of books totaled just over £1,420 for the twenty-four months covered in his daybook. As was the case with his predecessor, book sales nearly equaled the value of all nonbook income, and the bookstore remained the single most important branch of the printing office business. Royle's credit book sales amounted to 68.4 percent more than Hunter's combined credit and cash sales. If only credit sales are considered, Royle's book business surpassed Hunter's by nearly 144 percent. Although Hunter's daybook covers a period one month shorter than Royle's, it is clear that a substantial increase in sales at the Williamsburg bookstore occurred between the early 1750s and the mid-1760s. This conclusion obscures an important change in the type of books sold during the two periods, however, which can only be alluded to here. In the 1750–52 period, Hunter recorded selling books on credit to 230 different individuals. Royle's daybook includes the names of 335 purchasers. In both periods, however, a number of people bought only an almanac. Excluding almanacs, Hunter sold 2,028 copies of 355 different titles. Royle's ledger records the sale of 395 different titles, but the number of copies sold totaled only 1,827.[44] Thus, despite the expanded inventory of titles stocked by Royle, the principal reason his bookstore grossed more than when Hunter was proprietor was not due to a surge in the number of book buyers, nor because purchasers were buying more books—they actually bought fewer—but because of different exchange rates and because his inventory included a larger proportion of higher-priced titles.

Analysis of the printing office ledgers shows that the books William Hunter and Joseph Royle offered for sale in Williamsburg were either imported from England or printed in America, principally on the local press. Most Williamsburg imprints were relatively inexpensive and some enjoyed enormous popularity, but imported books predominated in the bookstore's inventory and accounted for most of its income. Both Hunter and Royle operated the bookstore for profit, and each priced imported and locally printed books sufficiently high to realize a gain for himself. Locally printed books that had a large volume of sales could be sold more cheaply than imported titles because their price included only the printer's profit in addition to the costs of production. But demand was insufficient to enable Hunter or Royle to print more than a few books and pamphlets each year, so a Virginian who desired variety in his reading had to turn to imported titles. The selling price of imported books included not only a profit for the bookstore's proprietor, but also the charges of English printers, book-dealers, and middlemen, and transportation costs. Virginians therefore paid a high price for the imported books they purchased in Williamsburg, but the alternative of importing books directly from England, which was an option open to large planters and others with direct commercial ties to the mother country, resulted in minimal savings and inevitable delays and disappointments.

[44] Gregory A. Stiverson and Cynthia Z. Stiverson, 'Books Both Useful and Entertaining: Literary Culture in Late Colonial Virginia' (unpubl. report, Research Department, Colonial Williamsburg Foundation, [1976]), pp. 94–95, 183.

The daybooks provide information concerning the source of the books Hunter and Royle sold in the bookstore, as well as data that indicate the profit made on their sale. By comparing the price of imported books with the value of wages and the cost of other commodities, some conclusions can be reached concerning the relative costliness of books and about the effect price had on limiting the size of the reading audience in mid-eighteenth-century Virginia.

II

Importing books into eighteenth-century America required skill and a willingness to take financial risks. The distance between the colonies and England posed problems for everyone involved in transatlantic commerce, but the situation was especially difficult for the bookdealer. Many books published during the seventeenth and eighteenth centuries remained popular for decades, but the larger colonial booksellers also attempted to stock a selection of recent publications in addition to standard works of proven salability. The American bookdealer not only had to predict which available books would suit his customers, but he also had to have a trusted correspondent in the English book trade to select the most promising titles from recently published works. The English agent became even more important in the second half of the eighteenth century with the rise in popularity of novels. Current novels were a high-profit item in the bookseller's inventory, and he could not afford to wait to receive word of a book's publication, order it by a returning ship, and then obtain it via another vessel several months later. Every colonial bookseller was dependent on an English agent, and if that agent was not honest and informed the results might be disastrous.[45]

45 For examples of colonial booksellers relying on London agents to supply them with recently published titles, see Benjamin Franklin to William Strahan, Feb. 12, 1744/45, in Leonard W. Labaree et al., eds., *The Papers of Benjamin Franklin*, 22 vols. (New Haven, Conn., 1961), 3: 13–14; and Robert D. Harlan, 'David Hall's Bookshop and Its British Sources of Supply,' in *Books in America's Past: Essays Honoring Rudolph H. Gjelsness*, ed. David Kaser (Charlottesville, Va., 1966), pp. 10–12. William Allason, a Virginia tobacco factor and storekeeper, concluded an order to the

Correspondence between Hunter and Royle and their English book-sellers has not survived, but both men appear to have been adequately served by reputable London firms during the years covered by the daybooks. Because the colonial bookseller had to know and trust his English supplier, most dealt with a small number of correspondents who had proven themselves reliable and capable. Hunter's daybook mentions only three London booksellers—Samuel Birt and Thomas Waller, who supplied him books on consignment, and Thomas Osborne, one of the principal men in the London book trade, who sold him books outright.[46] Parks had initiated the correspondence with all three, and Hunter acquired inventory from them when he became manager, and later owner, of the printing office. When Parks died, the bookstore stock included titles supplied by Waller and Birt, and a shipment Parks had ordered from Osborne arrived a few months later.[47]

During the period covered by his daybook, Hunter reordered books from only one of Parks's booksellers, receiving a large shipment from Samuel Birt in June 1752.[48] Birt remained Hunter's major supplier of imported books until late 1754 or early 1755, when Hunter was enticed by promises of higher profits into changing to another London bookseller, James Rivington. Rivington had begun expanding his busi-

Glasgow bookseller James Knox with the statement: 'If any New Books worth reading [you] may send a Copy of a few.' Allason to Knox, Oct. 23, 1769, Allason Letter Book.

[46] Thomas Osborne entered the colonial book trade in 1748, and one of his first shipments went to William Parks in Williamsburg. Wroth, *William Parks*, p. 25.

[47] Each book sale in Hunter's daybook indicates the account from which the title was sold. Until Apr. 1751 books from Samuel Birt and Thomas Waller comprised the majority of sales of imported books. On Sept. 6, 1751, Hunter recorded purchasing £57.0.3 sterling worth of Thomas Osborne's books from Parks's estate. The books had arrived some weeks earlier, however, because on July 23, 1751, Hunter credited himself £4.10.0 currency for 'Packing and taking an Account of Osbornes Books.' Because the books had been ordered by Parks, they became part of his estate, thus accounting for the delay before Hunter could acquire possession of them for sale. Daybook, 1750–52, fols. 55, 64.

[48] The order was sufficiently large—£293.18.10 sterling—to warrant publication of a special catalogue to advertise the collection. In the *Virginia Gazette* for June 5, 1752, Hunter announced that the book catalogue would be published the following week, and on June 10 he charged the Birt account £3.5.0 for the cost of printing it. No copy of the catalogue is known to have survived. Daybook 1750–52, fols. 121, 127.

ness in the early 1750s by offering provincial booksellers a substantial discount from the prices they were charged by other London book-dealers. One reason Rivington was able to sell books so cheaply was that he pirated books owned by other printers. Rivington's unscrupulous practices earned him general enmity in the London book trade, but he continued to attract provincial booksellers because of his low prices.[49]

William Hunter's decision to drop Samuel Birt in favor of James Rivington was discussed by William Strahan, a prominent London printer, in a letter he wrote early in 1755 to David Hall, Franklin's partner in Philadelphia. Strahan characterized Hunter as 'a very sensible Man and a good Judge of Books,' but he was convinced that Hunter would regret having changed correspondents. The terms Rivington offered Hunter were 'never heard of till now,' wrote Strahan, but he concluded that the low prices were 'only an Artifice to wrest him [Hunter] from his old Correspondent Mr. Birt.'[50]

Strahan's prediction that Hunter would be ill-served by Rivington proved accurate. Hunter was in England in 1758, and he told Strahan that although Rivington gave him a 16 percent discount on his orders with the right to return what he did not sell, the shipments he had

---

[49] For a contemporary account of Rivington's pirating activities, see the letter from William Strahan to David Hall, Mar. 24, 1759, quoted in Leroy Hewlett, 'James Rivington, Loyalist Printer, Publisher, and Bookseller of the American Revolution, 1724–1802: A Biographical-Bibliographical Study' (Ph.D. diss., University of Michigan, 1958), p. 15. James Rivington was the son of Charles Rivington, founder of the London publishing house of that name. Upon his father's death in 1742, James and his brother John succeeded to the business and remained in partnership until 1756. James then formed a new partnership with James Fletcher, an arrangement that was exceedingly profitable due in large part to their publication in 1758 of Tobias Smollett's *History of England*. By 1760, however, Rivington was in financial distress and decided to recoup his fortunes in America. He first became a bookseller in Philadelphia, and later had stores in New York and Boston as well. Rivington was a loyalist printer in New York during the War for Independence. See Septimus Rivington, *The Publishing Family of Rivington* (London, 1919), pp. 40–51; Frank Arthur Mumby, *Publishing and Bookselling: A History from the Earliest Times to the Present Day*, 4th ed. (London, 1965), p. 198; and Leroy Hewlett, 'James Rivington, Tory Printer,' in Kaser, ed., *Books in America's Past*, pp. 166–93.

[50] William Strahan to David Hall, Mar. 3, 1755, quoted in J. A. Cochrane, *Dr. Johnson's Printer: The Life of William Strahan* (Cambridge, Mass., 1964), p. 81.

received had included 'a great many extreme dull Books' that were overpriced compared to what they sold for in England. Hunter had therefore concluded that the discount Rivington gave was actually far less than it appeared on paper.[51]

Because Hunter was in England at the time of his disenchantment with Rivington, he probably selected a new bookseller to supply his Williamsburg shop. Whom Hunter chose is uncertain, but at the time of his death in August 1761 the only bookdealer known to have been shipping books to the Williamsburg printing office was William Johnston of Number 16, Ludgate Hill.[52] Hunter's executors credited Johnston for £50 sterling worth of books that Hunter had ordered before his death, and when Joseph Royle became manager of the printing office he continued to employ Johnston as his sole agent. On May 25, 1764, Royle credited Johnston with £59.5.6 sterling for books received on the ship *Ruby*, and on October 8, 1765, he entered a charge of £242.3.0 sterling for books Johnston had sent to him aboard the *Charming Molly*.[53]

Both Hunter and Royle augmented their inventory of imported books with titles printed in the colonies. William Parks had frequently received books and supplies from Benjamin Franklin, and Hunter continued to do so.[54] In a daybook entry for July 1751 Hunter credited Franklin £14.4.8 sterling for unbound books in sheets and some unidentified bound volumes, and in December of the same year Franklin sent Hunter 100 copies of James Hervey's *Meditations and Contemplations* and 45 copies of George Fisher's *American Instructor, or Young Man's Best Companion*. In a memorandum to the last account, Hunter noted that he was not crediting Franklin for the copies of the *American Instructor* because he had previously sent Franklin a parcel of books of

---

51 Strahan to Hall, July 11, 1758, ibid., p. 84.

52 When Rivington went bankrupt in 1760, William Johnston was one of the principal creditors who filed suit against him. Hewlett, 'James Rivington, Loyalist Printer, Publisher, and Bookseller,' p. 16.

53 Daybook, 1764–66, fols. 58, 203. See also 'Statement of Wm. Johnston,' T. 79/114, pp. 196–99.

54 Mary Goodwin, 'Printing Office,' pp. V—V–E; R. Goodwin, *William Parks Paper Mill*, pp. 12–13.

equal value, indicating that there was at least some exchange of books between Williamsburg and Philadelphia.[55]

Franklin is the only colonial printer known to have supplied Hunter with books during the twenty-three months covered by his daybook. Hunter sold books and supplies to two other colonial printers, however, and he may have received some of their publications in payment. The largest account was with James Davis of North Carolina. Davis, a Virginian, was appointed North Carolina's first public printer in April 1749, and soon after set up a press in New Bern.[56] Davis opened a bookstore in his printing office, and Hunter became one of his major suppliers. In April 1751 Hunter sent more than £48 worth of supplies to Davis, all but £3 of which was for books. The only book listed by title in the account was George Webb's *Justice of Peace*, a book printed in Williamsburg in 1736 by Parks. Hunter charged Davis £0.6.8 per copy for Webb's book, a one-third discount from the regular retail price. The remaining volumes in the shipment were from the bought books, Waller, Birt, and Bible accounts, all of which Hunter had imported from England. Hunter sent another order to Davis in May 1752. The invoice totaled nearly £92, with books accounting for over £30.[57]

Jonas Green of Annapolis was the other colonial printer who received books and supplies from Hunter. Hunter shipped Green £25.11.6 worth of books in September 1751, allowing him 'Liberty of returning those unsold.' Green also purchased a 'box of Printing Letter[s]' from Hunter in January 1751, for which he was charged £7.16.10½ sterling.[58]

Joseph Royle did not receive books from other colonial printers during the years covered by his daybooks, and only one shipment of books from Royle to another colonial bookdealer, a single sale to the

---

[55] Entries for July 25 and Dec. 16, 1751, Daybook, 1750–52, fols. 55, 81.

[56] George Washington Paschal, *A History of Printing in North Carolina* (Raleigh, N.C., 1946), pp. 23–26; Robert N. Elliott, Jr., 'James Davis and the Beginning of the Newspaper in North Carolina,' *North Carolina Historical Review* 42 (Jan. 1965): 1–20.

[57] Entries for Apr. 15, 1751, and May 16, 1752, Daybook, 1750–52, fols. 32, 112.

[58] Entries for Jan. 23 and Sept. 3, 1751, ibid., fols. 21, 64.

firm of Rivington and Brown, was recorded. The Rivington in the partnership was the same London bookseller with whom William Hunter had corresponded in the mid-1750s. James Rivington moved to America in 1760, and Royle shipped him and his partner £28.16.0 worth of books in June 1765. The order consisted of four copies of John Cleland's *Memoirs of a Woman of Pleasure*, a title that even Rivington with his close ties to the London book trade may have had difficulty procuring, as well as a selection of prints, including five sets of plates illustrating Cleland's book.[59]

Although Hunter received books from Franklin, and both he and Royle may have occasionally acquired publications from other colonial printers, most of the American imprints sold at the printing office were produced on the Williamsburg press. The *Virginia Almanack*, published late each summer, was the overwhelming favorite among local publications, but both Hunter and Royle printed a small assortment of other books and pamphlets that they offered for sale at the printing office.[60] During the period covered by his daybook, Hunter printed Samuel Davies's *Miscellaneous Poems* and William Stith's *The Sinfulness and Pernicious Nature of Gaming*, both of which were extremely popular, as well as E. Smith's *Compleat Housewife*, a reprinting from the sixth London edition, as well as a variety of proclamations, laws, and acts of assembly in fulfillment of his duty as public printer.[61]

Pamphlets presenting opposing views in the Parsons' Cause controversy dominated Royle's publications. The first contribution, Landon Carter's *Letter to the B----p of L----n*, had been printed by Hunter in 1759. During the months covered in his daybook, Royle printed four

---

59 Entry for July 2, 1756, Daybook, 1764–66, fol. 182. Rivington and Brown had stores in Boston, New York, and Philadelphia by mid-1765. *Maryland Gazette* (Annapolis), May 20, 1765. Royle's account does not specify which of Rivington and Brown's stores received the shipment of books and prints he sold them, but one would hope that the *Memoirs* were not destined for Boston.

60 A comparison of Hunter's cash and credit almanac sales indicates that he printed about 2,000 copies annually during the period covered by his daybook. Royle's credit sales of almanacs are unknown, but assuming that they represented about the same percentage as Hunter's, he printed at least 5,000 copies of the *Virginia Almanack* annually during the years covered in his daybook.

61 For a discussion of these titles and of books published by Royle, see Stiverson and Stiverson, 'Books Both Useful and Entertaining,' chap. 3.

additional Parsons' Cause pamphlets: Landon Carter's *Rector Detected*, John Camm's *Review of the Rector Detected*, Camm's later contribution entitled *Critical Remarks*, and Richard Bland's *Colonel Dismounted*. In addition to the Parsons' Cause pamphlets, Royle printed several treatises and sermons by residents of the colony, as well as a number of government publications.

A final source of stock for the bookstore was used books, although they are mentioned only in Hunter's daybook. In September 1750 Hunter recorded buying a 'Parcel of Books' for six shillings from the estate of Robert Stevenson. The titles were not listed, and only one sale of a used book is mentioned later in the daybook, that being Col. Littleton Eyre's purchase in April 1752 of a '2nd Hand' copy of Virgil.[62] Hunter and Royle may have acquired other books from individuals or estates, but the single mention of the sale of a used book in the daybooks suggests that most volumes stocked at the printing office were new copies.

III

Although Hunter and Royle provided a valuable service by making available to the public a wide variety of imported and locally printed books, their incentive for operating the bookstore was profit. Unfortunately, the printers rarely listed the wholesale price of imported

---

[62] Entries for Sept. 1, 1750, and Apr. 1, 1752, Daybook, 1750–52, fols. 51, 101. The only other indication of used books being sold at the printing office comes from an advertisement Hunter inserted in the May 24, 1751, issue of the *Virginia Gazette*. The advertisement listed 195 titles, among which were a number of sixteenth- and seventeenth-century books. Because of their age, the books were probably second-hand copies, and this was certainly the case with several law books described as having 'Manuscript References, which render them very valuable.' The source of the old books is not recorded in the daybook, although they may have come from Hunter's London correspondent, Thomas Osborne. Osborne had purchased the large and valuable library of Edward Harley, Earl of Oxford, in 1742. Osborne printed an elaborate five-volume sale catalogue for the Harleian collection in 1744–46, but he found the library difficult to sell. If the old books advertised by Hunter were part of the Harleian collection, they may have been among the rarest and most important books ever handled by a Virginia bookseller. The books in the collection excited little interest among patrons of the bookstore, however, and there is no evidence in Hunter's daybook that 42 of the titles printed before 1700 were ever sold.

books in their daybooks, and the cost of producing locally published works was not regularly recorded. A few entries do specify the wholesale price, however, and permit some judgment to be made concerning the profit on books sold at the printing office.

Because of the expense and risks involved, goods imported from England frequently sold at a high rate of advance. The rate of advance —the difference between the cost of an item and the price at which it was sold—varied according to the state of the economy and the amount of competition among retailers of the same commodity. The proprietors of the printing office had a virtual monopoly on the Virginia retail book trade, so one might expect that their profit margin on books would be at least as high as that of merchants who retailed other kinds of imported merchandise.

William Allason, the Virginia-based factor of the Glasgow tobacco firm of Baird and Walker, reported to his employers in 1757 that he was selling goods at the company's store for 85 percent above cost. In June 1761 Allason wrote that he was paying for half of the tobacco he purchased for the firm in goods that were marked up 100 to 150 percent. Three years later, in June 1764, Allason wrote that 'Goods in the retail way sells at a very great profit, very few articles sold for less that 200 p[er] Cent advance and often higher.'[63]

The daybooks indicate that the gross profit on imported books sold at the printing office was far lower than the figures mentioned by Allason. For the first six months of 1751, Hunter entered the sterling cost of the books he sold from the Birt and Waller accounts. Because the value of Virginia currency was rarely equivalent to English money, the sterling price of the books must be adjusted in order to compare their cost with what they sold for in Virginia money. In 1751, for example, the exchange rate was 30 percent. Therefore, in order to break even, Hunter would have had to charge thirteen shillings Virginia currency for a book that cost him ten shillings sterling.[64] After

---

[63] William Allason to A[lexander] Walker, Oct. 1, 1758, Allason to brother, June 25, 1761, and Allason to Alexander Walker, June 24, 1764, Allason Letter Book.

[64] Virginia currency stood at par with English sterling when the exchange rate was 25 percent. For a discussion of exchange rates, see Soltow, *Economic Role*, pp. 156–76; and McCusker, *Money and Exchange*, p. 211.

adjusting the sterling value of the Birt and Waller books to Virginia currency, the profit Hunter made on their sale for the six months can be determined.

TABLE 5

PROFIT ON BOOK SALES FROM BIRT AND WALLER
ACCOUNTS, JANUARY–JUNE 1751

Month and account	*Wholesale cost in pence sterling*	*Wholesale cost in Va. currency**	*Retail sales in Va. currency*	*% profit on sales*
January				
Birt	—	—	—	—
Waller	156.0	202.8	254.0	25.2
February				
Birt	204.0	265.2	374.0	41.0
Waller	264.0	343.2	480.0	39.9
March				
Birt	318.0	413.4	558.0	35.0
Waller	—	—	—	—
April				
Birt	201.0	261.3	342.0	30.9
Waller	1,134.0	1,474.2	1,776.0	20.5
May				
Birt	—	—	—	—
Waller	—	—	—	—
June				
Birt	2,490.0	3,237.0	4,274.0	32.0
Waller	378.0	491.4	650.0	33.1
Totals				
Birt	3,213.0	4,176.9	5,544.0	32.7
Waller	1,932.0	2,511.6	3,170.0	26.2

SOURCE: Daybook, 1750–52.

NOTE: All monetary values are expressed in pence or fractions of pence.

*Sterling has been converted to currency at an exhange rate of 30 percent, based on averages in Soltow, *Economic Role*, Table xv.

As Table 5 shows, the rate of advance ranged from 20.5 percent for the Waller books sold in April 1751 to 41.0 percent for the Birt books sold in February of that year. Hunter's average profit on the Birt books for the six-month period was 32.7 percent, while his profit on the Waller books averaged only 26.2 percent. The Waller books were exclusively legal titles, however, a type of book that traditionally brought low profits in the English book trade.[65] But even the profit from the mixed assortment of books Hunter received from Samuel Birt was low compared to the rates of advance reported by Allason at about the same period.

Hunter sold the books from Birt and Waller on commission, so he may have made more profit on sales from the bought books account, which consisted of those volumes that he imported at his own risk. The rate of advance can be determined for only a few of the titles in the bought books account, but the figures indicate that even on those titles Hunter made only a moderate profit.

Hunter purchased several titles for the bought books account from Hugh Crawford, the captain of a ship engaged in the Virginia tobacco trade.[66] Crawford probably bought the books in London in the hope that by selling them in Virginia he could make some extra money on the voyage. Hunter bought £7.18.10 worth of books from Crawford in February 1751. By comparing the amount Hunter paid Crawford with the price he later charged for the books, the percentage of profit he made on their sale can be established.[67]

Hunter sold the copy of the *Spectator* he purchased from Crawford at a 30.5 percent advance, while Thomas Gordon's collection of essays, *The Humorist*, brought 35.7 percent more than it cost. Henry Fielding's *Joseph Andrews* sold for a 42.9 percent advance, and another novel, *The History of Charlotte Summers, the Fortunate Parish Girl*, brought 36.9 percent above cost. These books represent only a few of the titles in the bought books account, but they suggest that the rate of advance on books from that account little exceeded the profit on Samuel Birt's commission books.

---

[65] See Cochrane, *Dr. Johnson's Printer*, pp. 79–80.

[66] Crawford was employed by the London firm of Buchanan and Hamilton. Francis Jerdone was the company's factor in Virginia. Several letters from Jerdone to Crawford are printed in the 'Letter Book of Francis Jerdone,' *William and Mary Quarterly*, 1st ser. 11 (Jan. and Apr. 1903): 158–60, 239–42.

[67] Entry for Feb. 4, 1751, Daybook, 1750–52, fol. 24.

Hunter occasionally offered customers a special price on books, especially when a purchaser bought a large number of expensive volumes or when he wanted to reduce his inventory of hard-to-sell titles. On July 4, 1751, for example, Hunter held a one-day sale at the bookstore. Public response was less than enthusiastic, but Hunter appears to have restricted the price reduction to books that were in limited demand. During the course of the day, eight individuals purchased a total of twenty-seven books, many of which were very expensive titles that would have appealed to few people. Hunter charged a flat rate of 50 percent over the sterling cost of the sale books, and since the exchange rate was 30 percent his profit on the sales amounted to just 20 percent.[68]

Royle's daybook also provides some information concerning the profits on book sales. In one shipment Royle received from his London supplier, William Johnston, three volumes listed on the invoice were never received. By comparing the amount Royle deducted from Johnston's account to the retail price he charged for other copies of the same titles, the profit Royle made on the books can be established. The last two volumes of the novel *Chrysal* retailed in Williamsburg for either £0.12.6 or £0.13.0, between 56.3 and 62.5 percent more than the wholesale price Johnston charged Royle.[69] Laurence Sterne's *Tristram Shandy*, another novel, sold for 33.9 percent over its cost. The book was unbound, however, and Royle could have increased his profit by adding a leather binding. The rate of advance was highest on William Mather's *Young Man's Companion*, a popular conduct and instructional book for juveniles. Bound copies of the book retailed at the printing office for £0.5.9, or 136.6 percent more than what Johnston charged Royle. This book may also have been unbound, how-

---

[68] Ibid., fols. 51–52.

[69] Hunter occasionally, and Royle frequently, charged two prices for the same title. The usual variation was three pence on a six shilling book (e.g., £0.6.0 or £0.6.3) and sixpence on a book that cost over ten shillings (e.g., £0.12.6 or £0.13.0). The price differential probably reflected assessment of the credit risk involved in the sale, or the amount of time the purchaser had been allowed in which to pay for the book. See Soltow, *Economic Role*, p. 152.

ever, and if it were the cost of binding would have to be deducted from Royle's profit.[70]

Royle, like Hunter, sold some books at a flat rate of advance over his cost. On February 4, 1764, Royle sold the twenty-year-old law student Thomas Jefferson £12.15.6 sterling worth of books, charging him a 100 percent advance. The exchange rate in 1764 was 60 percent, however, so Royle's profit on the sale to Jefferson actually amounted to only 40 percent. John Mercer purchased £6.14.3 sterling worth of books on May 5 of the same year, also at a 100 percent advance, or 40 percent profit for Royle. Because the wholesale cost of each title purchased by Mercer and Jefferson is given, the profit Royle made on retail sales of other copies of those volumes can be determined.[71]

Royle sold two copies of M. Duhamel's *A Practical Treatise of Husbandry* in addition to the one purchased by Jefferson. Royle made a 40 percent profit on the sale to Jefferson, but only 36.7 percent on the other two. Most of the books in the lot Jefferson purchased from Royle were written in Italian, however, so the slight premium he paid for the Duhamel probably reflected the fact that it was included in a list of titles that Royle had ordered specially for him.[72]

Eight of the titles Royle sold to John Mercer were also purchased by other persons at their regular retail price. Mercer achieved only minimal savings by purchasing at a flat rate, because half of the books on his list retailed at less than a 40 percent rate of advance. The profit margin was least on Sarah Scott's *Millennium Hall*, a volume that sold for between £0.6.0 and £0.6.3 at retail, representing a profit of between 25.0 and 30.2 percent for Royle. Mercer saved most on Edward Montagu's *Reflections on the Rise and Fall of Ancient Republics* and on the novel *Maria*, books that regularly retailed at the Williamsburg bookstore for 56.3 percent over their wholesale cost.

If the profits that can be determined from the books sold to Jeffer-

---

[70] Entry for Oct. 8, 1765, Daybook, 1764–66, fol. 203.

[71] Ibid., fols. 7, 51.

[72] In addition to the Duhamel, Jefferson purchased Francesco Guicciardini's *Delle Istoria d'Italia*, Johann Scapula's *Lexicon*, Enrico Davila's *Istoria delle Guerre Civili di Francia*, *Opera di Machievelli*, and Giuseppe Baretti's *Dictionary of the English and Italian Languages*. Ibid., fol. 7.

son and Mercer are typical, Royle marked up most imported books between 30 and 45 percent, with the average being about 40 percent. Thus Royle's profit margin was higher than the approximately 30 percent Hunter made on his book sales. The principal reason Royle averaged higher profits than Hunter was that he sold fewer low-profit law books and a larger number of novels, a lucrative category in both periods covered by the daybooks.[73]

Although a gross profit of from 30 to 40 percent on imported books is less than might have been expected considering the rates of advance reported by William Allason, the bookstore was nonetheless an important source of income for the Williamsburg printers. Estimating a 30 percent markup, Hunter made approximately £110 currency per year from his cash and credit sales of imported books. Royle's cash sales cannot be determined, but at a 40 percent rate of advance his profit from credit book sales alone would have averaged nearly £240 currency per year for the period covered by his daybook.[74] The figures are only approximate, and do not include deductions for operating expenses and uncollectible debts, but bookselling nevertheless appears to have been a profitable business for the proprietors of the Williamsburg printing office. Furthermore, these figures are limited to the profits made on the sale of imported books and pamphlets, and the sales ledgers indicate that locally published titles provided Hunter and Royle with an important additional source of income.

Hunter's daybook best indicates the profit that could be made from local publications. Hunter calculated the cost of producing the *Virginia Almanack* for 1752 as follows: paper, £5.0.0; printing and composing,

---

[73] Royle's average profit was about the same as the rate of advance charged by the College of William and Mary on books that were imported for sale to students. In 1756 the president and masters of the college directed Emanuel Jones, faculty secretary, to sell students books at 75 percent above cost, which amounted to a 40 percent advance in terms of Virginia currency. Jones was permitted to charge an extra 10 percent for his trouble, however, so that if the same title was available at the printing office it might have been slightly cheaper to purchase it there. John M. Jennings, *The Library of the College of William and Mary in Virginia, 1693–1793* (Charlottesville, Va., 1968), pp. 52–53. The exchange rate in 1756 averaged 35 percent. Soltow, *Economic Role*, Table xv.

[74] Based on sales figures given in Tables 2 and 4.

£1.6.0; press work, £2.2.8; wear and tear, £0.11.4; payment to the philomath, £5.0.0; for a total of £14.0.0.[75] The almanac went on sale in October 1751, and while a few copies were still being sold as late as the following May, when entries in the daybook end, it is probable that virtually all sales of that edition had been made by then. If so, the edition numbered just over 2,000 copies. Cash and credit sales for the 1752 almanac credited to the *Almanack* account totaled £70.6.6½. Deducting the publication costs of £14.0.0, Hunter netted £56.6.6½ from the almanac, or a substantial 402.3 percent profit.

The *Virginia Almanack* enjoyed the largest circulation of any title published in Williamsburg, and as a result the costs of production undoubtedly represented an unusually small percentage of gross sales. Evidence from Royle's daybook indicates that impressive profits could be made on other local publications as well—margins far in excess of what prevailed on the sale of imported volumes. For example, Royle charged the Reverend John Camm £20 for printing and binding 500 copies of his pamphlet *A Review of the Rector Detected*. Camm's pamphlet sold for £0.2.6 per copy, and the net profit would have amounted to more than 212 percent if all 500 copies were sold.[76] In this case, Camm paid the printing costs and assumed liability for unsold copies, while Royle included a profit for himself in the sum that he charged. Therefore, Camm's potential profit of 212 percent may well have been less than what Royle could have made on popular books and pamphlets that he printed for himself.

In light of the high profit that could be made on local publications, the fact that Hunter and Royle published little, preferring instead to import most of their inventory from England, might seem incongruous. Actually, neither Hunter nor Royle could afford to print many books, because a large volume of sales was required for a locally

[75] Entry for Aug. 14, 1751, Daybook, 1750–52, fol. 60. The philomath was the person who compiled the astronomical, astrological, and meteorological calculations for an almanac. The philomath's name does not appear on the 1752 edition of the *Virginia Almanack*, but the Bears believe that he was the Pennsylvanian Theophilus Grew. James A. Bear, Jr., and Mary Caperton Bear, *A Checklist of Virginia Almanacs, 1732–1850* (Charlottesville, Va., 1962), pp. xi–xiii, xvi–xvii.

[76] Entry for Apr. 11, 1764, Daybook, 1764–66, fol. 33.

printed title to be profitable. Only a copy or two of most books stocked at the printing office were sold, and even sales of popular school books rarely exceeded a dozen copies per year. Unless a publication had wide popular appeal—such as an almanac, a cookbook, or a pamphlet on a subject of local concern—there was little chance that sales would cover publication costs. Furthermore, the printing of those perennial best sellers, the Bible, the New Testament, and the Book of Common Prayer, was restricted by the Bible patent. Even if they could have been legally printed in America, no colonial printer, working with inadequate equipment and a limited supply of type, could have produced these books as cheaply as they could be imported from high-volume English publishers.[77]

A final factor contributing to book profits requires brief mention. The overwhelming majority of imported books were sold in leather bindings. Most were bound in London, but if they were not, an additional profit could be made by binding the books prior to sale. One of the few cases recorded in the daybooks of an imported book being sold unbound indicates just how much binding added to the cost of a book. On November 11, 1765, Robert Bolling, Jr., purchased volumes 7 and 8 of Laurence Sterne's *Tristram Shandy*. The two volumes were stitched, meaning that the collated pages were sewn together with a plain paper cover rather than being bound in leather. Bolling paid £0.7.6 for the two books. The regular price for leather-bound copies of these two volumes ranged from £0.12.6 to £0.13.0, or about two-thirds more than what Bolling was charged.[78] Since the local binder was employed at the printing office, some of the cost for adding covers to unbound imported books would have gone to Hunter or Royle in the form of a profit on the operation of the bindery.

Locally printed pamphlets were usually sold stitched rather than bound. Such was the case with the *Virginia Almanack*, and in both the early 1750s and the mid-1760s a paper-covered copy cost only

[77] P. M. Handover, *Printing in London from 1476 to Modern Times* (Cambridge, Mass., 1960), pp. 73–95; Hellmut Lehmann-Haupt et al., eds., *The Book in America*, 2d ed. (New York, 1951), p. 40; Wroth, *Colonial Printer*, p. 186; Winterich, *Early American Books*, pp. 64–65.

[78] Daybook, 1764–66, fols. 211, 212.

£0.0.7½. Individuals who desired a more durable copy could purchase an almanac bound in leather. Hunter charged £0.2.6 for a leather-bound copy of the *Virginia Almanack*, four times the price of a plain copy, and Royle raised the price to £0.5.0, eight times more than a stitched copy. The difference in price between a stitched copy of the *Virginia Almanack* and one bound in leather again illustrates the high cost of leather bindings and suggests that binding books provided an important additional source of profit for the owners of the printing office bookstore.[79]

While neither Hunter nor Royle made an exorbitant profit on his book sales, it is important to note that imported books, which constituted the bulk of titles stocked by both men, bore in their selling price the charges of English middlemen and the cost of transporting the volumes across the Atlantic. Almost anyone could afford a paper-covered copy of the locally printed *Virginia Almanack*, but the number who could afford school books, novels, histories, and the vast majority of other imported books stocked in the printing office might well have been much smaller. To determine what effect the price of books might have had on limiting the size of the reading audience and on restricting the number of books that an individual could purchase, the relative costliness of books in late colonial Virginia must be ascertained.

IV

The cost of books in eighteenth-century America has only rarely been the subject of research, and no consensus exists on the subject. One leading authority concludes that 'the cost of books to the eighteenth-century American reader was not greatly different, relative money

[79] Leather-bound almanacs may have been interleaved with writing paper, however, which would have slightly reduced the difference in price between bound and stitched copies. Hunter charged £0.1.0 for paper-covered, interleaved almanacs, and Royle raised the price to £0.1.2. In addition to leather-covered and interleaved almanacs, copies could be purchased in the 1750–52 period that were covered with marbled paper at a cost of £0.1.0 each, and in the 1764–66 period a few copies interleaved with blotting paper were sold for £0.1.6 each. In both periods covered by the daybooks, plain copies selling for £0.0.7½ each were overwhelming favorites.

values considered, than to his descendant of the present day,' but another scholar contends that many books, especially those on religion, science, and law, were 'priced at ten times as much' as they would sell for at the present time.[80] Establishing how expensive books were in colonial Virginia is particularly important because, unlike several other colonies, there were no circulation or subscription libraries in the province, and the opportunities for receiving a free or inexpensive education were so limited that many people were never exposed to books in the context of a public school. Unless he inherited books or was able to borrow them from another individual, a Virginian had to purchase books if he wanted to read them.

The daybooks list the price of most books sold at the printing office, and the relative costliness of books can be determined by comparing their prices with other commodities of known value. Thomas Ruddiman's *Rudiments of the Latin Tongue*, one of the least expensive and most popular school books sold in Williamsburg, cost £0.2.6 per copy during the period covered by Royle's daybook. At the other end of the price spectrum was Tobias Smollett's *Complete History of England*. The eleven-volume *History* and its four-volume *Continuation* was the most frequently purchased history book sold at the printing office in the mid-1760s. The price for the fifteen-volume set was £9.[81]

80 Lawrence C. Wroth, writing in Lehmann-Haupt et al., eds., *The Book in America*, p. 42; Clarence S. Bingham, 'American Booksellers' Catalogues, 1734–1800,' in *Essays Honoring Lawrence C. Wroth* (Portland, Me., 1951), p. 33. Lawrence Cremin refines Wroth's statement, concluding that the price of books in the 1760s was 'about equivalent to the cost of hardcover books in the twentieth century.' Lawrence A. Cremin, *American Education: The Colonial Experience* (New York, 1970), p. 395. George Smart, on the other hand, considers books 'sufficiently expensive' in the eighteenth century so that it was 'extremely unlikely' that anyone would purchase a book unless he regarded it as particularly valuable and useful, considerations that hinder few bibliophiles today. 'Private Libraries,' p. 25n. See also John Tebbell, *A History of Book Publishing in the United States*, vol. 1, *The Creation of an Industry, 1630–1865* (New York, 1972), pp. 131–33.

81 Entry for May 23, 1764, Daybook, 1764–66, fol. 57. Although Smollett's *History* was the most frequently purchased of the twenty-nine history titles known to have been sold at the Williamsburg printing office in the 1764–66 period, it is important to note that no history sold in large numbers. A total of eighteen individuals are recorded as purchasing the *History* or the *Continuation* in Royle's daybook. See Stiverson and Stiverson, 'Books Both Useful and Entertaining,' pp. 94, 149–50.

In the early 1760s a pair of shoes for an adult slave cost one shilling. The shoes were strictly utilitarian, but they were made entirely of leather.[82] The majority of the white population probably wore shoes of similar price and quality. At one shilling per pair, more than 2 pairs of shoes could have been purchased for the price of Ruddiman's school book, and 180 pairs for the price of Smollett's *History* and *Continuation*.

Nearly every family in colonial Virginia had at least one cow and several hogs. A hog cost about £0.6.0 and a cow cost about £1.10.0 in the early 1760s.[83] At these prices, a hog could have been purchased for a little more than twice the price of Ruddiman's *Rudiments*, while Smollett's *History* represented the value of six head of cattle or thirty hogs.

The value of wages provides another means of gauging the cost of books. Peter Fontaine, writing to his brother in 1757, noted that common laborers, white or black, could be hired for £0.1.3 per day, although carpenters received what he believed to be the exorbitant wage of £0.2.6 per day.[84] At these rates, the common laborer would have had to invest the proceeds of 2 days' work to buy Ruddiman's *Rudiments* and his wages for 144 days—over five months—to purchase Smollett's *History*. The carpenter, one of the higher-paid laborers in colonial Virginia, would have had to work an entire day for the school book and nearly three months for the history.

The colonial price of books, shoes, and cattle cannot be directly equated with what they cost today, nor are wages exactly comparable. But in terms of purchasing power, books clearly cost a great deal in

[82] 'Account for Shoes for Moss Neck,' Dec. 5, 1761, E. W. Hubard Papers; 'Account for Making 21 Pairs of Negroe Shoes,' [1764], Charles W. Dabney Papers, vol. 4, both in the Southern Historical Collection, Louis Round Wilson Library, University of North Carolina, Chapel Hill (available on microfilm, Research Department, Colonial Williamsburg).

[83] Inventories of Gerrard Sandefur, William Powell, and Edmund Stuckey, York County Wills and Inventories, 1760–71 (typescript, Research Department, Colonial Williamsburg), pp. 133, 142, 144.

[84] Peter Fontaine to Moses [Fontaine], Mar. 30, 1757, Feinstone Collection, American Philosophical Society, Philadelphia, Pa. (available on microfilm, Research Department, Colonial Williamsburg).

eighteenth-century Virginia, many times more than they do at the present time. People who were able to import books directly from England achieved some savings by avoiding the profit charged by the proprietors of the local bookstore, but they still paid dearly for books. London prices were already high, and private purchasers, unlike book dealers who received wholesale discounts, generally paid full retail price. In addition, the Virginian who imported his books directly had to pay shipping charges, duties, and commissions that added considerably to their cost, and he had to wait months before his volumes arrived.[85]

[85] George Washington purchased many of his stepson's school books through his London agent, Robert Cary. Cary's invoices show that he added 2.5 percent for insurance to the retail price of the books, in addition to 2.5 percent for his commission and 3 to 4 percent for searchers' fees, freight, and miscellaneous charges. The extant invoices are for books ordered during times of peace when insurance rates were very low, but when war threatened, transatlantic shipping insurance charges added a great deal more to the cost of importing books directly from England. 'Invoice of Cost and Charges on Goods,' Nov. 17, 1766; 'Invoice of Cost and Charges on Goods,' Jan. 23, 1770, Custis Papers, 1765–79, Virginia Historical Society, Richmond. Cary appears to have charged Washington the regular retail price for the books he ordered, but some colonists may have paid a premium price in addition to the commission, insurance, and other charges for shipping books across the Atlantic. In an invoice dated July 21, 1770, from the London firm of Edward Hunt and Son, Robert Carter of Nomini Hall was charged £1.4.0 sterling for William Falconer's recently published *Universal Dictionary of the Marine* (London, 1769), although the *Gentleman's Magazine* 39 (Mar. 1769): 156 reported that the retail price of the volume was only £1.1.0 sterling. Even when Virginians were not charged a premium price for the books they ordered directly from England, shipping charges and fees added so much to the cost of a volume by the time it reached Virginia that books were considered a bargain if they could be purchased at London prices. As a result, when Dr. John Mitchell of Urbanna decided to return to England he advertised that his 'choice Collection of *Books*, both ancient and modern' could be purchased 'at prime Cost, or [the] Value of the Books in *England*.' *Virginia Gazette*, Nov. 21, 1745. Because of commissions, fees, and shipping charges, only small savings could be achieved on most books by importing them directly rather than purchasing them in Williamsburg at the printing office. There was one exception, however, because Joseph Royle frequently charged nearly double the London price for novels that he stocked at the bookstore. John Hawkesworth's *Almoran and Hamet*, for example, sold for £0.4.0 sterling in London, but Royle charged £0.12.6 currency, or a 95.3 percent increase over his cost after adjusting currency values. Royle made the same profit on Laurence Sterne's *Tristram Shandy*, charging £0.6.3 currency per volume compared to the London price of £0.2.0 sterling. Royle was able to charge such a high rate of advance on novels because devoted readers were unwilling to wait the year or more that would have been

V

To summarize, William Parks's establishment of a bookstore in Williamsburg by the mid-1740s, and the continuation and expansion of the business by his successors, William Hunter and Joseph Royle, afforded Virginians throughout the colony an opportunity to peruse and purchase a wide variety of both locally printed and imported books and pamphlets. Analysis of the daybooks kept by Hunter and Royle reveals the importance of book sales as a component of gross income of the Williamsburg printing office, although the margin of profit on books, where known, was modest compared to the rate of advance borne by other kinds of imported goods. The cost of imported books, which constituted the bulk of titles available at the printing office bookstore, was nonetheless high, while inexpensive productions from the local press were, due to lack of demand, limited in number.

Because of the dearth of inexpensive, locally printed works, access to a variety of reading materials was dependent, to a significant degree, on a person's economic condition. Illiteracy, still not adequately measured in colonial Virginia but significant among women, blacks, and poor white males, further curtailed the extent of the active reading public, as did inadequate or nonexistent artificial lighting in most dwellings. In addition, many people simply lacked the necessary leisure to engage in time-consuming, nonproductive pursuits of any kind. The tedious nature of much of the literature available—from works of practical piety to the turgid prose of metaphysical writers—undoubtedly further limited reading, even by those who were functionally and financially able to do so.

The Williamsburg bookstore's role as a conduit of culture in colonial Virginia was undoubtedly important, but it must be emphasized that it served a select clientele, much the same as Williamsburg's

-----

required for them to order the book from London. Royle's profit margin on most other books was far more modest than on novels. Royle sold the eleven-volume *New and General Biographical Dictionary*, for example, for only 13.6 percent more than the London price, so that the Virginian who ordered it directly would have achieved almost no savings over purchasing it in Williamsburg.

peruke maker, milliners, and purveyors of other costly or imported goods. For the privileged few in colonial Virginia—perhaps the upper quarter of the white population—school books and other practical volumes were an affordable necessity, while books purchased solely for enjoyment were an accessible luxury. For most Virginians, however, the Williamsburg bookstore offered little of use or interest, and except for an inexpensive almanac, prayer book, or Bible, neither books nor the local bookstore figured prominently in their search for information, instruction, or entertainment.

Bibliography and the Cultural Historian:
Notes on the Eighteenth-Century Novel

ROBERT B. WINANS

BIBLIOGRAPHY, as that term is used in this essay, refers to the knowledge of books as physical artifacts, including knowledge of the production of and trade in books. In a recent article, John Feather discusses various meanings of bibliography, and contrasts the Anglo-American tradition of the study of the book with recent French studies.[1] He suggests that while Anglo-Americans have been concerned solely with the physical book and literary studies and have not looked for historical or sociological significance, the French scholars have been cultural historians without enough concern about the physical book. Feather recommends a consolidation of these approaches and mentalities, to achieve a total history of the book as a cultural artifact. He urges bibliographers to look at book distribution as well as (perhaps even more than) book production, to look at the book trade as a trade, to understand its commercial arrangements and the central motivating factor of profit.[2] I have attempted to follow his advice in this essay, the main themes of which are the rise of the novel in eighteenth-century America and the relationship of the length of a given work to the prospects of its American publication.

The novel represented new and important developments in the eighteenth-century world of books. The novel came of age in the eighteenth century: it took its modern form(s), and it became the era's dominant form of literature. But the novel was not only a literary

---

[1] John Feather, 'Cross-Channel Currents: Historical Bibliography and *l'Histoire du Livre*,' *The Library*, 6th ser. 2 (1980): 1–15.

[2] Ibid., p. 8.

development; it also brought a change in the English book publishing and distributing industry. Before the ascendancy of the novel, the book trades were geared to books with steady, long-term sales. The novel created a different marketing situation, with very short-term, but high-volume, sales. Publishers certainly still hoped that any given novel might have long-term popularity, and although some did, the vast majority of novels came and went quickly. The novel also helped to bring about major changes in reading style, as David Hall notes in the introductory essay to this volume.

In a previous essay, I discussed the growth of novel reading in eighteenth-century America based on demographic evidence and evidence from the book trades.[3] Here I would like to present a different kind of evidence, and a different kind of bibliographical argument, to trace that same growth.

One of the problems in enumerative bibliography is the creation of 'bibliographical ghost' entries, based on 'circumstantial evidence,' for books that did not actually exist. For instance, Charles Evans's *American Bibliography*, a primary tool for studying books in eighteenth-century America, contains many such ghosts. Knowing something about how and why these ghosts were created can make them yield useful information.

Evans examined myriad advertisements and based many of his entries on them even when he had not seen the book nor had any other evidence of its existence, and to this practice are due most of the ghosts in his *American Bibliography*. The ghosts were created because Evans apparently assumed that when a bookseller's advertisement noted that books were 'just published,' or even 'printed by' or 'printed for' the advertiser, an edition of each of these books had been published, with the imprint of that bookseller and at about the date of the first advertisement of the work by that bookseller. This turns out to be a faulty assumption because of the exchange system which the booksellers used. American printer-booksellers frequently exchanged copies of books they had printed for copies of books printed by others

---

[3] Robert B. Winans, 'The Growth of a Novel-Reading Public in Late Eighteenth-Century America,' *Early American Literature* 9 (1975): 267–75.

in order to broaden the selection they could offer their customers. Editions of foreign works were especially likely to be exchanged because 'the legal right to reprint any foreign work at any time was gradually restrained by the "courtesies of the trade." These unwritten laws of the book trade upheld the prior rights of the person who first advertised a specific foreign work in the press and forbade this work to be "printed upon." The laws made taboo the issuance of another edition until the advertised one was exhausted or the claim to it relinquished.'[4] Books that a printer-bookseller acquired by exchange he then advertised and sold as though they were his own; his investment and potential for profit (or loss) were the same as though he had printed them himself. Many of the advertisements that Evans saw were for such exchange books.

Among the foreign works affected by this practice were English novels. Compared to other subject categories of books, not many English novels were printed in America at the time, for reasons to be noted shortly. But among the ghosts in Charles Evans's *American Bibliography*, ghosts of English novels far outnumber those of any other category of book for the late eighteenth century. This phenomenon suggests that English novels were in greater demand than other kinds of books as items of exchange among printer-booksellers, reflecting in turn the booksellers' perception of greater demand from the reading public, their customers.

In the essay on the growth of novel reading noted above (see fn. 3), I based my argument partly on the general growth of the reading public, demonstrated through the growth of the book trades, and more specifically on the increase of one segment of the distribution system, the circulating library. These points can be turned around to make a different kind of point: these effects are evidence of the increase in novel reading because they are the result of that increase. The increase in the number of circulating libraries was largely the result of the increasing demand for novels; the general growth of the reading public was caused primarily by the novel. In an essay on English

4 Rollo G. Silver, *The American Printer 1787–1825* (Charlottesville, Va., 1967), p. 104.

books in eighteenth-century Germany, Bernhard Fabian states that the sources for the later decades of the century 'indicate the seminal role of the novel in extending the reading public and establishing the habit of extensive reading' in Germany.[5] All the evidence confirms that this was also true in late eighteenth-century America. David Hall, in his introductory essay to this volume, outlines a shift in the 'style of literacy' in America from intensive to extensive reading, and sees fiction as a major cause of this shift.

To return to Feather's point about the importance of the distribution of books, as opposed to their production, if this is important for England in the eighteenth century, it is much more so for America. Books produced in America probably constituted less than half of the books distributed in America. As Lawrence Wroth observed many years ago, in the eighteenth century 'the function of the American bookseller . . . was largely the sale of the imported book.'[6] Though not new, this observation bears repeating, since over the years many discussions of American reading tastes of the time have been based mainly on what was printed in America. The best evidence for studying what books were distributed in eighteenth-century America, and the most dramatic display of the primacy of the imported book, is found in the catalogues of books published by booksellers and libraries.[7] One must turn to these catalogues for a full picture of the mixture of imported and domestic books available to the American reading public.

Such catalogues provide the data for determining which novels were the most widely and continuously distributed, the 'best sellers.'

[5] Bernhard Fabian, 'English Books and Their Eighteenth-Century German Readers,' in *The Widening Circle: Essays on the Circulation of Literature in Eighteenth-Century Europe*, ed. Paul J. Korshin (Philadelphia, 1976), p. 171.

[6] 'Book Production and Distribution from the Beginning to the American Revolution,' part 1, *The Book in America*, ed. Helmut Lehmann-Haupt, Lawrence Wroth, and Rollo G. Silver, 2d ed. (New York, 1951), p. 46.

[7] Robert B. Winans, *A Descriptive Checklist of Book Catalogues Separately Printed in America, 1693–1800* (Worcester, Mass., 1981), lists and describes in some detail both the physical aspects and the nature of the contents of all book catalogues printed as separate publications in America between 1693 and 1800, including booksellers', book auction, social library, circulating library, college library, and publishers' catalogues.

TABLE 1

The Novels Most Frequently Listed in American Catalogues of Books, 1750–1800

Novel	(Author, date)	Length (12°)*	Number: dates of American eds.†
Fool of Quality	(Brooke, H., 1765)	5 v.	1: 1794
Don Quixote	(Cervantes, 1605–15)	4 v.	—
Vicar of Wakefield	(Goldsmith, 1766)	1 v.	8: 1767, 1772, 1780, 1791, 1791, 1792, 1795, 1795
Gil Blas	(Le Sage, 1715–35)	4 v.	— (2 abridged)
Tom Jones	(Fielding, 1749)	4 v.	1: 1794–95 (+ 11 abridged)
Roderick Random	(Smollett, 1748)	2 v.	1: 1794
Peregrine Pickle	(Smollett, 1751)	4 v.	— (1 abridged)
Chrysal	(Johnstone, 1760–65)	4 v.	—
Evelina	(Burney, 1778)	2 v.	3: 1792, 1796, 1797
Sir Charles Grandison	(Richardson, 1754)	7 v.	— (6 abridged)
Humphry Clinker	(Smollett, 1771)	2 v.	—
Robinson Crusoe	(Defoe, 1719)	2 v.	— (39 abridged)
Sentimental Journey	(Sterne, 1768)	1 v.	6: 1768, 1770, 1790, 1792, 1793, 1795 (+ in Works, 1774
Joseph Andrews	(Fielding, 1742)	2 v.	1: 1791 (+ 1 abridged?)
Devil on Two Sticks	(Le Sage, 1707)	2 v.	3: 1791, 1791, 1795
Citizen of the World	(Goldsmith, 1762)	2 v.	1: 1794
Sorrows of Werther	(Goethe, 1774)	1 v.	6: 1784, 1789, 1795, 1796, 1796, 1798
Clarissa	(Richardson, 1748)	8 v.	— (6 abridged)
Pamela	(Richardson, 1740)	4 v.	1: 1744 (+ 13 abridged)
Tristram Shandy	(Sterne, 1760–67)	9 v.	— (included in 1774 ed. of Work
Emilius and Sophia	(Rousseau, 1762)	4 v.	—
Rasselas	(Johnson, 1759)	2 v.	3: 1768, 1791, 1795
Capt. Robert Boyle	(Chetwood, 1726)	1 v.	4: 1792, 1794, 1796, 1799
Man of Feeling	(Mackenzie, 1771)	1 v.	5: 1782, 1791, 1791, 1794, 1795

*Most of these novels went through many English editions, with different numbers of volumes; th length given here is the most common one found in the catalogues. *Vicar of Wakefield, Sentimen Journey*, and *Sorrows of Werther* (in English) were all originally published in two volumes. B they were such slim volumes that subsequent editions, including the American ones, tended print them in one volume, and this is how they are most often listed in the catalogues.

†This table includes only full-length adult editions, and does not count children's abridgemen although these are noted.

Table 1 presents the twenty-four novels, including European novels in English translation as well as strictly English novels, most frequently listed in a balanced sample of 140 American catalogues published between 1750 and 1800. The sample of catalogues is balanced in the sense of including both long and short catalogues, from as many different places as possible, spread as evenly as the extant catalogues allow over the whole time period. Multiple catalogues from the same bookseller or library have been eliminated so as to avoid the possibility of counting books that just stayed, unsold or unborrowed, on the shelves year after year. These precautions allow me to say with confidence that these twenty-four novels were the most widely distributed, and therefore the most 'popular,' ones. All of them except *Evelina* and *The Sorrows of Werther* were published early enough to have been highly popular before the Revolution as well as after. It is notable that most of these novels maintained their popularity over a long period of time (this was true of them in England also), making them proven candidates for reprinting in America. But as the right-hand column of Table 1 shows, the record of full-length American editions of these novels is very irregular.

This inconsistency reveals a particularly interesting facet of American printing history at the time, one which needs to be kept in mind when evaluating the output of American presses. Some novels which were frequently listed in the catalogues were not printed here at all. American printers published no editions of Cervantes's *Don Quixote* (questionably a true novel, but always listed with novels in the catalogues), Sterne's *Tristram Shandy*, Smollett's *Humphry Clinker*, or Charles Johnstone's *Chrysal or the Adventures of a Guinea*, and no full versions of Defoe's *Robinson Crusoe*, Smollett's *Peregrine Pickle*, Richardson's *Sir Charles Grandison*, or his *Clarissa*, to mention only the most glaring cases. In addition, several popular novels were printed in only one American edition while other novels of roughly similar popularity, according to listings in the catalogues, were printed many times. The catalogues show that Goldsmith's *Vicar of Wakefield* and Sterne's *A Sentimental Journey* were highly popular; the first appeared in eight American editions, the most for any English novel up to 1800, and the second had six American editions. But Fielding's *Tom Jones*, Smollett's *Roderick Random*, and Henry Brooke's *Fool of Quality* were also highly popular and they appeared in only one American edition. Richardson's *Pamela*, Fielding's *Joseph Andrews*, Goethe's *Sorrows of Werther*, and Mackenzie's *Man of Feeling* were also popular. But while *Pamela* and *Joseph Andrews* each appeared in only one complete American

TABLE 2
NOVELS WITH THREE OR MORE AMERICAN EDITIONS

N of eds.	Novel (Author)	Length
8	*Vicar of Wakefield* (Goldsmith)	150–340 pp. (most ~260)
6	*Sentimental Journey* (Sterne)	120–250 pp. (most ~200)
6	*Sorrows of Werther* (Goethe)	~150 pp.
5	*Man of Feeling* (Mackenzie)	~200 pp.
4	*Capt. Robert Boyle* (Chetwood)	250 pp.
4	*Sanford and Merton* (Thomas Day, 1783–89)	3 v. or 2 v. (+3 abridged)
4	*Blind Child* (Mrs. Pinchard, 1791)	190 pp.
4	*Baron Munchausen* (Raspe, 1786)	~100 pp.
4	*Man of Real Sensibility* (Sarah Scott, 1766)	~80 pp.
3	*Gaudentio di Lucca* (Simon Berington, 1737)	100–300 pp.
3	*Evelina* (Burney)	2 v.
3	*Ela or Delusions of the Heart* (Mrs. Burke, 1787)	~140 pp.
3	*History of Louisa* (Elizabeth Helme, 1787)	100–160 pp.
3	*Rasselas* (Johnson)	190 pp.
3	*Man of the World* (Mackenzie, 1773)	160–300 pp.
3	*Julia, or Adv. of Curate's Daughter* (Mr. McMillan, 1773)	~100 pp.
3	*History of Belisarius* (Jean Marmontel, 1767)	135 pp.
3	*Emma Corbett* (Samuel Pratt, 1780)	3 v. or 2 v.

NOTE: Children's abridgements are not included here, although some of the abridged versions of the longer popular novels are in the same length range as novels in this table. Other abridged versions of those same novels are in the chapbook range of around thirty pages.

edition, *The Sorrows of Werther* appeared in six and *The Man of Feeling* in five. One concludes that, while the American printing of a novel, especially in multiple editions, probably bespeaks its popularity, the lack of American editions by no means indicates that a novel was not popular in eighteenth-century America.

Why were some of the English novels which were apparently widely read in America printed in many editions, while others were not printed at all or in only one edition (and at that not until the end of the century)? As Table 2 shows, the novels printed in three or more American editions have one thing in common: they are all rather short. Only one was in three volumes, two were in two volumes, and most were in one not very bulky volume. *A Sentimental Journey*, *The Vicar of Wakefield*, *The Sorrows of Werther*, and *The Man of Feeling*, for instance, are all quite short. On the other hand, the English novels which were popular in America but printed only once or not at all in a full American edition are long, some of them very long. *Sir Charles Grandison* is a seven-volume opus, *Clarissa* came in eight volumes, and *The Fool of Quality* in five; only *Joseph Andrews* and *Robinson Crusoe* (both in two volumes) in this group spanned less than four volumes. The longer the novel the less likely it was to have been printed in America in even one unabridged edition.

The difference in length seems to indicate that popularity and length, rather than popularity alone, determined which English novels were reprinted with any regularity in America. In fact, Table 2 suggests that perhaps length was the most important consideration; of the eighteen novels listed, only eight appear among those most frequently found in the catalogues, and many of the others are quite obscure and seem to have not been very popular. Even those long popular novels that were printed in one full American edition were not printed until 1794 and after, although they all had been around for a long time (e.g., *Tom Jones*). Apparently American printers, at least until near the end of the century, could not compete profitably with imported English editions of longer novels. The greater the length of a novel, the more crucial became its cost of production, and therefore its potential profitability, in the face of competition from English

imports. Cost and profitability determined what books would be imported rather than reprinted, materially affecting the choice of novels
to be reprinted in America.

Because of the importance of the cost factor, some of the novels
popular in America in complete versions, but not, or rarely, printed
in such versions, were printed in abridgements; these were nominally
children's books, though their readership was undoubtedly not limited to children. Those abridgements most often printed in America
were *Robinson Crusoe* (39 editions), *Pamela* (13), *Tom Jones* (11), *Gul-
liver's Travels* (7), *Clarissa* (6), and *Sir Charles Grandison* (5). Children's
abridgements of these novels were profitable while full versions apparently were not.[8] Charles Mish has pointed out, with regard to seventeenth-century fiction in England, that works of fiction popular over
a long time tended to generate abridgements, and these abridgements
ultimately replaced the full versions.[9] This is also partly true for the
novel in the eighteenth century. Popular novels did generate abridgements, but these did not replace the full versions, in terms of what was
produced and read in England and imported and read in America.
However, in terms of what was produced in America, abridgements
did in some sense replace full versions, because of the financial limitations of the American printing industry.

The idea that potential profitability contributed to the decisions
about which British works would be reprinted in America is, of course,
not surprising. But that length, and the competitive cost advantage
of the London book trade, should be as important as popularity in
determining that profitability, and that this factor should introduce
such a high degree of selectivity, are not immediately obvious without
comparing the printing output to the catalogues.

This phenomenon was not limited to novels, but affected other
classes of books as well, for instance, modern history books. The modern history books most widely distributed in America (those most

---

[8] Some of these abridgements were extreme condensations of the original novels.
Try to imagine *Tom Jones* in thirty pages, for instance, or *Pamela* in ninety.
[9] Charles C. Mish, 'Best Sellers in Seventeenth-Century Fiction,' *Papers of the
Bibliographical Society of America* 45 (1953): 372.

frequently listed in American book catalogues) between 1750 and 1800 were nearly all rather long books. Their longevity of popularity (since at least the 1760s) made them prime candidates for reprinting, but only two of the top eighteen not written in America were printed here, and those in one edition only, in the last five years of the century.

To conclude by returning to the issue of the rise of the novel in America, the information in Table 1 can be used to briefly explore some specific aspects of that rise. To begin with, those 24 titles represent the very peak of a mountain consisting of a total of more than 2,000 novel titles found in the catalogues. They are entered, from the top down, in descending order according to the frequency with which they were listed in the catalogues; the novel at the top of the table was clearly more 'popular' than the one at the bottom, but by how much it would be difficult to say. Nevertheless, some conclusions can be drawn.

According to most scholars who have written on the reading of novels in eighteenth-century America, Richardson was unquestionably the most popular novelist with American readers, Sterne was second, and then off in the far distance were Fielding, Smollett, Defoe, Goldsmith, and a few others.[10] Table 1 suggests that although Richardson was certainly popular he was not in sole possession of 'first place,' the other novelists noted above being more popular than they have been given credit for, as were several other novelists not even mentioned by those scholars—Brooke and Johnstone, for instance. The earlier misassessment was probably due to an inadequate concern with distribution (vs. production) and with full versions (vs. abridgements).

The novel at the top of Table 1, Henry Brooke's *The Fool of Quality*, is particularly interesting, especially in relation to the issue of the composition of the 'popular' reading public at the time. As David Hall points out in his essay in this volume, the concept of a 'popular'

[10] Frank L. Mott, *Golden Multitudes; The Story of Best Sellers in the United States* (New York, 1947); James D. Hart, *The Popular Book: A History of America's Literary Taste* (New York, 1950); Herbert R. Brown, *The Sentimental Novel in America, 1789–1860* (Durham, N.C., 1940).

reading public has been stretched to fit what really were several reading publics. Hall suggests three broad groupings within the popular reading public of the time: (1) readers of devotional literature; (2) readers of fashionable books, especially fiction; and (3) readers of traditional prophecies, fairy tales, and romances. *The Fool of Quality* is a didactic book, promoting both a fundamentalist religious outlook close to eighteenth-century Methodism and a Rousseauistic educational program. It also drowns tearfully in overwrought sensibility, and is filled with amazing coincidences, all put together in a rather chaotic style. *The Fool of Quality* is not great literature, but it contains some elements of nearly all the fictional genres of the century and, more importantly, contains something to appeal to all levels of the popular reading public—which probably explains why it is at the top of the list.

Despite the overwrought sensibility of *The Fool of Quality*, the novel of sensibility in general was not as paramount in America as has been supposed. Substantiating this point again raises the issue of distribution vs. production. The four novels produced in the greatest number of American editions, *The Vicar of Wakefield*, *A Sentimental Journey*, *The Sorrows of Werther*, and *The Man of Feeling*, are the key expressions of the eighteenth-century sentimental ethos, which could lead one to conclude that the ultrasentimental mode had the greatest appeal with American readers. These novels certainly appear among those the catalogues indicate were the most widely distributed, but note how many of the titles in Table 1 are *not* novels of sentiment or sensibility —*Don Quixote*, *Gil Blas*, *Tom Jones*, *Roderick Random*, *Peregrine Pickle*, *Chrysal*, *Humphry Clinker*, *Robinson Crusoe*, *Joseph Andrews*, *Devil on Two Sticks*, *Citizen of the World*, *Rasselas*, and *Capt. Robert Boyle*—a total of thirteen out of the twenty-four. The appeal of sentimental vs. unsentimental novels is not just an issue of literary preference; such preferences say something more general about the 'mind' of the popular reading public, or at least that segment of it that had moved from intensive to extensive reading.

A final point involves the notion of 'steady sellers.' It has been suggested that the novel eroded the market for steady sellers in the eighteenth century, which is true; but at the same time some novels themselves essentially became steady sellers. *Robinson Crusoe* would certainly seem to fall into this category, and two novels of the 1740s, *Tom Jones* and *Roderick Random,* continued popular long enough for American printers to publish an edition of each, for the first time, as late as the mid-1790s. A look at shorter time periods within the last fifty years of the century would show other novel titles rising for a day in the sun before fading away again, but the novels that remained popular throughout that period become a new kind of steady seller.

The rise of the novel in the eighteenth century was an important cultural phenomenon, but in order to understand that phenomenon, especially in America, one needs the bibliographer's approach as well as the cultural historian's. Such an approach has led to a central conclusion of significance to the world of books beyond just the novel: that the length of a book had a large impact on whether it was reprinted in America.

Early American Music Printing and Publishing

RICHARD CRAWFORD *and* D. W. KRUMMEL

COLONIAL AMERICA is seldom thought of as a place where the art of music flourished. Historians have tended to look for a standard of musical development in Europe, where well-established musical traditions with recognized composers, formal training, substantial patronage for musicians, and a sophisticated system of musical notation have been in evidence since the Middle Ages. In comparison to this elaborate structure, musical life in the American colonies looks thin indeed. However, if the European standard is set aside and the surviving glimpses of colonial American musical life are observed rather than judged, it becomes clear that music served the colonists in many of the same ways that it has always served human society: as a participatory aspect of worship; as recreational and expressive song; and as an accompaniment to dancing, marching, and other physical activity. From such origins—heightened by the work of printers and publishers—our country's subsequent musical institutions, practices, and values came to be developed.

A duality between early American secular and sacred music has long been taken for granted, influencing the work of scholars from Oscar Sonneck to today. The primary evidence for this duality is distinctive: secular music survives in the form of sheet music, and sacred music exists chiefly in tunebooks. But the duality has fundamental cultural bases as well. The most important sacred music, at least by the 1780s, was a distinctively native expression, provincial and rural in spirit; while secular music was characteristically European in content, cosmopolitan and urban in spirit.

The present essay explores the impact on these musical traditions of two events which are, broadly speaking, bibliographical. Both events called for a reconception of the working relationship between publisher and printer; and both presumed, or at least found, a ready audience of purchasers and musicians, in such a way as to pose the classic question of the chicken and the egg: did the new publications fill or create a demand? The events in question are, first, Isaiah Thomas's publication of *The Worcester Collection* in 1786, using his newly imported music type; and second, the establishment of sheet music publication in 1793–94, together with the founding of a continuous tradition of American theater. The purpose of this essay is to suggest the ways in which these two essentially bibliographical events might be seen as landmark events in music history. In the case of Thomas's type, the bibliographical event is, at least on the surface, easy to understand; it is the specifics of the musical (and thus also the cultural) impact that need to be brought out. With sheet music publication, the musical and cultural impact is obvious; it is the specifics of the bibliographical event that need to be explored.

During the colonial period, most Americans learned their music orally. Psalm tunes for the meetinghouse, composed to be sung by a congregation, were simple by design and could easily be picked up by ear. Of the secular songs that circulated in early America, a good many were catchy, revealing their theatrical roots. As for dance music, the performer who played by ear—who could not read music because he never needed to learn how—is a familiar figure in both European and American cultures. Given the informality of early American musical life and the easy oral accessibility of much of the music that Americans sang and played, musical notation was scarcely needed.

If most colonial Americans got their tunes by ear, this does not mean that they were forced to rely entirely on memory for the words they sang. Congregational psalm singing, a fundamental emblem of Protestantism, assumed a literate congregation. From early in its European history, worshipers could obtain printed copies of the metrical songs sung in public worship.[1] As for the secular song, the practice

---

[1] Nicholas Temperley, *The Music of the English Parish Church* (Cambridge, 1979), esp. pp. 53–57, discusses the role of the printed metrical psalter in English Protes-

of printing and selling ballads established itself in England in the Renaissance, and was taken up by the American colonists.[2] Moreover, by the eighteenth century the lyrics of new popular songs were often being printed in newspapers and periodicals.[3] Printed collections of song texts, bound up in books called songsters, were also available.[4] Thus, by the middle of the eighteenth century, metrical psalters, broadsides of song lyrics, and songsters were commonly being issued from a number of colonial presses.

As the seventeenth century drew to a close, the first music was printed in the English-speaking colonies: a supplement of tunes to the Bay Psalm Book, ninth edition (1698). From a distance of nearly three centuries the event may seem simply one more natural step in the long history of American cultural 'progress.' In the context of this volume and the conference from which it originated, however, its significance looms larger. Here it can be understood as the start of a transformation of American musical life—a transformation that, by incorporating written music into musical publications, laid the groundwork for an American musical life open to European influence and also capable of developing its own composers and performance tradi-

---

tant worship. Charles Evans's *American Bibliography*, 14 vols. (Chicago and Worcester, Mass., 1903–59), lists more than 250 American editions and issues of extant metrical psalters before 1801. See Clifford K. Shipton and James E. Mooney, *National Index of American Imprints through 1800: The Short-Title Evans*, 2 vols. (Worcester and Barre, Mass., 1969), esp. under 'Bible, O.T., Psalms,' and 'Watts, Isaac.'

[2] For Massachusetts materials, see Worthington Chauncey Ford, 'Broadsides, Ballads, &c. Printed in Massachusetts,' *Collections of the Massachusetts Historical Society* 75 (1922); also Carleton Sprague Smith, 'Broadsides and Their Music in Colonial America,' in *Music in Colonial Massachusetts 1630–1820*, vol. 1: *Music in Public Places* (Boston, 1980), pp. 157ff. Other materials are listed in such library catalogues as the *Catalog of Broadsides in the Rare Book Division of the Library of Congress* (Boston, 1972).

[3] These are accessible through J. A. Leo Lemay, *A Calendar of American Poetry in the Colonial Newspapers and Magazines . . . through 1765* (Worcester, Mass., 1972), and discussed and transcribed in Gillian B. Anderson, *Freedom's Voice in Poetry and Song* (Wilmington, Del., 1977). References may also be found in Oscar Sonneck, *A Bibliography of Early Secular American Music*, rev. and enl. by William Treat Upton (Washington, D.C., 1945), a particularly important reference work hereinafter cited as Sonneck-Upton.

[4] Irving Lowens, *A Bibliography of Songsters Printed in America before 1821* (Worcester, Mass., 1976).

tions. The role of printing in sacred music can be brought into focus by examining three issues: the introduction of notation into an essentially oral practice; the economic support of sacred music publication; and the changing technology of early American sacred music printing.

It is not entirely clear why music was added to the 1698 edition of the Bay Psalm Book when none had been included in the earlier editions. Surely the intent was not to have the worshipers in the congregation sight-read the psalm tunes from the book. The printed tunes were almost certainly known to the people who sang them; and if they were not, they were few enough in number and uncomplicated enough in style to be learned simply by ear. It seems more likely that the tunes were included, in this and all later editions, in order to record, for the few who could read music, an official version of each tune. When carried on as an oral tradition, as it was in England and America during the seventeenth century and also in many places in the eighteenth, congregational psalmody had turned into a highly improvisatory practice. Sung with decorations at extremely slow tempos, the psalm tunes tended to lose their melodic shape. Printing a tune, no matter how few could read it, at least established one form of it, fixing its identity and making it accessible to some—especially to leaders of congregational singing.

By 1720, religious leaders in the colonies had begun a reform of congregational singing. Convinced that the reigning oral practice was failing to foster true devotion in congregational worship, a group of Massachusetts clergymen recommended that 'regular singing'—singing the psalm tunes as they were set down in the book—replace 'the usual way.' Instruction in psalm singing was offered in singing schools, and instructional books were printed. The Reverend Thomas Walter's *Grounds and Rules of Musick* (Boston, 1721, and later editions) and the Reverend John Tufts's *Introduction to the Singing of Psalm-Tunes* (Boston, 1721, and later editions) offered instructions on how to read musical notation and sing properly. They also carried selections of psalm tunes, harmonized for three voices.[5]

[5] The 1721 edition of Tufts, not now extant, apparently contained only the melodies of the psalm tunes. The earliest surviving edition, the third (1723), set the

The music in Walter and Tufts served different functions than that of most earlier editions of the Bay Psalm Book. Since the later works were designed as textbooks for singing schools, the tunes in them were obviously used to teach note reading. Since their tunes were set in three-part harmony, Tufts and Walter specified far more musical detail than had the earlier work. Rather than simply a melody, Tufts and Walter provided a musical composition, with three separate voice parts coordinated both vertically—where different notes blended to produce a richness of sound—and horizontally—where the different voices were instructed to proceed from note to note within a specified set of rhythmic values.

Wherever notation established its authority, as it gradually was to do with certain groups of musicians in certain locales during the course of the eighteenth century, sacred music grew more specialized, more artistically elaborate. Notation, never commanded by congregations, was the property of the smaller, more musically committed group which sang in harmony. By the 1760s, choirs had begun to spring up all over New England, and their repertories had begun to introduce anthems and fuging tunes with texture changes and voice overlaps as well as standard congregational fare. The music that choirs sang depended upon notation—on a composer's controlling of a group of singers by setting down his sonic inventions in a form that they could understand and realize. Without notation, psalmody was a true popular music: plain people singing whatever sacred melodies they knew and could remember. With notation—and most commonly the notation was set down and circulated in printed tunebooks—psalmody owned the means of developing into a composer's art. The steady and impressive increase in the number of sacred publications testifies that during the course of the eighteenth century sacred music making in America came to be a written, not an oral, practice for many people.

The engagement of the printing industry in sacred music introduces a second matter for study: the economic support for sacred music

---

tunes for two voices. From the fifth edition (1726) through the eleventh and last (1744), Tufts provided three-voice settings. See Irving Lowens, *Music and Musicians in Early America* (New York, 1964), chap. III, passim.

printing. Like any other books, tunebooks were bought and sold, and hence were subject to the uncertainties of the market. But if they were to be sold, they first had to be printed, and printing entails financial risk. Thus, the economic support of sacred music depended first and foremost upon publishers—upon persons who were willing to assume the financial risk of printing a tunebook, either by enlisting support from others or by supplying the capital themselves.

TABLE 1

AMERICAN SACRED MUSIC IMPRINTS, BY DECADE

Decade	N of items*	Decade	N of items	Decade	N of items
1690s	1	1740s	5	1790s	107
1700s	5	1750s	7	1800s	222
1710s	6	1760s	23		
1720s	14	1770s	20	Total number	
1730s	5	1780s	58	of imprints	473

SOURCE: Based on information drawn from a forthcoming (1984) bibliography of sacred music printed in America through 1810, by Richard Crawford in collaboration with Allen P. Britton and Irving Lowens, to be published by the American Antiquarian Society.

*An 'item' is here defined as a separate title, a designated edition, or a significantly altered later issue of a work of sacred music. The totals include unlocated items whose publication can be verified.

In the early days of American sacred music publishing, booksellers took the lead as publishers. The first issues of the Bay Psalm Book were printed for Boston booksellers like Michael Perry and Nicholas Buttolph. Both Tufts's and Walter's instructional tunebooks of the early 1720s were printed for Samuel Gerrish, also a bookseller in Boston. The sponsorship of these items fits Rollo Silver's description of the way the early American book trade worked: 'Because they spoke of themselves as booksellers, it is somewhat difficult to remember that certain members of the colonial Boston book trade were also publishers. They secured the manuscript, contracted for the printing, paid for the production, and marketed the finished work which bore their imprint on the title-page.'[6] During the course of the eighteenth

---

[6] Rollo G. Silver, 'Publishing in Boston, 1726–1757: The Accounts of Daniel Henchman,' *Proceedings of the American Antiquarian Society* 66 (1956): 17.

century the role of American booksellers in the publication of sacred music changed. Most issues of the first half-century—and there were not many—were published by booksellers. After the 1760s the book-sellers' sponsorship declined in proportion to that of other agents, although it did not die out completely.[7]

From the 1760s on, American compilers of tunebooks took an active role in publishing them. James Lyon, Daniel Bayley, William Billings, Andrew Law, Daniel Read—leading American musicians of their day—all assumed a publisher's stake in their works. Their involve-ment did not necessarily depend upon their own financial means. Rather, at the start of their careers, it required organizing support for their works by subscription—a standard procedure of the book trade that allowed for an unknown author to spread the risk of publishing a new work among subscribers, who promised before publication to buy a certain number of copies at certain prices.

At first glance, it may seem a quaint example of colonial self-suffi-ciency that many early American authors of tunebooks also published them. At second glance, their motives look less quaint. As Rollo Silver and others have shown, the concept of authors' royalties was new in the eighteenth century and hardly existed in the United States until very late in the period, and then only in exceptional cases.[8] In fact, in the early American book trade, the author's chance to profit was slim. Printers and engravers, the producers of the physical book, were customarily paid for their services as professional craftsmen. The dis-tributor of the book, the seller, earned a commission on his sales. The sponsor of the book, in effect the publisher, took the greatest risk, paid the bills, and stood to gain or lose the most. The author, how-

---

[7] Booksellers' names continued occasionally to appear on title pages up into the early nineteenth century. Where they do appear, it probably signals the seller's acceptance before publication of some part of the financial risk of the work. Note, for example, *The Village Harmony*, 5th ed. (Exeter, N.H., 1800), printed and sold by Henry Ranlet, and 'sold also by Thomas & Andrews, David and John West, and Caleb Bingham, Boston; Thomas C. Cushing, Salem; Edmund M. Blunt, Newburyport; Stephen Patten, Portland; David Howe, Haverhill; William A. Kent, Concord; and Charles Peirce, Portsmouth.'

[8] See Rollo G. Silver, *The American Printer, 1787–1825* (Charlottesville, Va., 1967), pp. 102–3, 106.

ever, was likely to work for a token amount or even for nothing in this tradition of bookmaking. Financial benefit was tied more closely to financial risk than to creative contribution. Only by assuming some risk, usually in either the publisher's or the seller's role or both, did most authors or compilers stand to profit from their labors. Thus it was that so many American composers and compilers took an active role in the publishing of their tunebooks, and that so many books bear the title page legend 'Printed for the author.' During the eighteenth century, an American-born musician usually made a living from his art only by selling tunebooks or by teaching music to others.

Appearing first after the Revolution, and growing stronger in influence in subsequent years, was a third agent of musical sponsorship. If the compiler's goals were, first, to make an artistic statement—or perhaps a pedagogical one, or a combination of the two—and only then to hope to make some financial gain from it, the new agent's goal was less complicated: simply to turn a profit. He was the professional printer—not the man who, like William Law of Cheshire, Connecticut, ran off tunebooks for his brother at home, but the man who followed the printer's trade, whose livelihood depended on it, and who saw sacred music as a market ripe for exploitation by a knowledgeable businessman.

Isaiah Thomas of Worcester, Massachusetts, and Henry Ranlet of Exeter, New Hampshire, were the two professional printers who involved themselves most heavily in sacred music during the eighteenth and early nineteenth centuries. Both were publishers of newspapers, and Thomas was the foremost printer-publisher of the era, his various partnerships extending over New England and beyond and his catalogue covering a wide range of printed matter: sermons, psalters, songsters, textbooks, broadsides, government proclamations, novels. As businessmen first and foremost, Thomas and Ranlet could approach tunebook making somewhat differently than their compiler-rivals. Their printing technology and approach to repertory, outlined below, are manifested in Thomas's *Worcester Collection* (eight editions, 1786–1803) and Ranlet's *Village Harmony* (seventeen editions, 1795–1821). Both books were published by their printers; both were apparently compiled under their supervision; and, we may safely speculate, they were commercially the most successful tunebooks of the time.[9]

Sacred music was published in different shapes and sizes, ranging from small supplements to metrical psalters, through end-opening oblong tunebooks to folio-sized sheet music and bound volumes. Differences in format suggest differences in function. Tune supplements usually contain simple, unaccompanied music designed for congregational singing; oblong tunebooks are likely to be more diversified in content, adding to the conventional psalm tunes some more elaborate pieces suitable for singing schools or choirs; the sheet-music–sized publication, intended for church or parlor use, most often includes a keyboard part and emphasizes music in 'modern' European style.

Another physical difference also helps to divide sacred music publications into different classes: the process by which the music in them was printed. At the end of the seventeenth century, when tunes were added to the Bay Psalm Book and the history of American music printing began, the tunes were reproduced by relief cut. Once a tune was cut into a block, the block could be fitted into a form along with a text set in movable type, and printed from the typical letterpress. All music printed in the English-speaking American colonies before 1721 was executed in this way.

A broadside in the Massachusetts Historical Society, dated 'Boston, 12 November 1720,' announces a process of music printing new to the colonies. Preparing to bring out 'a small Book containing Instructions for the Easy attaining to the Art of Skill of singing Psalm Tunes, with about Twenty Tunes,' the author reported that the music would 'be curiously ingraven in Copper plates.' When Thomas Walter's *Grounds and Rules of Musick* appeared in the winter of 1721, it included, after the title page, twenty-eight pages of typeset front matter and sixteen

[9] Karl D. Kroeger, 'The Worcester Collection of Sacred Harmony and Sacred Music in America, 1786–1803' (Ph.D. diss., Brown University, 1976), pp. 88–92, describes how Thomas used his advisors on the third (1791) and later editions, and speculates on their possible contributions to the first edition; see also pp. 66–67. A newspaper advertisement notes that Ranlet relied for musical advice on 'several Gentlemen, who are Teachers of Musick'; see *The American Herald of Liberty*, Exeter, N.H., July 30, 1795.

leaves of music, printed from engraved plates. From that time through the 1780s, most sacred tunebooks followed a plan similar to Walter's: most began with a theoretical introduction—the longer it was, the more likely that at least part of it was printed from type—and continued with engraved music. Thus, a typical eighteenth-century sacred tunebook called for both letterpress and intaglio printing.

A third method of printing music was tried by various American printers from the 1750s on, but did not firmly establish itself until the 1780s. The key figure in its establishment was, of course, Isaiah Thomas, who, calling himself 'unskilled in musick,' brought out a tunebook with the help of musical advisors. Thomas's *Worcester Collection* (1786) was printed from music type that he had imported from the Caslon foundry in London. According to him, typographical printing would cut the price of tunebooks, which had previously been 'high-charged, owing to their being printed from Copperplates.'[10] Having purchased a type font, Thomas needed only to find someone to set it before he was ready to begin running off tunebooks on a standard letterpress. In the two decades that followed the appearance of *The Worcester Collection*, Thomas, mostly through his Boston partnership with Ebenezer Andrews, issued nearly forty sacred music books. His example changed the field. Noting Thomas's success, others acquired their own fonts of music type and set about printing other tunebooks. As Table 2 shows, the new method of music printing caught on quickly.[11] During the first decade of the nineteenth century, typo-

---

[10] 'Preface,' *The Worcester Collection* (Worcester, Mass., 1786). See Kroeger, 'The Worcester Collection,' pp. 63–64, for more on Thomas's purchase of music type.

[11] Other printers in other places acquired music type fonts as well, and began to print sacred tunebooks typographically. John M'Culloch of Philadelphia brought out *A Selection of Sacred Harmony*, the first of his many typographical issues to survive, early in 1788. (As the following note in the collection shows, M'Culloch hoped to keep his type from gathering dust: 'Any Piece of Music, (not larger than four pages of this book) will be printed at 6 *d.* each, Provided that Six Dozen are taken by the employers.') In Exeter, N. H., Henry Ranlet entered the field with *The Village Harmony* in 1795. By 1797, Daniel Wright, soon thereafter followed by his nephew, Andrew Wright, had brought typographical printing to the Connecticut Valley—perhaps using Thomas's first font to print music in Northampton, Mass. See Paul R. Osterhout, 'Music in Northampton, Massachusetts, to 1820' (Ph.D. diss., University of Michigan, 1978), pp. 202–5. After the turn of the century, such printers

graphically printed tunebooks, which had held only 15 percent of the market in the 1780s, outnumbered engraved tunebooks by nearly three to one.

TABLE 2

PROCESSES OF PRINTING SACRED TUNEBOOKS

	Total number of issues	Issues printed from engraved plates	Issues printed typographically
1780–89	52	44	8 (15%)
1790–99	102	54	48 (47%)
1800–10	214	59	155 (72%)

The engraved tunebooks that dominated American sacred music between 1720 and 1790 occupied a less secure place in the book trade. 'It is probably safe to say,' Lawrence Wroth has written, 'that the printing of copperplate engravings was a separate industry in this country in the colonial period as it has been, in general, ever since.'[12] Since most eighteenth-century American tunebooks had their music printed from plates rather than type, and since the evidence suggests that few letterpress printers had either the equipment or the skill to print from a rolling press, tunebooks were somewhat unconventional items by the standards of the early American book trade.

To begin with, while the printers of typographical tunebooks are almost invariably named on their editions, the printers of engraved tunebooks are not. Of the printers of engraved tunebooks who have been identified, few are associated with the mainstream of the book trade. Moreover, some of the engraved collections were actually printed by their compilers. That may not seem unusual for works whose com-

---

as Manning & Loring and Joseph T. Buckingham in Boston, Herman Mann in Dedham, and the musician-printer John Cole in Baltimore were issuing sacred music printed from type.

[12] Lawrence C. Wroth, *The Colonial Printer*, 2d ed., rev. (New York, 1938), p. 286. Support for Wroth's point appears in Rita Susswein Gottesman, *The Arts and Crafts in New York, 1726–1776* (New York, 1938), pp. 9–12, 365–73, where newspaper advertisements for copperplate printers are listed separately from notices of letterpress printers.

piler-engravers are men identified with the graphic arts: John Burger and Cornelius Tiebout of New York, for example; or Thomas Johnston, James A. Turner, and John and William Norman of Boston; or perhaps even Amos Doolittle of New Haven.[13] But the list of tunebook printers also includes a number of musicians who seem to have been pressed into that role simply by necessity, among them Daniel Bayley, William Billings, Daniel Read, Oliver Brownson, and Thomas Atwill.[14] The quality of these men's craftsmanship aside, their involvement in the printer's role makes it clear that the technology of plate printing was relatively uncomplicated, and rolling presses were mechanically simple and quite inexpensive.[15] It also suggests the relative informality and lack of specialization in copperplate printing, as op-

[13] Turner and Johnston each engraved and printed an untitled collection of psalm tunes designed to be bound as a supplement to a metrical psalter—Turner in 1752 and Johnston in 1755. John Norman and his son William were very active as engravers and copperplate printers from the 1780s on, and William Norman also engraved and printed secular music. See David P. McKay and Richard Crawford, *William Billings of Boston* (Princeton, 1975), p. 141n; also Sonneck-Upton. Burger and Tiebout's *Amphion* appeared in New York around 1789. Among Doolittle's many musical ventures was his collaboration with Simeon Jocelin in bringing out *The Chorister's Companion* (New Haven, Conn., 1782; also a later ed.) and with Daniel Read in issuing *The American Musical Magazine* (New Haven, Conn., 1786–87). Turner, Johnston, John Norman, Tiebout, and Doolittle are all mentioned in Daniel McNeely Stauffer, *American Engravers upon Copper and Steel* (New York, 1907).

[14] From 1769 on, all of Bayley's many musical publications are designated 'Printed and sold by Daniel Bayley.' Several of Billings's tunebooks are printed by others, but *Music in Miniature* (1779) was 'printed & sold by the author at his house in Boston,' while *The Psalm-Singer's Amusement* (1781) carries a similar legend. Read normally hired a printer to work for him, but his *Supplement to the American Singing Book* (New Haven, Conn., 1787) is marked on the title page as 'printed and sold by Daniel Read.' Brownson's *New Collection of Sacred Harmony* (Simsbury, Conn., 1797) was 'printed and sold, by the author at his dwelling house.' Finally, a note printed in Thomas Atwill's *New York and Vermont Collection*, 2d ed. (Albany, [1804]), p. [9], claims that it was 'printed by the author's own hands.'

[15] By way of showing that copperplate printing could even be done with makeshift equipment, Wroth notes that in 1784 John Fitch 'printed his copperplate *Map of the Northwest Part of the United States* on a cider press.' See his *Colonial Printer*, p. 286. Clifford K. Shipton, *Isaiah Thomas: Printer, Patriot and Philanthropist, 1749–1831* (Rochester, N.Y., 1948), p. 86, prints part of 'Isaiah Thomas's Account of Stock, 1796.' The list includes an inventory of the twelve presses in Thomas's shop and their worth. Thomas places values on the letterpresses ranging from $50 to more than $100; and he also mentions '1 Laye Rolling Press $10' and a 'small rolling press' valued at $4.

posed to the more structured environment of the letterpress printing trade.

However separate copperplate and typographical printing may have been, the title pages of some tunebooks whose music is printed from engraved plates do name letterpress firms as their printers. This would seem to mean either that the printers named dealt in both techniques, or that they printed only the letterpress portions of the books, leaving the plate printing to someone else. Circumstantial evidence in most cases argues for the latter thesis. Most of the works in question, especially in the years before 1790, have fairly extensive typeset introductions—long enough to seem to justify identifying the printer, even if he did not print the entire book. Moreover, for some books we know of a person other than the printer, but still connected with the shop, who was qualified in engraving. For instance, Daniel Bayley's third edition of William Tans'ur's *Royal Melody Complete* (Boston, 1767) is marked on the title page 'Printed and sold by W. M'Alpine.' Yet an inner leaf carries a contradictory colophon: 'Printed and Sold by Daniel Bayley of Newbury-Port.' Bayley is known to have acquired a rolling press by 1769 and to have printed all of the tunebooks he brought out from that year on. Perhaps he had the press in his possession as early as 1767 and did the plate printing himself; or perhaps John Ward Gilman, the work's engraver—who engraved and printed a collection of his own in 1771[16]—ran off the plates, and M'Alpine printed only the typeset introduction.

Similar examples can be found. According to its title page, William Billings's *New-England Psalm-Singer* (Boston, 1770) was 'printed by Edes and Gill.' Yet Josiah Flagg, listed as a seller on the title page, had engraved and printed a collection of his own in 1766,[17] and Billings printed some of his later engraved tunebooks himself. So either, or both, might have had a hand in the plate printing—the book's imprint notwithstanding. Jocelin and Doolittle's *Chorister's Companion* (New Haven, 1782) names no printer, the imprint reading 'Printed for and sold by Simeon Jocelin and Amos Doolittle.' However, Part

16 *A New Introduction to Psalmody* (Exeter, N.H.).
17 *Sixteen Anthems* (Boston).

III, a subsequent addition, was 'Printed by T. and S. Green, for Simeon Jocelin and Amos Doolittle.' There is good reason to speculate that the Greens, members of Connecticut's leading family of letter-press printers, produced the sixteen pages of typeset front matter, while some other printer did the thirty-two pages of engraved music. Copublisher Doolittle, who almost surely engraved the work, and who did print at least one more later work that he engraved,[18] could also have assumed the printer's role.

Rather than contradicting the supposed separation of the engraving and the letterpress trades, many of the engraved tunebooks purportedly printed by letterpress printers seem instead to confirm it; although no extant tunebook names two printers, a number do leave reason to suspect that two were involved. That suggestion, in turn, dramatizes that the compiler's role was central and the printer's peripheral in arranging for the physical production of these books. It would appear that in early America no well-marked path led from a tunebook's conception to its final printed form. Rather, it seems to have been the lot of each compiler to blaze his own trail: not only to select the repertory, but then also to arrange for the economic support of his collection, to hire an engraver, to find a printer (and perhaps even two) and a binder, and then to find outlets beyond his own singing schools where his books might be sold. (It is probably significant that fewer than ten engraved tunebooks before 1811 that were printed by letterpress printers are identified on their title pages as having also been sold by them. That would seem to indicate that letterpress printers seldom retained any financial interest in the engraved tunebooks that they printed, hence that those books were not simply as a matter of course accepted into the distribution network that printers had set up.) These factors, taken together with the rest of the evidence, mark the engraved tunebook as a production of early American entrepreneurial activity, the result of a cooperative alliance of agents and craftsmen that was temporary—assembled most likely by the compiler himself but unlikely to outlive his own involvement.

---

[18] Stephen Jenks, *The Musical Harmonist* (New Haven, Conn., 1800).

If the publication of sacred music proceeded somewhat sporadically throughout most of the eighteenth century, the publication of secular music during this time was even more sparse and fitful. Prior to the mid-1790s, the bibliographical record is strewn with an assortment of musical editions. Some are clearly songbooks, like Chauncey Langdon's *Select Songster* (1786), engraved in Connecticut by Amos Doolittle and essentially an extension of sacred music engraving practice. There are also the broadside ballads, without musical notation, for which no publication pattern has yet been detected. Of the songsters listed in the Lowens bibliography, sixty-nine items were issued between 1734 and 1792, nearly half of these prior to 1783. There are also the music supplements to magazines—engraved, printed by blocks, or typeset—probably beginning to proliferate in the 1790s; and the musical texts, almost always without musical notation, which appeared in the newspapers. Completing the bibliographical record, in a sense, are the manuscript texts, although their extent is much more conjectural as their circumstances of creation are more variable.[19]

Such documents are interesting in their own right, as individual instances. What they lack seems to be any suggestion of a continuity of production practice: they are not part of any discernible music printing and publishing 'industry.' The fact that they give no evidence of any such aspirations is perhaps not surprising; after all, how exactly do any documents do this, except perhaps in the presence of implicit advertising or explicit stylistic similarities of 'house practices'? If such an answer begs the question, the larger and more serious issue is why there should have been any concern for the establishment of a music printing and publishing industry at this particular time, but not before. There are obvious abstract and idealistic explanations: in a stable and optimistic cultural environment, to create lasting monuments; in a thriving economic and political environment, to circulate texts more widely; and in the spirit of mercantile activities, simply to

[19] Lowens, *Bibliography of Songsters*; James J. Fuld and Mary Wallace Davidson, *18th-Century American Secular Music Manuscripts: An Inventory*, MLA Index and Bibliography Series, 20 (Philadelphia, 1980).

handle funds and commodities, assuming the citizenry's rights of musical self-determination and wagering one's stake as entrepreneur and reader of public taste in an enterprise aimed at financial survival and capital appreciation. There are also obvious models in the 1780s and 1790s for the aspiring music merchant: the extended success of several literary publishers, as well as the emerging continuity of businessmen in the field of music itself, as reflected in the rise of concert and theater management.

An attempt at publishing continuity may or may not be reflected in several remarkable books that came out of Philadelphia beginning in 1787, including a Roman Catholic liturgical book of that year; Francis Hopkinson's song collection of the very next year; and four collections by Alexander Reinagle, three vocal and one instrumental, undated but datable from 1789.[20] Behind this activity were men of conspicuous and varied talents, so as to make the question of one single prime mover seem almost irrelevant. Presumably Hopkinson was the patron, whether through cash or blessings and good words. Reinagle must have been the main musical advisor, whether as composer or consultant. John Aitken, a goldsmith late from Scotland, engraved the plates, thus beginning his off-and-on but nonetheless ground-breaking career in music printing;[21] while Thomas Dobson ran off the plates and Henry Rice sold most of them in his bookshop. The significance of these editions in general, and of Aitken's contribution in particular, lies in the introduction of a fourth music printing technology in early America. Here for the first time is music of the kind that European professional musicians commonly worked with: folio in format,[22] on heavy paper, printed on a rolling press, and,

---

[20] The books in question are cited in Sonneck-Upton, pp. 66–69, 403, and 439; see also p. 377 for another possible title, unlocated. The 1787 liturgical book, entitled *A Compilation of the Litanies and Vespers, Hymns and Anthems*, was issued in reprint by Alfred Saifer (Philadelphia, 1954).

[21] Sonneck-Upton, pp. 6, 59, 206, 212, 285, 318, 422, and 448, for instance.

[22] Typically the sheets measure about 33 x 25 cm; and they are usually gathered in twos, as was the common European plan as well. Since the chain lines almost invariably run horizontally, however, it scarcely seems right to view them as folios, at least until such time as the full sheet can be shown to be in the idiosyncratic dimensions of 33 x 50 (which, curiously, nobody has so far undertaken either to

most significantly, using soft punched pewter plates.[23] Patronage and high culture are suggested both by the name of Hopkinson and by the fact that these items were in several gatherings, not single sheet music pieces of one or two leaves (although several selections were run off separately as sheet music). These books may have introduced into America the technology of a continuous music publishing industry; but they did not introduce the continuity itself, since the activity ceased after two years, leaving a five-year hiatus before any further such music was published. Conditions, for whatever reasons, were not quite right yet.

Five years later, in 1793 and 1794, a continuous tradition was indeed established, first by Moller and Capron in Philadelphia, and later by George Willig, Benjamin Carr, and others; by James Hewitt in New York in 1793, followed soon by George Gilfert and others; in 1794 by Thomas Carr in Baltimore; and in 1798 by Peter Albrecht von Hagen in Boston.[24] Music publishing was to flourish almost immediately, and a direct lineage was to persist to today. The two obvious necessary conditions for this activity, printing technology and a musical interest, clearly existed. Why then would publishing have flourished in 1794 when it failed seven years earlier? Surely the increased economic stability of the new nation has something to do with the answer. But there is another factor, a more dramatic event to be considered; and the pedantry of advancing it as a 'sufficient cause' has the special virtue of suggesting the cosmopolitan character of the secular repertory in question, in contrast to the somewhat rural and provincial character of the indigenous sacred music repertory.

---

establish or disprove). Nor is it any more than a bibliographical preciousness to call them quarto half-sheets, since the huge full sheets (66 x 50) would almost certainly have been cut in two *before* printing.

[23] Earlier American use of punches is conjectured by Karl D. Kroeger in his introduction to *The Complete Works of William Billings* (Charlottesville, Va., 1981), I : xxx–xxxi; and while he is probably correct, the punches in question seem to have been used mainly for note-heads, rather than for the other musical or alphabetical signs.

[24] Summarized in D. W. Krummel, 'Philadelphia Music Engraving and Printing' (Ph.D. diss., University of Michigan, 1958), pp. 78–80.

The event in question is the beginning of what Oscar Sonneck calls the 'fourth period' of early American theater.[25] It is a series of events, in fact: the opening of the Chesnut Street Theatre in Philadelphia on February 17, 1794, and of the Park Street Theatre in Boston two weeks earlier; the establishment of a permanent home for the Hallam and Henry 'Old American Company' in New York at this same time; the high point of theater activity in Charleston, and the earliest tours to Baltimore and Hartford; but above all else, the London recruitment trips of the managers of the several companies, of John Henry in 1792, Thomas Wignell in 1793 (most conspicuously), and Charles Stuart Powell in 1794. The importance of these events is reflected in some of the characteristics of the early sheet music repertory itself— for instance, the origins of the repertory in imported London opera; the evidence of contributions from local theater musicians; and the similarities to the practices of publishers in London at this same time.

An analysis of the sheet music repertory must follow rather arbitrary categories, and must be constructed in rounded estimates; the statistical evidence is rather 'soft.' There are roughly 1,200 titles cited in the Sonneck-Upton bibliography, reflecting the output of the country in all areas of secular music prior to 1801. Wolfe has additions which do not significantly alter the picture, since the unit of consideration here is the title, rather than the edition or variant.[26] (In all likelihood, republication and reissue would serve mostly to make the popular titles even more so.) Of these 1,200 titles, roughly 800 are for the sheet music which was published beginning in 1793; and of these 800, no fewer than 600 represent works which were imported from the London stage. Most are songs from the comic operas; some are from dramatic works, which often included musical interpolations— for instance, the 'Witches' Chorus' in *Macbeth* or Ariel's songs in *The Tempest*—on over to the special ballets and marches, which kept the theater's small company of musicians active for a good part of the season. Of the composers, by far the best represented was James Hook·

---

[25] Oscar Sonneck, *Early Opera in America* (New York, 1915), esp. pp. 84–161.
[26] Richard J. Wolfe, *Secular Music in America, 1801–1825* (New York, 1964), hereinafter cited as Wolfe.

From his prolific output, over 200 titles were reissued in America. Down the list, in order, came four more London stage composers: William Shield, Charles Dibdin, Stephen Storace, and Samuel Arnold. Together these five Londoners account for perhaps 500 of the 800 sheet music titles issued in the United States before 1801.

The Americans who bring up the rear still serve mostly to strengthen the basic point, since most of them were musicians in the theaters. Of those who were major figures in 1800, only a few had lived in the New World ten years before: Alexander Reinagle, for instance, now one of the managers of the theater; and J. C. Moller, Henri Capron, and Peter Albrecht von Hagen, all of whom were early music publishers but who faded quickly from the scene. Of those who came between 1792 and 1796, a number were recruited specifically for the theaters, including George Gilfert, later to become a major music publisher; William Priest, an actor who advertised his services as a music engraver, apparently without very much success; and George Gillingham, mainstay for many years in the Philadelphia Theatre orchestra. Other immigrants within this period came under different auspices, but within a few years were prominent names in the theater. Their number includes most of the celebrated turn-of-the-century American musicians—Benjamin Carr, James Hewitt, Victor Pelissier, and Raynor Taylor—not to mention William Dubois and Gottlieb Graupner, both important music publishers of the next decade.

As members of theater orchestras, these men wrote occasional songs, and were also announced in newspaper notices as the creators of the 'accompanements' for the theater; that is, the reorchestrations of works which were presumably being imported from London in sheet music. London publishers had already found that songs were best issued in the form of a vocal line or lines with keyboard accompaniment, a practice which American music publishers quickly learned to follow. For other music layouts, one must look instead to typographical printers. The first orchestral score, of sorts—Hans Gram's 'Death Song of an Indian Chief'—appeared in the 1791 *Massachusetts Magazine*, while the first set of performance parts are in the *National Martial Music*, printed by William M'Culloch (Philadelphia, 1809).

What exactly do we mean by 'sheet music'? Its distinctive appearance was suggested earlier. Even more important is its special manner of production. Most of the process as it involves printing is discussed, and as it involves publication is implicit, in Richard J. Wolfe's new book, *Early American Music Engraving and Printing*.[27] The present discussion serves mainly as a reflection on that text. The original source material consists of thousands of extant editions, as described in Sonneck-Upton and Wolfe; a miscellany of newspaper notices, many of them cited in modern scholarly writings; and a paucity of original archival records, highlighted by the account book of Simeon Wood in the Library of Congress, the papers of Gottlieb Graupner at Brown University, and the correspondence of John Rowe Parker at the University of Pennsylvania.[28] It is curious but probably coincidental that all of these sources pertain to Boston music publishers.

Sheet music, reflecting the fourth technology of American music printing, was typically engraved rather than typeset, and run off on a rolling press rather than by letterpress. Through several major innovations which were apparently developed in London around 1700,[29] the intaglio plates were not of a hard copper, but of a soft pewter alloy of tin, lead, zinc, and antimony. The texts were incised on these plates, partly by hand, but as much as possible by being struck by specially designed hard-metal punches. As a result, there are none of the minute variations which would result from the same text having been drawn at different times by hand.

Music engraving techniques were learned presumably through an apprenticeship. As he acquired his tools, the apprentice craftsman learned the precise mixture of metals in the plates; the formula for the particularly thick ink; and some idea of the appropriate kinds of paper, the appropriate heat of the plate during the printing process,

---

[27] Richard J. Wolfe, *Early American Music Engraving and Printing* (Urbana, Ill., 1980).

[28] These are cited in *Resources of American Music History* (Urbana, Ill., 1981), entries 227-J, 1402, and 1352.

[29] The reconception of European music publishing, based on the decline of music typography and the revolutionary changes in music engraving, is discussed in D. W. Krummel, *English Music Printing, 1553–1700* (London, 1975), pp. 166–70.

the speed with which the pressure roll needed to be turned, the efficient use of body weight in turning it, the optimum conditions for drying, and the efficiencies in cleaning, reinking, and wiping the plates. In addition to the printing process itself, he learned the practices for gathering the sheets, and the requisite imposition practices; the right thread needed for sewing the gatherings for those infrequent editions comprising more than one leaf; and the appropriate wrappers. In all such matters, Wolfe's discussion is particularly instructive, as supplemented by several other writings.[30]

This basic method of sheet music production was to persist into the mid-twentieth century. One reason for its persistence is the engraver's expertise in the subtleties of musical notation and layout. The peculiarities of the placement of signs, the use of optical space to convey the sense of the melodic line, and the relationship of sound as a means to interpretation for the reader-performer are all coming to be recognized as major reasons why the cumbersome technology was to survive for so long. Around 1800, the subtleties of layout—what music engravers and publishers know as the *Stichbild*—were first coming to be understood, most notably in London, with a full century of experience with engraved music. On the other hand, coming from Vienna, the early editions of Mozart and Beethoven are conspicuously difficult for a performer to read.

Glancing over the American music itself will suggest some of these nuances. The early engraved religious music, for instance from the hand of Amos Doolittle or John Norman, is variously cramped, badly aligned, and altogether crude in its effect. It commits a text to record, as the 1698 Bay Psalm Book had done, but it could not be sight-read, even by an experienced performer. In contrast, American sheet music of the 1790s was of a quality approaching that of London, and by 1810 the two are almost indistinguishable (partly, to be sure, as a

---

[30] For other discussions of the technology of music engraving, see in particular 'Printing' by H. Edmund Poole, assisted by D. W. Krummel, in *The New Grove Dictionary of Music and Musicians*, 6th ed. (London, 1980), 15: 232–60. Karl Hader, *Aus der Werkstatt eines Notenstechers* (Vienna, 1948) includes good pictorial material; while Hal Ross, *The Art of Music Engraving and Processing* (Miami, Fla., 1970) goes into valuable detail relevant to the subsequent discussion of music layout.

result of American publishers having pirated so much English sheet music, copying particulars of detail so as to leave no doubt that an English exemplar was in hand as the copy). Whoever they were, the American engravers learned how to imitate British layout, thereby learning how to produce reasonably handsome and craftsmanlike editions. In a few instances from the last years of the eighteenth century —from Shaw and Trisobio in Baltimore and Philadelphia, or Goldberg in Albany, or several of the New York and Boston shops—the workmanship of the continent is suggested by an awkwardness of layout and heaviness of signs; but soon after 1800 the London 'image' was conspicuously present.

The point is relevant to the use and development of the art music repertory in early America. Briefly put, the sacred repertory was one of performers trained through group methods in singing schools, in a sense thus still emerging from oral tradition; the sheet music repertory was for those who were taking, or had taken, private lessons—mostly children and adults with leisure time. They were also persons with a piano at home, an object costing in the general vicinity of $100. These purchasers were presumably interested in a 'progressive' musical repertory, moving toward either the technically more difficult or the socially more fashionable (being in a sense, perhaps, precursors of Richard Hoggart's 'earnest minority'). As an indigenous repertory, and apart from Handelian imports and imitations, the religious repertory was circumscribed and poorly suited to increasing refinements —whether for reasons having to do with the limited capacities of composers, masters, or performers, or the limited range of the musical notation as controlled by its typography. The sheet music image was capable of notational growth (whether into the transcendental pianism of Franz Liszt, or the music dramas of Richard Wagner, or the notational innovations of John Cage). Around 1800, the typical sheet music song was notated on two staff lines. The keyboard performer doubled the melodic line of the singer in the right hand, adding the bass and chords in the left. Already by 1810 the layout was almost always on three staves, the singer often being left on his or her own, while the pianist added interesting and usually more complicated

patternwork in both hands. Such notational complications were hard
to envision in the modest graphic conceptions of the early tunebooks.
As for movable type, its fonts as used in the United States were not
amenable to the complications of art music, at least until European
'mosaic' type was introduced in the middle of the nineteenth century.
As early as 1817, however, a Beethoven sonata was issued in Philadelphia—naturally in an engraved sheet music edition.

The cumbersome music-engraving process—and it was indeed cumbersome, as Wolfe's book amply describes—served not only to make
the music more functional and attractive. It also encouraged the music
publisher to speculate with the repertory. In a time when labor was
cheaper than today and paper more expensive, it was important for
the music publisher to be able to issue small press runs, keeping the
plates available when the music proved to be successful. Setting music
type, running off a fixed number of copies, and then distributing type
was appropriate when the press run could be reckoned with some
exactitude, on the basis of an estimated financial break-even point
and a safe prediction of a profitable overrun. But the fashions of music
scarcely allowed for so predeterminable a practice. They demanded
a wider range of possibilities. For a book, the financial break-even
point might be 2,000 copies, with 1,500 known or likely orders and
4,000 copies a likely maximum, in which case the publisher might
produce 2,500 copies in uncertain times or 4,500 under optimistic
circumstances. With sheet music the break-even point could be as
few as 25 or 30 copies, with 10 or fewer known or likely orders and a
likely maximum of 2,000.[31] Under the circumstances, what the pub-

[31] The evidence of large press runs for sacred tunebooks is considerable. The
Dutch Reformed psalter of 1767 was issued in 1,800 copies. See Carleton Sprague
Smith, 'The 1774 Psalm Book of the Reformed Protestant Dutch Church in New
York City,' *Musical Quarterly* 34 (1948): 89. Andrew Law's press runs, as cited by
Crawford, *Andrew Law, American Psalmodist* (Evanston, Ill., 1968), pp. 215n, 220,
237n, ran to 2,000 or 3,000 copies; Daniel Read's *Columbian Harmonist*, in a second
edition (1804–5), ran to 3,000 copies, and a third (1807) to 2,000, as cited in Bush-
nell, pp. 299, 328. As for Thomas's *Worcester Collection*, Kroeger, 'The Worcester
Collection' (pp. 72n, 104, 133, and 140), suggests and quotes evidence for editions
of from 1,000 to 4,000 copies. The 'Introduction' to the seventh edition of Ranlet's
Village Harmony (1806) mentions 'the sale of about 27,000 copies . . . in the course
of nine years.'

lisher needed was something comparable to standing type; and for a catalogue of 200 editions running to 500 folio-size pages, committing this much type would have been prohibitively expensive. Such specific figures, of course, are mostly speculation. The plate book of Simeon Wood, however, does suggest typical press runs and reruns of 25 to 50 copies, with frequent reruns of some titles. The wide range of variation in press runs of some European publishers—even the large ones—and the number of reruns for fewer than 10 (!) copies is even more striking.[32] Graupner's account books further suggest such practices—orders for 2, 3, or 6 copies, only occasionally as many as 100—although these citations refer to single orders and not a cumulative demand which would be the basis for press reruns. In any event, flexibility was no doubt necessary if the music publisher was to succeed in his business; and in turn it accommodated and encouraged a rapidly changing and growing musical repertory.

Timeliness, currency, and fashion thus became bywords for the music publisher. And from this very attitude, alas, came the practice of omitting dates in the imprint statements, thus leaving the bibliographer with a special task in establishing the catalogue's chronological bearings. He can make guesses of varying degrees of plausibility and reliability, based on references in the song texts, bibliographical characteristics of the physical object, or external citations. But the large portion of a publisher's catalogue still often remains pinned down to no more precise a span than a decade or so, offering no way for the modern scholar to identify fashions, often even trends, in music publishing. 'Fine tuning' (in the economist's, not the musician's, sense) was what kept the publisher going. This would be important to study, but thanks to the very phenomenon under consideration, it is impossible. There do seem to be fewer marches published after ca. 1800; American song composers seem to have been quite well recognized in the period 1806–8; and apart from Francis Scott Key's venerable text, there seems to have been very little national music issued during

---

[32] For examples of European press runs, see the International Association of Music Libraries' *Guide for Dating Early Published Music*, comp. D. W. Krummel (Hackensack, N.J., 1974), p. 38.

the period 1812–14, certainly far less than appeared as words only in the newspapers and periodicals. Instrumental 'tutors' (method books with tunes) seem to have shown up at a slow but steady rate, perhaps two or so a year, especially after 1815. Such impressions would be worthwhile and interesting to establish with some degree of conclusiveness; and often even the year would help. In other instances, even more exact dating would be helpful. For instance, an edition of a song announced 'as sung by Mrs. French at the Chesnut Street Theatre,' the performance being verifiable to the exact date, might have been issued within a period of weeks, months, or even years; nor should we exclude the most interesting possibility of all—of the sheet music having been specially timed so as to be for sale the very day after the performance mentioned. Lacking almost all of the official records of the publishers, we usually have only guesswork, theories, and instinct to lead and mislead our scholarship.

The pricing of sheet music suggests editions intended not only for a cosmopolitan audience, but also generally for a wealthy one. The typical practice, from 1793 on up into the 1830s and 1840s, was to charge twelve and a half cents per plate. That is, one plate (on one sheet) for twelve and a half cents, two plates (typically on two sheets rather than one back to back, so as to remove the performer's page turn) for twenty-five cents, and three plates (almost always also on two sheets) for thirty-seven and a half cents. There could be some discount for larger editions, but seldom very much. Furthermore, the practice of selling at half the announced price, said to have been common in England at this time,[33] seems not to have found its way to America. From the Graupner account books we learn of discounts of a mere 20 percent, on orders of as few as 4 or as many as 100 copies, with the purchaser covering transportation. Often there was no discount at all. In the close-knit music community, it would seem to have made sense for the publisher to do what was common 100 and

---

[33] Frank Kidson, *British Music Publishers, Printers, and Engravers* (London, 1900), p. 134. The practice of concealing a price through a number inside a symbol (usually a star), common in the United States around 1850, suggests a similar practice, but needs further investigation.

1 50 years later: sell to the teacher at half price, giving him some incentive to promote the edition by pocketing the difference as a form of commission. The fact that published music was extremely expensive, by any standards, is attested by comparisons with the cost of commodities and other durables and services, with the price of books in general, and even with the cost of music lessons. (In Philadelphia in 1820, for instance, prominent local musicians rarely charged more than a dollar a lesson.)

Under the circumstances, manuscript copying ought to have flourished. There is some evidence of it, but not really very much.[34] A kind of 'demand publishing,' especially among music teachers, perhaps did exist, although the evidence, in the form of commonplace books and other manuscript documents, is scanty indeed. If the financial situation in general sounds hard to believe, one should also remember that phonographs in the 1910s usually cost several hundred dollars; and that throughout history expensive music has flourished in general as well as inexpensive music, if not better. Economic realities are obviously important to publishers of all kinds, but they can go only so far in explaining the circulation and the appeal of music.

Many purchasers of the luxury-oriented sheet music went to the further trouble of having it bound. At least, the evidence of extant copies suggests this. Of those copies which are not still found in bound volumes, almost all of them show stab marks which tell us that they were removed from disbound volumes, presumably by a strangely matched conspiracy of antiquarian dealer-collectors and library cataloguers. These parties may indeed be guilty of destroying interesting historical evidence; but meanwhile, the prosecution has been less than convincing. What really is the value in preserving the evidence of a binder's volume? In theory, the configurations of the repertory, together with the biographical facts about the owner, ought to tell us what music was used, by whom, perhaps even how. It could even suggest some dimensions to the cosmopolitan/provincial dichotomy which runs as an undercurrent through this essay. In practice, how-

---

[34] For instance, the plan of E. Lilly in Philadelphia, 1820, as mentioned in Krummel, 'Philadelphia Music Engraving,' pp. 135–36.

ever, the owners' names, as stamped on the front label, seem always to have been as distinctive as Nancy Brown and Mary Wilson; and their repertory came from a variety of publishers, in different cities, probably issued over a wide spread of time, with marches and ballads, English opera tunes, and American patriotic music all mixed together. If the binders' volumes do tell us anything, it is that the typical American sheet music owner usually had unflatteringly catholic tastes. She bound anything she could lay her hands on. The fact that she was almost always a she is presumably of considerable interest, although the implications are yet to be seriously explored. In any case, the American secular music 'consumer' needs yet to be identified. That study will probably need to be based on the surviving evidence of bound volumes. Until that time, a moratorium on dismemberment—even over the ardent sentiments of library cataloguers in particular—seems called for.

Evidence of the music's cosmopolitan character thus is one mostly of production rather than consumption. Who exactly were the publishers? As a group, a few of them were respected musicians, like Benjamin Carr, James Hewitt, or Gottlieb Graupner. Most of them were in the picture from the beginning, in the 1790s, but withdrew a decade or so later. Others were faceless businessmen, like George Willig, George Blake, or John Paff. In the world of conspicuous talent, a shadowy existence was probably an asset; few of these men, for instance, would have dared the impertinence of signing an introduction to one of their own publications, as both Isaiah Thomas and Henry Ranlet did.

Edward Riley, of New York, seems to have been well established in London as a music publisher before emigrating; but few of his colleagues show specific evidence of European music-publishing ties. The publishers who were basically businessmen must have needed a close working relationship with musicians; someone had to read proof and offer advice in matters of repertory. We may conjecture from the pattern of publication of his original music, for instance, that the Philadelphia theater musician John Bray filled this post for the music publisher George Blake between ca. 1807 and 1814. Of the successful publishers, most will be seen to have British names. The several Germans seem to have come directly from Europe rather than through any of the American German settlements in Pennsylvania and to the south. Above all, these were music specialists. Apart from publishing music, they sold music supplies, not books on other subjects—a fact which further accounts for their position on the periphery of the world of early American books and bibliography. Their output is statistically summarized in Table 3.

Quite obviously the totals in Table 3 correlate rather highly with the population totals from the 1800 census, which report Philadelphia with 70,000 inhabitants; New York with 60,000; Boston and Baltimore with 25,000 each; and Charleston with 20,000. These cities, of course, were also the centers of American theater at that time. Their nearest rivals in size are far in the distance: Providence with 9,000 inhabitants; Salem with 8,000; Richmond with 6,000; Portsmouth with 5,000; and New Haven with 4,000. There is some evidence of the dissemination of sheet music in the Graupner account books, in the form of payments in 1802 from Portland, Salem, Providence, and Newport. But the account books for 1815 show an even greater traffic between publishers in other major cities: with Blake and Willig in Philadelphia; Geib, Gilfert, Riley, and Dubois in New York; and a detailed order list with Bacon in Philadelphia which suggests that Graupner may even have subsidized much of Bacon's early publishing activity.

Sheet music publishing, in sum, needs to be viewed as something which was superimposed on existing American cultural patterns, achieved through a new and relatively ingenious method of printing and publishing. Many of the advantages of the method, and much of its success, can be seen as broadly Jeffersonian; and while in time the industry became a powerful force in American cultural life, its modest capital investment and the flexibility of its product always demanded that it respond to subtle market pressures. Its limitations are obvious: it could scarcely accommodate and encourage heroic musical works in extended forms—operas, symphonies, and the like, such as were indeed being performed and composed at this time in Moravian Amer-

TABLE 3

SHEET MUSIC PUBLISHING IN THE U. S. BEFORE 1825:
ESTIMATED CHRONOLOGY AND PRODUCTION

Publisher	Years	N of issues	Publisher	Years	N of issues
Philadelphia			Boston		
Carr	1793–1824	600	Von Hagen	1798–1801	90
Willig	1794–	1,250	Graupner	1803–	600
Blake	1802–	1,200	Hewitt	1812–	70
Aitken	1806–11	200	Jackson	1821–	110
Bacon/Klemm	1816–	280	Other		100
Other		250	Total		970
Total		3,780	Charleston		
New York			Siegling	1819–	70
Hewitt	1793–1810	600	Other	1807–	30
Gilfert	1795–1806	310	Total		100
Paff	1799–1816	650	Albany (mostly Goldberg,		
Riley	1808–	400	1813–19)		34
Willson	1811–20	230	Providence (mostly Shaw,		
Geib	1815–	400	1823–)		30
Dubois	1817–	750	Alexandria, Va.		2
Other		410	Brooklyn, N.Y.		1
Total		3,750	Charlestown, Mass.		1
Baltimore			Frankford, Pa.		1
Carr	1794–	670	Greenfield, Mass.		2
Cole	1821–	200	Hartford, Conn.		1
Willig	1824–	40	Hudson, N.Y.		1
Other		70	Norfolk, Va.		10
Total		980	New Haven, Conn.		3
			Petersburg, Va.		1
			Washington, D.C.		4

SOURCES: Sonneck-Upton (1945), pp. 575–89; Wolfe (1964), pp. 1133–72. These totals supersede those cited in Krummel, 'Counting Every Star; or, Historical Statistics on Music Publishing in the United States,' *Yearbook for Inter-American Musical Research* 10 (1974): 179–80.

ica. Nor, in time, as the sheet music firms developed and as competition between them became keener, could the firms do much more than to gear their catalogues to timely pressures from their audiences, and thus magnify the pressures. Thus, while graphically the sheet music publisher could be committed to an increasingly complex musical repertory, commercially he remained committed to a publishing medium resembling Schopenhauer's conception of the newspaper: 'a second-hand in the clock of history, . . . not only made of a baser metal than the hands which point to the minute and the hour, but also one which seldom goes right.' Such sentiments, applied to music, might be imagined as coming from such diverse persons as Alexis de Tocqueville, Matthew Arnold, or Theodor Adorno; while Thomas Jefferson in particular, one suspects, would have been conspicuously saddened.[35] The characteristics of the music publishing industry thus came to heighten—to reflect, then to encourage—works in short forms. But there are other basic considerations to be acknowledged as well: British as well as American composers toward the end of the century, for instance, are among those who lamented that they had to go to the Continent to get their best music published.[36]

In the case of sacred music publishing, a continuity of different dimensions was also being established, in fact some seven years before the sheet music paradigm of 1793–94. Isaiah Thomas's introduction of movable music type in 1786, though it may seem less dramatic than the events that formed the sheet music publishing industry, was to prove no less revolutionary in its impact. When sacred tunebooks were moved into the letterpress shop, the compiler's task was greatly simplified. For, once he had completed his manuscript and enlisted financial support, he could strike a bargain with a printer and turn

[35] Jefferson's predilection for music was no doubt enriched by his experience with the engraved music which he acquired in Paris, as reflected in his collection extant today in Charlottesville, Va. See Helen Cripe, *Thomas Jefferson and Music* (Charlottesville, Va., 1974), esp. pp. 77–87.

[36] Discussed in D. W. Krummel, 'Music Publishing,' chap. 3 in Nicholas Temperley, *The Romantic Age, 1800–1914*, Athlone History of Music in Britain, vol. 5 (London, 1981), pp. 56ff.

over the book's physical production to him. By relieving the compiler of the responsibility of arranging his own network of agents for the printing of his work, the advent of typographical music printing helped to open up the field of sacred music to compilers who lacked the contacts or the physical resources to see their own books into print. In short, even though a great deal of sacred music had been printed in America before 1786, it took Isaiah Thomas's typographical publication of *The Worcester Collection* in that year to establish a continuous sacred music publishing tradition.[37]

The trend toward typographical printing influenced some of the most active American compilers. Daniel Read, whose *American Singing Book* (5 editions, 1785–96) and *The Columbian Harmonist* (numbers 1–3, 1793–1801) were executed on copper plates, had the second and all subsequent editions of the latter printed from type.[38] Andrew Law, whose career as a compiler spans more than forty years, switched to typographical printing in 1803 in order to accommodate a new musical notation that he had devised.[39] Little and Smith's *Easy Instructor* went through several engraved editions (1801–8) before its publishers had a type font made and began to turn out a stream of typographical editions that ran through the 1820s.[40]

The new printing technology was not without its effect on the content of sacred tunebooks. A look at Thomas's *Worcester Collection* (1786) reveals a new approach to compiling, one that was swiftly taken up by others. Drawn from many sources—no fewer than twenty-five different composers or sources are named, and American pieces outnumber foreign by more than two to one—it also includes a handful of (eight) tunes that were being printed for the first time. Of the older repertory, more than a third comes from a group of pieces that achieved special acceptance in early American tunebooks: the 101 sacred compositions most frequently printed in American tunebooks between

---

[37] See discussion above for evidence of continuity.
[38] See Vinson C. Bushnell, 'Daniel Read of New Haven (1757–1836): The Man and His Musical Activities' (Ph.D. diss., Harvard University, 1978).
[39] See Crawford, *Andrew Law*.
[40] See Lowens, *Music and Musicians*, chap. 6: 'The *Easy Instructor* (1798–1831): A History and Bibliography of the First Shape-Note Tunebook.'

1698 and 1810, here referred to as the Core Repertory.[41] Thus, *The Worcester Collection* brought together under one cover a range of music selected from other tunebooks already in print, emphasizing American compositions and the most popular sacred pieces of the day, but also with a dash of novelty in the form of a few new pieces.

Before the decade was out, the influence of *The Worcester Collection* as a model was firmly established. Similar tunebooks were published in Boston, Newburyport, and Philadelphia, some specifically intended to compete with Thomas's work.[42] Table 4 provides comparative figures on the repertories of tunebooks of the years 1786–89 that seem to have been issued to appeal to the market addressed by Thomas and his associates. The figures suggest that perhaps the most striking feature of *The Worcester Collection* was its definition of something of a formula for a successful tunebook.

[41] Richard Crawford, 'Massachusetts Musicians and the Core Repertory of Early American Psalmody,' in a volume on early Massachusetts music forthcoming from the Colonial Society of Massachusetts, lists the tunes constituting the Core Repertory. An edition of the music, edited by Crawford, will appear in the series Recent Researches in American Music, ed. H. Wiley Hitchcock (A-R Editions, Madison, Wis., forthcoming.)

[42] In Aug. 1788, Thomas, noting that the first edition had quickly sold out, brought out a second in which he referred to a 'spurious edition.' Irving Lowens has identified that work as *Sacred Harmony* (Boston, [1788?]), a clear-cut plagiarism; it mentions *The Worcester Collection* as a source in boldface type on its title page, and includes all but three of the pieces in the earlier work. See Lowens, *Music and Musicians*, pp. 76–77. In the same year, *The Federal Harmony* also appeared in Boston, identifying itself as a rival of *The Worcester Collection* by claiming in its introduction, 'The whole is Engraved on Copper, the superior advantages of which to musical printing Types, none conversant in matters of this sort, can be ignorant of.' Though less obviously based on *The Worcester Collection* than *Sacred Harmony* had been, *The Federal Harmony* contains seventy-nine of the same pieces, and its adoption of some of the earlier work's traits—very little new music, a mixture of American and English pieces with a preponderance of the former, and a substantial group of Core Repertory pieces—demonstrates this influence. Two more tunebooks that appeared in the same year outside the Worcester-Boston axis may also have been influenced by *The Worcester Collection*, though neither refers to it: Daniel Bayley's *New Harmony of Zion* (Newburyport, Mass.) and *A Selection of Sacred Harmony* (Philadelphia). Both outdid Thomas in their devotion to familiar repertory, for neither contained any new music at all, and both carried an even higher proportion of Core Repertory tunes. Both also gave greater emphasis to foreign music. Another Philadelphia tunebook published the next year followed a similar path: Adgate and Spicer's *Philadelphia Harmony*.

TABLE 4
Contents of Early 'Formula' Tunebooks, 1786–89

	Number of pieces	Provenance			Core Repertory	New pieces
		American	English	Unknown		
The Worcester Collection (1786)	108	73 (68%)	33 (31%)	2 (1%)	39 (36%)	8 (7%)
Sacred Harmony ([1786–88])	132	79 (60%)	49 (37%)	4 (3%)	54 (41%)	4 (3%)
Bayley, The New Harmony of Zion (1788)	102	52 (51%)	47 (46%)	3 (3%)	49 (48%)	0
The Federal Harmony ([1788])	129	94 (73%)	32 (25%)	3 (2%)	43 (33%)	8 (6%)
A Selection of Sacred Harmony ([1788])	62	26 (42%)	32 (52%)	4 (6%)	40 (69%)	0
The Worcester Collection, 2d ed. (1788)	118	82 (69%)	34 (29%)	2 (2%)	50 (42%)	8 (7%)
Adgate and Spicer, Philadelphia Harmony ([1789])	61	30 (49%)	30 (49%)	1 (2%)	48 (79%)	3 (5%)
A Selection of Sacred Harmony, [2d ed., 1789]	60	31 (52%)	27 (45%)	2 (3%)	42 (70%)	0

As Table 4 shows, the fundamental element in the approach to compiling that Thomas followed in *The Worcester Collection* was an emphasis on familiar music. That emphasis is measured both by a relative scarcity of new music, and by the presence of a healthy share of Core Repertory pieces. The former established the tunebook as primarily a compiler's statement rather than a composer's; the latter ensured that the book would carry a substantial ballast of pieces judged to be the most widely known, hence the most popular and presumably the most salable. A corollary element is the mixing of pieces of different origins and hence of different styles. Whether American pieces are emphasized, as in *The Worcester Collection*, or foreign pieces, as in *A Selection of Sacred Harmony*, or, as in Adgate and Spicer, the two stand in equal proportion, a commitment to familiar music led the tunebook compiler inevitably to a rather eclectic mixing of styles.[43]

The presence of a recognized model by the 1780s is suggested by Table 4. That model's survival into the next decade and beyond argues strongly that, indeed, some notion of a formula did exist. A comparison of tunebooks that seem to follow the formula helps to provide some statistical definition, however approximate.

Between 1790 and the end of 1810, no fewer than fifty books of sacred music were published in America which follow the lead established by the works noted in the table above. With minor exceptions, all of them fall within the following guidelines: *size*—fifty or more pieces; *new music*—10 percent or less of the pieces are first printings or first American printings; *sources*—a mixture of American and non-American compositions, with no less than 35 percent American and no less than 15 percent foreign; *Core Repertory*—at least one-third devoted to these pieces. Included in the list of 'formula' tunebooks from the years 1790–1810 are four more editions of *The Worcester Collection*, three more of *A Selection of Sacred Harmony*, four more of *The Federal*

---

[43] The idea of the sacred tunebook as an eclectic mixture of compositions in different styles had been established by two Connecticut collections from which Thomas borrowed: Andrew Law's *Select Harmony* (Cheshire, Conn., 1779) and Simeon Jocelin's *Chorister's Companion* (New Haven, Conn., 1782). See Richard Crawford, 'Connecticut Sacred Music Imprints, 1778–1810, Part II,' *Music Library Association Notes*, n.s. 27 (1971): 676–77.

Harmony, and nine more of Adgate's *Philadelphia Harmony*, as well as ten editions of *The Village Harmony*, four issues of Read's *Columbian Harmonist*, two of Little and Smith's *Easy Instructor*, and two of Law's *Rudiments of Music*—in short, a list of most of the tunebooks of the period that enjoyed more than a single edition, and hence presumably the most successful tunebooks of the day. It is surely significant that the conception behind these books was introduced and imposed upon the tradition by a professional printer, not a musician.

The Worcester Collection symbolizes the entry of the letterpress printer into the field of sacred music as a new and powerful force. Professional printers like Thomas and Ranlet involved themselves in different ways in the business of sacred music. They arranged for the compiling and publishing of works like *The Worcester Collection* and *The Village Harmony*, which they also printed; they helped to sponsor the publications of other compilers by acting as sellers of these works, in some cases accepting books rather than cash as payment for their printing services; and they accepted other tunebooks for printing, presumably on a cash basis.[44] Their presence gave musicians an access to print that they had never enjoyed before. Established letterpress printing firms with the equipment and reputation for printing music made the works of prolific composer-compilers like Oliver Holden and Samuel Holyoke available to singers throughout New England and southward as well. Moreover, they were beacons for other musicians such as Timothy Swan of Suffield, Connecticut, who compiled and delivered for printing a collection of his own compositions;[45] or Daniel Belknap of

[44] The assumption here is that when the imprint of a tunebook reads 'printed for the author by . . . ,' as with Samuel Babcock's *Middlesex Harmony* (Boston: Thomas and Andrews, 1795), the author is in essence the publisher, and the printer owns no financial stake in the enterprise. If, however, the item is listed as 'printed and sold' by the printer, as in Ranlet's *Village Harmony*, then the printer is counted as the publisher. A work like Supply Belcher's *Harmony of Maine* (Boston: Thomas and Andrews, 1794) claimed to be both printed and sold by Thomas and Andrews, 'and by said Thomas in Worcester,' indicating that the printers were acting, at least in part, as sponsors of the book's publication. From the evidence of his imprints, Ranlet seldom contributed to the support of the tunebooks he published; Thomas and Andrews seem to have been more inclined in that direction.

[45] Timothy Swan, *New England Harmony* (Northampton, Mass.: Andrew Wright, 1801).

Framingham, Massachusetts, who published several compilations of his own and his neighbors' music;[46] or Abraham Maxim of Turner, Maine, who lived far from the centers where music publishing commonly took place.[47] The relatively large press runs and distribution networks of the letterpress trade helped to widen the circulation of music. The economic advantage of the process—a page of a typical typeset tunebook sold for roughly half the cost of a typical engraved one—made typographical tunebooks affordable to more people.[48] Finally, as entrepreneurs with capital as well as agents of the musicians who brought manuscripts to their doors, printers could influence the field to a degree beyond what their musical expertise might suggest. In particular, Thomas, who seems to have reaped some financial reward from *The Worcester Collection*, which was built around a core of familiar pieces, acted as publisher for other books whose content was less tried and true.[49] Thus, the presence of the letterpress printer helped to give sacred music a new solidarity and continuity, a more

[46] For example, *The Evangelical Harmony* (Boston: Thomas and Andrews, 1800); *The Middlesex Collection* (Boston: Thomas and Andrews, 1802); and *The Village Compilation* (Boston: J. T. Buckingham, 1806).

[47] Maxim made his debut with *The Oriental Harmony* (Exeter, N.H.: Henry Ranlet, 1802), a collection of his own compositions. In 1805 he compiled a work drawn from many sources, *The Northern Harmony* (Exeter, N.H.: Henry Ranlet), which came out in a second edition (Exeter, N.H.: Norris & Sawyer, 1808).

[48] The figures suggested here are necessarily rough, because tunebook prices are not consistently available, because those that are show less consistency than the scholar might wish, and because it is hard to know how constant monetary values remained over time. Per-page prices on Andrew Law's *Select Harmony* (Cheshire, Conn., 1779) range from a high of 1.6 cents to 1.09 cents. Daniel Read's *American Singing Book*, smaller in page size than Law's work, sold for approximately a penny a page, or slightly less. In contrast, *The Worcester Collection*, printed on large octavo pages, was introduced into the market in 1786 at .76 cents a page retail and .66 cents wholesale, shrinking in 1794 to .53 cents retail and .48 cents wholesale. *The Village Harmony* was selling in 1798 at .49 cents retail and .41 cents wholesale, declining by 1806 to .45 cents retail and .37 cents wholesale.

[49] Belcher's *Harmony of Maine* (cited above in fn. 44) was made up entirely of the compiler's own music, all previously unpublished. So was Jacob Kimball's *Rural Harmony* (1793). Both were published and sold by Thomas and Andrews. Similarly, a work like Walter Janes's *Harmonic Minstrelsy* (Dedham, Mass., 1807)—with almost no Core Repertory pieces and nearly half filled with new music—was sold by its printer, Herman Mann, again suggesting some share in sponsorship. Other examples could be cited, showing that printers sometimes assumed a large part of the risk of collections whose market potential would seem to have been limited.

or less standard set of publishing and distributing procedures, standards of pricing, and approaches to repertory. Together with the church and the individual chorister (and potential book buyer), the letterpress printer came to serve as a patron of psalmody.

The outline of early American music publishing given here identifies secular music with engraving and, at least from the late 1780s onward, sacred music with letterpress printing. In fact, the dichotomy was less clear-cut. In sacred music, engraved issues continued to appear after the advent of typographical printing, increasing in number during the 1790s and again in the decade of the 1800s. In secular music, although typeset song sheets were rare, the letterpress printers who issued sacred tunebooks also brought out a few secular songbooks printed from type. Neither kind of item, however, taken as a group, appears to represent a characteristic sample standing in the forefront of its genre.

During the 1790s, engraved sacred tunebooks held their own in comparison with typographical items, even outnumbering them slightly. However, in the next decade (as shown in Table 2 above) typographical items outstripped them by far. Moreover, especially after 1805, almost all the engraved items were either provincial and somewhat old-fashioned, or they were products of the urban music-publishing trade, where the older printing technology continued to flourish. The locations in which engraved items of that decade were issued dramatize the shift. Boston, long the center of the tunebook-publishing business, produced exactly one engraved tunebook between 1800 and 1810. In contrast, New Haven produced eight and Albany seven; towns like Cheshire and Danbury, Connecticut, Lansingburg, New York, and Hopewell, New Jersey, contributed a scattering of their own. When one observes that most engraved sacred items of the period came from New York (eighteen) and Philadelphia (fifteen), it might appear that the center of the industry was shifting southward. However, since more than fifty sacred music items were issued typographically in Boston during the decade, it seems clear that it was the technological fashion, not the center of the industry, that had changed.

More than a third of the sacred items printed between 1800 and 1810, including many of the New York and Philadelphia imprints, were products of the professional urban music trade. Together with a few oblong tunebooks, such as Peter Erben's *Selection of Psalm and Hymn Tunes* (New York, 1806) and Charles Woodward and John Aitken's *Ecclesiae Harmonia* (Philadelphia, [1806]), were quarto-sized items like the Reverend William Smith's *Churchman's Choral Companion* (New York, 1809), designed for Episcopal churches, and Benjamin Carr's folio-sized *Masses* (Philadelphia, 1805), for Roman Catholic worship. In addition, a few pieces of sacred sheet music were issued: Raynor Taylor's edition of 'Hotham' (Philadelphia, 1807) and James Hewitt's of 'The Dying Christian' (New York, 1806) represented as separate items individual pieces that were already available in many tunebooks. The prices of some of these issues of the professional music trade identify their market as the wealthy, presumably urban musician. Sacred sheet music sold at standard sheet music prices, as discussed above—in other words, ten times as much as one would pay for the tunes as part of sacred tunebooks. Carr's *Masses* sold for as much as $10.00 bound ($.075 per page); Smith's *Churchman's Choral Companion* brought $3.75 per copy (nearly $.08 per page). In general, the repertory of the provincial and nonprofessional engraved collections appears to be quite similar to that of most typeset books, while that of the professional urban music trade runs toward the unusual. In particular, the latter emphasizes non-American music over American. Table 5 illustrates how strong a disparity existed between the two groups of engraved tunebooks.

Conversely, secular music also came to be printed by letterpress, as printers with movable music type looked for new markets. The spread

TABLE 5

PERCENTAGES OF AMERICAN AND FOREIGN MUSIC
IN ENGRAVED SACRED MUSIC ITEMS, 1800–10

Printer	American	Foreign	Unidentified
'Nonprofessional'	65%	32%	3%
'Professional'	19%	72%	9%

of type, and the transmission of old fonts from printer to printer, can easily be traced through extant copies and archival records—much more easily, in fact, than the evidence of the shadowy music engravers.[50] All of the printers used the same Caslon music face, which remained unchallenged until the emergence of new forms from the Binny and Ronaldson firm soon after 1800.

How much of the music in these typographical books of secular music can also be found in sheet music editions? A comparison of the repertories is not yet quite manageable, though the invaluable *National Tune Index*[51] should greatly facilitate the task. But it is already possible, in a highly tentative way, to distinguish several repertories based on the form of the document: sheet music, songster, typographical songbook, and manuscript repertories, for instance. Tunes like John Moulds's 'Sterne's Maria,'[52] or the Scottish ballad 'John Anderson,'[53] appeared mostly in songsters and typographical songbooks, and perhaps in manuscripts as well, but rarely or never in sheet music editions.

A study of the contents of the best known of the typographical secular music books, Daniel and Andrew Wright's *American Musical Miscellany* (Northampton, Mass., 1798), suggests a repertory somewhat different from that of the sheet music publishers, however close to it in spirit. Of the 112 texts, at least 68 seem to appear in no other form in Sonneck-Upton. Another 44 are found in sheet music; while 50 of the titles were published in other sources like songsters, periodicals, and newspapers (26 of the 50 are in sheet music as well, but 24 are not). What is surprising, in light of this only partial overlap with the sheet music repertory, is that half of the tunes still come from the London theater repertory, with the very same five composers mentioned earlier accounting for three-fourths of the total. Native American composers come far down the list, although they might account

---

[50] In addition to those cited in fn. 11 above, Daniel Steele of Albany was among the important early publishers of typographical music.

[51] Kate Van Winkle Keller and Carolyn Rabson, *National Tune Index* (New York, 1980).

[52] Wolfe 6165–69; cf. 8606.

[53] Wolfe 4632–39.

for a goodly share of the unidentified texts. In considering both repertories, the early effects of America's copyright laws may help to explain the predilection for foreign works.

In their search for purchasers, the typographical printers seem to have begotten and fostered a bibliographical mongrel. Most common among their books was the 'half-songster,' basically a pocket-sized book of texts with tunes added, as in the *American Miscellany*. Other books, like Samuel Holyoke's *Instrumental Assistant* of 1800 and 1807,[54] were designed specifically for string and wind performers, the books often amounting to songsters with tunes but no words. In most of these books, the format is small, for several interrelated reasons: type was unsuited to keyboard accompaniment, which took space; pianists would need larger books for the music stand, with pages which would not need to be turned so often; and persons with pianos presumably also had money, which they would prefer to spend on sheet music, which, being larger in format, was more conspicuous. Typographical printing favored ensemble music, whether for use in church, by chorus, by a local band, or in group or family song. And, of course, ensemble music, in the modest dimensions of early American practice, was better suited to the economics of letterpress printing. Consequently, for reasons already suggested, the letterpress repertory in general came to favor sure-sale, established music, at the expense of the innovative and speculative musical work. Thus it was possible for the engraving and the letterpress music printers to coexist, if not always culturally and ideologically, at least technologically and economically.

In the course of the nineteenth century the established institutions of music printing and publishing, as discussed here, tended to weaken, evolve, and disappear under the impact of new tastes, technology, and publishing arrangements. In the 1820s and 1830s, for instance, sheet music publishing showed conspicuous signs of a new provincialism. No longer could the output be viewed as distinctively urban and

[54] The contract between Samuel Holyoke and Henry Ranlet for the 1800 edition of *The Instrumental Assistant* is reproduced between pp. 116 and 117 in Frank J. Metcalf, *American Writers and Compilers of Sacred Music* (New York and Cincinnati, 1925).

cosmopolitan when the repertory leaned strongly toward the vogue of blackface minstrelsy, and even less when the publishers worked out of Pittsburgh, Cincinnati, and Louisville. The particular interest of this development for bibliographers lies in the fact that the new (perhaps vaguely 'Jacksonian democratic') repertory was customarily printed from the new process of lithography, leaving the engravers to handle the more cosmopolitan tradition of guitar songs and sentimental ballads. The bibliographer should probably not attempt to make too much of this convenient dichotomy, however, partly because the tradition of music lithography proved in fact to be rather short lived. Through the course of these events the basic practices of music publishing appear to have varied little, from one repertory to the other, or from the model established in 1793.

In sacred music, meanwhile, the tradition of William Billings and Andrew Law began to lose its momentum in the 1810s and 1820s, as it also came to split into rural and urban camps of its own. Shape-note music, set in movable type, was to persist as a backwater tradition, moving into the South, where it has persisted to today in Sacred Harp practice. Sacred music set in round-note movable type, in contrast, became increasingly cosmopolitan, flourishing under the intense promotion of the master music organizer Lowell Mason. Here obviously was a prime target for stereotype printing. But above all, the basic presswork distinction between engraving and letterpress soon collapsed; Mason's popular hymn, 'From Greenland's Icy Mountains,' first appeared as sheet music, while Stephen Foster's *Social Orchestra*, and many of his songs as well, showed up in movable type.

The character of American music printing and publishing, however —as reflected in the two formative events discussed here—was to persist, in varying ways and degrees, up into the twentieth century. Such distinctions can perhaps all be taken for granted by those general historians who are satisfied to view music exclusively as a diversionary pastime, or by those musicologists who can be satisfied to conceive and to evaluate this music in terms of the concert experience. But for the scholar seeking richer cultural contexts, the advent of typographical and sheet music publishing must be viewed as landmark events.

The workings of early American music publishers, dependent on printing technology and links with particular segments of the public, are an important aspect of the character of early America's musical practice and repertory. The present essay may thus be seen as a contribution to this thesis, based on a fusion of the specialized antiquarian interests of the music bibliographer and the generalized interests of the cultural historian in studying the role of books and music in American life.

　◆ ◆

Books and the Social Authority of Learning: The Case of Mid-Eighteenth-Century Virginia

RHYS ISAAC

IN JULY 1744 an otherwise unknown Virginia gentleman celebrated the fact that Mr. William Parks, the Williamsburg printer,
had set up in town the necessary equipment to make paper from rags:

> Tho' sage Philosophers have said,
> *Of nothing can be nothing made:*
> Yet *much* thy Mill, O *Parks*, brings forth
> From what we reckon *nothing worth.*
> Hail kind *Machine!*—The Muse shall praise
> Thy Labours, that receive her Lays.
> Soon as the *Learn'd* denounce the War
> From pratling Box, or wrangling Bar,
> Straight, Pen and Paper range the Fight;
> They meet, they close, in Black & White. . . .
> 　Ye *Brave*, whose Deeds shall vie with Time,
> Whilst Mill can turn, or Poet rhime.
> Your Tatters hoard for future Quires;
> So Need demands, so *Parks* desires.
> (And long that gen'rous Patriot live
> Who for soft Rags, hard Cash will give!)
> 'The Shirt, Cravat, the Cap, again
> Shall meet your Hands, with *Mails* from *Spain*;
> The *Surplice*, which, when whole or new,
> With Pride the Sexton's Wife could view,
> Tho' worn by Time and gone to rack,
> It quits its Rev'rend Master's Back;

> The same again the Priest may see
> Bound up in Sacred Liturgy.
>   Ye *Fair*, renown'd in *Cupid's* Field,
> Who fain would tell what Hearts you've killed;
> Each Shift decay'd, lay by with Care;
> Or Apron rubb'd to bits at—Pray'r,
> One Shift ten Sonnets may contain,
> To gild your Charms, and make you vain; . . .
>   Nice *Delia's* Smock, which, neat and whole,
> No Man durst finger for his Soul;
> Turn'd to *Gazette*, now all the Town,
> May take it up, or smooth it down. . . .
>   The Bards, besure, their Aids will lend;
> The Printer is the Poet's Friend;
> Both cram the News, and stuff the Mills,
> For Bards have Rags, and—little else.[1]

The very triteness of such verse can be a help to us in evoking a vanished ethos and in reconstructing the relationships and ideas that sustained it. We encounter a series of stock characters and symbolic figures from the world of parish, county, and provincial town: the disputative man of learning, whether wordy parson or 'wrangling' lawyer; the ardent young man, dreaming of martial glory, himself the victim of a cruel 'Fair' who contrives conquests of another kind; and the poet, whose dedication to the muse presages rags for his fortune. Attention is also drawn to the medium itself, in the images of the public-spirited printer and the worthy reader who takes up his *Gazette* to find in it the news; the controversies of the learned, closed 'in Black & White'; and, to be sure, the odes and elegies that idealize this world.

The polite verses represented a precious genteel order of things. The humblest person whose stylized icon appears here is the sexton's wife, predictably female and subservient as she viewed with homely pride the results of her skill as a laundress. She represents the bulk of society—the unlettered many upon whom the cultivated few depended not just for economic support but for their sense of having a special

---

[1] The original *Gazette*, it seems, is not extant. The text of J. Dumbleton's 'The Paper Mill' was reprinted in the *Virginia Magazine of History and Biography* 7 (1899–1900): 442–44.

role in life. This highly conventional poem might have come, except for the references to Mr. Parks, from anywhere in the Anglo-American world. To that extent it conforms to the social and cultural patterns of the whole region.

There is, however, a particular problem raised by the case of Williamsburg and the Virginia society of which it was the cultural center: how could a colony in which libraries were small and the output of learned writing even smaller have produced the incisive intellects of the generation that contributed so much to the formulation of their new nation's revolutionary ideology and its enduring constitution? Attempts have been made (most notably by Prof. Louis B. Wright) to unriddle the riddle by denying the facts—by showing how many great works of learning were available in private libraries (though with expressions of dismay at the small number of works from the canon of great English literature).[2] The model offered here, by contrast, will be one designed to suggest how and why books and the interpretation of them could be a source of real authority on account not of their number but of their symbolic potency in the life of the whole community.

I

THE BOOK IN THE SYSTEM OF ORAL FOLK CULTURE

In a world where illiteracy and semiliteracy were widespread, the culture of common folk was transmitted and sustained in ways very different from those prevailing in an urbanized society where schooling is compulsory. Furthermore, special authority was vested in those who had facility in writing and were conversant with books. Virginia society in the eighteenth century, like that of much of Western Europe at that time, was under the influence of *both* the oral-dramatic and the script-typographic media of communication, each generating its distinctive sense of the nature of language and of the world itself. The presence of the written word was felt throughout the society—even

---

[2] Louis B. Wright, *The First Gentlemen of Virginia, Intellectual Qualities of the Early Colonial Ruling Class* (San Marino, Calif., 1940).

slaves were required to carry 'passes' (i.e., letters from their masters) before they could lawfully go off the plantation. Nevertheless, levels of literacy were not high. The best and most carefully corrected measurements of the ability of persons to write their own names show a close correlation between signature rate and social rank. Calculating ratios between signed names and marks made in lieu of signatures, it is estimated that the level of literacy among white males rose markedly from 46 percent in the 1640s to 62 percent by about 1710. After that date it seems not to have altered much until some time in the nineteenth century. About two-thirds of adult white males could sign; among females the signature rate was much lower. The internalization of the alphabet by Anglo-Virginians had stabilized at a low level during the eighteenth century. The influence of the written word upon the perceptions of most persons remained comparatively weak. For them, access to knowledge could not be attained through print. Slaves who could forge a 'pass' certainly feature in the records, but blacks who found the opportunity to acquire such skills must have been a tiny proportion of the whole population. In aggregate, then, some three out of every four persons whom a growing child would encounter in Virginia were largely or entirely confined within the oral medium. Yeomen's offspring would have found minimal literacy fairly general in their world, but they continually experienced total or near-total illiteracy among slaves and women. The children of the gentry would have had their skills and sensibilities informed by a divided experience: they were confronted by books and the more literate speech of parents, neighboring gentlefolk, and teachers on the one hand, and by the altogether orally conditioned language usages of slaves, some servants, and other humbler Anglo-Virginians on the other.[3]

[3] The most recent, critically appraised figures are to be found in Kenneth A. Lockridge, *Literacy in Colonial New England: An Enquiry into the Social Context of Literacy in the Modern West* (New York, 1974), pp. 73–87. The modest title of this book belies the importance of its wide-ranging comparative data and broad interpretation. For a lively commentary on the place of 'talk' in the lives of the gentry, and indeed for what are probably the best few pages on old Virginia to be found anywhere, see Douglass Adair's review of Robert D. Meade's biography of Patrick Henry, in the *William and Mary Quarterly*, 3d ser. 16 (1959): 589–93.

The social and cultural patterns surrounding developed literacy were complex and multilayered. At one extreme, very little removed from the realm of the wholly oral, were the minimal skills that made possible the scrawling of an awkward note to a storekeeper or the painstaking decipherment of a recipe for a cure from a farrier's manual. At the other extreme was cosmopolitan, 'polite' literature—the slow creation of 200 years of the development of printing. Within this expansive realm 'individualistic' personalities could come into existence free from the direct pressures of the immediate presence of others. Access to this realm was limited to the few who had the opportunity to immerse themselves intensively in the reading of books. Coexisting with this comparatively new world of silent literary communications was another cultural form that was ancient and in the process of being superseded but that still retained much of its power. 'Speaking books' is a suitable term to convey the function of the highly important bodies of written words, such as the Bible and the common law reports (together with the extensive commentaries surrounding each), that derived from manuscript traditions in which the written word was closely tied to formal speech. Such texts had originated in oral performance settings, and their constant recitation in churches and lawcourts ensured their exalted authority in the word-of-mouth culture of common people. Within this tradition, 'learning' (in this respect distinct from 'education') consisted of the skills to interpret the Scriptures and other authoritative writings and to communicate to an audience the customary and indispensable knowledge that had been stored within these writings from ancient times.[4]

Basic forms of oral culture, and some of the ways in which they interlocked with the valued wisdom contained in printed books, can best be traced in the only substantial Virginia account of the childhood and youth—the socialization—of a humble son of the soil. From

[4] For a more extended application of the concept of oral and literate cultures to early Virginia, see Rhys Isaac, 'Dramatizing the Ideology of Revolution: Popular Mobilization in Virginia, 1774–1776,' *William and Mary Quarterly*, 3d ser. 33 (1976): 358–61, and the references cited there. See also Harry S. Stout, 'Religion, Communications and the Ideological Origins of the American Revolution,' ibid., 3d ser. 34 (1977): 519–41.

the vantage point of the social eminence to which the Reverend Mr. Devereux Jarratt had climbed, he was moved in his declining years to look back on the world of his boyhood, and on the steps of his advancement. Jarratt's recollections of the processes by which he acquired, first, common literacy, and then access to higher learning, provide outlines of the relationship between popular culture—with its large oral component—and the authoritative realm of great books.

The young farm boy(born in 1733) soon showed particular talents which, while exceptional, reveal the forms of verbal expression that contributed to the shaping of the outlook of the countryfolk among whom he grew up. Oral cultures are dominated by mnemonic formulas that enable their traditions to be remembered and thus to survive. The boy excelled in memory, and, as he had also a 'voice . . . remarkably tuneable, and soft, or sonorous; as the case required, . . . [he] could sing . . . with an air and grace, which excited attention and admiration,' so that he was encouraged to learn 'the longest *songs*' by ear. A version of 'the old song of *Chevy Chase*' was evidently current in Tidewater Virginia, and this the young Devereux 'learned to repeat, and sing, by hearing it a few times only, though it contained near a hundred stanzas.' The lad can have experienced little difficulty when his parents saw to it that he was 'made . . . very perfect in repeating the *Church Catechism*,' for he early found that 'before [he] knew the letters of the alphabet, [he] could repeat a whole chapter in the Bible, at a few times hearing it read.' From the 'pregnancy of genius' thus revealed, the youngster was dubbed '*parson*.'[5] His mastery of Scripture evoked an archetypal symbolic figure.

Low levels of literacy and an agrarian way of life evidently worked to sustain a vital English oral culture in Virginia during the eighteenth century. Yet that culture had for a thousand years been contained within a book-defined cosmology, bounded at critical points by the written word whose highest forms were Divinity and Law. The Bible was evidently the source of some of the most powerful oral performances that helped mold the consciousness and establish the prom-

[5] Devereux Jarratt, *The Life of the Reverend Devereux Jarratt* (Baltimore, 1806; facsimile reprint, New York, 1969), pp. 19, 16–18.

ise of the little 'parson.' He heard it read aloud by the elders; he
assimilated it through his ear; then he recited it aloud again. Catechism and Bible lessons were common exercises where authoritative
forms of the written word met with, and contributed to the shape of,
oral culture.

In the world of farmers who grew tobacco for an export market,
minimal literacy skills were a practical asset. 'My parents,' recalled
the aged Jarratt, 'neither sought nor expected any titles, honors, or
great things, either for themselves or children. Their highest ambition
was to teach their children to read, write, and understand the fundamental rules of arithmetic. . . . They wished us all to be brought up
in some honest calling, that we might earn our bread, by the sweat
of our brow, as they did.' Thus, at age eight or nine, young Devereux
'was sent to an English school [i.e., not a Latin one] in the neighbourhood: and . . . continued to go to one teacher or other, as opportunity
served, (though not without great interruptions),' till he was twelve
or thirteen years old. 'In this time,' the boy whose ear and tongue had
been so apt to master the stanzas of ballads and the sonorous phrases
of the Authorized Version 'learned to read in the Bible (though but
indifferently) and to write a sorry scrawl.' In the confines of a school-
house, in the drudgeries of intermittent formal instruction, the promising virtuoso of oral performance became a clumsy tyro in the world
of letters. At this point, long before he had developed any ease or
mastery in the written medium, all schooling ceased. Jarratt's case
was not singular. The measurements (cited above) of men's and wom-
en's ability to sign their names to legal documents suggest that about
half of his contemporaries among the farm boys failed to get as far as
he had. Few indeed went appreciably further—while their sisters in
general were left incapable of forming letters at all.[6]

Both of Jarratt's parents had died by the time he was thirteen, and
with the expectation of a meager twenty-five pound patrimony when
he came of age, the lad was left in the care of his older brothers, who
were farmer-artisans like their father—the one a millwright, the other
a carpenter. The youngest brother, although he later idealized his

6 Ibid., pp. 15–16, 19–20.

yeoman parents' acceptance of their lot, was unwilling to follow any of these callings: 'I was not contented with the small degree of learning I had acquired, and wished for more knowledge, especially in figures. . . . To understand figures well, we reckoned the height of learning. Philosophy, Rhetoric, Logic &c. we never heard of. . . . *Arithmetic* was all and all. To acquire this, I borrowed a plain book, in manuscript; and while the horse, with which I harrowed or ploughed, was grazing an hour or two at noon, I frequently spent the time in application to that book.'[7]

Such rudimentary texts may have been quite widespread. One at least has survived and is now to be found in the manuscript collection of the College of William and Mary. Since this specimen dates from the 1760s, it may even be a direct lineal descendant, by the process of repeated copying, of Jarratt's text.[8]

At age nineteen the young field-worker was 'called from the *ax* to the *quill*.' (The use of these metaphors is itself evocative of a close-bounded world with its clearly discernible symbolic hierarchies of function.) His attainments in applied arithmetic won him such renown that he received an invitation to go and teach in Albemarle County, making his home with Jacob Moon, formerly of New Kent County. It almost goes without saying, however, that disappointment awaited the young hopeful in the west. Jacob Moon could not perform as well as he could promise, for he was but the overseer in charge of the Bremo quarters of Col. Richard Cocke and so lacked the influence to gather many children under the new schoolmaster's care. The fees, at one pound per child per year, were the teacher's sole cash income, and only nine children attended his school.[9]

During the course of Jarratt's stay at Moon's house, 'Mr. White-field's eight sermons, preached in *Glasgow*, were left, by some one,' and since it was the first sermon book he 'ever had seen, or, perhaps, heard of [he] had the curiosity to look into it.' The young schoolmaster, however, was still 'a poor reader, and understood little' of what

[7] Ibid., pp. 24–27.
[8] Earle Gregg Swem, 'Sublet's Arithmetic Book,' Manuscript Collection, Library, College of William and Mary, Williamsburg, Va.
[9] Jarratt, *Life*, pp. 25–27.

he found in the work. Books and religion impinged only to a small degree on his awareness. The consciences of those around him were unencumbered by formal piety. 'The Sabbath day was usually spent in sporting and whether *this* was right or wrong... no one questioned.'[10] A decisive change occurred in Jarratt's career after he had been somewhat over a year in this western region. The authority that the gentry derived from their superior command of book learning and refined manners appears plainly in the narrative of the next stages in the young schoolmaster's life:

I went now to board with a gentleman, whose name was *Cannon.* He was a man of great possessions, in lands, slaves, &c. &c. As I had been always very shy of *gentlefolk* . . . imagine, how awkwardly, and with what confusion, I entered his house. . . . It was on a Sunday, P.M. when I first came to the house—an entire stranger, both to the gentleman and his lady. . . . The interview, on my part, was the more awkward, as I knew not . . . what style was proper for accosting persons of their dignity. However I made bold to enter the door, and was viewed, in some measure, as a phenomenon. The gentleman took me . . . for the son of a very poor man, in the neighbourhood, but the lady, having some hint, I suppose, from the children, rectified the mistake, and cried out, *it is the school-master.*[11]

The rough-mannered retainer, who had come to live in the 'great house,' had another cause for trepidation, since he 'had been told that the lady . . . was a *New-light,* and of sentiments so rigid and severe, that all levities of every kind must be banished from her presence.' Evangelical dissent was just beginning its spectacular rise to prominence in Virginia. Jarratt therefore now faced religious doctrines and a discipline that were entirely unfamiliar to him. His mind became engaged in 'some serious reflections . . . how to demean [himself], in her presence,' and his social ambition manifested itself in 'a *project* entirely new to [himself] . . . to act the *hypocrite.*' He 'had no intention of being religious, but wished to appear so, in order to gain her good opinion.' So the young man sat by while the lady 'read a sermon, in *Flavel,* every night . . . though [he] understood not the

10 Ibid., p. 28.
11 Ibid., pp. 31–32.

tenth part of what was read.' Sometimes in furtherance of his plan of winning favor, he would even 'ask her to read another.' At first, 'when she was weary of reading,' she would ask him to read in his turn. 'But so poor a hand did [he] make of the business, that...she soon desisted asking.'[12]

There came a night, however, when the conscience of the bored young acolyte was 'imprest'—or was it his ambition, in subtle form? 'The text of the sermon was, *"Then opened he their understanding."* From which words were pointed out, what new discoveries would open to the eye of the mind, by means of spiritual illumination, &c.' He was led to ponder his ignorance of such things. He forsook sinful frivolity, and embarked on the course of study in divinity that elevated him in time to the status of a gentleman parson in the Church and earned him minor celebrity in the English Atlantic world as a tract writer and correspondent of John Wesley.[13]

As yet Jarratt remained a poor schoolmaster. The patronage of a gentlewoman (who was not at one with her husband in religious matters) was not sufficient to spare him the vicissitudes to which his humble rank left him prey. His second school dwindled, and he was forced to return to Moon's, where he found that his new earnestness concerning the salvation of the soul met only with rebuff:

They made light of it—turned all off with a laugh—imputing the whole to *new-light cant.* . . . Moon and his wife, being *Church people,* as they said, could listen to nothing but what came through that channel. . . . I was myself . . . but little acquainted with the principles of the church. Nor did I understand the meaning of many scriptures, which I read, but I understood . . . that . . . except a man be *born again,* he cannot see the kingdom of God. . . . This they did not deny, 'We must all be *born again,*' said they, 'but that is to be after we are dead.'[14]

The pursuit of higher learning was not encouraged. The ambitious young man had to seize opportunities as they chanced his way. He

---

12 Ibid., pp. 31–34. Douglass Adair identifies the author named as John Flavel (1630?–1691), a Presbyterian divine whose many religious writings were noted for a 'fine play of fancy and dramatic imagery.' Douglass Adair, ed., 'Autobiography of Devereux Jarratt,' *William and Mary Quarterly,* 3d ser. 9 (1952): 370.

13 Jarratt, *Life,* p. 34.

14 Ibid., pp. 38–39.

'had not a single book in the world,' and was too poor to order any. Fortunately for his purpose, pious tracts were to be found here and there, often little cared for, and so 'by some means, . . . [he] got hold of a little old book, in a smoky condition, which [he] found to be *Russel's* seven sermons.' He borrowed it, and read it again and again, but found himself still in need of some 'help in understanding the scriptures.' Jarratt's quest for a means to enter into the interpretation of the Bible shows the awed relationship of common people to the higher learning that towered dimly but authoritatively over them. He mentioned his need for 'an expositer' of the sacred word to an acquaintance, who told him 'of a *very large book*, belonging to a *gentleman*, about five or six miles *distant across the river*, which explained *all* the New Testament.' After 'living so long with Mr. Cannon, and [by] the resort of gentlemen to his house,' Jarratt found that he 'had worn off some of [his] clownish rusticity, and had become less shy of persons in the upper ranks of life.' He therefore went more readily to secure a loan of this awesome book whose fame was spread so wide. It was a folio volume 'called *Burkett* on the New Testament,' and made the borrower 'wonderfully pleased . . . because [he] found the *writer* to have been a minister of the Church.' To the diligent study of this great authority the poor schoolmaster now devoted himself. He may be pictured at his pious labours: 'As I had no candle, my custom was, in an evening, to sit down flat on the hearth, erect the volume on the end of a chest, which stood near, and, by the light of the fire, read till near midnight. . . . [By] these means . . . I soon became, what was called a good reader, and my relish for books and reading greatly increased.'[15]

Sometime later a return visit to his home neighborhood brought about a lapse from his newfound piety and asceticism. Back in the place where he had once been an awkward plowboy he found that now that he wore linen instead of osnaburg, had a veneer of culture,

15 Ibid., pp. 39–41 (some of the italics added). The authors named were William Russel (d. 1702), a Baptist minister, and William Burkitt (1650–1703). The prized volume was *Expository Notes, with Practical Observations, on the New Testament* (London, 1724). Adair, ed., 'Autobiography of Jarratt,' pp. 373–74.

and enjoyed some command of genteel manners, his virtuosity in the convivial style promised to win him social advancement: 'As I possess a great degree of vivacity, and was extremely jocose, my company was very acceptable . . . and courted by persons much my superior, in family and fortune.'[16]

Jarratt's career was not to be consummated in the profane mode— perhaps by a marriage into a New Kent gentry family?—but was again deflected onto its former course when Mr. Cannon, now having a young son (in place of a daughter and a niece) to be educated, engaged him as a resident teacher at fifteen pounds a year. Under this renewed influence he returned both to study and to evangelical piety. His patrons secured for him the Latin education that provided the indisputable cachet of gentility. With this qualification he was engaged as a tutor at forty pounds per annum in the household of Mr. Thompson Swann. With the help of patrons he went on from there to be ordained by the bishop of London as a clergyman of the Church of England.[17]

From Devereux Jarratt's description of his early education, from his accounts of the circumstances in which he came across books, and from his narrations of the responses of those around him, we can perceive both how limited was the actual acquaintance of humble churchfolk with print, and how great was the ultimate authority of learning in their cosmological scheme. Such volumes as were found among the common planters, rather than supplying means for readers to make confident pronouncements, seemed to point to a realm of erudition whose orthodox interpretations were only vaguely appre- hended and were assumed to be beyond the scrutiny of simple persons. A review of the social arrangements on the most significant occasions when authority was ceremoniously displayed may help explain this apparent paradox of immediate unconcern and ultimate respect.

16 Jarratt, *Life*, pp. 44–45.
17 Ibid., pp. 54–82.

II
RITUAL DISPLAYS OF THE AUTHORITY OF LEARNING

Divine Service

Churches were the important centers for community assembly, dispersed at the most frequent intervals in the countryside. The parishes of the established religion were sometimes, in the western part of the colony, coterminous with counties, but usually they were considerably smaller. In both cases the parish would have a number of houses of worship—churches and 'chapels of ease.' Each person, except those who formally dissented (and they were very few in the settled parts before mid-century), was deemed a member of 'the Church of England as by law established.' All were required to attend divine service at least once in four weeks, under penalty of a fine of five shillings or fifty pounds of tobacco for failure to comply.

In the 1730s a new church design was introduced whose rapid spread is a clear sign that it was felt to be appropriate by those who dominated decision making at the parish level. The first of these new-fashioned edifices, Christ Church in Lancaster County, has somehow survived the triumph of the sectaries and the ravages of the three wars that have laid waste parts of Virginia. With nearly all of its woodwork and most of its original glass intact, it stands in its wall-enclosed green among the trees on the northern shore of the Rappahannock River, lovingly restored as a silent reminder of the religious observances and the social exchanges that it was built to contain.

Entering Christ Church, Lancaster (and other churches following its design), one is suddenly in a lofty, light-filled, enclosed space. The high-vaulted interior would certainly be the largest 'room' or hall that most parishioners ever entered. The effect was not—as with the form of Gothic churches—to channel the devotions of the faithful through the clergy and the sanctuary to the heavens, but rather, in the Protestant spirit, to make the community-congregation worshipfully present to itself.

The plan maximized the visibility to the assembled community of a numerous emulative gentry. In the center the four arms of the Greek cross united to form a great focal space. Great oak-walled pews reserved for magistrates and leading families stood at the front of each arm of the church, delimiting the central area. High within the space thus defined stood the pulpit with its grand, ornately canopied sounding board, or 'tester,' above it. The pulpit was the obvious point of attention in the design, symbolizing, again in the Protestant spirit, the central importance of the explication of the Word of God. Only a clergyman who had been examined, ordained, and licensed by a bishop, successor to the Apostles, could mount the elevated rostrum to unfold the divine revelation. In tiered hierarchy beneath the pulpit were the desk from which the scriptural lessons were read, and the clerk's desk from which the parson's lay assistant 'lined out' the psalms for communal intonation. Behind pulpit and desks, and hence symbolically and dramaturgically in the lowest position, was a gallery for a small number of slaves, entered by a steep narrow stairway just inside the south door.

On the far side of the central space stood the altar. Above it on the end wall, the words of the Ten Commandments and the Apostles' Creed shone out in gold lettering from black tablets, keeping the people mindful of the cosmic framework within which their community was contained and of the moral absolutes to which it was subject.

Worship consisted almost entirely of the reading of the services from the Book of Common Prayer, whose use was sanctioned by law. The mode was thus liturgical and alien to modern sensibilities. We of the antiformalistic twentieth century are ill attuned to appreciate the meanings expressed through the weekly repetition of set words, with appointed variations marking the seasons of the year and the rotations of the ecclesiastical calendar. The potentialities of these rituals may best be revealed to us in the pronouncements of a late seventeenth-century English bishop who defended the liturgy against the criticism to which it was already subject from proponents of creative individualism:

Whatsoever good things we hear only once, or now and then, though perhaps upon the hearing of them, they may swim for a while in our brains, yet they seldom sink down into our hearts, so as to move and sway the affections, as it is necessary they should do in order to our being edified by them; whereas by a set form of public devotions rightly composed, we are continually put in mind of all things necessary for us to know or do, so that it is always done by the same words and expressions, which, by their constant use, will imprint the things themselves so firmly in our minds, that . . . they will still occur upon all occasions, which cannot but be very much for our Christian edification.

The bishop's words indicate not only the manner in which the familiar phrases of the liturgy might be savored, but convey powerful resonances of a traditional, ordered community, in which persons were expected to aspire to become inwardly what the social constraints of their lives (including the intoning of the formulas of the Prayer Book responses) required them to be outwardly.[18]

The seating plans of the Virginia churches—accentuated by the manner of entry and exit—exhibited the community to itself in ranked order. The form and tone of the liturgy reinforced the demonstration inherent in the physical setting. The services of the Book of Common Prayer had been given their vernacular shape in the sixteenth century and expressed strongly an ethos of English Christian gentility. The appointed set of words, read in the midst of a community ranged in order of precedence, continuously evoked postures of deference and submission. Liturgy and church plan thus readily combined to offer a powerful representation of structured, hierarchical community under the authority of great books and of those who understood them. The ceremonial of the county court—as will be seen—asserted similar, complementary values and relationships. Church and courthouse, each

---

[18] The quotation is from Bishop William Beveridge, *Sermon Concerning the Excellency and Usefulness of the Book of Common Prayer* (London, 1681), cited in Horton Davies, *Worship and Theology in England: From Watts and Wesley to Maurice, 1690–1850* (Princeton, N.J., 1961), pp. 26–27. For an exploration of the origins of the particular form of Christ Church, Lancaster, see Alan Gowans, *King Carter's Church* ([Victoria, B.C., 1969]), pp. 7–32. Gowans attributes the design to Christopher Wren, but omits discussion of the perfect conformity of this building to Wren's sense of the requirements of churches as 'auditories.' See G. W. O. Addleshaw and Frederick Etchells, *The Architectural Setting of Anglican Worship: An Inquiry into the Arrangements for Public Worship in the Church of England from the Reformation to the Present Day* (London, 1948).

in its proper way, exhibited symbols and formulas expressing the orientation of the local community to the larger social world.[19]

Court Day

In the eighteenth-century Virginia landscape, the courthouse occupied a unique place. It can be pictured in its physical setting—usually an isolated brick structure with a simple round-arched, loggia-style porch on the front. Not uncommonly it stood at a crossroads in the midst of woods and fields, since most counties were without towns, and central location was the prime consideration in choosing a site. The courthouse, however, was never quite solitary, for it was invariably accompanied by supporting buildings—always at least one ordinary (i.e., tavern), a lockup, and often a store. With the holding of something like a county fair, a great deal besides the court proceedings drew the county's inhabitants together on court day, but the sessions in the courthouse were at the center of all activity. A society dominated by landholders, jealous of their independence and litigious in the defense of their boundaries and entitlements, could not but attach great importance to the arena in which conflicts over matters of this kind were joined and their issue determined. The importance of the arbitrator's function conferred considerable dignity on those who exercised it. We must picture the gentlemen justices, bewigged and in their fine coats and waistcoats, seated on the raised 'bench'— His Majesty's commissioners engaged in the communal dispensation of 'justice.'

It would be hard to overemphasize the importance of the ceremonial at the center of the coming together on court day. In the cultural context of the time it served not only to make the community a witness to important decisions and transactions but also to teach men the very nature and forms of government. There was no written constitution; Anglo-Virginians could only conceive of law and authority in their society as extensions and adaptations of English custom. (Modern Americans are so dependent on the idea of a constitution as a

[19] For a brief commentary on the tone of the liturgy see John E. Booty, ed., *The Book of Common Prayer, 1559: The Elizabethan Prayer Book* (Charlottesville, Va., 1976), pp. 379–82.

document that they readily misconstrue colonial charters, and even governor's 'Instructions' in the case of Virginia, as instruments functioning in the manner of written fundamental law.) There were no elementary textbooks on 'government'—and not many schools to teach from them had they been available—while few, even among the more literate gentry, would have studied learned volumes giving systematic explication of the English customary 'constitution.' For most men the primary mode of comprehending the organization of authority was through participation in courthouse proceedings. Its oaths and ritual forms were so many formulas, diagrams, or models, declaring the nature of government and its laws. Its executions were fearful demonstrations of the consequences of putting oneself outside the protection of those laws. Although there was no single great volume to embody 'the Law' and render it ritually present in the courthouses as the Bible did for divinity in the churches, the bound collections of legal manuals —and even the forms of the justices' pronouncements—were evident tokens of a complex realm of erudition raised above the common knowledge of simple folk.[20] Indeed, some knowledge of the law was a badge of gentility.

III

THE CREDIBILITY OF DISPLAYS

The public representations of authority would not have been convincing if there had existed the kind of cultural chasm in society that is suggested by terms like 'educated' and 'uneducated' or 'inarticulate.' The effectiveness of the ritual occasions depended on profound continuities between the culture of 'learning'—the capacity to bring alive the great texts that I have called 'speaking books'—and the folk culture. These continuities appeared in the accounts given of the liturgy, and of the young Devereux Jarratt's early encounters with Scripture and the catechism. It was for these reasons that some degree of

[20] For a slightly fuller explication of the blending of oral and learned forms in the county courts see Isaac, 'Dramatizing the Ideology,' pp. 364–67. The subject is given excellent, fuller treatment in A. G. Roeber, 'Authority, Law, and Custom: The Rituals of Court Day in Tidewater Virginia, 1720–1750,' *William and Mary Quarterly*, 3d ser. 37 (1980): 29–52.

learning was not only professed by the true gentleman, but was expected of him by the populace. The unities in the system were sustained by the mediating role of the gentry.

The defining characteristics of gentility are elusive. At first sight being a gentleman resided in the fact itself—a claim made upon the world and accepted by the world. A complex of behaviors and attributes were required to support the claim, and deficiency in some would require balancing by a fuller measure of the others. Appropriate demeanor, dress, manners, and conversational style were essential. These might confer a presumption of gentility, especially if accompanied by a familiarity with the sources of sacred, classical, or legal learning, but the status of gentleman could only be confirmed if one unmistakably possessed the means of personal independence. In this slaveholding colony customary English valuation of manly independence was carried to very great heights.[21]

The quality that most nearly epitomized what was needed in a gentleman was 'liberality.' This word was rich in connotations deriving from its Latin root: first and foremost, it denoted *freedom* from material necessity and the grubbing for subsistence that poverty entailed; second, it meant *freedom* from the servile subjection that the quest for satisfaction of material want imposed; third, it evoked *freedom* from the sordid subordination of considerations of honor and dignity to calculations of interest that lack of independence was presumed to involve; and fourth, most relevant to this discussion of print and social authority, it was associated with *freedom* to elevate the mind by application to the great books that contained the higher learning (as in the expression 'liberal arts'). Ultimately the idea of 'liberality' had reference to a certain disposition in the soul that all these freedoms made possible—the disposition willingly to undertake important responsibilities in the community at large.[22]

[21] See Jack P. Greene, *All Men Are Created Equal: Some Reflections on the Character of the American Revolution* (Oxford, 1976).

[22] For a dated but still valuable discussion of gentility (with references), see Wright, *First Gentlemen of Virginia*, esp. pp. 1–37. A profoundly insightful exploration of genteel sensibility in a nurturing and social context is presented in Philip J. Greven, *The Protestant Temperament: Patterns of Child-Rearing, Religious Experience, and the Self in Early America* (New York, 1977), pp. 265–331.

The 'liberal principles' of gentlemen, and their assumed role as mediators between higher learning and common culture, made them the only proper trustees of the institutions that dispensed the authority of great books—the parish churches and the county courthouses. The squires who ruled the vestries were willing to tax themselves heavily in order to maintain the dignified reading of the liturgy and exposition of scriptural texts that made up the divine service that all heads of household were obliged to attend at least once a month. The importance attached to this control of the Book, and to the erudition that surrounded it, was clearly revealed in the escalating conflict that resulted in the 1760s and 1770s, when many of these squires attempted to repress popular dissenters who presumed to interpret Scripture outside of the churches—where the assignment of pews and the elevation of the pulpit so clearly expressed hierarchical social order. The Separate Baptists, who encouraged the most humble men (even slaves) to go forth and preach if they showed powerful signs of 'the gift' of the Holy Spirit, were contemptuously designated 'New Lights' with unmistakable reference to their outrageous disregard for the authority—the true light—of ancient higher learning. Popular dissenting meetings were broken up and their evangelists arrested as disturbers of the peace.

Only the circumstances created by the Revolution were able to force the gentry to concede defeat in this hard-fought struggle to maintain the symbolic public authority of a learned clergy. The strong continuance of gentry dominance after the collapse of their parish church organization served as a conclusive demonstration that the control exercised by the elite through their command of great books had always derived less from their place in an ecclesiastical system than from their roles in the courts. 'They diligently search the Scriptures,' wrote one bitter satirist of the squires, 'but the Scriptures which they search are the Laws of Virginia: for though you may find innumerable families in which there is no Bible, yet you will not find one without a Law-book.'[23] The exaggeration is palpable, but the observation behind it was certainly accurate. The law was the most valued

[23] Richard Beale Davis, ed., 'The Colonial Virginia Satirist,' *Transactions of the American Philosophical Society* 57 (1967): 52.

branch of higher learning in this society of assertive, litigious land-owners. It was, then, in court sessions that the most persuasive displays of the power to be derived from book learning occurred; and it is to the law, as Virginians made and applied it, that we must turn in order to understand the power of those displays.

The General Court, to which appeals went within Virginia, was the King's Council acting in a judicial capacity, and so was made up of great landowners not specially trained in law. It was presided over by a governor who was never drawn from among the gentlemen of the bar. At the county level, the commissioning of squire justices, unsu-pervised by assizes of learned judges, encouraged the 'determining of every thing by the Standard of Equity and good Conscience,' as Rob-ert Beverley noted. Beverley took pride in the way Virginia courts spurned 'the Impertinences of Form and Nicety.' Col. Landon Carter thought that issues should be decided rather by 'Good reason and Justice' than by 'Precedents,' and sneered at the 'Mechanical knowl-edge' of attorneys. In this the colonel was not disparaging law, but expressing a Virginian's view of its nature. He was setting his face against a mere technical application of law as found in law books, and asserting a substantial role for the common-sense judgments of men of affairs—gentlemen who would bring their experience of life and the wisdom of a generalized higher learning to bear on the cases before them. The tendency was to emphasize the social authority of the gentlemen justices rather than the formal authority of texts.[24]

The court was central to the organization of society in ways that went deeper than the conduct of business or the distribution of patron-age. The court was the guardian of the law, and the law maintained rights and enforced obligations. Rights meant property, above all in land and slaves. Obligations meant, essentially, the monetary regula-tion of relationships between landowners (as in trespass cases) and of relationships that arose from trade in the produce of land (mainly debts and credits). The connections linking the patriarchal household

[24] Robert Beverley, *The History and Present State of Virginia*, ed. Louis B. Wright (Chapel Hill, N.C., 1947), p. 255. Landon Carter, *The Diary of Colonel Landon Carter of Sabine Hall, 1752–1778*, ed. Jack P. Greene, 2 vols. (Charlottesville, Va., 1965), 1: 75.

units of plantation society to the maritime exchange system were formalized and secured in the courts. At the sessions of the county commissioners a powerful form of high culture—the law—met with a compelling local need—security of property. Without security of property there could be no effective independence of persons, a supreme value in this age. In the courthouse, the royal arms and the form of justice in the king's name expressed the descent of authority from above, while the character of the justices as leading landowners of the county represented the patriarchal property system and affirmed the basis of English law in the needs and consent of the governed.

This essay has sought to reveal some of the most important social contexts of books in a by no means bookish part of the Anglo-American world: the world of the oral performances that impressed Devereux Jarratt as a boy; the world of occasional schooling designed to impart minimal skills in writing and ciphering; the world of plain folk in awe of great books and satisfied, like Jacob Moon, that their authority reinforced conventional wisdom—'We must all be born again, but that is to be after we are dead.' This was also the world of the unitary parish congregation assembled beneath the great pulpit, where the supervisory presence of the great gentlemen added weight to the authority of the parson, himself a gentleman, expounding the Bible; the world of the bewigged justices presiding in county courthouses where the prestige of their book learning was merged with communal consensus arrived at through jury deliberations. These forms of the most significant communication—these ways of being, one might say—provided the larger context to which the precious literary configurations of the *Virginia Gazette's* ode to the paper mill belonged. This system of relationships was already ancient when the first Englishmen came to settle on the Chesapeake shores; it was already weakened and partially superseded by the middle of the eighteenth century. The developments of the next fifty years—developments whose analysis lies beyond the scope of this essay—were to occasion the system's ultimate dissolution. The Great Awakenings, and the popular dissent they promoted, effectively wrested the Bible and its interpretation from the custody of the learned; the republican principle of popular sovereignty subverted the conception of higher authority embodied in the wisdom of learned justices; newspapers and pamphlets (increasingly promulgating divisive ideologies, and more and more frequently involving the vulgar in affairs formerly the preserve of the learned)[25] combined with the newly invented boom product of the 1750s, the sentimental novel, to turn the flow of print into a flood.

The Virginians who penned the Revolutionary documents that set forth the fundamental principles of the new republic wittingly and unwittingly contributed to the processes of accelerated transformation enumerated above. They were, however, men schooled in the old order which it has been the purpose of this essay to delineate—the order in which the higher learning imputed to gentlemen resonated with the culture of plain folk at churches and courthouses, where the authoritative 'speaking books' were displayed or felt to be present. In conclusion, it may be suggested that it was the tradition of combining erudition with consensus in the context of the courthouse that gave the Virginian penmen of the emergent republic the assertive confidence to carry out the task of expressing 'the mind of the people' in bold formulations such as the Declaration of Independence, the Constitution, and the Bill of Rights.

[25] Gordon S. Wood, 'The Democratization of Mind in the American Revolution,' *Leadership in the American Revolution*, Library of Congress Symposia (Washington, D.C., 1974), pp. 63–88.

Elias Smith and the Rise of
Religious Journalism in the Early Republic

NATHAN O. HATCH

I

A RELIGIOUS NEWSPAPER would have been a phenomenon not many years since,' a Methodist journal noted in 1823, 'but now the groaning press throws them out in almost every direction.'[1] Virtually nonexistent in 1800,[2] religious periodicals had by 1830 become the grand engine of a burgeoning evangelical culture, the primary means of promotion for and bond of union within competing religious groups. The Universalist denomination alone cranked out 138 different periodicals in the three decades after 1820.[3] Between 1826 and 1834, Anti-Masons brought their message to virtually every hamlet in New York through a network of over 100 newspapers.[4] By 1840, the Methodists, turning every circuit rider into a colporteur, could claim 15,000 subscribers to their weekly periodical, *The Western Christian Advocate*. A decade later the Western Methodist Book Concern in Cincinnati employed twenty-five printers and forty-six binders to produce five different periodicals with a combined circulation of

---

[1] *Methodist Magazine* 6, no. 6 (Jan. 1823); quoted in Frank Luther Mott, *A History of American Magazines, 1741–1850* (New York, 1930), p. 136.

[2] At the turn of the century, the idea of a religious newspaper was still nowhere entertained. See David Benedict, *Fifty Years Among the Baptists* (New York, 1860), p. 25. For the severe difficulties that the Methodists had in sustaining a viable religious periodical before 1800, see Millard George Roberts, 'The Methodist Book Concern in the West, 1800–1870' (Ph.D. diss., University of Chicago, 1947), pp. 1–50.

[3] Russell E. Miller, *The Larger Hope: The First Century of the Universalist Church in America, 1770–1870* (Boston, 1979), pp. 285–87.

[4] Milton W. Hamilton, 'Anti-Masonic Newspapers, 1826–1834,' *The Papers of the Bibliographical Society of America* 32 (1938): 71–97.

85,000.[5] Even these figures paled before the extraordinary publishing exploits of William Miller and the Adventists, who blitzed the nation with an estimated 4 million pieces of literature within four years.[6] The early missionary movement was likewise transfixed by the potential of publishing,[7] as were reformers such as Alexander Campbell and John Humphrey Noyes. The latter made it clear that he would have sacrificed his communal experiment rather than his newspaper.[8] Bemused by such infatuation with the printed word, Horace Bushnell concluded that Americans operated 'as if God would offer man a mechanical engine for converting the world, . . . or as if types of lead and sheets of paper may be the light of the world.'[9]

Despite this outpouring of print, or perhaps because of it, cultural historians have not seriously explored the rise and significance of religious journalism in America. Historians of journalism likewise have neglected the task, their interest fixed on tracing the rise of the modern newspaper and magazine.[10] How are we to understand the transition between an eighteenth-century world of religious print—learned, circumspect, oriented to authority figures—and an age of competing

5 John C. Nerone, 'The Press and Popular Culture in the Early Republic: Cincinnati, 1793–1843' (Ph.D. diss., University of Notre Dame, 1982), pp. 197–98.

6 The Adventist leader Josiah Litch gave this estimate in a letter in 1843. See *Signs of the Times*, Nov. 15, 1943, p. 11; quoted in David Tallmadge Arthur, 'Joshua V. Himes and the Cause of Adventism, 1839–1845' (M.A. thesis, University of Chicago, 1961), p. 106.

7 The most sensitive study to date of the cultural significance of the rise of religious journalism is Joan Jacobs Brumberg, *Mission for Life: The Story of the Family of Adoniram Judson* (New York, 1980), esp. chap. 3, 'Does the Bibliomania Rage at Tavoy?', pp. 44–78.

8 For the primary importance that the press had for Noyes, see Lawrence Foster, 'Free Love and Feminism: John Humphrey Noyes and the Oneida Community,' *Journal of the Early Republic* 1 (1981): 178–79; and Robert Fogarty, 'Oneida: A Utopian Search for Religious Security,' *Labor History* 14 (1973): 202–27.

9 Horace Bushnell, *New Englander and Yale Review* 2 (1844): 605–7; quoted in Brumberg, *Mission for Life*, p. 67. The Abolitionist use of the press is another clear example of effective religious journalism. See Leonard L. Richards, *Gentlemen of Property and Standing: Anti-Abolition Mobs in Jacksonian America* (New York, 1970), pp. 47–81.

10 Two bibliographies that are helpful in beginning to address this issue are Henry S. Stroupe, *The Religious Press in the South Atlantic States, 1802–1865* (Durham, N.C., 1956); and Wesley Norton, *Religious Newspapers in the Old Northwest to 1861: A History, Bibliography, and Record of Opinion* (Athens, Ohio, 1977).

sects and denominations, each campaigning for popular support with the printed word? What possible implications does the harnessing of print technology to the cause of religion have for the shaping of American culture and religion in the Early Republic?

Such questions are particularly intriguing, if no less complex, in that religious print became much more a popular medium and agent of change in America than in Great Britain. There, the flood of religious print after 1800 was largely the product of elites working to shore up an ordered religion.[11] In France popular religious movements, still smarting from the Revolution's violent attack, faced the new century with a reactionary, if not royalist, bent.[12] The religious press in America, by contrast, sprang from an explicit faith in reason and popular opinion. Having done little battle with either a democracy stigmatized by 'infidelity' or a Christianity yoked to aristocratic privilege, Americans could easily declare that common folk could challenge their betters without violation of conscience, that the working out of democracy was a sacred cause.

This essay represents a modest introduction to a complex story: the rise in America of a democratic religious culture in print. A useful window on these developments is the communication strategy of one obscure American, Elias Smith, who in the wake of the democratic revolutions became enthralled with the press as a catalyst for achieving religious democracy. Despite a style that was often eccentric and exaggerated, Smith's efforts suggest certain contours that religious journalism was to assume in the Early Republic, and provide significant clues to the Christianization of American popular culture.

II

In the fall of 1814 an alarmed Stephen Porter, the Presbyterian minister of Ballston, New York, called together his congregation to warn

[11] Richard D. Altick, *The English Common Reader: A Social History of the Mass Reading Public, 1800–1900* (Chicago, 1957), pp. 67–77.

[12] For the reactionary cast of much of French popular religion in the early nineteenth century, see Thomas Kselman, *Miracles and Prophecies in Nineteenth Century France* (New Brunswick, N.J., 1983).

them of the 'awful delusions' that were spreading among them. Two objects, in particular, drew his fire: the band of 'false teachers'—one of them a woman—who railed against all kinds of orthodoxy, 'aiming the poisoned arrows of ridicule and reproach against all the regular ministers of Christ'; and, second, the pamphlets and books that these radical sectarians 'engaged in circulating.' Porter vented his wrath against one publication entitled *A New Testament Dictionary*, a 'pocket volume' which offered people the chance to discover for themselves the true 'meanings of more than eleven hundred words as they are used in the New Testament' and at the same time dismissed all Protestant denominations as limbs of Antichrist.[13]

After Mr. Porter finished reading his sermon and had pronounced the benediction, those Presbyterians in the audience who had heard only secondhand about these dissenters had the chance to see them in action. Jabez King of Woodstock, Vermont, one sectarian who had deigned to attend the service, rose to his feet and began to sing. Despite repeated interruptions, including the fact that 'one man shook his fist at him, [and] another collared him, to prevent his singing,' Jabez King proceeded to voice the words of 'The World Turned Upside Down':

> When Paul went to Ephesus,
> He Preached to them Jesus,
> Who died to redeem us,
> From an Indignant frown:
> They knowing not the stranger,
> Once cradled in a manger,
> Cry'd out our craft's in danger,
> They turn the world upside down. . . .
>
> Priests follow this example,
> Although it is not ample,
> That they should on us trample,
> And turn us out of town;
> But when a soul engaged,
> The Clergy cry enraged,
> They pull our churches down.

[13] Stephen Porter, *A Discourse, in Two Parts, Addressed to the Presbyterian Congregation in Ballston* (Ballston Spa, N.Y., 1814), pp. 2, 7, 10, 16, 42, 45. A description of the incident is found in *Herald of Gospel Liberty*, June 23, 1815, pp. 693–94.

O What a sad commotion,
On Babylon's broad ocean,
The Clergy and each notion,
With their surplice and gown;
Can be no longer smother'd,
Not people by them bother'd,
Since light has now discover'd,
That they are wrong side down. . . .

In the time of reformation,
The Clergyman's vexation,
For losing their taxation,
They often sue the town;
They hate a gospel preacher,
And cry out a false teacher,
A wolf an active creature,
Turns our church upside down.

They have found out our tinkling,
And upset infant sprinkling,
And set the people thinking,
O dear what shall we do?
If the President and Congress,
Don't have some pity on us,
And drive those run-a-gates from us,
We all to work must go.[14]

The gusty defiance of this incident serves as a fitting introduction to the career of the religious firebrand Elias Smith, the promoter of these sectarians, and to the kind of communication techniques he employed to stimulate people to think for themselves. Until 1800, Smith filled the pulpit of the respectable Baptist Church in Woburn, Massachusetts, and gave little attention to political and social questions. During the election of 1800, however, he fell under the powerful influence of the radical publicist Benjamin Austin, Jr., who wrote regularly for the Boston *Independent Chronicle*. Smith quickly imbibed Austin's heady wine, which made much of popular self-determination and raised serious questions about the authority of elites, formal education, and received tradition. Resigning from his church—as a

14 *Herald of Gospel Liberty*, June 23, 1815, p. 694.

manifesto of his own liberty—and denouncing formal religion of all kinds, Smith became a radical publicist par excellence.[15] In addition to a style of unremitting itinerancy, Smith cranked out an avalanche of pamphlets, tracts, books, and newspaper copy which, in form and content, conspired against social distinction. Noting the following that Smith was building in Essex County, Massachusetts, the diarist William Bentley noted in 1805 that 'the press has lately vomited out many nauseous things from this writer.'[16] After publishing a quarterly magazine for two years, in 1808 Smith launched the first religious newspaper in the United States, a fortnightly entitled the *Herald of Gospel Liberty*. Self-conscious of his innovation, he confessed on its opening page that its utility had been suggested by the explosion of popular print all around. 'In a short and cheap way,' he asserted, 'general knowledge of our affairs is diffused throughout the whole.' By promoting in common language the idea that 'right is equal among all,' Smith knew he would incur the judgment that he was 'stirring up the people to revolt' and 'turning the world upside down.'[17] By 1810, Smith had recruited for the 'Christian Connection' fifty or so itinerants who went about discomfiting respectable churches not by positing a tension between oral and written communication—burning books, for example—but by reinforcing the spoken word with bundles of books and pamphlets. Smith's commitment to democracy in the church was clearly wedded to the notion of the transforming power of the printed word, and his career represents an ingenious, if eccentric, crusade to short-circuit the hierarchical flow of information.[18]

[15] For a brief sketch of Smith's life, see William G. McLoughlin, *New England Dissent, 1630–1833: The Baptists and the Separation of Church and State*, 2 vols. (Cambridge, Mass., 1971), 2: 745–49. For the influence of Austin ('old South') upon Smith, see Elias Smith, *The Life, Conversion, Preaching, Travels and Sufferings of Elias Smith* (Portsmouth, N.H., 1816), pp. 341–42. See also Nathan O. Hatch, 'The Christian Movement and the Demand for a Theology of the People,' *Journal of American History* 67 (1980): 545–67.

[16] William Bentley, *The Diary of William Bentley, D. D.*, 4 vols. (Salem, Mass., 1911), 3: 291.

[17] Between 1805 and 1808, Smith published a thirty-six page quarterly, *The Christian's Magazine, Reviewer, and Religious Intelligencer*, in Portsmouth, N.H. *Herald of Gospel Liberty*, Sept. 1, 1808, p. 1.

[18] On Smith's movement, the Christian Connection, see the memoir of Smith's

Nothing makes this point more forcefully than the two accounts, Smith's and Porter's, that describe the tumultuous entrance of the Christians into Ballston, New York. Smith, understandably enough, used this specific incident in the *Herald of Gospel Liberty* to broadcast the technique of common folk successfully challenging established authority. In this affair, the 1,400 subscribers to the *Herald* witnessed a powerful interpretive framework in which day-to-day events became part of larger cosmic questions, in this case the battle to overthrow Antichrist. What is striking, however, is that Smith was also committed to assisting Stephen Porter with publishing his sermon railing against the Christians. Smith explained that he and several followers subscribed to the publication of the discourse 'fearing that it might not come to the birth.'[19] Smith's absolute confidence that people could decide issues for themselves led him to welcome an open exchange of opinion, however conflicting. Attacks against the democratic force of his arguments, as far as he was concerned, could only serve to confirm them in the forum of public opinion. Smith relished both the freedom to publish his own case and also the kind of verbal combat in the press that would excite common folk to reexamine fundamental issues of authority and social organization. He could only chuckle at the hyperbolic tone of the attacks against 'the poison' of his writings. How could common people, many of whom had reason to lash out at vested interests, avoid taking note of what elites were calling 'the most wretched trash that ever issued from the press'?[20]

Smith's brazen confidence followed the conviction, of unmistakable Enlightenment vintage, that truth was self-evident. The process of clearing away superstition and ecclesiastical privilege, first of all, brought the truth into plain view, simple and undefiled. This liberating knowledge was kept from popular acceptance by a combination

colleague, Abner Jones, *Memoirs of the Life and Experience, Travels and Preaching of Abner Jones* (Exeter, N.H., 1807); and Thomas H. Olbricht, 'Christian Connection and Unitarian Relations,' *Restoration Quarterly* 9 (Sept. 1966): 160–86.

[19] *Herald of Gospel Liberty*, June 23, 1815, p. 694.

[20] Thomas Andros, *The Scriptures Liable to be Wrested to Men's own Destruction, and an Instance of This Found, in the Writings of Elias Smith* (Taunton, Mass., 1817), pp. 10, 21.

of mere ignorance and the intent of authorities to retain their control; in the words of Smith, to keep people in 'mental bondage.'[21] But, because people were capable of discerning truth for themselves, they would flock to its standard if only rightly informed. What stood in the way of popular enlightenment, then, was simply a lack of communication. This being the case, Smith saw the task before him with penetrating clarity: to publish the good news abroad was ipso facto to liberate people from the ignorance in which many had perished.[22]

III

The real intrigue is to understand how Smith came to graft a zeal for democratic publishing onto the revivalistic Christianity he had inherited. What kind of cultural ferment moved this talented, if obscure, preacher toward such strong convictions about communicating, particularly through the periodical press?

Born in Lyme, Connecticut, in 1769, and raised in Woodstock, Vermont, after 1782, Elias Smith came to maturity at a time when many of the people of the United States—those, like him, who had not enjoyed formal education, wealth, or social standing—had many occasions to question the kind of authority that should hold sway over the individual. From the debate over the Constitution to the election of Jefferson, a second and explicitly democratic revolution united many who suspicioned power and many who were powerless in a common effort to pull down the cultural hegemony of a gentlemanly few. In a complex cultural process that historians have just begun to unravel, people on a number of fronts began to speak, write, and organize against the authority of mediating elites, of social distinctions, and of any human tie that did not spring from volitional allegiance.[23] This raising of popular consciousness gained momentum

---

[21] *Herald of Gospel Liberty*, Sept. 15, 1808, p. 5.

[22] Much of the preceding discussion is influenced by valuable insights in Nerone, 'The Press and Popular Culture in the Early Republic: Cincinnati, 1793–1843.'

[23] For the importance of the idea of volitional allegiance in this period, see James H. Kettner, *The Development of American Citizenship, 1608–1870* (Chapel Hill, N.C., 1978), pp. 173–309. On these developments, generally, see Gordon S. Wood, *The Creation of the American Republic, 1776–1787*, pp. 483–99; Alfred F. Young, *The Demo-*

from a variety of sources: the conflict and confusion over establishing republican governments, the social implications of the French Revolution, the growth of overt electioneering, the formation of democratic clubs and popular organizations, and the explosive growth and popularization of American newspapers.[24] By the late 1790s, the attempts by various elites to reassert their moral authority only riveted public attention upon the different interests of rich and poor and played into the hands of radical Jeffersonians. With a fiendish delight they took note of how elites, by struggling to put distance between themselves and the people, actually began to live out the parodies that had been used to mock them.[25]

This crisis of confidence in a hierarchic and ordered society led to demands for root and branch reform: in politics, in law, and in religion. In each of these areas, radical Jeffersonians, seizing upon issues close to the hearts of the people, resurrected 'the spirit of 1776' to protest the control of elites and the force of tradition. Rhetoric which had once unified people across the social spectrum now drove a powerful wedge between rich and poor, elite and commoner, privileged classes and the people. Federalists, members of the bar, and the professional clergy also heard the wisdom of the ages ridiculed as a mere connivance of the powerful to maintain the status quo.

These reforms gained a new intensity between 1798 and 1800 from the perceived threat that Federalists would muzzle the printing of dissent. The American Revolution, as Thomas C. Leonard suggests,

cratic Republicans of New York (Chapel Hill, N.C., 1967); and Edmund S. Morgan, The Challenge of the American Revolution (New York, 1976), pp. 211–18.

[24] Jackson Turner Main, The Antifederalists: Critics of the Constitution, 1781–1788 (Chapel Hill, N.C., 1961); Eugene Perry Link, Democratic Republican Societies, 1790–1800 (New York, 1942); Philip S. Foner, ed., The Democratic-Republican Societies, 1790–1800 (Westport, Conn., 1976); Donald H. Stewart, The Opposition Press of the Federalist Period (Albany, N.Y., 1969); David Hackett Fischer, The Revolution of American Conservatism: The Federalist Party in the Era of Jeffersonian Democracy (New York, 1965).

[25] Alan V. Briceland, 'The Philadelphia Aurora, the New England Illuminati, and the Election of 1800,' The Pennsylvania Magazine of History and Biography 100 (1976): 3–36.

had done much to make newspaper reading a way of life for many.[26] At the same time, freedom of the press, as Stephen Botein notes, was coming to stand less for impartial reporting and more for taking tough stands against tyranny in whatever form. In short, the Revolution had seen the press expand its role as a medium to express a politics of tension and dissent.[27] The Sedition Act, then, by clamping down on the kind of dissent that had become the hallmark of the press during the Revolution, served to make the issue of freedom of the press anything but an abstract constitutional issue in the election of 1800. Threats against a free press riveted the attention of many on the necessity of countering Federalist propaganda with a literature of the people.[28]

One has only to sample the Jeffersonian press in the decade after 1798 to note how many average Americans came to see it as a patriotic duty to begin speaking their own minds and breaking into print. A writer identifying himself as 'Baptist' wrote in *The Patriot, or Scourge of Aristocracy* (Stonington-Port, Connecticut) in 1801 to explain how he could no longer remain 'neuter in opinion in politics. I have formerly been what is generally called a federalist, a lover of order . . . duped to believe that we must follow the old beaten track laid down by our rulers and priests, without examining whether it was right or wrong.' The tyranny perceived in the administration of John Adams, however, convinced him to move beyond a posture of deference: 'But of late I began to suspect that every class of people have a right to shew their opinions on points which immediately concern them.'[29] In the same journal, another writer argued that because 'the people are the ultimate judges' of government, they must interpret freedom

[26] Thomas C. Leonard, 'News for a Revolution: The Expose in America, 1768–1773,' *Journal of American History* 67 (1980): 26–40.

[27] Stephen Botein, 'Printers and the American Revolution,' in *The Press and the American Revolution*, ed. Bernard Bailyn and John B. Hench (Worcester, Mass., 1980), pp. 11–57.

[28] Richard Buel, Jr., 'Freedom of the Press in Revolutionary America: The Evolution of Libertarianism, 1760–1820,' in Bailyn and Hench, eds., *The Press and the American Revolution*, pp. 59–97.

[29] *The Patriot, or Scourge of Aristocracy*, Oct. 2, 1801, pp. 85–86.

of the press to mean the actual process of disseminating information: 'This information can only be obtained in two ways: by speaking, or publishing freely our sentiments; for no one will question the inability of the great mass of the people of any nation to be enlightened without one or another, or both of these means. In our country, we believe both to be necessary, and particularly the liberty of the press. There is not a republican citizen among us, who does not consider the liberty of the press as the palladium of his rights.'[30]

Between 1790 and 1810 the United States witnessed an explosive growth in the number of newspapers, from 90 to 370. More important, an overt popularization changed the very character of the medium. Responding to a wider democratic public, papers increasingly employed communication strategies that conspired against any form of social distinction: blunt and vulgar language, crude oratory, and sharp ridicule of mediating elites such as lawyers, physicians, and clergymen.[31] Studies by Alfred F. Young and Howard B. Rock, for instance, have demonstrated the crucial role that the press played in New York City in drawing mechanics into the political process and firing them with a new sense of electoral power and self-esteem.[32] Given these qualitative changes going on within journalism, it is little wonder that elitists such as Timothy Dwight came to equate the reading of newspapers with tavern-haunting, drinking, and gambling; or that Washington Irving, after his experience as an active Federalist politician in 1807, ridiculed New York City as having capitulated 'to the tongue and the pen: to the puffers, the bawlers, the babblers and the slang-whangers: I have seen . . . that awful despot the people, in the moment of unlimited power, wielding newspapers in one hand, and with the other scattering mud and filth about. . . . I have seen liberty! I have seen equality!'[33]

---

30 Ibid., p. 149.
31 Gordon S. Wood, 'The Democratization of Mind in the American Revolution,' in *Leadership in the American Revolution*, Library of Congress Symposia on the American Revolution (Washington, D.C., 1974), pp. 63–89.
32 Young, *The Democratic Republicans of New York*; Howard B. Rock, *Artisans of the New Republic: The Tradesmen of New York City in the Age of Jefferson* (New York, 1979).
33 Rock, *Artisans of the New Republic*, p. 70.

IV

The career of the Boston radical Benjamin Austin, Jr., superbly captures the interrelated protests against elite control of politics, law, religion, and the press, and provides the clearest introduction to the shaping of Elias Smith's communication strategy. As successor to Samuel Adams as the leader and favorite of the Boston crowd, Austin held various town offices during the 1780s and frequently contributed to the popular press. He opposed the Constitution in 1787, led a democratic club, and sat in the state Senate. During the 1790s, this 'Democratic *enragée*' incurred the wrath of Federalists more than any other man in Massachusetts on account of his talents as a writer—he was probably the ablest polemicist in the state. Austin gained national reputation in 1786 for a series of articles attacking the legal profession in Boston's *Independent Chronicle*. Later published together as *Observations on the Pernicious Practice of the Law*, Austin's articles became the single most effective protest in the broader move for legal reform.[34]

Throughout the 1790s, Austin kept egalitarian principles before the people with regular articles in the *Independent Chronicle*. He continued to argue for 'the benevolence and dignity of the people' and to assail the tyranny of the Federalists and the legal profession. Yet by the late 1790s he came to identify another threat to democracy. He redirected his fire to take in the Standing Order of New England, who had come to align the cause of God with that of high-toned Federalism. Austin called for common people to throw off the yoke of 'proud priests' who attempted to enslave their conscience: 'It is degrading to an American to take every thing on trust, and even the young farmer and tradesman should scorn to surrender their right of judging either to *lawyers* or *priests*.'[35] With an exegesis of Scripture that bordered on a class analysis of society, Austin insisted that the people had always had an

[34] For an extensive treatment of the role of Austin, see Richard E. Ellis, *The Jeffersonian Crisis: Courts and Politics in the Young Republic* (New York, 1971), pp. 184–224. Austin's *Observations*, originally published in 1786, are reprinted in the *American Journal of Legal History* 8 (1969): 244–302.

[35] Benjamin Austin, Jr., *Constitutional Republicanism in Opposition to Fallacious Federalism* (Boston, 1803), p. 173.

instinct for truth and virtue. The multitude had received Christ with great acclaim, with shouts of hosanna, while 'the *monarchical, aristocratical* and *priestly* authorities cried crucify him.' The Scribes and Pharisees would have killed Jesus sooner, 'but they feared the people.' In this scenario, the elites were the ones prone to evil and poised to violate principles of social order.[36]

What underscores the significance of Austin's polemic is clear evidence that people—common people—were listening. The cases of William Manning, an unlettered farmer, and Elias Smith, an uneducated preacher, serve as graphic illustrations of the influence upon common people of Austin's paper, the *Independent Chronicle*.

William Manning's *The Key of Libberty* represents the rarest kind of historical evidence, a window on the mind of a man who would generally be considered among 'the inarticulate.'[37] An uneducated farmer from Billerica, Massachusetts, Manning put pen to paper in 1798—forming letters one by one like a child—to protest a supposed Federalist plot to renege on the principles of the American Revolution. Manning, who admitted to 'have bin a Constant Reader of publick Newspapers,'[38] hoped to have the piece published in the *Independent Chronicle*, the primary catalyst of his own thought. Too crude and too radical even for that out-and-out Jeffersonian paper, the manuscript illustrates the power of the popular press to crystallize for common people impulses which they may not have had vocabularies to express. To a remarkable degree, Manning's indictment of elites in the name of the American Revolution parallels the views of *Chronicle* publicists such as Benjamin Austin.

In the first place, Manning insisted that what troubled the Republic was a fundamental conflict between the few and the many: 'a Conceived Difference of Interests Between those that Labour for a

36 Ibid., p. 212.

37 Samuel Eliot Morison edited *The Key of Libberty* in 1922; it is reprinted with a suggestive introduction in the *William and Mary Quarterly*, 3d ser. 13 (1956): 202–56. Manning's spelling and punctuation in Morison's edition and in this essay remain unaltered.

38 Samuel Eliot Morison, 'William Manning's *The Key of Libberty*,' *William and Mary Quarterly*, 3d ser. 13 (1956): 211.

Living & those that git a Living without Bodily Labour.' Manning
was incensed that those who did an honest day's work stood powerless
before the well-organized 'ordirs'—'the marchent, phesition the lawyer and divine and all the literary walkes of Life, the Juditial & Exec-
utive oficeers & all the rich who live without bodily labour.' What
Manning found most galling was the condescension of these gentlemen: 'these ordirs of men generally associate together and look down
with too much contempt on those that labour. . . . they cant bare to
be on a leavel with their fellow cretures.' In order to destroy free
government, Manning argued, common people had only to continue
the pattern that had been drummed into them, to submit to 'a few
leeding men.' Most of all, this agitated soul feared that people would
continue to recognize authorities, 'to take for truth whatever they
[the elites] say without examining for themselves.'[39]

The conviction that people had the task of sorting out truth for
themselves led Manning to propose new forms of organization and
new means of communication. Impressed by the power of association,
Manning proposed that 'the many' follow the lead of the elites in
banding together for common purpose. He even went so far as to
suggest that farmers and laborers use the Society of the Cincinnati as
a model for their own organizations. Manning hoped that these popular associations would be instrumental in bringing about a communications revolution; he charged them to bypass the regular press—
too expensive and too Federalist for the multitudes—and 'to invent
the cheepest & most expeditious meathod of conveying' knowledge
to the people. These plans projected upon society the same process
of political awakening that Manning had experienced through the
popular press.[40]

The other self-confessed disciple of Benjamin Austin, Elias Smith,
came to discard orthodox Calvinism through reading Austin's articles
in the *Chronicle* in 1799 and 1800.[41] In method, substance, and style,
Smith championed the cause to which Austin and Manning were

---

39 Ibid., pp. 212, 213, 218, 220, 221.
40 Ibid., pp. 253, 232, 248.
41 See fn. 3 above.

committed: an appeal to class as the fundamental problem of society, a refusal to recognize the cultural authority of elites, a disdain for the 'lessons' of history and tradition, a call for root and branch reform using the rhetoric of the Revolution, and a utopian hope that the American republic had set the stage for all of this to be realized. Smith's primary interest, of course, was the spread of evangelical religion, yet he could never divorce that message from the egalitarian principles that the frantic pace of the 1790s had made self-evident.

Smith translated his zeal for reform into an agenda of radical activities, most noticeably in turning the press into a sword of democracy: 'As truth is no *private man's property*, and all Christians have a right to propagate it, I do also declare, that every *Christian* has a right to publish and vindicate what he believes.'[42] And publish Smith did. In 1803, after stirring up considerable controversy with a biting satire on the clergy in the *New Hampshire Gazette*, he followed up with four different pamphlet editions of this attack, *The Clergyman's Looking-Glass*, two editions of a well-received political speech, and two pamphlets of doctrinal controversy.[43] The next year he brought out three new editions of *The Clergyman's Looking-Glass*, three new controversial pieces, and a substantial hymnbook.[44] In addition to publishing five new pamphlets and two more hymnbooks in 1805, Smith began his career as a journalist with a quarterly, *The Christian's Magazine, Reviewer, and Religious Intelligencer*, which he later confessed had 'greatly enraged the *clergy* and their subjects.'[45] This magazine gave way in 1808 to the keystone of Smith's career as a publicist, the *Herald of*

---

[42] Smith, *Life*, p. 353.

[43] Elias Smith, *The Clergyman's Looking-Glass: Being a History of the Birth, Life, and Death of Anti-Christ* (Portsmouth, N.H., 1803); Smith, *A Discourse Delivered at Jefferson Hall, Thanksgiving Day, November 25, 1802: and Redelivered (by Request) the Wednesday Evening Following, at the Same Place: The Subject, Nebuchadnezzar's Dream* (Portsmouth, N.H., 1803); Smith, *A Reply to This Congregational Methodistical Question* (Portsmouth, N.H., 1803); and Smith, *The Doctrine of the Prince of Peace and His Servants, Concerning the End of the Wicked* (Boston, 1803).

[44] The new editions of *The Clergyman's Looking-Glass* were published in Boston. Elias Smith, *Five Letters* (Boston, 1804); Smith, *A Letter to Mr. Daniel Humphreys* (Portsmouth, N.H., 1804); and Smith, *A Reply to This Question, How Shall I Know That I Am Born Again* (Boston, 1804).

[45] Smith, *Life*, p. 309.

Gospel Liberty, a fortnightly newspaper which he edited for a decade and which served as the primary means of communication among his followers as well as a forum for a wide variety of religious radicals throughout the country. In the meantime, he continued flooding the market with pamphlets and issued several lengthy books, among them *A New Testament Dictionary, Containing the New Testament Meaning of Eleven Hundred and Eight Words, Pocket Volume* (Philadelphia, 1812)— 384 pages; *The Age of Enquiry: The Christian's Pocket Companion and Daily Assistant* (Exeter, N.H., 1807)—155 pages; *The History of Anti-Christ* (Portland, Me., 1811)—120 pages; *Sermons, Containing an Illustration of the Prophecies* (Exeter, N.H., 1808)—300 pages; and his memoirs, *The Life, Conversion, Preaching, Travels and Sufferings of Elias Smith* (Portsmouth, N.H., 1816)—406 pages.[46] After 1818 Smith moved beyond the Christian Connection, which he had founded, to embrace Universalism and sectarian medicine. As a promoter of the former he began two short-lived journals, *The Herald of Life and Immortality* (1818–19) and the *Morning Star and City Watchman* (1827–29).[47] As a rebel against conventional medicine, Smith became the hired publicist of Samuel Thomson, the most effective proponent of sectarian medicine in Jacksonian America. The links between these movements of protest against respectable clergymen and physicians will be clarified by examining first the no-holds-barred approach to communication that Smith employed in the *Herald of Gospel Liberty*.

---

[46] Smith seemed to have little trouble getting his work printed once he became well known. He recollected in 1816: 'When I first began to publish my thoughts in books, the printers and booksellers were willing to print and sell them; but at this time, many were afraid to print them or keep them in their stores. Two men agreed to print and sell whatever I brought them; but when I proved their denomination and doctrine unscriptural, they fell from their argument; and sent my books away from their store, which was a great damage to me, and disgrace to them. Being treated in this manner, I went to Mr. Henry Ranlet, of Exeter, and told him how I was treated, by the printers and booksellers; and wished to know if he was a man of courage. He observed that printing and bookselling were the business he followed for a living; that he was not accountable, where the author's name was known. The greater part of my printing from that day, to this, has been done in that office.' Smith, *Life*, p. 387.

[47] Smith published both of these monthly magazines in Boston.

V

One qualitative index of Elias Smith's skills as a communicator is the large number of sermons and pamphlets put forward by others to limit his influence. In their attempts to assess the popularity of his movement—'a matter of astonishment to see how many go after them,' one critic confessed[48]—these warnings offer valuable insight into Smith's communication techniques. Walter Harris, for instance, the Congregational minister at Dunbarton, New Hampshire, answered the question 'why they make such easy and rapid progress?' by referring to the tantalizing theme of liberation which Smith was able to drive home to common people:

Liberty is a great cant word with them. They promise their hearers to set them at liberty. And to effect this, they advise them to give up all their old prejudices and traditions which they have received from their fathers and their ministers; who, they say, are hirelings, keeping poor souls in bondage, and under oppression. Hence to use their own language, they say, 'Break all these yokes and trammels from off you, and come out of prison; and dare to think, and speak, and act for yourselves.'[49]

The broader manifestations of this 'theology of the people' I have discussed elsewhere, and it is not necessary in this context to reiterate the pervasive revolt against history, learned theology, and professional elites that the *Herald of Gospel Liberty* represents.[50] What is significant about the *Herald's* content, from the perspective of communications, is the extent to which traditional folk themes are linked to attempts to draw people into rational deliberations about their own beliefs. Apocalyptic themes, for instance, long resonant in the popular culture of New England, reappear laced with Jeffersonian political thought,

[48] Walter Harris, *Characteristics of False Teachers* (Concord, N.H., 1811), p. 18. For other attacks upon Smith, see Isaac Braman, *The Spirits That Are Not of God* (Haverhill, Mass., 1810); Andros, *Scriptures Liable to be Wrested to Men's own Destruction*; Samuel Shepard, *An Examination of the Account Lately Published by Mr. E. Smith, in two Pamphlets Respecting Original Sin* (Exeter, N.H., 1806).

[49] Harris, *Characteristics of False Teachers*, pp. 5, 19.

[50] Nathan O. Hatch, 'The Christian Movement and the Demand for a Theology of the People,' *Journal of American History* 67 (1980): 545–67.

even heavy doses of Jefferson's prose;[51] traditional resistance to elite positional codes and to local religious taxes takes on the ideological imperative of Enlightenment attacks against a state religion and against the use of all religious creeds.[52] Most important, the *Herald* served to weave specific examples of common people protesting the paternalism and condescension of their 'betters' into a convincing rationale that the age of hierarchy was tottering and about to collapse of its own weight. 'To be reproached as a friend of Democracy,' Elias Smith exhorted people of meager social position, 'is the same as though a cripple, with one leg gone, his hands trembling, and his tongue struck with the palsy, should, while moving slowly with his crutches, ridicule a strong well built man, who in his presence moves on his way, performing with ease, whatever he undertakes to do.'[53] The election of Thomas Jefferson, seen from this perspective, became the prophetic sign that all forms of hierarchy were on their way to extinction.[54]

Elias Smith's format in the *Herald* reinforced this democratic message in at least two respects. First, his newspaper served as a vehicle of communication among a variety of radical dissenters. Some, like Barton Stone and James O'Kelly, made informal alliances with Smith and came to call themselves merely 'Christian';[55] others, like Abel M. Sargent and the Rogerene Quakers, despite their own distinctive positions, were glad to relate to a larger movement committed to an assault upon privilege.

Abel M. Sargent began a radical religious sect in Marietta, Ohio, around 1805 and came to identify strongly with the Christian Connection after he read about it in the *Herald*. In extended letters to

---

[51] *Herald of Gospel Liberty*, Feb. 2, 1809, p. 45. Upon Jefferson's reelection in 1804, Smith delivered a sermon declaring that the millennial kingdom was about to dawn. See *The Whole World Governed by a Jew: or the Government of the Second Adam, as King and Priest* (Exeter, N.H., 1805).

[52] For Smith's use of Voltaire in attacking Protestant 'tyranny,' see *Herald of Gospel Liberty*, Oct. 11, 1811, p. 308.

[53] Elias Smith, *The Lovingkindness of God Displayed in the Triumph of Republicanism in America: Being a Discourse Delivered at Taunton, (Mass.) July Fourth, 1809; at the Celebration of American Independence* (n.p., 1809), pp. 13–14.

[54] Smith, *The Whole World Governed by a Jew*, pp. 51–58.

[55] Hatch, 'The Christian Movement and the Demand for a Theology of the People.'

Smith's newspaper and in his own religious periodical, which he began
in 1807, Sargent ridiculed religious tradition, lambasted any human
attempt to mediate God's government, and championed the right of
people to think for themselves. Sargent's comments are particularly
incisive in analyzing the religious turmoil of the period, the 'general
agitation now prevailing in the intellectual and religious world,' and
in attacking the subjugation of the poor to the rich—whose goal, he
feared, was 'to establish a hidden aristocracy and . . . to engross the
power and usurp the rights of the common people and thus to render
the poor subservient to their hidden purposes . . . by rendering the
poor and common citizens tenants, by preventing them of a situation
of independence and by placing them in a state of dependence on
their oppressors.'[56]

In an equally radical attack on the oppression of the poor, the Rogerene Quaker Timothy Waterous wrote a pamphlet entitled *The Battle-Axe* which he printed on a homemade press after no printer in the
vicinity of Mystic, Connecticut, would publish the work. In this highly
apocalyptic pamphlet, Waterous yoked republican politics and a class
analysis of society to the coming of the end. On several occasions
Elias Smith used passages from *The Battle-Axe*, one of them a poem
entitled 'Priest-Craft Float Away':

> Why are we in such slavery, to men of that degree;
> Bound to support their knavery when we might all be free;
> They'r nothing but a canker, we can with boldness say;
> So let us hoist the anchor, let Priest-craft float away.
>
> It is a dark confusion, that the people welters in;
> To harbour such delusion, to plead for righteous sin;
> If truth could just come forward, and justice bare the sway;
> The Priests would sink in horror, and Priest-craft float away.
>
> The Priests are on a nettle, to see their glory cease;
> Because they cannot settle on any terms of peace:

[56] Sargent published six issues of *Halcyon Itinerary and True Millennium Messenger*
in 1807. Quotations are from *Halcyon Itinerary*, pp. 13, 127, 195. For a letter from
Sargent to Smith, see *Herald of Gospel Liberty*, Aug. 16, 1811, p. 310. On Sargent,
see John W. Simpson, *A Century of Church Life* (Marietta, Ohio, 1896), p. 3.

Therefore with maze and wonder, they languish in the fray;
For truth shall fetch them under, and Priest-craft float away;
For truth and her communion, which they do soarly hate;
Shall break that horrid union, of devil, Church, and State.

Though we make our appearance, to execute this plan;
Yet we give our adherence, the sacred rights of man;
To every sect and nation, their tenets to display;
Yet may the whole creation, let Priest-craft float away.[57]

The format of the *Herald* also reinforced an egalitarian message in a second sense: by setting forth a new style of leadership radically dependent upon popular will and remarkably attuned to it. Starting with the assumption that leaders had no authority except 'as the people consider them useful,'[58] Smith became a master of the democratic art of persuasion, drumming up support for his cause by appealing to popular sentiment. Without any recognized denominational forms or ecclesiastical regulations, the persuasive words of the *Herald* became the primary means of retaining a measure of coherence within the Christian Connection. By striking down all normal lines of authority in the name of the people, dissenters such as Smith exalted the printed page as the primary means to convey a sense of direction to widely dispersed congregations, each groping to find its own way.[59]

VI

Alexis de Tocqueville noted that the popular newspaper in America facilitated a new form of association that allowed individuals, keenly aware of their own autonomy, to pursue a common purpose. Only

[57] Timothy Waterous, *The Battle-Axe and Weapons of War: Discovered by the Morning Light, Aimed for the Final Destruction of Priestcraft* (Groton, Conn., 1811). The poem is quoted by Elias Smith in *Herald of Gospel Liberty*, June 21, 1811, p. 296. On the Rogerene Quakers, see Ellen Starr Brinton, 'The Rogerenes,' *New England Quarterly* 16 (1943): 3–11; and Brinton, 'Books by and About the Rogerenes,' *Bulletin of the New York Public Library* 49 (1945): 627–48.

[58] *Herald of Gospel Liberty*, Oct. 13, 1809, p. 117.

[59] Smith and other leaders of the Connection used the *Herald* to identify churches and ministers within their fellowship, to announce itinerant schedules, to clarify disputed points of teaching, and to endow the overall movement with a grand, if not cosmic, significance.

the newspaper, he said, could drop 'the same thought into a thousand minds at the same moment . . . without distracting men from their private affairs.'[60] From 1810 to 1828 newspaper circulation in America increased twice as rapidly as the population, and religious periodicals kept pace with, if not exceeded, this advance.[61] In Jacksonville, Illinois, for example, the postmaster charge account books for 1831 and 1832 reveal that more than half of the 271 subscriptions (to 133 different periodicals) were distinctly religious publications.[62] If Jacksonian America witnessed the advent of 'an ERA OF PAPER, and the AGE OF PRINT,' as Grenville Mellen suggested to a Harvard audience in 1838, evangelical denominations were its most enthusiastic celebrants. They took a back seat to no one in their commitment to the transforming power of the printed word.[63]

This outpouring of ink, to be sure, did not always bring into question established authority. The religious press reflected the full spectrum of American churches. Yet even those who longed for a return to an era of less sectarian wrangling could not avoid using the artillery of a free press to drive home their position. The resulting tumult of opinion, which Joseph Smith called 'this war of words,'[64] clearly served to erode traditional forms of religious authority and to place at a decided disadvantage those who still expected a hierarchical flow of information. Traditionalists could not begin to compete with those who, in the words of a critic of Elias Smith, 'came to measure the progress of religion by the numbers, who flock to their standard; not by the prevalence of faith, and piety, justice and charity, and the public virtues in society in general.'[65] Those who found the printed word a way to change the status quo excelled as publicists, as Whitney Cross noted when he began to sort through the 'tons of tracts, Bibles,

---

[60] Alexis de Tocqueville, *Democracy in America*, trans. Henry Reeve, 2 vols. (New York, 1959), 2: 111.

[61] Brumberg, *Mission for Life*, p. 67.

[62] Frank J. Heinl, 'Newspapers and Periodicals in the Lincoln-Douglas Country, 1831–1832,' *Journal of the Illinois Historical Society* 23 (1930–31): 371–438.

[63] Ibid., p. 73.

[64] Joseph Smith, *The Pearl of Great Price* (Salt Lake City, Utah, 1891), pp. 56–70.

[65] Andros, *Scriptures Liable to be Wrested to Men's own Destruction*, p. 6.

pamphlets, sermons, and periodicals' that flourished in western New York in the 1820s and 1830s.[66] The success of movements such as the Mormons, the Anti-Masons, and the Abolitionists, and of reformers such as William Miller, John Humphrey Noyes, and Charles Finney, can be explained, in part, by the power of the printed word to reinforce the spoken word and to extend the message beyond the local audience.

The communication strategy of Elias Smith certainly had no direct bearing upon most of these later movements except insofar as they all reflected an application to communications of certain underlying shifts in the norms of popular culture. Many came to similar conclusions, even if they did not imitate Smith's pioneering attempts to mobilize popular opinion by the printed word. The legacy of Elias Smith is far more than casual, however, in two movements that swept through the 'Burned-Over District': the Thomsonian system of sectarian medicine, and the campaign by Joshua V. Himes to convince America of the value of William Miller's Adventism. A brief examination of these movements, both revealing shrewd manipulation of the printed word, suggest the ongoing significance of the strategies that Smith had employed with such effect.

At the close of his memoirs, published in 1816, Elias Smith concluded that there were three issues to which Americans should devote their attention: religion, government, and medicine.[67] Convinced that a common democratic winnowing would transform each of these spheres, Smith had little difficulty in redirecting his energies to champion democratic medicine after a serious illness in 1816 brought him into contact with Samuel Thomson, a practitioner of natural remedies and botanic medicine.

Thomson learned his botanic medicine in rural New Hampshire at the close of the eighteenth century. After 1800 he extended his practice into Essex County, Massachusetts, where he became embroiled in a series of personal and legal conflicts with the regular medical

---

[66] Whitney R. Cross, *The Burned-Over District: The Social and Intellectual History of Enthusiastic Religion in Western New York, 1800–1850* (Ithaca, N.Y., 1950), p. 105.
[67] Smith, *Life*, p. 362.

profession. At the behest of one of their number, a grand jury indicted Thomson for murder in 1809 after one of his patients died. Although the Supreme Judicial Court of Massachusetts acquitted Thomson of the charges, the trial steeled him to broadcast his open defiance of the medical profession.[68] His contact with Smith in 1816 offered just such an opportunity. He hired Smith as his general agent to sell 'Family Rights' and to assist 'in preparing for the press, a work to contain a narrative of my life, and a complete description of my whole system.'[69] Although Smith and Thomson quarreled repeatedly and in the early 1820s developed competing systems of natural medicine, both championed the idea that Americans must throw off the oppressive yoke of clergymen, lawyers, and physicians. Americans, argued Thomson, 'should in medicine, as in religion and politics, act for themselves.'[70] Returning to natural remedies, common people were to break the stranglehold of the medical profession and resist such treatments as bleeding and blistering and such drugs as mercury and opium.

What makes Samuel Thomson far more significant than a mere 'quack' is the fact that by 1840 he had sold over 10,000 patents to practice his medicine, and in states as diverse as Ohio and Mississippi perhaps a third of the citizens preferred the Thomsonian way of medicine. Thomson and a host of other sectarian doctors who followed in his wake battled with numerous state legislatures to withhold from

[68] On the Thomsonian movement, see Alex Berman, 'The Thomsonian Movement and Its Relation to American Pharmacy and Medicine,' *Bulletin of the History of Medicine* 25 (1951): 405–28; Joseph F. Kett, *The Formation of the American Medical Profession: The Role of Institutions, 1780–1860* (New Haven, Conn., 1968), pp. 97–131; and Ronald L. Numbers, 'Do-It-Yourself the Sectarian Way,' in *Medicine Without Doctors: Home Health Care in American History* (New York, 1977), pp. 49–72. For Thomson's trial, see Dudley Atkins Tyng, *Reports of the Cases Argued and Determined in the Supreme Judicial Court of the Commonwealth of Massachusetts*, vol. 6 (Newburyport, Mass., 1811), pp. 134–42.

[69] Samuel Thomson, *New Guide to Health: or Botanic Family Physician* (Boston, 1825), p. 155; and Samuel Thomson, *An Earnest Appeal to the Public Showing the Misery Caused by the Fashionable Mode of Practice of the Doctors at the Present Day* (Boston, 1824). Elias Smith's medical publications are *The Medical Pocket-Book, Family Physician and Sick Man's Guide to Health* (Boston, 1822); and *The American Physician and Family Assistant* (Boston, 1826).

[70] Numbers, 'Do-It-Yourself the Sectarian Way,' p. 50.

regular medical associations the exclusive right to license physicians.[71]

What is significant for our purposes are the methods by which Thomson came to advance the cause of democratic medicine. In a flurry of pamphlets and journals, Thomsonians made their case by weaving together three powerful themes. In the first place, their system drew upon folk beliefs of rural society, where a great deal of medical practice was inevitably domestic. Lobelia, for instance, Thomson's primary medicine, had been used as an emetic by the Penobscot Indians, who communicated knowledge of its functions to Yankee settlers.[72] What made the system appear anything but traditional, however, was that it was linked to a second theme, the egalitarian rhetoric of the Revolution; in particular, a flouting of the authority of elites and a rejection of the 'speculative' norms of traditional medical education —'the refined taste of the learned Latin and Greeklings of this learned age.'[73] Thomsonians also expressed a buoyant faith that in medicine, as in other matters, 'people are certainly capable of judging for themselves' and thus should break the habit of relying on others and develop a 'spirit of inquiry' into medical practice.[74] In the end, each person had the potential to become his or her own physician.

The affinity of Smith's religion and Thomson's medicine suggests the correlation in the Early Republic between sectarian medicine, radical republican politics, and religious dissent. Thomson, like Smith, espoused republican politics in no uncertain terms. One of his defenders even made the claim that opposition to him in Essex County stemmed from his daring 'to be a republican in a hot bed of federalism.'[75] Thomson, for his part, once suggested that it was as impossible 'that one of the learned professions can be a republican, as it is for ice to produce heat.'[76] Given this posture, it is hardly surprising to find that Thomson's practice in Essex County thrived among religious

[71] Kett, *The Formation of the American Medical Profession*, pp. 105–11.

[72] Ibid., pp. 107, 131.

[73] *Boston Thomsonian Manual*, 1 (Nov. 1835), p. 8.

[74] Samuel Thomson, *New Guide to Health*, pp. 6–9, 165; Samuel Thomson, *An Earnest Appeal*, p. 2.

[75] John Thomson, *A Vindication of the Thomsonian System of the Practice of Medicine on Botanical Principles* (Albany, N.Y., 1825), p. 73.

[76] Samuel Thomson, *An Earnest Appeal*, p. 7.

dissenters and that a Thomsonian convert in Ohio could characterize his battle with 'doctorcraft' as a process of 'defeating this limb of Anti-Christ.'[77] Later, during the 1830s, New York state also provides considerable evidence that a common cultural revolution could bring together people of widely differing interests to wage a joint battle against what was perceived as 'King-craft, Priest-craft, Lawyer-craft, and Doctor-craft.'[78]

That religious dissenters nimbly stayed abreast of this ferment suggests one crucial reason why Christian belief retained its hold on the people of the Early Republic. Religious views that endowed common folk with dignity and responsibility and that balked at vested interests had obvious appeal; the charm multiplied, no doubt, by the availability of reading material that claimed to equip any person to become a self-regulating interpreter of truth.

If Elias Smith pioneered such adroit use of a democratic medium, his apprentice in the Christian Connection, Joshua V. Himes, perfected the method in his crusade to spread the Adventist message of William Miller. A formative influence in the Connection for the two decades after 1820, Himes made the Chardon Street Chapel in Boston a hotbed of social reform, and became closely associated with William Lloyd Garrison, Bronson Alcott, Henry C. Wright, and Edmund Quincy.[79] In 1839, Himes met the Adventist William Miller and became enamored of the 'humble farmer of Low Hampton' who had discarded learned theology, set out to understand the Bible for himself, and challenged common people that, if they would do the same, the truth of Christ's advent in 1843 would leap from the pages of prophetic Scripture.[80] Along with two other influential Christian leaders, Joseph Marsh and L. D. Fleming, Himes led scores of Connection churches into the Adventist camp.[81]

More important, he turned his relentless energy to the cause of mak-

---

[77] John Thomson, *A Vindication of the Thomsonian System*, p. 58.

[78] Kett, *The Formation of the American Medical Profession*, pp. 105, 111.

[79] Arthur, 'Joshua V. Himes and the Cause of Adventism,' pp. 1–20.

[80] *Signs of the Times*, Sept. 28, 1842, p. 13; Joshua V. Himes, *A View of the Prophecies and Prophetic Chronicles* (Boston, 1841), pp. 9, 11.

[81] Olbricht, 'Christian Connection and Unitarian Relations,' pp. 184–85.

ing Miller's predictions a national cause. To that end, he launched an unprecedented media blitz. Prior to meeting Himes, Miller had been a rather obscure preacher known only in pockets of rural New York and New England. Himes opened the cities to Miller by pioneering in the use of an immense tent and extended his influence in rural areas with large camp meetings. In addition, he flooded the country with cheap literature. Himes claimed to have distributed 50,000 copies of the Boston fortnightly *Signs of the Times* in 1840 alone. His New York–based *Mid-Night Cry*, a daily two-cent newspaper, claimed to have distributed 600,000 copies in five months of 1842, sending at least one copy to every clergyman in the state of New York. Both of these publications regularly sent issues free of charge to postmasters throughout the country and frequently advertised the array of pamphlets, tracts, and books that Himes brought from the press. Many of these were collected into the 'Second Advent' or 'Cheap' Library, which could be purchased for under ten dollars to circulate in local communities.[82] Those who opposed the Adventist crusade poured endless ridicule upon Himes for his insistence upon hawking cheap and popular literature.[83]

The overriding message of Adventist publications is the familiar theme that people should resist the authority of the clergy and learn to prove everything 'by the Bible and nothing but the Bible.'[84] Like Elias Smith, Miller and Himes attacked all denominations for not acknowledging the right of the people to '*interpret* it [the Bible] for themselves.'[85] 'The Divinity taught in our schools,' protested Miller,

is always founded on some sectarian creed. It may do to take a blank mind and impress it with this kind, but it will always end in bigotry. A free mind

---

[82] On these developments, generally, see David L. Rowe, 'Thunder and Trumpets: The Millerite Movement and Apocalyptic Thought in Upstate New York, 1800–1845' (Ph.D. diss., University of Virginia, 1974). See also Arthur, 'Joshua V. Himes and the Cause of Adventism,' p. 105; and *Mid-night Cry*, Aug. 24, 1843, p. 1. The vast quantity of Adventist literature is evident in Jean Hoornstra, ed., *The Millerites and Early Adventists: An Index to the Microfilm Collection of Rare Books and Manuscripts* (Ann Arbor, Mich., 1978).

[83] *Signs of the Times*, Sept. 28, 1842, p. 16.

[84] Ibid., Mar. 20, 1840, p. 2.

[85] Ibid., May 15, 1840, p. 25.

will never be satisfied with the views of others. Were I a teacher of youth in divinity, I would first learn their capacity, and mind. If these were good, I would make them study bible for themselves, and send them out free to do the world good. But if they had no mind, I would stamp them with another's mind, write bigot on their forehead, and send them out as slaves.[86]

To encourage people to develop their own minds, the Adventists encouraged the formation of Bible classes so that they could ply clergymen with questions about the interpretation of prophecy. Confident of the power of their own arguments, Miller and Himes, like Smith, regularly reprinted attacks against their movement, assuming that theologies premised on the traditions of men could not stand up to a democratic alternative.[87]

VII

By 1840, of course, it had become the convention to premise religious arguments on the rights of the people and to view religious leaders as the agents of popular will—in Tocqueville's words, politicians instead of priests. The communication strategy of Elias Smith serves as a useful window on a movement by which people struggled to gain control of those sources of information to which they were subject. The religious press in America invited dissent, exalted leaders attuned to popular concerns, and made it possible for Americans by the thousands to speak their mind in print. Self-educated men with a thirst for knowledge may not have retained control of their own fate, as Edward Pessen or Paul E. Johnson would remind us,[88] but they did alter, for better or worse, the kind of information sources that were available and the style of leadership that people were willing to acknowledge. The freedom of the press, as popularly understood and practiced, accelerated a process by which democratic forms of religion came to resonate powerfully within American popular culture.

[86] Ibid., May 15, 1840, p. 26.
[87] Ibid., Sept. 21, 1842, p. 8; Sept. 28, 1842, p. 16; Oct. 15, 1840, p. 112.
[88] Edward Pessen, *Jacksonian America: Society, Personality, and Politics* (Homewood, Ill., 1978); Paul E. Johnson, *A Shopkeeper's Millennium: Society and Revivalism in Rochester, New York, 1815–1837* (New York, 1978).

This is not to suggest that the communication strategies of Elias Smith remained the driving force behind religious periodicals or that his utopian hopes for popular enlightenment were fulfilled. A profound irony, in fact, surrounds the success of religious printing. Instead of the press serving as truth's herald, it often amplified a welter of competing voices, proving, if anything, that no truth had inherent power. Instead of erasing the distinction between leaders and followers, the press gave ample opportunity for religious demagogues to expand their influence. Instead of sounding the death knell for organization and structure, religious periodicals remained successful largely to the extent they became yoked to organizational programs.

The ultimate irony of a democratic religious press was that it came to reverse the link that Elias Smith had envisioned between the truth and popular opinion. Smith assumed that truth was inherently powerful. By conveying it, the press became almost sacred; by beholding it, people could think for themselves and find enlightenment. Given these assumptions, Americans easily came to correlate truth with what proved to be successful in the free marketplace of ideas. A message unable to win public support was a contradiction in terms; conversely, to be read was to deserve to be read. In such a climate, the freedom of the press did not necessarily lead to freedom of thought, as Tocqueville would observe.[89] People kept in step with their fellows not from fear of authority but from a hesitancy to transgress public opinion. Religious periodicals over time became no less submissive to public taste, a process encouraged by dependence on continued subscriptions. As a medium, then, religious journalism conspired to make the sovereignty of the audience the final test of truth. Americans thereafter would find it more difficult to identify with truth when spoken by a still, small voice.[90]

---

[89] Tocqueville, *Democracy in America*, 1: 269–78.
[90] This discussion of the relationship between truth and popular opinion depends heavily upon the provocative conclusion of John C. Nerone, 'The Press and Popular Culture in the Early Republic: Cincinnati, 1793–1843.'

Print and the Public Lecture System, 1840–60

DONALD M. SCOTT

I N 1856 THE EDITOR of *Harper's Monthly* made one of his
periodic assessments of the American cultural landscape:

A few years since, when the steam-engine was harnessed into the service of
the printing-press, we were ready to conclude that oral instruction would
have to yield the palm, without dispute, to written literature. . . . When
we saw steam made to do the bidding of editors, publishers, and the whole
host of bookcraft, we began to think that speaking intellect had seen its
best days. Oratory would be doomed either to obsoleteness or to decay;
authors would rise into the ascendant, and readers would far outnumber
hearers. We even imagined, in the first shock of amazement, that the ear
. . . would retire on a pension, and that the eye . . . would literally become
the most perfect of the senses.[1]

As the editor looked 'over the varied panorama of life and society in
our country,' he found that his initial expectation was mistaken. Far
from driving the speaker out of the field of public influence, the age
of the steam press had created a powerful new institution, the 'popular' or 'public' lecture, and the lecturer had gained 'a prominent
position among those agents who work in the present and herald the
future.'[2] The editor's discovery raises directly the issue of the relationship between the world of print and traditional forms of public discourse in mid-nineteenth-century America. This essay examines that
issue by focusing on the public lecture system that had forced him to
revise his first assessment of the triumph of eye over ear.

Much of the scholarship concerning the social history of print has
shared the *Harper's* editor's initial assumption that oral forms belong
to a disappearing past and that print is a dynamic cultural force which

1 'Lectures and Lecturing,' *Harper's Monthly Magazine* 14 (Dec. 1856): 122.
2 Ibid., p. 122.

carries all before it. Orality and print are seen as fundamentally different technologies of communication, appropriate for very different societies. Orality is considered a defining characteristic of 'traditional' or 'premodern' societies; and print, as one of the essential technologies of modernization, is viewed by its very nature as an innovative and disruptive force which inevitably undermines the patterns of life and belief associated with traditional societies. Once print invades a society, moreover, it is oral forms which preserve the remnants of traditional culture and which permit the 'popular classes' to define and maintain an identity and culture separate from the culture of the elite. The precept that informs this approach is certainly a useful one, namely, that the differences between orality and print are significant because forms of cultural expression are ultimately social forms that, in part at least, define the relations between persons and groups in society. In addition, this particular line of interpretation may well provide a compelling account of the introduction of print into fifteenth- and sixteenth-century Europe.[3] But as David Hall has argued recently, insistence upon the dichotomy between orality, tradition, and the lower orders on the one hand, and print, modernity, and elites on the other, is a misleading way to go about understanding the cultural history of even seventeenth-century New England. He contends that since print had been around for nearly two centuries, the 'folk' culture of New England was not encased in pure oral forms but was made up of a 'continuum between print and oral modes.'[4] More important, he shows that print was itself attached to traditional culture as well as to the ideas that were undermining it, and he warns against the 'presumption' that elites and the lower orders automatically think differently and express themselves in different modes.[5]

Further modification of the approach seems to be in order when we

[3] See, for example, Natalie Zemon Davis, *Society and Culture in Early Modern France* (Stanford, Calif., 1975), chaps. 7, 8.

[4] David D. Hall, 'The World of Print and Collective Mentality in Seventeenth Century New England,' in *New Directions in American Intellectual History*, ed. John Higham and Paul Conkin (Baltimore, 1979), p. 169.

[5] Ibid., pp. 171–77; and see David Hall's essay in this volume for a more precise distinction between 'oral' and 'verbal' modes.

look at the relationship between the world of print and forms of oral expression in mid-nineteenth-century American society. The society as a whole, as well as most groups within it, participated fully in both oral and printed modes of cultural expression, and there appears to have been considerable similarity in much of the content expressed in the two modes. In addition, many Americans of the mid-nineteenth century were both hearers and readers, and what they read influenced how they listened as well as what they heard, and vice versa. Thus, it does not seem particularly useful to think in terms of oral *versus* printed media. Instead of construing print and orality as belonging to inherently separate social and cultural worlds, it might be more useful to approach them as different parts of an overall system of cultural expression, a system containing a variety of printed, oral, and visual genres.[6] This in no way minimizes the difference between orality and print as cultural forms, nor does it deny the social significance of that difference. It is, after all, the face-to-face immediacy of the relationship between speaker and audience, and the sense of collective participation that the occasion creates, that at once distinguishes the oratorical form (whatever its particular content or genre) from the medium of print (whatever its particular content or genre) and gives the oratorical form historical significance as a social institution. But it would be a mistake to conjecture too hastily about just what that significance might be. That an oratorical form has social significance is partly inherent in its character as a rhetorical occasion, but precisely what its significance is depends on how, in form as well as content, it is embedded in a particular social and cultural context. It is within this framework that the present essay approaches the public lecture system of the 1840s and 1850s as a 'case' for illuminating some of the dimensions of the larger issue.

When the *Harper's* editor made his discovery that oratory was alive and well in countless towns and cities around the country, lectures for the 'diffusion of useful knowledge' had been part of the American cul-

---

[6] It is useful to distinguish between *modes* of communication, denoting the general forms, and *genres*, denoting different styles of expression.

tural scene for decades. Lectures before exclusive or specialized audiences—literary and philosophical societies, missionary and benevolent associations, and reform societies—had originated in the late eighteenth century and the early decades of the nineteenth, as had the 'itinerants' who went around peddling their cultural wares to anyone who would pay a few cents to listen. In the late 1820s and early 1830s a somewhat broader kind of lecture developed as lyceums, young men's associations, library societies, and mechanics' institutes began to sponsor lectures on a wide variety of subjects given by their members (often aspiring young tradesmen and professionals), local ministers, doctors, teachers, and notables. These lecturers were rarely paid for their efforts and were not necessarily noted for their skills as speakers. To a large extent, speaker and audience alike perceived the lectures as essentially instructional and informational rather than oratorical occasions, as a kind of schooling or continuing education.[7]

Though such lectures certainly continued into the 1840s and 1850s, the 'popular lecture system' that emerged then was a new and very different kind of cultural institution.[8] In the first place, it was a coherently organized, national *system* that centered on a core of 'professional' lecturers—people like Henry Ward Beecher, Oliver Wendell Holmes, Bayard Taylor, Ralph Waldo Emerson, Henry Giles, Louis Agassiz, Ormsby Mitchell, Park Benjamin, Starr King, Horace Greeley, Wendell Phillips, Anna Dickinson, and George William Curtis, to name some of the most prominent ones. They were paid between $50 and $150 plus expenses for each lecture and ordinarily spent four or five months of each year traveling across the country, giving lectures in

[7] For discussion of these earlier lectures and lyceums see Carl Bode, *The American Lyceum: Town Meeting of the Mind* (New York, 1956), pp. vii–viii; Robert J. Greef, 'Public Lectures in New York, 1851–1878: A Cultural Index of the Times' (Ph.D. diss., University of Chicago, 1941), pp. 1–9.

[8] By the 1840s there were a number of fairly coherently organized lecture 'circuits'—reform, health, and evangelical circuits as well as the circuit referred to as 'the popular lecture system' upon which this essay concentrates. There was some crossing over between the special emphasis circuits and the lyceum or popular lecture. Moreover, some of the analysis of the popular lecture system offered here would also be applicable to those circuits. In the interests of brevity and coherence, however, I have given my attention exclusively to the popular lecture system.

hundreds of small towns, villages, and cities.[9] In the spring and summer, before the lecture 'season' (mid-November to early April), the
lecture committees of the various sponsoring societies would send out
letters in their desire 'to spare no pain to give the public a course of
lectures from the first men in the country.'[10] Ordinarily a society's
course, consisting of ten to twelve lectures, would take place at the
same time and place each week. Often the secretaries of a particular
locale—say, the Connecticut Valley—would coordinate their efforts
so that Bayard Taylor, for example, could lecture in Northampton on
Tuesday, Chicopee on Wednesday, and Springfield on Thursday of
the same week; and lecturers often sent out circulars to the various
societies indicating what lectures they had available for that season.[11]

Second, the 'popular' lectures were more explicitly oratorical occasions than most other lectures. Although they were expected to be
serious and moral in their ultimate intent (wit, irony, and satire were,
of course, widely used as rhetorical devices) and had to be 'instructive'
and 'ennobling,' great emphasis was placed upon their character and
effectiveness as oratorical performances.[12] Newspaper accounts as well

[9] A widely quoted and variously attributed statement put the standard fee of the
late 1840s and early 1850s at 'F.A.M.E . . . fifty and my expenses.' Edward Everett
Hale, *James Russell Lowell and His Friends* (Boston, 1899), p. 107. The leading lecturers ordinarily gave between 75 and 140 lectures each year, earning between
$3,500 and $6,000. See Eleanor M. Tilton, *Amiable Autocrat: A Biography of Dr.
Oliver Wendell Holmes* (New York, 1947), pp. 440–41; and Richmond Croom Beatty,
Bayard Taylor: Laureate of the Gilded Age (Norman, Okla., 1936), pp. 146–48.

[10] *Hampshire Gazette*, Feb. 17, 1852, p. 1.

[11] See, for example, the correspondence of the secretary of the Northampton
Young Men's Institute, Forbes Library, Northampton, Mass.; and Lecture Com-
mittee Minutes, Albany Young Men's Association Papers, Albany Public Library,
Albany, N.Y. For examples of lecturers' circulars and correspondence see Park
Benjamin Papers, Butler Library, Columbia University, New York; and Elias Nason
Papers, 1831–84, American Antiquarian Society, Worcester, Mass.

[12] This essay is based heavily upon the advertisements and reports of lectures
contained in newspapers, esp. the *Hampshire Gazette*, the *Albany Argus*, and the *New
York Tribune*, for the years 1840–60. Several dissertations quote heavily from newspaper accounts and have been very useful: see esp. Greef, 'Public Lectures in New
York'; Robert Martin, 'The Early Lyceum Movement, 1826–1845' (Ph.D. diss.,
Northwestern University, 1953); and Richard L. Weaver II, 'Forum for Ideas:
The Lyceum Movement in Michigan, 1818–1860' (Ph.D. diss., Indiana University, 1969). David Mead, *Yankee Eloquence in the Mid-West: The Ohio Lyceum, 1850–
1870* (East Lansing, Mich., 1951) is based on a thorough canvass of Ohio news-

as notations in private diaries usually assessed the quality of elocution as well as the substance of the message.[13] Much of the audience was already familiar with many of the ideas that might be contained in a given lecture, and, as a number of commentators pointed out, more information could be gleaned more readily from books.[14]

Finally, the 'popular' lecture was very explicitly a public occasion.[15] It was ordinarily sponsored by a lyceum, lecture society, or young men's association which acted as a quasi-civic body in providing the public with suitable lectures. Lectures were delivered in at least ideologically neutral if not clearly designated public space, the town hall or another auditorium large enough to hold all who might wish to attend. The fanfare that surrounded a lecture enhanced its public character. At the beginning of each season, an article announcing and extolling the whole course would appear in the local newspaper and a special announcement, often accompanied by a plug, usually preceded each lecture—which was then reported as a newsworthy event. The intended audience, usually ranging from 200 or 300 to 2,000 or more when the lecturer was one of the stars, was the general public, drawn from across the community without regard to occupation, social standing, or political and religious affiliation. In addition, the genuine popular lecture was considered by lecturer and audience alike to be a disinterested public act, delivered as a service to the community out of commitment to truth rather than out of personal ambition. Access to the platforms of the system was strictly by invitation, and considerable care was taken to protect the forum from contamination either

---

papers; and Hubert H. Hoeltje, 'Notes on Lecturing in Iowa, 1855–1885,' *Iowa Journal of History and Politics* 25 (Jan. 1927): 62–131, also quotes extensively from newspaper accounts.

13 See, for example, the *Hampshire Gazette*, Mar. 17, 1846; Dec. 14, 1847; Feb. 25, 1850; Feb. 23, 1852; Mar. 15, 1853; Mar. 22, 1853; Jan. 24, 1854; Jan. 16, 1855; Dec. 2, 1856. See also the notations on lectures in Levi Lincoln Newton, Diary, 1839–42, Newton Family Papers; Brown Thurston, Diary, 1834–50, 1893; and Elisha Harkness, Diary, 1840–41—all located at the American Antiquarian Society.

14 'Lectures and Lecturing,' p. 123; J. G. Holland, 'The Popular Lecture,' *Atlantic Monthly* 15 (Mar. 1865): 367.

15 This paragraph is based on my article 'The Popular Lecture and the Creation of a Public in Mid-nineteenth Century America,' *Journal of American History* 66 (Mar. 1980): 791–809.

by sectarian, reform, or party zealots or by itinerants with their self-promotion, dubious nostrums, and humbuggery. Moreover, though the topics varied enormously, most lectures in the system followed what in another context I have called an 'interpretive imperative,' and self-consciously connected their immediate subjects to some universal truth or good.[16] As Josiah Holland put it: 'The man who takes the facts with which the popular life has come into contact and association, and draws from them their nutritive and motive power, and points out their relations to individual and universal good, and organizes around them the popular thought . . . and does all this with masterly skill, is the man whose houses are never large enough to contain those who throng to hear him. This is the popular lecturer, *par excellence*.'[17]

This popular lecture system was in many ways a creation of the world of print of mid-nineteenth-century America—the system could no more have operated without print than the railroad could have operated without tracks. The connections between the public lecture system and what might be called the popular press—especially the newspapers and the general monthlies like *Graham's*, *Putnam's*, *Harper's*, *MacMillan's*, and *Scribner's* (themselves products of the 1840s and 1850s)—can scarcely be exaggerated. The general magazines played an important role in describing and celebrating the public lecture as a significant new cultural institution, and at least two editors, George William Curtis from *Harper's* and Josiah Holland from *Scribner's*, were themselves prominent lecturers.[18] Moreover, the newspapers generated most of the publicity that oiled the operations of the system. In large measure, in fact, the success and prosperity of a local lecture society depended upon the support of the local press. The notices about who was lecturing when and where, the editorials declaring how valuable the institution was, and the stories preceding and following the particular lectures, by treating the lectures as important

16 Ibid., p. 803.

17 Holland, 'The Popular Lecture,' p. 367.

18 In certain ways the emergence of the popular lecturer as a new kind of public spokesman parallels the emergence of the editor as a public figure.

events, helped make them important events. Indeed, it appears that lecture societies only thrived in communities where there were local newspapers that actively supported them. When a town's newspaper withdrew its support and either attacked or simply ignored the institution, the lecture society had a difficult time surviving.[19]

The connection between press and platform was even subtler and deeper. In large measure it was the press which established the idea in the public mind that a particular figure was a legitimate popular lecturer whom they wanted to hear. The press was thus an essential instrument for turning a writer, educator, minister, statesman, journalist, scientist, or aspiring itinerant into an accepted 'professional' lecturer. The process by which people like Bayard Taylor, Ralph Waldo Emerson, Oliver Wendell Holmes, Henry Ward Beecher, Wendell Phillips, and others became avidly sought after and highly paid national lecturers was complicated and varied, but for all of them a fabric of publication and reportage played an important role in giving them access to the platform and in keeping them there. For some, lecturing came as a result of quick and dramatic attention. Bayard Taylor's letters to the *New York Tribune* on his travels to exotic lands brought invitations to lecture as soon as he returned,[20] and when Dr. Elisha K. Kane returned from an Arctic expedition that had been followed avidly by the daily and weekly press, he was immediately flooded with 'more than 100 invitations to lecture in various parts of the country.'[21] For figures like Henry Ward Beecher and Ralph Waldo Emerson, who began in the late 1830s and early 1840s by lecturing to local audiences and then published their efforts as essays or collected 'occasional addresses,' the fact of publication and the notice it brought

[19] When the *Hampshire Gazette* changed hands in 1845, the new editor appears to have been uninterested in the lyceum lectures, and the lecture courses died out for a year. Then another editor, J. R. Trumbull, an avid supporter of the system, took over the paper and continually supported the lecture system. Barbara Hinds, 'The Lyceum Movement in Maine' (M.A. thesis, University of Maine, 1949) describes a similar incident in which the editor of the *Bangor Gazette* attacked the lyceum course, leading to its demise for two years.

[20] Marie Hansen-Taylor and Horace Scudder, eds., *Life and Letters of Bayard Taylor*, 2 vols. (Boston, 1884).

[21] *Hampshire Gazette*, Feb. 17, 1952.

moved them into a wider orbit and gave them a general reputation which carried them into the system as professional lecturers. The publication of Beecher's *Lectures to Young Men* (originally delivered to the Indianapolis Young Men's Lyceum when he was a minister there) brought him the attention that gained him the pastorate of the newly established Plymouth Church in Brooklyn Heights. Once he was strategically located in what was rapidly becoming the major communications center of the nation, his growing reputation as a preacher and orator (and his considerable skills at self-promotion) quickly led to the notices in the press that propelled him to fame and onto the lecture circuit as one of its stars.[22] Emerson's essays, the newspaper reviews and excerpts, and the use of some of his most apposite aphorisms as a kind of moral filler in newspapers bit by bit built his reputation among the general public as America's leading philosopher. Indeed, by the early 1850s, the idea of Emerson as the 'Sage of Concord' and 'a true genius' was so firmly embedded in the public consciousness that even those who roundly criticized his ideas (and his oratorical style) had to pay obeisance to it.[23]

The press, then, not only was essential for gaining access to the system, it was equally important for spreading reputation and keeping the system operating. Several key metropolitan newspapers, particularly the *New York Tribune* and the *Boston Herald*, played an enormously important role in nationalizing reputation. Boston and New York were the lecturing centers—in Boston, for example, twenty-six different courses were held in 1846, and on January 26, 1853, the

[22] William C. Beecher and Samuel Scoville, *A Biography of Rev. Henry Ward Beecher* (New York, 1888), pp. 199–224.

[23] Emerson's lecturing has been followed almost step by step by modern scholars: the state historical journals are filled with accounts of his lectures and the reception of them in numerous places. See, for example, Louise Hastings, 'Emerson in Cincinnati,' *New England Quarterly* 11 (1938): 443–51; Russel Nye, 'Emerson in Michigan and the Northwest,' *Michigan History Magazine* 26 (1942): 158–72; Hubert Hoeltje, 'Ralph Waldo Emerson in Minnesota,' *Minnesota History* 11 (1930): 145–59; Lynda Belz, 'Emerson's Lectures in Indianapolis,' *Indiana Magazine of History* 60 (1964): 269–80; Donald F. Tingley, 'Ralph Waldo Emerson on the Illinois Lecture Circuit,' *The Journal of the Illinois State Historical Society* 64 (1971): 192–205.

Tribune listed eleven different lectures for a single night[24]—and these two newspapers reported, excerpted, and commented on a great many of the lectures held in these two cities. The *Tribune* had a special section entitled 'Sketches of Lectures' which summarized the lectures from various courses in New York City. These reports, moreover, were in effect syndicated far and wide; the *Weekly Tribune*, for example, had a press run of about 175,000, a large portion of which was distributed to newspapers all over the country, providing them with an important source of copy for filling their pages. Thus the Boston and New York newspapers played a role in making someone a nationally known and sought-after lecturer. In fact, it appears that very few, if any, of the stars entered the national system without first breaking into the Boston or New York circuit. But it was not only the metropolitan press that sustained the system. As is well known, newspapers 'exchanged' with each other; the editors of papers in towns like Northampton, Massachusetts; Kalamazoo, Michigan; Davenport, Iowa; or Kenosha, Wisconsin took their copy from two or three dozen newspapers. The readers in such far-flung places were thus regularly supplied with information about lectures, audiences, and lecturers from across the country. The *Hampshire Gazette*, for example, routinely reported on lectures in Boston and New York, but also occasionally printed accounts from Philadelphia, Cincinnati, or New Orleans. It paid particular attention to lecturers as they entered the region and spoke before audiences in Springfield, Hartford, Worcester, and Pittsfield. As a consequence, its readership was not only made familiar with, say, Theodore Parker's 'Progress of Mankind,' it could also follow Parker's activities and the responses to them as he traversed the circuit.[25]

This system of reportage was thus essential in creating the corps of popular lecturers and securing their acceptance as legitimate, author-

24 Greef, 'Public Lectures in New York,' pp. 4–7; *New York Tribune*, Jan. 26, 1853.

25 This statement is based upon careful examination of the *Hampshire Gazette*. The broader study I am currently working on, tentatively entitled 'Theatre of the Mind: Ritual and Authority in Mid-Nineteenth-Century America,' will examine the process that is sketched so briefly here in far greater detail.

itative spokesmen for 'universal' truth and good. Once this conception
of a lecturer was firmly implanted, it was not easily dislodged—as the
persistence of the idea of Emerson's genius suggests. It became, in
short, the presupposition with which the public approached a lecture
by one of the national figures; the presupposition that in large measure
drew them, for example, to Beecher's 'Ministry of the Beautiful' and
kept them away from a lecture on the same topic by a local, unknown
'amateur,' one who had not been legitimated and certified by the
skein of publicity that surrounded the system and created and sustained the professional lecturers.[26] Similarly, the system of reportage
extended the boundaries, as it were, of the lecture beyond the oratorical performance itself. In a sense, the event began with the public
heralding and anticipation of the lecture—the creation of the sense
that a significant cultural event which people would want to partici-
pate in was about to take place in their town—and did not end until
it had been publicly assessed and its importance certified in print.
Moreover, a lecture by one of the national figures was not an isolated
event of only local importance; by its reportage in local, regional, and
sometimes national press, it became an occasion in the overall system,
an event for a broader, unseen public as well as for the immediate audience. Indeed, part of the attraction and appeal of, for example, Wendell Phillips and his 'Lost Arts of Egypt' or John Saxe and his 'The
Money-King' for the people of Delaware, Ohio, or Bangor, Maine,
was their knowledge that lecture and lecturer had played and would
play to full houses in towns all over the country.[27]

[26] Most societies had to rely on local 'amateur' talent for at least some of their
lectures. The response to these figures was at best lukewarm, and societies that
relied too heavily upon them often fell into debt. Both newspaper and diary accounts
seem to indicate that the nature of the expectation in the two instances differed
radically. See, for example, *Hampshire Gazette*, Dec. 2, 1856, for a 'disappointing'
performance by one of the stars and the notations in Levi Lincoln Newton's Diary,
American Antiquarian Society. Hale, *James Russell Lowell*, p. 70, makes the distinction very clearly.

[27] The way in which a single lecture gained some of its meaning as an event
in relation to previous knowledge of the lecture and lecturer and in relation to other
lectures in a season or seasons appears to be similar to the way in which the meaning
of a single major league baseball game is derived in large measure from its relation
to other games in the season.

Description, of course, is not explanation; the question still remains of why a new oral medium with the scope and character of the public lecture emerged at a time when widespread literacy and the ready availability of inexpensive printed material were revolutionizing communications. The answer lies in part in what could be called a crisis of cultural form, a crisis stemming from changing social conditions as well as from the emergence of new agencies which dispensed new kinds of information and asserted new kinds of cultural authority. Generally speaking, most seventeenth- and eighteenth-century Americans had been oriented to place, and the institutions of church, polity, and class within which and against which they had defined themselves had promulgated a collective *mentalité* which situated everyone in an appropriate place within the local community. The extraordinary mobility of Americans and the unrelenting spread of settlement over the first half of the nineteenth century obliterated the familiar points of reference and undermined traditional habits of thought.[28] The town or rural locale—taken as social wholes—had atrophied as the frame of reference and order, and, instead, people sought community and identity increasingly through party, sect or denomination, voluntary association, and lodge—institutions that brought people together, but in collectivities that situated them very differently in social and cultural space. These were all institutions which largely transcended local boundaries and possessed the specialized languages, codes, and rituals by which Baptists, Democrats, and Masons, for example, from one place could find compatriots whenever and wherever they moved. By the same token, however, they were institutions which divided and separated people, locally and nationally, and thus they transformed ministers and officeholders into spokesmen for party and sect rather than guardians of the community or polity as a whole.[29]

[28] A number of historians have argued that it was during the first decades of the nineteenth century that American society became unhinged from the institutions and cultural assumptions that had directed it through the eighteenth century. See, for example, Gordon S. Wood, ed., *The Rising Glory of America, 1760–1820* (New York, 1971); David Hackett Fischer, *The Revolution of American Conservatism* (New York, 1965); and Donald M. Scott, *From Office to Profession* (Philadelphia, 1978).

[29] Fischer, *Revolution of American Conservatism*, pp. 1–50; Scott, *Office to Profession*, pp. 18–75.

By the 1830s and 1840s, moreover, America was a society that seemed
in constant motion, continually spreading out and fragmenting into
more and more units of all kinds: new towns, new sects, new associations, new parties. The result was a national society—under such conditions 'Americanness' became an ever-important badge of identity—
but one, in a sense, without a clear and coherent cultural center, without obvious institutions which clearly embraced the national community or figures who were widely and readily accepted as legitimate
spokesmen for a common, public culture.

Various agencies developed to fill the vacuum. The new, democratic party system that emerged in the 1820s and 1830s drew the
far-flung populace into active participation in a set of rituals that were
organized around the symbols and ideals of democracy and individualism. The evangelical transformation of American religion in these
years, with its revivals and its tract, Bible, education, and missionary
societies, steadily indoctrinated Americans with inclusive, nondoc-
trinal forms of piety and moralism. Finally, the press itself was perhaps
the most significant force of all for nationalizing the ever-expanding
American republic. Subjecting people from Texas to Maine, Florida
to Wisconsin, and New York to Iowa, to many of the same tracts,
books, political speeches, and newspaper copy, the world of print provided the essential mechanism not necessarily for unifying Americans
around the same opinions and beliefs but for inducting them into a
common field of discourse.

If, however, all these things fostered national cohesion and identity,
they were also paradoxically instruments of disorder, divisiveness, and
disintegration. The party system itself might have been integrative,
but on the most immediate level it seemed to enthrone partisanship
and, under the electoral conditions and culture of the Jacksonian
period, seemed less to order public life than to embroil it, to translate
every fissure of discontent and difference into shrill contention. As one
commentator put it, 'in a republican government, where discourse is
free, and where all great measures are to be decided by popular suf-
frage, there will often be violent conflicts of opinion, nor will any

department of society or class of men escape the occasional visitation of a storm of passion.'[30] Similarly, the efforts to spread evangelical hegemony unleashed intense sectarian rivalry, intolerance of Roman Catholics, and strident and often angrily resisted attempts to impose particular standards of belief and behavior on American society as a whole.[31] Moreover, the press itself was a profoundly unsettling force —unsettling in the enormous variety and volume of printed material with which it almost literally inundated the public, in the number of new sources from which it came, and in the variety of new forms in which it was housed.

Neil Harris has written of how the 1880s and 1890s experienced an 'explosion of information' which affected every aspect of life and society.[32] But in many ways the explosion of information in the 1830s and 1840s appears to have been almost as dramatic. The newspapers of the day were compendia of information of all sorts.[33] In addition to local, national, and sometimes international news events, they often contained compilations of statistics and commercial data, tidbits of historical and scientific fact, and accounts of travelers and missionaries among exotic peoples in distant lands. Their pages of advertisements were full of information about new products, new business opportunities, new health cures, and still other sources of knowledge and information. In addition, each issue had a large number of short items, undigested notations of 'miscellaneous,' 'curious,' and 'bizarre' facts. There was a vast proliferation of new genres which further expanded the world of available fact and image: journals devoted to specialized topics or conducted by particular groups; magazines and miscellanies (like newspapers, essentially anthologies of various kinds of articles and fictional forms); tracts, addresses, and pamphlets by the hundreds

---

[30] James Hall, 'Education and Slavery,' *Western Monthly Magazine* 2 (1834): 270.

[31] Leonard L. Richards, *Gentlemen of Property and Standing: Anti-Abolition Mobs in Jacksonian America* (New York, 1970); Scott, *Office to Profession*, pp. 95–111.

[32] Neil Harris, *Land of Contrasts* (New York, 1970), pp. 1–30.

[33] The notion that newspapers of this period might be construed as a kind of cultural anthology, a mid-nineteenth-century equivalent of the almanac, was first suggested to me by David J. Rothman.

of thousands; novels and romances; 'universologies' offering keys to all knowledge; manuals of advice on almost every aspect of life; and, finally, various kinds of taboo and immoral literature.[34]

Almost as confusing as the sheer amount and variety of fact and opinion created by the revolutionary new world of 'cheap print' was the babble of voices competing for the attention and allegiance of the public. There were, of course, the traditional opinion makers—the ministers, officeholders, gentlemen of letters and learning, college presidents, and professors—who continued to act as guardians of the culture.[35] But their voices were in danger of being drowned out by a vast array of reformers, lecturers, and pundits of all sorts, 'crying,' as one commentator put it, 'lo here and lo there.'[36] There were, first, the various societies with their agents, lecturers, colporteurs, and tracts, all of which insisted upon the great significance and far-reaching importance of their particular cause. In addition to these voices, which had at least the sanction of their particular society, there was the horde of people who offered their intellectual wares to the public in what amounted to a vast cultural bazaar. The combination of greatly reduced printing costs, easier travel and new systems of distribution, and a public eager for anything that might seem to satisfy its craving for 'useful knowledge' on the one hand, and the presence of a swarm of young men forced to try to carve a career out of the possession of some kind of knowledge rather than from soil or craft on the other, had produced a large number of people for whom ideas literally had become commodities which they tried to merchandise. The Fowler brothers, with the assortment of phrenological wares which they peddled in numerous books and in widely advertised and extravagantly

[34] There is as yet no adequate study of underground literatures in the United States in this period, although a few studies do suggest some of the characteristics of the demiworld of urban intellectual and literary life in this period. See, for example, Merle M. Hoover, *Park Benjamin: Poet and Editor* (New York, 1948); and Cortland P. Auser, *Nathaniel P. Willis* (New York, 1969).

[35] See Wilson Smith, *Professors and Public Ethics* (Ithaca, N.Y., 1956); Thomas Haskell, *The Emergence of Professional Social Science: The American Social Science Association and the Nineteenth-Century Crisis of Authority* (Urbana, Ill., 1977); and Scott, *Office to Profession.*

[36] Parsons Cooke, *Moral Machinery Simplified* (Andover, Mass., 1839), p. 4.

promoted lectures, were perhaps the most successful exemplars of the type.[37]

Such then was the cultural condition out of which the popular lecture emerged. There was what might be called a communications overload, the problem of sorting out and assimilating the quantity and variety of fact and opinion one encountered. It was partly a problem of quantity, but it was also a problem of form: creeds, orthodoxies, and traditional schema for classifying and ordering knowledge seemed to many to be outmoded and inadequate to express or contain the 'spirit of the age.'[38] There was also the problem of intellectual legitimacy and authority. How among the babble of voices, so many of which asserted that their particular views provided the 'key' to understanding 'the age,' could one locate what Thomas Haskell, in writing of the crisis of authority of this period, has referred to as 'sound opinion'?[39] Where in the society was it to be found, who were its legitimate spokesmen, and upon what did their claim to speak for the culture at large rest? It is against the backdrop of this cultural situation that we can best understand the significance of the popular lecture system as a new cultural institution, oral in form, but firmly embedded in the new world of print.

The popular lecture system was at once authoritative and comprehensive. It embraced people of different parties, sects, occupations, and stations in towns all over the country, and was widely accepted as a legitimate agency for expressing a common culture.[40] But where did this legitimacy come from, where did the professional lecturers get their credibility as 'the intellectual leaders of an intelligent progress in the country.'[41] As has been suggested, both the practice of

[37] Although there are biographies of some figures of this type, no study of how this style of intellectual career emerged and operated exists.

[38] 'Lectures and Lecturing,' p. 123; 'Lectures and Lecturers,' *Putnam's Monthly* 9 (Mar. 1857): 317–21; 'Popular Lectures,' *Galaxy* 9 (Mar. 1870): 418–20.

[39] Haskell, *The Emergence of Professional Social Science*, pp. 63–90.

[40] Although the system was fairly inclusive and surrounded by a myth that it was all-inclusive, it was largely a 'middle-class' institution. Moreover, by the mid-1850s it had become largely a Northern institution, as many of the lecturers became identified with antislavery sympathies.

[41] 'Lectures and Lecturers,' p. 318.

lecture by invitation from bodies which were accepted as representing the good of the whole community and the system of reportage and publicity that supported the system fostered some of its legitimacy. (Occasionally lecture committees were thought to have broken this trust by acting exclusively or partially, and an aggrieved group would organize a counter course which they invariably called 'the people's course' but which drew its lecturers from the same overall list of speakers.)[42] The deliberate exclusion of partisan and sectarian discourse and the convention that the genuine popular lecturer addressed themes of 'general interest' directed to 'individual and universal good' also enhanced legitimacy. To be sure, many of the lecturers came from traditional positions of intellectual leadership—professorships, pastorates, public office, editorships—that still conveyed some legitimacy as the possessors of important knowledge. But their acceptance as public spokesmen depended upon their conformity to the conventions; for Henry Ward Beecher to preach evangelical doctrine or advocate guns for Kansans, for Daniel Webster to spout Whig doctrine, or for Wendell Phillips to push abolitionist programs (things they did quite acceptably in other forums) would have been immediately perceived and condemned as a violation of the rules of the system.[43]

The system also derived some of its legitimacy from the notion that it was a democratic institution—open to all, under the domination of or serving the good of no special interest, and ultimately under the control of the people. Lecturers, it was believed, could neither gain nor maintain their position and influence by the exercise of privilege or authority. Only those who were able to attract and hold their audiences could succeed. This very dominion of 'popular opinion and taste' led some critics to condemn the system and scoff at its intellectual pretensions. Celebrants of the system, however, insisted that truly sound, democratic opinion was that opinion which could pass 'the severe test of repeated delivery before lyceum audiences in different parts of the country.'[44] Indeed, Josiah Holland, declaring that 'there

[42] Albany, Worcester, and Northampton all had 'people's courses' at various times in the 1850s.

[43] See, for example, *Hampshire Gazette*, Jan. 16, 1849.

[44] 'Reviews and Literary Notices,' *Atlantic Monthly* 6 (July 1860): 120.

is no literary tribunal in this country that can more readily and justly decide whether a man has anything to say, and can say it well, than a lecture audience,' concluded that the public lecture system was 'the most purely democratic of all our democratic institutions.'[45]

Finally, its specific character as an oratorical occasion played a crucial role in establishing the system's legitimacy to speak to and for the democratic community as a whole. Ernest Bormann and Michael McGee, among others, have suggested that 'speech occasions' often create among their participants a 'rhetorical vision' of themselves as 'the people.'[46] In this sense, the lecture's standing as a fully legitimate 'popular' institution was enhanced both by the manifest and symbolic content of the lecture—the paraphernalia heralding it as a democratic institution and a public occasion and its appeal to universal truths— and by the sense of collective participation and belonging that is created by an oratorical performance which is built upon shared expectations.[47] Both of these aspects fostered the feeling that the immediate audience as well as the larger public which participated in the institution did so not as believers in different creeds and parties or as people with different interests but as a community standing, as one commentator put it, 'on common ground.' Indeed, Thomas Wentworth Higginson captured this dimension of the system when he characterized the popular lecturer as 'moving to and fro, a living shuttle, to weave together this new web of national civilization.'[48]

The rhetorical dimension of the event, operating within the context

---

[45] Holland, 'The Popular Lecture,' pp. 365, 363.

[46] The following analysis has been greatly aided by recent work in rhetorical theory and analysis, much of it following the lead of Kenneth Burke. See esp. Lloyd Bitzer, 'The Rhetorical Situation,' *Philosophy and Rhetoric* 1 (Jan. 1968): 1–14; Karl R. Wallace, 'The Substance of Rhetoric: Good Reasons,' *Quarterly Journal of Speech* 49 (1963): 239–49; Michael C. McGee, 'In Search of the People: A Rhetorical Alternative,' *Quarterly Journal of Speech* 61 (1975): 235–49; Ernest G. Bormann, 'Fantasy and Rhetorical Vision: The Rhetorical Criticism of Social Reality,' *Quarterly Journal of Speech* 58 (1972): 396–407; Barnet Baskerville, 'The Dramatic Criticism of Oratory,' *Quarterly Journal of Speech* 45 (1959): 39–45.

[47] McGee, 'In Search of the People'; Charles G. Finney, *Christian Affinity* (Utica, N.Y., 1827) is a superb discussion of how oratorical performance forges community.

[48] Thomas Wentworth Higginson, 'The American Lecture-System,' *MacMillan's Magazine* 18 (May 1868): 49.

of all the constraints that have been suggested, conferred cultural authority on the institution in still another way. Guarded by its particular rules, and surrounded by the vision of it as a genuine expression of democratic culture, the popular lecture was an occasion for what was widely referred to as 'true eloquence.'[49] True eloquence itself conferred intellectual authority, for it (as opposed to false eloquence) could serve only as a vessel of truth and understanding. The idea of eloquence—as opposed to simple oratorical skill—appears to have been reserved for the expression of truth. Moreover, it could only originate in the proper frame of motive and intent on the part of the speaker. In this sense, demagogues or charlatans could use all the tricks of oratory, the argument went, but could never be genuinely eloquent because their efforts were tainted by falsehood and evil motives. In addition, a lecturer could never be eloquent over mere fact or trivial subjects. As Daniel Webster put it, 'true eloquence must exist in the man, in the subject, and in the occasion.'[50] In its essential features, the lecture system met these criteria and thus gained much of its authority as a vehicle for sound and ennobling thought from the fact that its audience participated in it with the expectation that it was an institution devoted to 'true eloquence.' In this sense, it possessed a mode of authority comparable to that which the pulpit, when filled with an 'edifying' preacher, traditionally had been thought to possess.[51]

All this suggests how the popular lecture system gained its standing as an authoritative cultural institution attuned to a far-flung democratic republic, but it does not reveal whether or how it met the needs of a populace buffeted by an explosion of information. It was largely the intellectual comprehensiveness of the system that responded to

---

[49] See, for example, William Mathews, *Oratory and Orators* (Chicago, 1879); Henry Ward Beecher, *Oratory* (New York, 1876); 'Eloquence: Its Principles,' *Universalist Quarterly* 20 (Jan. 1863): 27–32; Edward G. Parker, *The Golden Age of American Oratory* (Boston, 1857); Ralph Waldo Emerson, 'Eloquence,' in *Works*, 14 vols. (Boston, 1898), 7: 59–100, and 'Eloquence,' 8: 108–34.

[50] Daniel Webster, *A Discourse in Commemoration of the Lives and Services of John Adams and Thomas Jefferson* (Boston, 1826), p. 35.

[51] See, for example, George W. Bethune, *The Eloquence of the Pulpit* (Andover, Mass., 1842). Scott, *Office to Profession*, pp. 112–32, discusses the ideal of edifying preaching.

this need. Over a few seasons, the typical lyceum would present an almost encyclopedic range of topics, covering, in effect, the broad new world of fact, information, knowledge, and event. A typical course would provide a lecture or two on a scientific topic; a travel lecture or two; some disquisition on a crucial American institution; an assessment of some troubling new phenomenon in American life, like the 'woman question'; a literary and a historical lecture; the exploration of a grand theme like the 'law of progress'; and several lectures on crucial matters of manners and morals, like marriage or money.[52] The system was also marvelously flexible, responsive to events as well as to startling new knowledge. After the Hungarian Revolution, for example, Charles Loring Brace, who had just traveled in Hungary and been captured for a time by the revolutionaries, was in great demand for his lecture 'Hungary: Its Fitness for Democracy.' As has been mentioned, E. K. Kane was flooded with invitations to lecture when he returned from his Arctic expedition, and after the Seneca Falls convention, the 'woman question' made its way rapidly onto the podium.[53]

But in addition to this intellectual scope and flexibility, as rhetorical performances the lectures gave their audiences a sense of broad intellectual comprehensiveness. A widely popular lecture by one of the stars usually drew upon an astonishing array of concrete references and allusions, taking its material from literature and history, from the most pressing news and startling facts of the day, and from the experiences of everyday life. The essential element, however, was what it did with this material. As Holland said in describing the lecturer 'par excellence,' 'American life is crowded with facts, to which the newspaper gives daily record and diffusion. . . . Men wish for nothing more than to know how to classify their facts, what to do with

[52] See Barbara Hinds, 'Lyceum Movement in Maine,' pp. 77–78, for a list of lectures in Bangor, Maine. Kenneth Cameron, *The Massachusetts Lyceum During the American Renaissance* (Hartford, 1969) reprints the year-by-year lists of lectures in Salem and Concord. The broadside collection of the American Antiquarian Society is a superb source for the offerings of each season in Worcester.

[53] *Hampshire Gazette*, Feb. 17, 1852; Jan. 22, 1856. See Doris Yoakeam, 'Woman's Introduction to the American Platform,' in *A History and Criticism of American Public Address*, ed. William Brigance, 3 vols. (New York, 1943), 1: 153–89.

them, how to govern them, and how far to be governed by them.'[54]
This is what the good popular lecture did. It took its particular subject—the Turks, the Beautiful, the Course of the Waters—and, drawing facts to it like a magnet, with great artistry and 'true eloquence'
connected it to broad themes.[55] Thus did it 'elevate and enlarge the
understanding and give broader, more comprehensive views' of the
self, the nation, mankind, the world, or nature.[56] In short, the crucial
thing that distinguished the lecture from 'Essay, Narrative, Disquisition, and Review' was the rhetorical experience.[57] As one commentator put it, the lecturer 'acts his drama before our eyes,' an intellectual
drama which gave its hearers not an intellectual system but an *experience* that provided a powerful sense of comprehension and carried
them to a state of 'enlarged understanding.'[58] Our editor from *Harper's*
put it this way in the same piece with which we began: Americans,
he wrote,

need living mind to place them in living contact with the whole living
world; and in no way can they have it as cheaply, as easily, and as effectively as in the right kind of Lectures. Books have their office; . . . Nothing
great or good was ever done that was not connected, in some way, with
the influence of books; say all this, and then say, too, books are not men.
. . . Books are broken fragments. Books are products of insulated hours—
dissevered nights—sundered years. . . . But the living speaker, commanding
subject and audience by fullness of knowledge and potency of will . . .
every pulse obedient to the intellect—what is like it?[59]

The public lecture system can thus be interpreted as an institution
situated, as it were, at a crossroads of American society, straddling a
number of contradictory tendencies and impulses in the culture. It
bridged some of the spatial, social, institutional, and intellectual diversity and fragmentation of the society; it drew upon some of the tradi-

[54] Holland, 'The Popular Lecture,' p. 367.
[55] See Scott, 'The Popular Lecture and the Creation of a Public in Mid-Nineteenth Century America,' pp. 802–5, for a more extended discussion of this point.
[56] Bayard Taylor, 'The Philosophy of Travel,' *Hampshire Gazette*, Dec. 25, 1855.
[57] 'Lectures and Lecturing,' p. 123.
[58] 'Popular Lectures,' p. 419.
[59] 'Lectures and Lecturing,' p. 123.

tional sources of intellectual authority while incorporating new styles of democratic legitimacy; it reflected the flood of print and information and at the same time provided a medium for assimilating it, thereby giving at least the illusion of comprehension and control; and it was firmly rooted in both the revolutionary new world of 'cheap literature' and in the older modes of oratorical discourse. In all these ways, then, at least to some extent and for a fairly broad (but by no means all-inclusive) American public, it did provide a much needed cultural center.

Afterword: From Cohesion to Competition

RICHARD D. BROWN

THE FOREGOING ESSAYS, whose subject matter spans nearly two centuries, make no pretense toward comprehensive coverage of the history of printing or its social importance in early America. Conceived independently, rather than commissioned, they represent in their variety some of the leading edges of research scholarship. The authors' approaches, ranging from analysis of auctions and the records of printers and booksellers to the methods of historical anthropology and bibliography, are as varied as their subjects. Quantitative and qualitative experiences of producers, distributors, and consumers of print have been examined. Though gaps remain, the essays illuminate central themes in American eighteenth- and nineteenth-century history, and help to explain the significance of printing in the historical process. By charting aspects of the production and distribution of books in the eighteenth century and going on to explore the new republican environment that emerged in the first half of the nineteenth century, they clarify key aspects of the social and intellectual history of early America. Together they illuminate the transition from a world where printed matter was scarce and commonly used intensively, to one where print was abundant and came to be valued and employed in different ways. In contrast to the colonial era, by the first decades of the nineteenth century printing had become a central vehicle of popular politics, both secular and religious. Forms of public expression—oratory and ceremony as well as print—were transformed as they took on new functions in a society whose structure and values were changing. To grasp the dimensions of change one need only compare the circumstances of readers in the early eighteenth century, as described by David Hall in an essay in this volume, with the readership a century later of Benjamin Austin's Boston paper, *The Independent Chronicle*, and Elias Smith's *The Gospel of Christian Liberty*, analyzed by Nathan Hatch.

Ultimately, of course, this transformation was bound to the economics of the production and consumption of print. Here, though a systematic examination of the economics of printing and its place in the domestic economy of early America has yet to be written, it is widely assumed that, relatively speaking, printed products became less expensive between 1750 and 1850, with the pattern of declining prices becoming visible between 1790 and 1830. This decline cannot be measured precisely; indeed, no dramatic technological advances comparable to the electric and photographic innovations of our own era can explain it. Since the techniques of stereotyping and pulp paper production, and steam and roller presses, appeared only toward the close of the period, these advances seem to be consequences rather than causes of the transformation. Small, incremental reductions in the relative cost of printed matter over several decades, owing to more and better presses and lower paper and distribution costs, helped provide a foundation for the explosion of printed matter in the early nineteenth century.[1]

Equally evident, but also uncharted in any systematic way, is the concomitant increase in consumption. People in nearly all walks of life enjoyed some increase in discretionary income as the American economy became more commercial. They may also have enjoyed more discretionary time. The number of personal libraries per capita was growing, as was their size. Moreover, collective 'social libraries,' mostly confined to a handful of port towns before Independence, became ever more common.[2] The use of low-cost ephemera, both commercial and recreational, was also on the rise. With the advent of the daily 'penny press' in the 1830s, cranking out tens of millions of copies yearly, the era of abundant, 'throwaway' printing had arrived.[3] The

---

[1] Michael Schudson, *Discovering the News: A Social History of American Newspapers* (New York, 1978), pp. 31–34.

[2] Jesse H. Shera, *Foundations of the Public Library: The Origins of the Public Library Movement in New England, 1629–1855* (Chicago, 1949), chaps. 3, 4.

[3] Schudson, *Discovering the News*, p. 18.

world of scarcity described by David Hall, charted in Williamsburg by Cynthia and Gregory Stiverson, and manifest in the Chesapeake social order depicted by Rhys Isaac was gone. As Nathan Hatch's and Donald Scott's studies demonstrate, the social context of printing had been shattered and its social functions had been radically transformed.

How are we to explain this seismic shift? Since literacy rates seem to have been relatively stable, the most direct explanation is that there was a pent-up thirst for print that had long been blocked by high cost and low availability; as these problems were solved after 1790, consumption escalated.[4] Such an argument is persuasive in part. Improved distribution of a cheaper product certainly enhanced consumption since many, perhaps most, adults had for generations valued printing as a source of religious and secular improvement as well as entertainment. But one key limitation to this view is the evidence that cheap print was not entirely new. Broadsides and almanacs had long been popularly consumed and, like devotional books, widely distributed. The colonial trade in printed goods had satisfied, though not satiated, this thirst for printing.[5]

Popular reading tastes of the early nineteenth century were different, as David Hall points out. The experience of reading itself changed, coming to emphasize extensive exposure to many printed texts rather than repeated, intensive examination of the same ones. Following Independence, Americans developed both a craving for varied reading material and a willingness to spend so as to satisfy it. The relation-

---

[4] Changes in literacy rates may have affected printing and reading, but evidence to support that view is presently lacking. See David Hall's introduction above; Schudson, *Discovering the News*, pp. 35–39; Kenneth Lockridge, *Literacy in Colonial New England* (New York, 1974); Harvey J. Graff, *The Literacy Myth: Literacy and Social Structure in the Nineteenth-Century City* (New York, 1979).

[5] There is some reason to believe that the increasing commercialization and specialization of economic life in the early republic increased people's discretionary or leisure time available for reading. The proliferation of carding and spinning mills, for example, altered female work patterns, and the increasing number of people engaged in nonfarm occupations and settled in villages suggests the possibility of increased leisure time. In the end, however, the central question is how people chose to spend their time—doing more in the endless succession of chores, or reading.

ship of people to print changed so decisively that a multifaceted new reading public emerged.

The Revolution acted as a catalyst for the new reading style. It had, in the first place, created an unprecedented demand for news and newspapers. In the New England countryside, clergymen who had rarely paid attention to events beyond their region, and who had relied chiefly on word of mouth to bring them such news as they needed, now took up newspaper subscriptions and avidly followed events in New York, Pennsylvania, and Virginia.[6] The clergy were not alone, and after 1783 the number of newspapers and their distribution networks burgeoned. People who had been satisfied with only an occasional paper, months old and passed from hand to hand, now became addicted to the continuous doses of reading which newspapers offered. The rush of public events during the Revolutionary era, and the pamphlet wars that extended into the 1790s, promoted a taste for extensive reading, both in the privacy of a clergyman's study and amid the hubbub of a country tavern.

The Revolution was also a catalyst at a deeper level of consciousness. In the colonial era extensive reading had been the prerogative of the urbane few who either owned large libraries or were members of select gentlemen's libraries such as the Redwood at Newport. To read widely was a badge of high status, one which the aspiring Benjamin Franklin displayed conspicuously as he propelled himself upward through the economic and social ranks.[7] Franklin, an innovator

6 Rev. James Cogswell, Diary, 1781–91, Connecticut Historical Society, Hartford, Conn.; Timothy Walker, *Diaries of Rev. Timothy Walker, The First and Only Minister of Concord, N.H., from His Ordination November 18, 1730 to September 1, 1782*, ed. and annotated by Joseph B. Walker (Concord, N.H., 1889). Ebenezer Parkman, a Boston native who became the minister at Westborough, Mass., was subscribing to a newspaper as early as 1727. *The Diary of Ebenezer Parkman, 1703–1782*, First Part, 1719–1755, ed. Francis G. Walett (Worcester, Mass., 1974), Jan. 4, 1727, p. 20.

7 In his autobiography Franklin reported that as a young man books gave him access to learned gentlemen. *The Autobiography of Benjamin Franklin and Selections from His Other Writings*, with an introduction by Henry Steele Commager (New York, 1950), pp. 39, 50. John Adams employed similar tactics, noting on Oct. 5, 1758, that 'by the Study of the Civil Law, in its native languages, . . . I shall gain the Consideration and perhaps favour of Mr. Gridley and Mr. Pratt.' *Diary and*

in so many ways, set a course in colonial Philadelphia that would
become common in post-Revolutionary America. His library company and mechanics institute were imitated widely after the Revolution when the impulse for wide-ranging, varied reading took hold
generally.

To a large degree the Revolution unleashed social aspirations, and
since learning was connected to social recognition, people expressed
their social ambitions in a new taste for reading. The old idea expressed
by opponents of the Revolution like Soame Jenyns—who claimed that
popular ignorance was a positive good, 'the only opiate capable' of
making the poor accept the 'miseries' and 'drudgeries' of their lives,
'a cordial administered by the gracious hand of providence, of which
they ought never to be deprived'—was swept away. More people than
ever before now believed that books and learning should be available
to them. Whether founding academies or lyceums and lecture series
later on, Americans were convinced that republicanism entitled everyone to have access to learning.[8] Learning was conceived as extensive knowledge derived from wide reading, according to the model
of such enlightened republican gentlemen as Franklin and Jefferson.
Mere reading of the intensive sort associated with Christian piety was
respectable, but it was no badge of status or honor. The new interest
in reading was tied, in Gordon Wood's apt phrase, to the 'democratization of gentility' that was evident in so many aspects of early
American physical and literary culture.[9] Leveling up, not down, was

---

Autobiography of John Adams, ed. Lyman Butterfield, 4 vols. (Cambridge, Mass.,
1961), 1: 44.

[8] Jenyns quoted in Richard D. Altick, *The English Common Reader: A Social History
of the Mass Reading Public 1800–1900* (Chicago, 1957), pp. 31–32. Carl F. Kaestle
and Maris A. Vinovskis, *Education and Social Change in Nineteenth-Century Massachusetts* (Cambridge, 1980), chap. 2; Richard D. Brown, 'The Emergence of Urban
Society in Rural Massachusetts, 1760–1820,' *Journal of American History* 61 (June
1974): 29–51, esp. data on education in Table I.

[9] Gordon S. Wood, Brown University, comment at the American Antiquarian
Society conference 'Printing and Society in Early America, 1640–1860,' Oct. 24–
25, 1980, Worcester, Mass. The phenomenon is evident in a wide range of consumer behavior, such as the replacement of wooden dishes and trenchers with
china, the embellishment of domestic architecture, and in forms of address with
the spread of the terms 'Mister' and 'Mistress' to common people.

a central cultural legacy of the Revolution, so the extensive reading pattern of the few became a model for the republican many.

Republican ideology reinforced this behavior by requiring informed citizenship. Traditional Christian virtue had always stressed piety and faith, so the intensive reading of the Bible and devotional works was fundamental to the discipline of virtuous Protestants. But the new republican ideology carried a different message, defining the virtuous citizen as one who was broadly informed about political doctrine and public affairs.[10] Whereas newspaper reading had been an entertaining diversion in the older context, it now became a duty. Because government was based on 'the opinion of the people,' Thomas Jefferson maintained, everyone must have 'full information of their affairs thro' the channel of the public papers, and . . . those papers should penetrate the whole mass of the people.' It was not enough that gentlemen and clergy were informed. 'Every man,' Jefferson asserted, 'should receive those papers and be capable of reading them.'[11] The mark of the virtuous citizen was his ability to converse knowledgeably about the changing political scene. The Revolution, therefore, had played a dual role in stimulating extensive reading: by generating news, and by requiring that citizens be well informed.

These changes in public taste generated a self-intensifying spiral of growth in the production, distribution, and consumption of print. Whereas the colonial market had been capable of supporting printers only in political capitals and port towns, after Independence printing flourished on an unprecedented scale in dozens of interior towns. Precociously, Benjamin Franklin had set up a chain of printing partnerships along the colonial seaboard. After Independence, Isaiah Thomas, whose headquarters were at Worcester, created a network reaching from Boston to Baltimore and far into the interior of New England

[10] The Massachusetts Constitution of 1780, chap. 5, sec. 2, displays this credo. Oscar and Mary Handlin, eds., *The Popular Sources of Political Authority: Documents on the Massachusetts Constitution of 1780* (Cambridge, Mass., 1966), p. 467.

[11] Thomas Jefferson to Edward Carrington, Paris, Jan. 16, 1787, in *Papers of Thomas Jefferson*, ed. Julian P. Boyd, 19 vols. (Princeton, 1950–77), 11: 49. The policy of encouraging newspaper distribution was written into postal rates from 1790 onward.

and New York. Thomas emerged as the leading entrepreneur in a highly decentralized commerce that mixed an inventory of old-fashioned 'steady sellers' with a lengthy, frequently changing list of current titles, in addition to newspapers and periodicals. Businessmen and printers like Thomas were discovering lucrative markets for print where scarcely any such trade had existed before.[12] By bringing their shops close to consumers they lowered prices while encouraging sales. Earlier, country merchants of the colonial era could not risk stocking any but the most staple steady sellers, merchandise that would be as salable one year as the next. In contrast, print vendors of the republican era could offer a wider selection, thereby stimulating further development of the new taste. In these circumstances a new standard of literacy that emphasized current and wide-ranging knowledge became a social reality in country villages and, more slowly, on farms as well.[13]

It was in this setting that revivalists of the second Great Awakening and their adversaries turned to print. The pamphlet wars of the first Awakening, between Jonathan Edwards and Charles Chauncy for example, had been aimed at limited audiences of clergy and gentlemen, with press runs numbering several hundred.[14] Now, in the republican era, religious controversy and competition generated an avalanche of print. The trailblazing sectarian journalism of Elias Smith came in the wake of the tract societies which by the 1820s had already distributed millions of moral tales.[15] If the first Great Awakening had

12 Isaiah Thomas, *The History of Printing in America*, 2d ed., 2 vols. (1874; reprint ed., New York, [1967]), 1: 182–83. Elizabeth Reilly, in her essay in this volume on Jeremy Condy's trade, notes that sales were exclusively along the most beaten paths of travel and trade.

13 Brown, 'Emergence of Urban Society in Rural Massachusetts'; William J. Gilmore, 'The Annihilation of Time and Space: The Transformation of Event and Awareness in American Consciousness, ca. 1780–1850,' unpublished paper given at the American Antiquarian Society conference 'Printing and Society in Early America,' Oct. 24–25, 1980; Robert A. Gross, comment on 'Development of the New England Village Center,' New England Historical Association meeting, Apr. 18, 1980, Old Sturbridge Village, Sturbridge, Mass.

14 Edward M. Griffin, *Old Brick: Charles Chauncy of Boston, 1705–1787* (Minneapolis, Minn., 1980), pp. 78–88.

15 American Tract Society, *Proceedings of the First Ten Years of the American Tract Society* ([New York], 1824), p. 208.

led to a transformation of oratorical style, then the second reinforced and extended the transformation in reading tastes and consumption of the printed word.[16] When leaders of religious culture followed the path of political (and more broadly secular) culture, they were acknowledging the dominance of the new pattern of reading. Here, in print, was a democratization of religious culture to parallel the democratization of genteel culture.[17]

By the 1830s and 1840s the widespread distribution of popular treatises on law, physiology, diet, and medical treatment produced a democratization affecting the other learned professions. Extensive printing and reading invited people to become their own doctors and lawyers as well as their own clergymen and political guides. The challenge to received cultural authorities was boundless.

Yet the central consequence of the shift from the traditional intensive pattern of reading to the extensive pattern was not necessarily democratization in one form or another. Alexis de Tocqueville's emphasis on democracy diverts us from the central issue, the transition from a coherent Christian culture to a competitive pluralistic one. Where there had once been a coherent Protestant culture in which, as David Hall explains, people of all ranks had in large part concentrated on reading the same texts intensively, with only a leisured few reading extensively beyond them, now a competitive marketplace of diverse values ruled. The prospect of a culturally united elite exercising hegemony as it led a culturally coherent population—as had once been the case in the colonial Chesapeake and much of New England —became, with few exceptions, unattainable and unrealistic. In contrast, the new reading environment of the republican era invited everyone to become an extensive reader, diluting if not destroying the old common core. Instead of a publications marketplace oriented to the comparatively unified tastes of gentlemen and clergy, a competitive mass marketplace developed.[18] Within it the competing judgments

[16] Harry S. Stout, 'Religion, Communications, and the Ideological Origins of the American Revolution,' *William and Mary Quarterly*, 3d ser. 36 (Oct. 1977): 519–41; Rhys Isaac's essay in this volume.

[17] Nathan Hatch's essay in this volume.

[18] Both Stephen Botein and Elizabeth Reilly note the connections between print-

of a miscellaneous media elite, including politicians like Benjamin
Austin, sectarians like Elias Smith, Whig entrepreneurs like Isaiah
Thomas, and a host of others determined the cultural matrix of the
reading public. When the public lecture system emerged near the
middle of the nineteenth century, it represented an extension of the
taste for extensive knowledge and urbanity that the transformation of
printing and reading had promoted. Indeed, as Donald Scott explains,
the lecture system helped people cope with 'information overload'
even as the lecturers added their voices to the rush of print. Ralph
Waldo Emerson oversimplified the situation when he groaned that
'the only aristocracy in this country is—the editors of newspapers.'
Touring speakers, who were often authors as well, and the people who
arranged their public appearances joined the motley ranks of the self-
selected media elite that, out of motives of conviction and/or profit,
was hawking all sorts of cultural wares to the hundreds of distinct
audiences or 'markets' that America had come to encompass.[19] The
character of this environment, where a wide variety of publications
was accessible to readers of all classes and tastes—in contrast to colonial times, when books were so scarce and choices so limited that the
American gentry would buy the residue of the English marketplace
and purchase copies of gentlemen's magazines that were several years
old—testified to the radical transformation of the role of printing in
society.[20] Indeed, even the emergence of mass marketing and the great
urban publishing houses, which standardized a portion of the market
and defined 'respectable taste,' operated to extend the divided, competitive world of print as the range of their titles multiplied. Where
printing had once been an instrument of cultural cohesion, it had now
become a principal agent of cultural fragmentation and competition.

This fact should not be surprising. During the first half of the nineteenth century competition emerged as one of the central features of

---

ers and clergy in their essays in this volume; Cynthia and Gregory Stiverson point
out the connections between printers and lawyers in their essay in this volume.

[19] Journal, 1837, in *Basic Selections from Emerson*, ed. Eduard C. Lindemann (New
York, 1954), p. 163.
[20] Stephen Botein's essay in this volume.

the new republic's culture, evident in nearly every aspect of activity as received perceptions of authority and hierarchy were challenged. Because printing was a prime instrument of cultural expression, its history was inseparable from the workplace, politics, religion, and the worlds of learning and literature. What should be surprising is that historians have for so long treated the history of printing and reading as if they were esoteric matters belonging at the periphery of scholarship. The American Antiquarian Society conference 'Printing and Society in Early America' and the studies drawn from it that have been presented here testify to an emerging awareness that the question of who reads what and why lies at the heart of understanding our history.

The Editors and Contributors

STEPHEN BOTEIN is Associate Professor of History at Michigan State University.

RICHARD D. BROWN is Professor of History at the University of Connecticut.

RICHARD CRAWFORD is Professor of Music at the University of Michigan.

DAVID D. HALL is Professor of History and American Studies at Boston University.

NATHAN O. HATCH is Associate Professor of History at the University of Notre Dame.

JOHN B. HENCH is Assistant Director for Research and Publication at the American Antiquarian Society.

RHYS ISAAC is Reader in History at LaTrobe University, Melbourne, Australia.

WILLIAM L. JOYCE is Assistant Director for Rare Books and Manuscripts at the New York Public Library.

D. W. KRUMMEL is Professor of Library and Information Science and of Music at the University of Illinois, Urbana.

ELIZABETH REILLY is completing a doctoral dissertation on books and readers in eighteenth-century New England at Boston University.

DONALD M. SCOTT is Visiting Associate Professor of History and Special Assistant to the Academic Dean at Brown University.

CYNTHIA Z. STIVERSON is the former Research Librarian for the Colonial Williamsburg Foundation.

GREGORY A. STIVERSON is Assistant State Archivist at the Maryland Hall of Records.

ROBERT B. WINANS is Associate Professor and Associate Chair of English at Wayne State University.

Index

PRINTED BY
THE STINEHOUR PRESS